DEMOCRACY'S CAPITAL

JUSTICE, POWER, AND POLITICS

The Justice, Power, and Politics series publishes new works in history that explore the myriad struggles for justice, battles for power, and shifts in politics that have shaped the United States over time. Through the lenses of justice, power, and politics, the series seeks to broaden scholarly debates about America's past as well as to inform public discussions about its future.

More information on the series, including a complete list of books published, is available at http://justicepowerandpolitics.com/.

DEMOCRACY'S CAPITAL

BLACK POLITICAL POWER IN WASHINGTON, D.C., 1960s–1970s

Lauren Pearlman

The University of North Carolina Press
Chapel Hill

This book was published with the assistance of the Authors Fund of the University of North Carolina Press and support from the University of Florida College of Liberal Arts and Sciences and Center for the Humanities and the Public Sphere (Rothman Endowment).

Designed by April Leidig
Set in Minion by Copperline Book Services
Manufactured in the United States of America

The University of North Carolina Press has been a member of the Green Press Initiative since 2003.

Cover illustration: Julius Hobson standing beside his station wagon equipped with loudspeaker. Star Collection, D.C. Public Library © *Washington Post*.

Library of Congress Cataloging-in-Publication Data
Names: Pearlman, Lauren, author.
Title: Democracy's capital : black political power in Washington, D.C., 1960s–1970s / Lauren Pearlman.
Description: Chapel Hill : The University of North Carolina Press, [2019] | Series: Justice, Power, and Politics | Includes bibliographical references and index.
Identifiers: LCCN 2019019895| ISBN 9781469653891 (cloth : alk. paper) | ISBN 9781469653907 (pbk : alk. paper) | ISBN 9781469653914 (ebook)
Subjects: LCSH: Washington (D.C.)—Politics and government—20th century. | African Americans—Washington (D.C.)—Politics and government—20th century. | Washington (D.C.)—Race relations—Political aspects. | Representative government and representation—Washington (D.C.) | Poor People's Campaign.
Classification: LCC F200 .P43 2019 | DDC 305.8009753—dc23
LC record available at https://lccn.loc.gov/2019019895

A portion of chapter 3 originally appeared as "More Than a March: The Poor People's Campaign in the District of Columbia," *Washington History* 26, no. 2 (Fall 2014): 24–41.

For Fletcher

CONTENTS

FIGURES

DEMOCRACY'S CAPITAL

INTRODUCTION

MAKE D.C. MEAN DEMOCRACY'S CAPITAL

By the late 1960s, Julius Hobson was tired. Tired of the white segregationists who crafted local policy from their perch on Capitol Hill. Tired of the white business and community groups who enforced the racial inequalities that stemmed from those policies and lobbied for urban renewal projects that overlooked the conditions of the neighborhoods where poor black Washingtonians lived. Tired of the District of Columbia's complacent black leaders, whom he had accused of selling out in the hopes of becoming part of the city's local government. Tired of the national politicians who used his city as an example of rampant lawlessness, the civil rights groups that came in to lead demonstrations to protest national injustices, and the local police officers who abused their powers.

Hobson was not alone. Despite local activists' unrelenting campaigns to break down racial barriers, and the national and international exposure afforded to Washington's segregation policies, Jim Crow still cast a long shadow over the District of Columbia. So, too, did the federal statutes that disenfranchised all Washingtonians and prevented them from securing local representation or creating the political infrastructure necessary to institutionalize temporary victories over employment and housing discrimination, school segregation, and police brutality. The 1963 March on Washington had helped generate support for what became the 1964 Civil Rights and 1965 Voting Rights Acts, which prohibited racial discrimination in public accommodations and voting. Yet these legislative victories did not have an immediate impact on D.C. residents. The passage of the Voting Rights Act in particular drew attention to the widening gulf between federal law and local reality: Washingtonians could not vote for president until 1961 and lacked national representation until Congress approved a nonvoting congressional delegate in 1970. Local representation was even more circumscribed: D.C. residents could not vote for school board members until 1968 or for mayor and city council members until 1974. Even after Congress approved the Home Rule Act in December 1973, granting some rights to self-government, the contours of D.C.'s local government remained clear: whether through "exclusive legislation," territorial governments, a commissioner system, or local elections, Congress still had broad powers over the capital. Because of this essential constraint, District residents have never achieved full citizenship rights.[1]

It was no wonder, then, that local activists were weary. "One of the problems of Washington is that you are always caught up being a proxy for the nation in making protests," Reverend Channing Phillips observed.[2] George Wiley, associate director of the Congress of Racial Equality (CORE), agreed. "I remember being very disenchanted with the March on Washington," he said. "I remember I—and the other tough activists in the nucleus of CORE—said 'the hell with that.' You know we're not going to any picnics down in Washington. We're going to do the nitty-gritty stuff here."[3] This book provides a detailed account of those who did "the nitty-gritty stuff" mere miles from the National Mall. It captures the transition from black protest to black political power on the municipal level under the Lyndon B. Johnson (1963–69) and Richard M. Nixon administrations (1969–74), an era during which the local movement underwent dramatic changes.[4]

By the 1960s, the national civil rights movement was becoming irrelevant to the needs of black Washington. District politics was caught up in the growing militancy of activists who were less patient than the city's traditional black leaders and more certain that the city's poor residents needed better advocates and newer methods to protect their interests. Their work previewed some of the larger ideological conflicts that took place within the national civil rights movement. In fact, many people in the civil rights movement, particularly younger activists sympathetic to the Student Nonviolent Coordinating Committee (SNCC), grew increasingly impatient with the pace of change in the country and with both the federal government and the older, more established civil rights organizations such as the National Association for the Advancement of Colored People (NAACP) and the Southern Christian Leadership Conference (SCLC). More left-wing groups like SNCC had grown openly critical of the systems that perpetuated inequality and were strongly opposed to the more hierarchical, bureaucratic, leader-centered organization of groups like SCLC. This new generation of activists called for "Black Power," not integration. New organizations such as the Black Panther Party, founded in October 1966, became known for their armed confrontations with police, their free education and health programs for poor urban communities, and their critiques of capitalism. Finally, from 1964 through 1967, uprisings spread through Harlem in New York; the Watts neighborhood in Los Angeles; Detroit, Michigan; and Newark, New Jersey.[5]

The move to more militant tactics and rhetoric, combined with the series of race riots that swept the nation in the years following the March on Washington, shifted national opinion against the civil rights movement as black visions of equality came closer to being realized. It was in part because of demands for self-determination and fears of black insurgency that President Johnson issued a reorganization plan in 1967 that promised D.C.'s black leaders a louder voice in local affairs. While Johnson originally intended for his reorganization plan to be a stepping-stone to full electoral representation, federal officials and white stakeholders capitalized on the limits of his home rule measure to dictate the implementation of Great Society and War on Poverty programming.

One cannot ask whether Washingtonians deserved a political voice without examining questions of whom the federal government deemed worthy of rights and resources. Scholars have begun to connect the history of the U.S. carceral state and that of the nation's welfare state. Specifically, they have started reckoning with the mechanisms that produced the dramatic welfare state retrenchment that arose concurrently with the dramatic growth of carceral institutions, largely on the state and federal level.[6] This book examines the intersection of the Great Society and the War on Crime on the municipal level and helps analyze how social programs developed alongside increasingly punitive law enforcement programs to limit radical political possibilities. But this outcome was not inevitable. As other scholars have documented, low-income residents in cities across the country seized on the political opportunities of the War on Poverty, and its emphasis on the "maximum feasible participation" of the poor, to claim new resources and challenge the power of local political elites. This was also true in D.C., and many black activists did harness the energy of the civil rights and Black Power movements to wage a grassroots assault on the political and economic foundations of black subordination.[7]

Studies of Washington, D.C., typically focus on the city as either a symbol of national politics or a mosaic of isolated neighborhoods.[8] Neither approach captures the ways that the fight for home rule undergirded fights over civil rights, law and order, and urban renewal and development during the 1960s and 1970s.[9] In Washington, more radical activists shifted to grassroots strategies to aggressively mobilize residents around the issue of home rule. During this time, local battles over War on Poverty programming—like the Community Action Program (CAP), Model Cities, employment training, tenant councils, and welfare expenditures—and high-profile anticrime efforts played out under strict federal oversight. Through intense fights over federal funds and programming, black Washingtonians fought for greater participatory democracy and community control under shifting and conflicting political regimes. Thus, the city's own struggle for self-determination reveals wide variations in the tactics and strategies taken up as the civil rights and Black Power movements intersected with the implementation of Great Society and War on Crime programming.[10]

Local antipoverty organizations reached their zenith in the mid-1960s. The absence of home rule provided the United Planning Organization (UPO), the local office charged with administering federal funds to District programs, with a great deal of autonomy. With a strong commitment to employing low-income residents, the UPO and other War on Poverty agencies funded projects at neighborhood centers and settlement houses, squeezing out independent grassroots movements but also opening up leadership opportunities, particularly for poor black women. Like Black Power activists in other cities, many of Washington's militant black leaders were at one time funded by federal dollars from Johnson's Great Society. Wanting a piece of this federal largesse, SNCC leader–turned–local home rule activist Marion Barry laid claim to his own antipoverty funds in 1967. But because the War on Poverty privileged issue-based activism and prioritized low-income and often female-driven mobilization, it diverted financial resources and the attention of militant activists away from grassroots movements around the larger issue of home rule until it reemerged as part of moderate black and predominantly male political platforms. As this book argues, the War on Poverty limited the democratic possibilities of the nation's capital. This was not exclusively the federal government's doing. Even black activists who took up the cause of home rule could not effectively convince poor residents that disenfranchisement was a more important citywide issue around which to mobilize. Accordingly, this book examines the ways in which black political power in D.C. reflected both the possibilities and limitations of the Great Society.[11]

Over the past decade, historians have increasingly analyzed the dramatic political, social, and economic shifts in the postwar era through the rise of the carceral state.[12] The effects of the carceral state include the growth of the physical apparatus of the criminal justice system, the expansion of America's prison population, and, most relevant to this book, the federal government's increasingly powerful role in crime-related policy making. *Democracy's Capital* examines the importance of punitive federal crime legislation, new surveillance methods, and the use of crime issues in national political campaigns to the marginalization of black radical politics and the undermining of self-determination during the 1960s and 1970s.[13]

Research about mass incarceration and the rise of punitive crime policy has largely focused on why political elites embraced law-and-order politics in the 1960s. Some scholars, for example, have examined the ways that Republican politicians and policy makers employed racially coded language about crime to mobilize white conservatives who were frustrated by the prevalence of urban disorder to gain electoral advantages.[14] Pushback against the idea that conservatives were solely responsible for "get tough" policies has fueled subsequent research on the crucial contributions of liberals to the War on Crime.[15] Other scholars have emphasized the role of grassroots pressure from white residents as a backlash against civil rights and urban uprisings and, on the opposite side of the spectrum, from communities of color over alarm about rising crime.[16] Most recently, political scientists and historians have argued that research on the War on Crime ignores black agency and that black politics did, in fact, play a pivotal role in crime politics. This work focuses on the black politicians, community leaders, and clergy across the country that responded to urban disorder by calling for more policing and more effective crime-control measures in their communities. Consequently, they claim, local black officials supported draconian law-and-order measures in major cities.[17]

In one of the more nuanced accounts of African Americans' influence on "get tough" politics, legal scholar James Forman Jr. argues that when it came to the issue of crime, black officials in Washington, D.C., "exhibited a complicated and sometimes overlapping mix of impulses."[18] This book examines the crucial era leading up to home rule, when the absence of self-government and the anticrime apparatus created by the Johnson administration shaped the parameters of the local black government's response to urban issues and marginalized black radicals. Moreover, the racialization of crime policies and crime discourse that began under the Johnson administration and was cemented under the Nixon administration compromised home rule and narrowed the policy solutions available to black residents to fight crime. When the first elected black officials took office in 1975, they were forced to fashion local crime policy out of failing federal crime fighting initiatives and in the face of an emerging drug epidemic.[19]

On the one hand, Johnson's limited home rule legislation made black leaders crucial stakeholders in debates over urban issues. On the other, it was representative of what urban historian Michael B. Katz has called mimetic reforms, "measures that respond to insurgent demands without devolving real power or redistributing significant resources." While it gave the impression that black leaders had the authority to make decisions about the city's governance, power resided indirectly with other constituents. For Katz, indirect rule meant that "powerful white Americans retained authority over cities through their influence on minorities elected to political office, appointed to public and social service bureaucracies, and hired in larger numbers by police forces." This was especially true in Washington, where Congress had the final say over the city's budget and laws, and white business and real estate groups had the ear of the House and Senate District Committees.[20]

Black politics also constrained the possibilities for self-determination. What had once been a radical proposition allowed for, instead, the selective incorporation of upper- and middle-class African Americans into the local political system.[21] As the city's more militant activists were pushed to the margins of city politics, they turned from the issue of home rule to activism around community control, riot rebuilding, police reform, and urban renewal—issues that were important to the city's black residents at a time when, at least one militant D.C. organization claimed, both local and national leaders had abandoned them.[22] As this book argues, Johnson's reorganization plan fractured black Washington politically, undermined grassroots activism, and prompted black municipal appointees to forge partnerships with local white business interests and conservative white lawmakers to implement a prodevelopment agenda and maintain traditional governing structures at the expense of the city's black residents. Along the way, the door opened to more moderate efforts at home rule. Those who were involved in the civil rights movement but were not part of the District's more militant cadre of radical activists sought to reclaim the city's rights to self-government, albeit in a watered-down version.[23]

Despite the burgeoning body of literature on the War on Crime, scholars rarely consider its effects on Black Power politics beyond its relationship to crime and drug policy. Black Power redefined black identity and American society from the mid-1950s through the mid-1970s, during which time the War on Crime devastated black communities. New works have helped historicize the Black Power era and its relationship to civil rights and other postwar phenomena. Demonstrating how Black Power activists waged political wars in the shadow of the civil rights movement and transformed struggles for racial justice has helped historians improve understandings of postwar American history and reframe the way in which a broad range of black activists attempted to redefine American democracy.[24] One of its lasting contributions was helping to usher in the first generation of black urban political leaders. But an examination of one of the first black-run cities reveals the limits of the popular argument that Black Power activists became part of the political mainstream through “nationalist appeals for racial solidarity in major metropolitan centers.”[25] While Black Power politics helped pressure the federal government to reconsider the city’s historic disenfranchisement, *Democracy’s Capital* demonstrates how tough-on-crime and prodevelopment politics undermined the struggle for black self-determination in the capital. The incorporation of black leaders into municipal politics and the prodevelopment coalition that coalesced in the capital took hold in cities from the urban Piedmont of North Carolina to New York, Los Angeles, Chicago, and Atlanta. Thus, Washington, D.C., a city that served as a bellwether for national policy and political shifts, also presaged local municipal policy and politics during the 1960s and 1970s.[26]

From the moment Congress arrived in the new capital city, it experimented with various arrangements to manage local affairs as it attempted to settle questions of self-government, federal representation, and financial support for the District. In 1801, Congress assumed jurisdiction over the federal district from territory ceded by Maryland and Virginia. To residents’ surprise, this dramatically changed their political status. No longer citizens of a state, they lost their national representation. As Congress became the equivalent of their state legislature, they also lost their self-determination. Slowly Congress afforded the city greater control over its own affairs. In 1802, it appointed a mayor to govern Washington but permitted white tax-paying males who had resided in D.C. for at least a year to elect a twelve-member city council. In 1812, it allowed the city council to appoint the mayor and, in 1820, permitted District residents to elect the mayor.[27]

New political, economic, and demographic changes prompted new experimentation. On account of the territorial retrocession of the Virginia portion of the federal district in 1847, the escalated pace of black migration into the District following the abolition of slavery in the capital in 1862, and the federal government’s unmet financial obligation to the city, Congress consolidated existing municipal and county governments into a large territorial government for the District in 1871. Following large-scale corruption and financial mismanagement of city funds, Congress abolished the territorial government and replaced it with a three-member commission appointed by the president. At the same time, it acknowledged its financial responsibility to the District and agreed to pay 50 percent of the District government’s expenses. The cementing of this political structure in the Organic Act of 1878 offered little opportunity for residents’ direct participation in local affairs.[28]

During this time, the District had become home to a large and influential free black population. By 1860, over three-fourths of the city's African American community was free and, overall, constituted nearly 20 percent of the city's sixty-one thousand residents. After the Civil War, the capital attracted many of the country's black elite, thanks to the unique social and economic opportunities available to them in Washington, including access to federal employment and the 1867 founding of Howard University, the nation's most prestigious black college. As a result, the city's black population grew by 44 percent from 1880 to 1900. At the turn of the twentieth century, the District claimed the largest urban concentration of blacks in the country. Many members of this sizable black community enjoyed a relatively high socioeconomic status, as evidenced by their occupations as university faculty, high school teachers, government workers, lawyers, and clergy.[29]

When President Woodrow Wilson and his progressive reformers took the capital by storm in 1913, they undercut the status of these prominent and prosperous black Washingtonians. Federal administrators insisted on racial segregation as part of their campaign to "clean up" the city and systematically dismantled many of the social and economic gains that African Americans had made during the late nineteenth and early twentieth centuries. By separating and isolating black civil servants and limiting their career prospects, the Wilson administration sharply eroded the city's prosperous black middle class. The president's successors followed patterns set by the Wilson administration. Consequently, government facilities remained segregated until the 1930s, when the Interior Department led federal efforts against racial segregation.[30]

From 1930 to 1950, Washington experienced a sustained period of growth as the city's population grew by 60 percent. The massive expansion of government and war-related bureaucracies during and after World War II provided new opportunities for blacks, who left the South in record numbers. The massive influx of African Americans from Alabama, Georgia, and the Carolinas outpaced other migrants as the proportion of black residents grew from 27 to 35 percent, more than doubling the black population during the same period. This dramatic growth compounded already-limited housing opportunities and added to inter- and intraracial tensions.[31]

The city's rigid housing segregation patterns forced black residents to double or triple up with other families in single-family units, search for new housing in restricted areas, and pay higher rents. Housing statistics from 1947 revealed glaring disparities between the city's white and black residents. Roughly two-thirds of all urban black Washingtonians lived within two and a quarter miles of the city's center. More than 20 percent shared living quarters with other families, as compared to 7 percent of white families forced to do the same.

Twelve percent lived in homes with more than one and a half occupants per room in D.C., while only 4 percent of whites did. Meanwhile, one of every nine black units in Washington lacked running water. Black families facing eviction notices or otherwise desperate to find adequate housing after months-long searches often wound up taking their chances in white neighborhoods protected by restrictive covenants.[32]

As housing conditions in D.C. and in cities across the country worsened, the federal government launched a groundbreaking national urban renewal program. The Housing Act of 1949, the first piece of legislation under this programmatic effort, offered cities funds to combat the twin trends of urban decay and suburban flight. Policy makers lobbied to implement this legislation in Washington, in part because the city had historically served as a laboratory for congressional implementation of urban policy and also because the city's postwar boom had exacerbated its housing problem. Affordable housing had become impossible to find—not just for the poor but also for members of Congress, thanks to the growth of government during and after World War II.[33]

The Redevelopment Land Agency (RLA) played an integral role in Washington's postwar redevelopment efforts. The federal government had created the five-member agency in 1946 and empowered it with the public authority to acquire and clear city property designated for redevelopment. In 1951, the RLA targeted Southwest D.C. as the city's first redevelopment site to be funded under the 1949 Housing Act. In 1954, the Supreme Court affirmed the RLA's legal standing to clear slums in the District, and the agency went ahead with its large-scale project to replace dilapidated housing inhabited by African Americans with high-rise apartments built for middle- and upper-income white residents, shopping centers, and restaurants. The project, which took another two decades to complete, forced the relocation of twenty-three thousand low-income black residents to housing projects around the city. Over a third of those displaced settled into public housing just outside the redevelopment area. Another two thousand families moved into private rental units in white middle-class neighborhoods east of the Anacostia River and in black neighborhoods like U Street, north of downtown. The Southwest renewal area's racial composition changed dramatically, from 70 percent black in 1950 to 70 percent white twenty years later.[34]

D.C.'s so-called slum removal paralleled efforts in nearly every major U.S. city at the time. But in the District, Congress and its appointed officials oversaw the decision, leaving Washingtonians without a voice in urban planning. The city's black residents were furious. In response to these massive demographic shifts, Walter Fauntroy, one of the District's black leaders, said famously, "Urban renewal means Negro removal." As dislocated Southwest residents moved to housing projects around the city, the government's overly ambitious 1955 report, *No Slums in Ten Years*, became a public mockery.[35]

By 1960, black residents were the majority in most census tracts east of 16th Street NW, with many of the poorest black residents clustered around Howard University and in historically black neighborhoods like Shaw, bounded by Massachusetts and Florida Avenues, 16th Street, and North Capitol Street. In addition to living with rat infestations and other slum conditions, these black residents sent their children to a school system neglected by the city, one where only one of three students entering ninth grade managed to graduate. Only Mississippi exceeded the District in infant mortality rates, and the city hospital routinely turned sick people away due to issues of overcrowding. Its gonorrhea infection rate was the highest in the nation, its syphilis rate the second highest, and its tuberculosis rate the sixth highest. More than one out of every four families had an income below the poverty line. But congressional overseers, while vocal in their horror over conditions in the city's ghettoized neighborhoods, failed to offer D.C. residents meaningful solutions.[36]

As the Second World War ushered a new wave of black migrants into the city, catapulting the city's black population into the majority in 1957, segregationists in Congress fought back to preserve white supremacy. The House and Senate Committees on the District of Columbia, two of the first standing committees created by Congress in 1816, wielded more power than the city's board of commissioners and had more authority over local affairs than even the president. Ever since the late nineteenth century, the House and Senate committees monitored black Washingtonians' struggles for employment and fair housing and against discrimination in restaurants and hotels. They oversaw the city's funds, managed its public services, and allocated money for slum clearance, highway construction, and new school buildings.[37]

Members of the House and Senate committees governed the District in a manner that conformed to their members' cherished images of Jim Crow. Elected to the Senate in 1934, Senator Theodore Bilbo (D-Miss.) was a self-professed Ku Klux Klan member. His vehement opposition to anti–poll tax and antilynching laws and his 1938 proposal of a work relief bill that threatened to deport twelve million African Americans to Liberia made him a notorious defender of white supremacy. When he assumed the chairmanship of the Senate District Committee in 1944, he used his position as the unofficial "Mayor of Washington" to preserve the city's Jim Crow culture. First Bilbo seized on issues of law and order, advocating for an expanded police force, programs to curb juvenile delinquency, and slum clearance—issues for which President

Richard Nixon would also advocate in Washington decades later. Bilbo also refused to entertain proposals to expand public housing in the city's black neighborhoods, recommended relocating black citizens to farms in Maryland and Virginia, and reviled the commingling of black and white federal workers in government offices.[38]

Bilbo's vigilant defense of segregation set the tone for the congressional governance of D.C. in the post–World War II era. When Bilbo's Senate career ended, Representative John L. McMillan (D-S.C.) carried on the mantle of white supremacy from his post as chairman of the House District Committee. From 1948 until 1972, the South Carolina representative refused to hold hearings on bills or proposals for self-government. McMillan was far from the only member of Congress to express disdain for the city's black residents. In the 1960s and 1970s, representatives and senators painted black Washington with broad criminal strokes, challenged the local government's authority, and leveraged the city's allegedly rampant crime problem to push for stronger law-and-order measures.[39]

In lieu of an elected city government, white business and civic groups also wielded a powerful influence over local affairs. Established in 1889 by prominent white business and civic leaders, the Washington Board of Trade (BOT) was the city's dominant commercial organization. The BOT drew members from Washington, northern Virginia, and suburban Maryland and represented the city's retailers, manufacturers, bankers, and attorneys on a host of issues ranging from economic development to public services. Primarily a civic group until the 1930s, its growing membership base and financial support allowed it to broaden its activities. It often sidestepped the city's local government appointees and appealed directly to the congressional committees and White House officials with recommendations on urban planning and development, transportation, residential zoning, crime, and local governance. It also spent considerable resources investing in the cultural infrastructure of the District; promoting the construction and maintenance of venues for professional sports, conventions, cultural events, and large festivals; encouraging businesses to move to the area; creating job training programs; and offering its expertise on urban issues from zoning to the minimum wage. In 1960, as its portfolio expanded and the city grew, it changed its name to the Metropolitan Washington Board of Trade.[40]

The *Washington Post*'s co-owner and publisher, Philip Graham, was also intent on aiding the city's economic development in the post–World War II era—so much so that in 1954 he spearheaded the creation of another group, the Federal City Council. From the outset, the Federal City Council's mission was "to develop, stimulate and encourage civic leadership in community development in the National Capitol."[41] Its membership was composed of leading businesspeople who believed that only an infusion of private sector money could improve the District and who agreed to work behind the scenes on projects that would have lasting effects on the city. The group backed a wide range of projects, beginning with the demolition of slums in Southwest D.C. to make way for a new urban center. Its forceful advocacy on behalf of the Southwest Redevelopment Project allowed the Federal City Council a central role in congressional deliberations and helped cement the alliance between House and Senate District Committees and local white business leaders. In 1959, to further cultivate business investment in the District, the group created Downtown Progress. Downtown Progress claimed a smaller, more elite membership that included the presidents and chairmen of the city's leading financial institutions, media outlets, utilities companies, and universities, and it advocated for the development of the central city above all other causes. The organization remained influential in real estate development and urban planning throughout the 1960s and 1970s.[42]

White citizens groups also had a powerful stake in local affairs. Comprising white male property holders, these groups cropped up in the 1880s and 1890s to uphold property values, lower taxes, and lobby for neighborhood services. In 1910, they consolidated into the Federation of Citizens Associations, an umbrella organization that used the defense of property values to maintain residential segregation. By the 1960s, it represented thirty-four neighborhood groups with a combined membership of about fifty thousand residents. In 1964, it voted to retain language in its constitution that restricted membership to "any white civic organization," thereby barring integrated homeowners associations from joining. The Federation finally excised the language from its constitution in 1972, but not before alienating its more progressive members. Throughout its existence, the Federation denounced any changes to the city's governance that threatened the interests of its white, middle-class, property-owning membership base, including home rule.[43]

Together, these business and civic groups formed the city's growth machine.[44] They privileged the construction of office buildings over low-income housing, interstate freeways over public transit, and the enlargement of the metropolitan police force over the amelioration of crime's root causes. Their partnership with the House District Committee bolstered crime prevention measures, redirected funds away from black neighborhoods and into downtown development, and prolonged the fight against home rule into the 1970s. The BOT, while supporting full voting representation in Congress for the

District, was one of the city's most powerful opponents of elected municipal representation. Fears of a government beholden to black voters guided its position. But it did not make its racial objections to home rule explicit. Instead, it couched its concerns about power shifting further toward the city's black population in broader arguments against the oppressive tax burden that home rule would usher into the city.[45]

White stakeholders continued to use the federal payment, which the government made to the city budget each year, as a reason to lobby against home rule. But Congress had been chipping away at the federal portion of the city's budget ever since agreeing to pay half the city's costs in 1878. Between 1919 and 1925, Congress abandoned the fixed percentage and set the federal payment at an annual fixed sum of $9 million, which in that year constituted about 30 percent of the total budget. As a result of federal budget cuts during the Depression, Congress reduced the 1934 federal payment to $5 million. Between 1957 and 1961, the federal payment never exceeded 16 percent of total District revenue, rendering that anti–home rule argument less persuasive.[46]

Until the mid-1960s, the fight for home rule did not have significant momentum behind it. Much of the city's early civil rights activity was led by the black middle class. They considered home rule an important component of a broader civil rights portfolio but had been enmeshed in fights for even more basic rights. In the preceding decades, they led demonstrations that mirrored those of national activists. They protested the Jim Crow laws that prevented African Americans from eating in local restaurants, staying in local hotels, shopping in downtown stores, or working in every sector of the federal government. They also challenged the racial covenants and discriminatory mortgage lending practices that had cemented Washington's segregated color lines. But until more radical activists took up the mantle of self-determination in the 1960s, the fight for home rule had lain fallow.[47]

During the 1960s, activists catalyzed Washington into a new phase of civil rights activism, one that allowed them to give expression to the frustrations of poor black residents while fighting for political and economic control of the city. Chapter 1 shows how the Washington CORE chapter led by Julius Hobson, the Free D.C. campaign run by SNCC leader Marion Barry, welfare rights activism by Etta Horn and other low-income black women, and the Black United Front (BUF), an organization formed to give activists a platform for more confrontational tactics and demands for autonomy, marked a strategic shift in the local movement toward self-determination. After almost a decade fighting for civil rights, black activists no longer wanted to live in a city whose terms were dictated by white stakeholders, federal officials, and unelected representatives. Due in part to the attention that radical campaigns brought to the issue of home rule, and also in part to Lyndon Johnson's own political calculus, the president issued Reorganization Plan No. 3 in 1967, replacing the city's three commissioners with a single mayor-commissioner and a nine-member council appointed by the president.

Johnson's plan, coupled with Congress's approval of popular elections for the D.C. Board of Education in April 1968, forged a new path for advocacy in the District. With revolutionary momentum on its side, groups like BUF were prepared to take control of the city. But Johnson's limited home rule measure, combined with the selective incorporation of upper- and middle-class African Americans with civil rights organizing experience into the local government, maintained the century's long tradition of indirect rule. Thus, while African Americans had ascended to local political office, powerful white stakeholders, along with members of the Johnson administration and Congress, retained control over the city.

While Johnson had issued his reorganization plan to give black residents more control over their affairs, he also implemented major crime fighting and riot prevention legislation on the local and national level. But on April 4, 1968, riots broke out in the capital and more than one hundred other cities following the assassination of civil rights leader Martin Luther King Jr. The uprising left thirteen people dead and more than twelve hundred injured, as well as an estimated $27 million in property losses, troop deployment, and city expenditures in Washington alone, catapulting the city to the center of national debates about civil rights and law and order.[48] Chapter 2 shows how Johnson's riot prevention and control measures—and particularly the ways in which they were implemented in the District—reordered the government around the problem of crime, challenged the local black government's authority, dampened the potential for radical change, and laid the groundwork for the conservative ascendance. In particular, local white business and civic groups and national lawmakers used the disturbance as a means to challenge the prudence of home rule legislation and pose questions about the future success of black self-determination—questions that remained long after the riots' duration.[49]

Five years after the March on Washington and just one month after the riots, SCLC returned to D.C. to stage the Poor People's Campaign (PPC), a national antipoverty campaign planned while King was still alive but executed after his assassination. Chapter 3 examines how the Poor People's Campaign unfolded in a city that operated with nascent black political power, federal oversight, and law-and-order measures that undermined grassroots activism. By ignoring the city's radical voices, racial tensions, and local organizations in planning the PPC, SCLC overlooked systemic injustices taking place just blocks beyond the monumental core. Quite the opposite, the campaign put a strain on local resources, sidetracked municipal government officials, increased tensions with the local police department, and provided fodder for a presidential candidate eager to make the city's lawlessness a focal point of his campaign. Meanwhile, in the shadow of the Poor People's Campaign, local activists battled the federal government over its War on Poverty efforts, revealing the ways Johnson's Great Society undermined black self-determination.

Although Johnson's anticrime initiatives paved the way for Nixon's presidential campaign, no president used law-and-order measures to curb Washingtonians' autonomy as vigorously as Nixon did. As his administration embarked on its anticrime crusade, it introduced a massive, overly punitive crime-control measure that Washingtonians themselves had limited ways to protest. As chapter 4 illustrates, the absence of home rule in Washington shaped the parameters of black municipal appointees' responses. While they felt immense pressure to reduce crime, they knew Nixon's legislation would disproportionally harm black constituents. They could not in good conscience support the D.C. Crime Bill and searched for alternatives to the White House's program. The Pilot Precinct Project, an ambitious program funded by the federal government to improve police-community relations in the inner city, presented such an opportunity. But as the city's municipal government tried to move out of the shadow of the riots, local white stakeholders partnered with national lawmakers and the Nixon administration to criminalize black Washingtonians and federalize policing efforts. Their efforts, combined with political compromises made by black municipal appointees and power struggles among black leaders, paved the way for the passage of punitive federal crime policy and the failure of community-based crime policy in the District.

After passing its sweeping omnibus crime bill for the District, the Nixon administration looked for a way to showcase its work in the capital. The upcoming Bicentennial celebration appeared to be the perfect occasion. The previous administration had already set in motion plans to commemorate the nation's two hundredth anniversary with extensive urban renewal efforts. However, as the celebration neared, the Nixon White House withdrew funds, decentralized Bicentennial programming, and minimized the importance of urban renewal to the overall celebration. Much like civil rights protests and law-and-order measures, chapter 5 shows how the urban development plans crafted during the Bicentennial planning period called into question the role of the federal government in local governance, shaped the parameters of Washingtonians' lives, and revealed the limits of community control under strict federal oversight.

In collaboration with both the Nixon administration and congressional representatives, the city's white boosters planned to use the national celebration as a platform for the redevelopment of downtown Washington. As they would discover, they had an ally in the city's black municipal leaders, who sided with the federal government and white developers in favor of the development of the city's downtown core. But the memory of earlier attempts at urban renewal shaped debates over urban development, including the building of the Eisenhower Convention Center and the redevelopment of Pennsylvania Avenue, which played out in the 1970s. Studies of these civic projects illustrate how, after decades of playing host to other groups, festivities, and protests, a new coalition of stakeholders tried to cash the Bicentennial's promissory note for permanent development. But in the end, the celebration revealed the unfulfilled promise of urban renewal efforts during the 1970s.

The April 1968 riots redirected the focus of Washington's more militant activists. While the District attempted to rebuild, they concentrated on the immediate problems of the city's low-income black residents rather than the issue of home rule. As the interracial coalition of local politicians and business groups strengthened, these activists found themselves pushed even further to the margins of traditional political power. During this time, more mainstream leaders and groups returned to the fight for home rule, opening up new, but gradualist, political possibilities during the Bicentennial planning period. Much like the 1968 riots, the Poor People's Campaign, and the D.C. Crime Bill, the Bicentennial became a battle not only over urban development but also over the leadership and direction of the city.

Democracy's Capital examines figures such as Stokely Carmichael, Marion Barry, Julius Hobson, Etta Horn, and Walter Fauntroy; local organizations like the Black United Front and United Planning Organization; and D.C. chapters of CORE, SNCC, SCLC, and the National Welfare Rights Organization (NWRO) as they confronted policies implemented by the federal government and racial barriers enforced by local groups like the Metropolitan Washington Board of Trade, the Federal Citizens Associations, and Downtown Progress. This account also captures the experiences of black Washingtonians who held federal jobs, participated in grassroots activism, and stood in line late into the night waiting to testify before the city council on neighborhood conditions. The focus is on how different constituent groups, including Black Power activists, white business groups and homeowners associations, national civil rights organizations, law enforcement officials, the White House, members of Congress, and an emerging black majority electorate negotiated the protests, political battles, and policy experiments of the 1960s and 1970s.

Self-government in the nation's capital was not a simple or arcane issue about representation but one that was central to conflicts between local and national powers. The implementation of the 1974 home rule legislation granted rights to self-government, but it did not change the U.S. Constitution. Legislative home rule allowed Congress to grant autonomy to the local government, while reserving the ability to intervene and overrule the District at any time.[50] This was not a fluke. Under the Johnson and Nixon administrations, local battles over the War on Poverty and War on Crime played out under strict federal oversight. Through intense fights and increased activism, Washingtonians fought for greater political control. But the racialization of crime policies and crime discourse, the use of new surveillance methods, and the implementation of punitive federal crime legislation curbed their efforts to achieve true self-determination. This ensured that the majority-black city with a strong civil rights tradition and hints of radical promise never fulfilled its democratic potential. It is no wonder, then, that black activists were fed up.

1

FROM CIVIL RIGHTS TO SELF-DETERMINATION

How do you accomplish change in a city where you don't have political power?
—Marion Barry, March 1966

On August 28, 1963, SCLC leader Martin Luther King Jr. delivered his renowned "I Have a Dream" speech on the steps of the Lincoln Memorial, calling for America to give black citizens "the riches of freedom and the security of justice." Arguably the greatest symbol of the civil rights movement, the image of King preaching to the peaceful crowd has been seared into public memory, providing visibility for racial justice issues and support for the 1964 Civil Rights Act. But what is not as well remembered is that just beyond the Mall, disenfranchised residents lived in a majority-black city that did not have political freedom or the channels to seek out justice.[1]

During the 1960s, a growing cohort of civil rights advocates was moving away from the integrationist ideology that had dominated earlier campaigns for civil rights. No longer were they satisfied protesting to protect basic rights that had been won decades before. Even so, local activists led a well-coordinated effort to support King's campaign when SCLC arrived in the District to stage the March on Washington. The Washington Coordinating Committee, chaired by local SCLC leader Walter Fauntroy and D.C. NAACP leader Edward Hailes, helped recruit upward of thirty-five thousand residents to march, arranged housing for out-of-towners, and assisted with crowd control. In addition, Howard University students helped with logistics, Washington CORE director Julius Hobson led the demonstrators' internal police force to help maintain order, and local civil rights leader Reverend Channing Phillips offered up his church, Lincoln Temple, as headquarters for volunteers to congregate.[2]

But national civil rights legislation had not improved their political status. Two years after the passage of the Voting Rights Act, for example, no more than one hundred counties had been protected from the egregious system of disenfranchisement maintained by white citizens. In Washington, the conflict was less violent but more striking. Even after the 1961 ratification of the Twenty-Third Amendment, which permitted District residents to vote for president, Washingtonians were still disenfranchised and financially and politically dependent on the government. So some activists shifted to grassroots strategies to more aggressively mobilize residents around the issue of home rule. Their actions helped catalyze the city into a new phase of civil rights activism, one that allowed them to give expression to the frustrations of low-income black residents while fighting for political and economic control of the city.

The D.C. CORE chapter led by Julius Hobson, the Free D.C. campaign run by SNCC leader Marion Barry, welfare rights activism by Etta Horn and other low-income black women, and the mere presence of a new organization called the Black United Front, formed to give activists a platform for more confrontational tactics and demands for autonomy, marked a strategic shift in the local movement toward self-determination. In the past, the city's black middle-class activists had been too busy waging battles against racial discrimination and too focused on traditional civil rights tactics to craft a sustained campaign to change Washington's political infrastructure. National civil rights leaders had not taken up the cause either. Instead, they routinely overlooked black residents' colonial status when they came to town to stage demonstrations on the National Mall.

There was another problem as well. Black residents did not necessarily connect their political disenfranchisement with the racial discrimination, systemic poverty, and poor infrastructure with which they lived. Activists like Hobson and Barry knew that without elected representation to protect the city's poorest residents, conflicts over the control of local resources would continue to emerge with public and private entities, white stakeholders, and government officials. They trusted that local sovereignty would amplify disenfranchised voices, prevent the federal government from dictating the parameters of their lives, and be the catalyst to institute permanent structural change. For them, home rule had to be at the center of local protests. As they articulated these new demands, the chasm between their fight for home rule, the black middle class's concern with respectability politics, national civil rights organizations' continued demonstrations for legislation, and the federal government's desire to manage the pace of desegregation deepened.

It was southern white segregationists in Congress and local white stakeholders, not competing civil rights groups, that presented the biggest obstacle to black Washingtonians who demanded self-government. Representative John McMillan, who chaired the House District Committee since 1948, governed the city as a personal fiefdom. McMillan, a staunch conservative with no sympathy regarding District residents' disenfranchisement, relied on allies in Congress to help hold the line against self-government.

To keep power out of black hands, the House District Committee also consulted with local white organizations like the Washington Board of Trade, the Federation of Citizens Associations, the Federal City Council, and Downtown Progress regarding decisions related to urban renewal, tourism, and infrastructure projects. Given their influence within Congress, these white-run business and neighborhood associations also vehemently opposed home rule measures that would give the city's majority-black population a greater voice in District affairs. The BOT claimed to speak on behalf of a diverse array of community members and interests. But in 1965, Julius Hobson accused the organization of perpetuating racial inequality in the District. The BOT, Hobson charged, opposed "all constructive actions that would help bring about equality between the poor and the affluent, the black and the white, using its considerable influence to oppose progressive measures."[3] Racial motivations similar to those undergirding their anti–home rule stances found expression in white community groups and business associations in cities across the country. But in the nation's capital, where out-of-state legislators rather than local elected officials governed, groups like the BOT wielded an immense amount of political influence. For decades, they succeeded in enforcing the racial inequalities that stemmed from federal policies.[4]

To counteract the power of these various stakeholders, activists zeroed in on the fight for self-government. In 1967, over the objections of the House District Committee and white business and real estate interests, President Johnson aided their fight by passing a reorganization plan that provided for an appointed municipal government. The shift that many civil rights leaders made to local office changed the political landscape. But it did not free Washington from federal control. Nor did it allow grassroots activism to find its footing in more formal politics. Instead, the president's limited home rule measure—enacted as a last resort in the face of obstructionist politicians—promoted elite African Americans into city functions and set up larger battles over civil rights, law and order, and urban development in the capital.

CORE IN THE CAPITAL

Dressed in a conservative suit, donning a fedora, and smoking his signature pipe, Julius Hobson did not fit the stereotype of a militant activist. Yet the

Birmingham, Alabama, native, born in 1922, fought relentlessly to eliminate racial inequality in the nation's capital and help loosen the federal government's strong oversight over residents' lives. Not only did he battle with the federal government. He also went toe to toe with national civil rights leaders over the direction of CORE. Through his leadership of the D.C. chapter, he showed Washingtonians an alternative to the staid civil rights activism for which the city was known, provided a new direction for social protest, and furthered the fight for black self-determination in the capital.

After graduating from high school, Hobson attended the Tuskegee Institute. During World War II, he enlisted in the army. He fought from northern Africa through Italy, flying in over thirty-five missions and winning numerous accolades. On returning to the states, Hobson headed north, first to Columbia University in New York and then to Howard University, where, drawn to Marxist theory, he studied with leftist professors while working toward a master's in economics in the late 1940s.[5]

Focused on radical ideas rather than radical action, Hobson did not participate in his first protest demonstration until after the 1954 Supreme Court's *Brown v. Board of Education* decision. Of an older generation than the college students who participated in the movement by staging sit-ins in Greensboro, North Carolina, and other college towns, Hobson initially eschewed grassroots work in favor of a professional career. In 1947, Hobson married Carol Smith, whom he met at Howard. He worked first as an economic researcher at the Library of Congress and then as a social science statistical analyst with the Social Security Administration, where he honed his research techniques. In 1949, Hobson had his first child, Julius Hobson Jr. Eight years later, he had a daughter, Jean. But despite job security and a growing family, Hobson was restless.[6]

Propelled to action by his children's experiences in Washington's public schools, Hobson took an interest in efforts to desegregate District schools in the wake of *Brown*. Shortly after, he became more involved in civic activities. By 1960, Hobson had ties to more than five civic and civil rights organizations, serving on his children's Parent Teacher Association (PTA) as well as on the Executive Committee of the D.C. branch of the NAACP.[7] In a town where congressional committees set education policy for the nation's capital and the president appointed its school board members, the PTA remained one of the few avenues available to pursue meaningful change. It served as Hobson's entrée into education reform, leading to his early efforts to desegregate his son's school, Woodridge Elementary School.[8] His work with the local NAACP branch, including a 1957 investigation into the Metropolitan Police

Department's (MPD) promotion practices, also helped shape Hobson's trademark blend of research and confrontation politics. Inspired by Hobson's work in local desegregation battles, members of CORE's Washington chapter recruited him to lead the organization in 1961.[9]

The early 1960s was a pivotal moment for CORE. Influenced by the writings of American philosopher Henry David Thoreau and the teachings of Mohandas Gandhi, activists had founded CORE in 1942. Members adhered to the belief that nonviolent demonstrations could be used as a tool to end racial discrimination, and they planned and implemented direct action campaigns to publicize the reality of racism in America. But CORE remained relatively unknown until 1961, when it made national headlines for sponsoring Freedom Rides in support of integrated interstate bus travel in the South.[10]

In the early 1960s, CORE was still a predominantly white, northern-based organization with fewer than thirty local chapters and six hundred active members. As it grew, its leaders faced two principal organizational dilemmas that paved the way for the D.C. chapter's success. First there was the challenge of ensuring that local chapters maintained a high level of discipline and understanding of CORE's methodology and philosophy as the organization expanded. As CORE discovered, local chapters wanted more independence than the national office wished to grant them. But with its headquarters located in Chicago, and chairman James Farmer based in New York, CORE leadership was too dispersed to verify that local chapters always complied with its values. Ultimately it had no choice but to officially grant them greater autonomy. This decision would give Julius Hobson greater freedom to adapt to different situations on the ground rather than rely solely on his commitment to CORE's national philosophy and tactics.[11]

The other issue CORE faced was how to increase the participation of African Americans within the organization. In its early years, Farmer described CORE as "small, Northern, middle-class, elitist, idealistic, and predominantly white."[12] Despite its pacifist leanings, Farmer believed that the group ought to allow nonpacifists to join, for "being Negroes for them is tough enough without being pacifist, too."[13] As CORE aggressively expanded its employment campaigns in the North, it attracted greater numbers of working-class blacks. In 1961 alone, the organization opened over twenty new chapters throughout the country. The selection of Hobson to run the D.C. chapter that year helped subdue black resentment against the national body's white membership and sent a message to the organization's base that African Americans would lobby for local leadership positions.[14]

Hobson's new position put him in direct competition with the leaders of the local chapters of the Urban League, NAACP, and SCLC. But unlike some of those activists, who saw their D.C. stations as potential stepping-stones to national positions, Hobson did not look toward greener pastures. When asked whether greater political ambitions motivated him to join CORE, Hobson responded quizzically, "Where would I go?"[15] Explaining why he chose to emphasize local problems, Hobson said, "I thought that the problems in the District of Columbia were big enough to take up the time of one person full-time. . . . I've always thought in terms of strong local leadership."[16] Hobson was not the only activist to think in these terms. But he was one of the first in Washington to articulate new demands for black self-determination.

From 1961 to 1964, Hobson poured his free time into fighting Washington's Jim Crow practices. During that time, he ran eighty-five picket lines at retail stores and businesses, negotiated nearly sixty agreements between employees and management to hire African American workers, and helped secure over four thousand jobs for African Americans in the District. Hobson's achievements included threatening a boycott that prompted the hiring of forty-four black bus drivers and clerks by D.C. Transit, forcing the hiring of the first black auto sales personnel and dairy employees, and waging a campaign to combat job discrimination by public utility companies. Washington CORE also demanded fair housing regulations. Hobson frequently staged "live-ins" at private apartment buildings that discriminated against blacks and, during the year of the March on Washington, led over four thousand protesters to city hall to urge the D.C. commissioners to prohibit discriminatory practices in rental housing. The commissioners got the message. After the demonstration, they enacted a housing ordinance desegregating D.C. rental units.[17]

Aside from tried-and-true civil rights strategies, Hobson favored unconventional tactics to overcome the city's racial disparities. When the commissioners responded too slowly to the inner city's rat infestation problem, Hobson launched weekend "rat catching rallies." To draw attention to his cause, he affixed cages to the roof of his station wagon, fondly called the "Rat Wagon," and threatened to release his haul each week in Georgetown. Shortly after he began these excursions, the city instituted a rat extermination program in Northeast D.C. The "Rat Wagon" doubled as the "Cop Watching Wagon" on Friday nights. To confront police brutality, Hobson tailed squad cars and yelled out to officers through a makeshift microphone to ensure that they behaved in accordance with professional standards. Through these confrontational tactics, Hobson provided residents with alternative methods to protest the conditions in which they lived while accelerating the pace of change in the capital.[18]

Rarely did black Washingtonians of Hobson's status risk their job security by causing such commotion. But Hobson, unafraid of the federal government and unwilling to make concessions to national CORE, chose to risk his job with the Social Security Administration to fight against racial injustice. As an *Ebony* reporter noted, "In the nation's capital, where government specialists generally are meek about insisting on civil rights gains and more interested in promotion to super-grades, the Birmingham, Alabama native is an eccentric."[19] His refusal to pander to his employer or to other civil rights organizations might have made him a radical in Washington, but it also made him a trusted representative to the black community—one of only a few at a time where, as Sam Smith, editor of the alternative *D.C. Gazette*, observed, "never had so many sold out for so little."[20]

Hobson felt no more beholden to the federal government than to CORE. Defying national leadership, Hobson honed an organizing tradition that he called "guerilla tactics in nonviolence." He also asserted that Washington CORE was not a nonviolent chapter, "in that it was not our philosophy." Furthermore, he refused to allow the local chapter to partake in what he believed were CORE's "religious ceremonies of nonviolence." Hobson's unconventional behavior frustrated national leadership but also made the D.C. chapter one of the most respected local chapters.[21]

Despite leadership's misgivings, Hobson's successful stewardship of Washington CORE, and Washington CORE's strategic location in the nation's capital, led him to work closely with national CORE leaders. Hobson trained northern civil rights activists in nonviolent techniques for participation in the 1961 Freedom Rides that departed from D.C. He also collaborated with founder and national director James Farmer during the Route 40 project, which aimed to desegregate restaurants along the route African ambassadors traveled from Washington to New York. Because of his hard work, and despite his obstinate ways, Hobson rose to the post of southeastern regional director for the national organization in July 1962.[22]

Despite Hobson's newfound success on the national level, local tensions brewed. In the spring of 1964, Hobson initiated his last protest as the director of D.C. CORE. That March, as local civil rights organizations strategized over what to do about the continued inequality of D.C.'s educational facilities—including overcrowding, inadequate school supplies, the assignment of too many temporary teachers to poor schools, the humiliation of black children before their white classmates, and the fact that some school personnel asked police officers to handle problems that should have been dealt with by administrators—Hobson abruptly called a local CORE-sponsored boycott of the D.C. school system.[23]

Eleven black leaders representing the city's major civil rights and religious groups spoke out against Hobson's plan. The group believed that Hobson had called the boycott preemptively, thereby jeopardizing their negotiations with D.C.'s superintendent. They wanted no part of his confrontational demonstration. The boycott made national headlines. "Here we are in the federal city, the nation's capital, where the schools have been integrated, where racial barriers have been dropped by law . . . and yet we are faced now with an impending school boycott," *Newsweek* reported, overlooking the actual state of affairs in D.C.'s school system.[24] On the heels of controversial school boycotts by Brooklyn CORE in February and early March 1964, the national body also spoke out against the proposed demonstration. At the end of March, Hobson capitulated. He called off the boycott, claiming that it was mainly a scare tactic to urge the school system to improve conditions. But by then, the activist's relationships with both local and national CORE leaders had soured.[25]

For some of D.C. CORE's members, Hobson's threatened boycott was the last offense in a series of unilateral decisions made by the leader, including boycotts against businesses that had been friendly toward the black community, theatrics when quiet meetings may have achieved the same results, and a zero-tolerance policy for dissent. His willingness to create change in the District by any means necessary wore on the rest of the chapter. Members hotly contested his tactics and leadership style, including his treatment of Roena Rand, one of the many women who comprised the local chapter's active membership. That spring, Hobson expelled Rand for allegedly disorderly conduct and canceled the employment campaign she had coordinated. His behavior toward Rand upset members, who rallied to the black woman's defense.[26]

Finally, on May 8, local chapter member Ethelbert Haskins wrote to James Farmer. Speaking on behalf of the anti-Hobson faction, he asked Farmer to expel the leader from the organization for administering the chapter in an undemocratic and irresponsible manner.[27] While awaiting Farmer's reply, the fractured body did not keep its loyalties secret. In June, pro-Hobson CORE members picketed against racial preferences at Casualty Hospital, while anti-Hobson members demonstrated against unfair housing practices four and a half miles away at Trenton Park Apartments.[28]

On June 19, 1964, CORE's national steering committee voted to expel the militant leader and place D.C. CORE under trusteeship. Hobson, under the impression that CORE's national leaders had conspired with the local chapter, wrote Farmer a scathing letter. "I really sympathize with you and the many problems you have. I am sorry to see you destroy your own organization in trembling fear. There is no room in this movement for a conservative activist even if it is profitable," he wrote. Unrelenting in his critique, Hobson continued, "The movement needs a CORE, not another NAACP or Urban League, and I hope that the watch-word of CORE will become, as it once was, human dignity and not acceptability and respectability."[29] Hobson was furious. It was not only one of the first times that the national organization had expelled an active member but also a sign to him that CORE was retreating from its own philosophy toward the kinds of civil rights politics for which the District had long been known.[30]

Although Hobson was one of the first casualties of CORE's national agenda, the tensions and cleavages within the organization revealed a state of crisis. Two years earlier, at its 1962 national convention in Miami, Florida, Farmer had expressed concern over the fact that local chapters had difficulties applying CORE's methods and philosophy to their desired outcomes. Additional conflicts over CORE's interracial membership, the erosion of the commitment to nonviolence, and the challenge posed by some chapters to the authority of the national office percolated within the organization.[31]

These issues intensified during the spring of 1964 as CORE feuded not just with Hobson but also with its Brooklyn chapter over militant "stall-in" tactics to disrupt the World's Fair in New York. Brooklyn CORE, a chapter that did not shy away from controversial tactics, had devised a plan for volunteers to disable their automobiles on major expressways on April 22, the fair's opening day. Farmer called the scheme "hare-brained" and suspended the chapter, causing a rift between CORE members. Hobson lent his support to the pro-stall-in Brooklyn contingent, which had decided to go forward with the protest despite their suspension. A last-minute counterdemonstration inside the World's Fair grounds, led by Farmer himself, drew greater member support. By waging a far more successful protest, Farmer proved, at least momentarily, that he could still exert discipline over the organization. But the damage had been done. The militant undercurrents Washington and Brooklyn CORE expressed were becoming part of the movement's dominant discourse.[32]

Hobson's expulsion foreshadowed larger problems for CORE nationally. Unable to contain the burgeoning militancy advocated by members, James Farmer resigned less than two years after Hobson's departure. When Floyd McKissick, a radical attorney and supporter of Black Power, replaced Farmer as national director in 1966, he brought CORE's philosophy more in sync with Hobson's. Firmly seizing upon the slogan of Black Power as its guiding philosophy, CORE rejected its interracial, pro-integration, nonviolent origins and affirmed support for self-defense when necessary.[33]

Hobson's expulsion sent ripples through the nation's capital. In a June editorial, the *Washington Afro-American* argued that Hobson's dismissal would have repercussions of importance to everyone involved or interested in the civil rights movement in the District.[34] Fed up with both local and national civil rights politics, Hobson viewed his expulsion as a chance to wash his hands of the "pasteurized, middle class, professional Negroes who were running the civil rights groups and the phony white liberals who were trying to find out what a Negro was."[35] Looking back, Hobson admitted that his contemporaries at the local Urban League, SCLC, and NAACP branches were more of a hindrance than a help. "They fought everything I did and did their damnedest to get rid of CORE," he said. "They were opposed to CORE and opposed to direct action."[36]

As Hobson test-drove his confrontation tactics, local civil rights organizations pushed back. They were wary of another black activist jockeying for space in a crowded field of established civil rights organizations that relied on the city's black middle class for support. However, what Hobson's work illustrated was that black residents had a wide array of demands—demands that had not been met through an accommodationist approach. The sophisticated urban problems that emerged in the postwar era demanded a more permanent solution than activists' protests had previously afforded. While they had spent decades demonstrating to win fights over employment and housing discrimination, school segregation, and police brutality, they could not convert them into permanent victories. Until the city was free to govern itself, civil rights leaders were forced to fight the same battles over and over again. As Hobson reflected on the issues that he believed most affected black residents, he recognized that the common methods of nonviolent direct action and protest would not preserve their dignity. Instead leaders would need to harness the economic might of the poor and lead them in efforts to direct their own destiny. The only way forward, he reasoned, was through structural change.

Yet after Hobson left CORE, the D.C. chapter enjoyed a short second life. CORE's national office reinstated Roena Rand, who in 1965 would go on to become the only black women elected to chair the chapter. The spring that Hobson was expelled, women represented one-third of the chapter's active members. His departure temporarily opened new leadership opportunities for them. In addition to Rand, women won five of eight elected positions. The chapter's new female leadership resolved to focus on the issues that plagued the city's poor black residents. To symbolize this, they moved the chapter from Northwest D.C. to the Southeast area across the Anacostia River. After relocating its office closer to the city's public housing, D.C. CORE prioritized campaigns for subsidized low-income housing and against highway construction in black neighborhoods. It even created a Freedom School in Anacostia to promote personal transformation. By facilitating these projects, the chapter emphasized political and economic empowerment without adopting all of Hobson's more provocative methods. However, when McKissick became the nation director, and as the Black Power philosophy became more explicitly articulated in masculine rhetoric, women were once again relegated to the sidelines. This was especially true in the D.C. chapter, where members elected black men to fill every position except recording secretary in 1966.[37]

Meanwhile, just one month after his expulsion, Hobson formed a chapter of the Associated Community Teams (ACT), an organization created in 1963 by activists Adam Clayton Powell Jr., Gloria Richardson, and Jesse Gray. ACT dramatically departed from the era's traditional civil rights organizations. It believed in abolishing the institutions that fostered oppression and exploitation and had as its motto "Research and Destroy." For Hobson, the institution that most oppressed and exploited D.C. residents was glaringly obvious. Therefore he used ACT as a vehicle to draw attention to Washingtonians' colonial status and to what he perceived was the most hypocritical institution in the country, the federal government, which from its headquarters in the capital crafted civil rights legislation that bypassed the black residents who lived there.[38]

While attacking the federal government, Hobson also vowed to distance himself from other local black leaders and work more closely with District residents. In 1966, he told the *Washington Star* that he was "not a Negro leader but a Negro with a direct line to ghetto people."[39] He ran what he called "the most militant citizen group with the smallest membership."[40] Sam Smith, editor of the *D.C. Gazette*, joked that ACT had just "six men and a telephone booth," but Hobson argued that that was all he needed to spark a revolution.[41] Yet Hobson's new affiliation with ACT made Washington's political and civil rights leaders uncomfortable. Known affectionately as the "eccentric" of the D.C. civil rights movement prior to 1964, Hobson quickly became a symbol of militancy. Descriptions of him ranged from "the Negro most feared in Washington" to part of the "lunatic fringe."[42] The *Washington Post* even described his organization as "a flat failure in the civil rights field."[43] The message was clear: controversial tactics and challenges to the city's central governing system were not as welcome as the nonviolent direct action campaigns of the past.

Acting as chairman of ACT, and without the support of other local civil rights leaders, Hobson embarked on the first legal challenge to de facto segregation in public schools since the Supreme Court's *Brown v. Board* ruling had outlawed legal segregation in them in 1954. During the summer of 1966, Hobson filed a lawsuit against D.C. School Superintendent Carl Hansen. To prepare for his case, the statistician conducted meticulous research and utilized copious amounts of data in support of his claim that black students received inferior educational opportunities in the city's public schools. It seemed that Hobson could not have found a more sympathetic judge than Judge Skelly Wright to test *Brown*'s legal teeth. President John F. Kennedy had appointed Wright to the U.S. Court of Appeals for the District of Columbia in 1962. Wright, an antisegregationist, was well known for his legal decisions enforcing the desegregation of public facilities in New Orleans. After a yearlong court battle that gained significant news coverage but left Hobson deeply in debt, the activist won his case. In June 1967, Judge Wright outlawed the school system's existing tracking system, desegregated faculty, and ended the differential distribution of books and supplies. Fittingly, the following year residents voted Hobson onto the city's first popularly elected school board.[44]

While Hobson poured his energy into his legal case, he attracted the attention of another militant group, the Deacons for Defense and Justice. The Deacons, a black, armed self-defense organization, had formed in 1964 in Jonesboro, Louisiana, to protect its community and visiting civil rights workers from racial vigilantes—mainly Ku Klux Klan members. National CORE members had engaged in strong philosophical disagreements with the Deacons over their pledge to use violent tactics to protect CORE volunteers who worked on voter registration projects down south. After Hobson severed ties with CORE, the Deacons approached him in March 1966 with a request to help develop a chapter in the District.[45]

The idea that the nation's capital would be on the Deacons' radar shocked both black and white residents, who associated Washington with more cosmopolitan cities north of the Mason-Dixon line. Why, African American *Washington Post* columnist William Raspberry wondered, did the Deacons want to move into the nation's capital, "where demonstrators almost never are subjected to violence and where there has been no reported KKK activity?"[46] For Hobson, the answer was obvious. Although demonstrators like those who came to D.C. for the 1963 March on Washington left unharmed, the city's black residents faced increased police brutality. Unlike those protesting on the Mall, the federal government had not passed legislation to protect them from the abuses they suffered. "Negroes can't expect justice from officials," Hobson said, "but middle-class Negro leadership acquiesces on this mistreatment," he added, taking a jab at local black civil rights leaders.[47]

Although the Deacons never moved to Washington, the very fact that they forged connections with Hobson in 1966 was significant. While there might not have been a Klan presence in the District, the Deacons made their point clear: federal oversight should also be cause for alarm. Hobson agreed. Within two years, Hobson, along with other local activists, created a new organization called the Black United Front, a group that gave him a platform for his confrontational style and demands for self-determination.

The work that Julius Hobson did as a local activist, "the nitty-gritty stuff" that flew under the radar of a nation captivated more by the capital's monumental symbolism than by the District's municipal problems, proved invaluable to the city's fight for racial justice. His confrontational approach shook up the District and redirected the local movement toward grassroots organizing. Hobson used D.C. CORE as a vehicle to run picket lines, stage "live-ins," and secure jobs for thousands of black residents. When national CORE's rigid structure did not accommodate the on-the-ground shifts in Washington's local struggle, Hobson did not surrender. Instead, he adopted his own organizing philosophy.

It was rare to see a black Washingtonian in Hobson's line of employment attack not just local institutions but also the federal government. But Hobson was not merely an "eccentric," as reporters claimed. He was representative of the growing tensions within CORE. His showdown with CORE chairman James Farmer previewed some of the larger ideological conflicts that took place within the national civil rights movement. For Hobson, his expulsion from CORE signaled that the city's poor residents needed better advocates and newer methods to protect their interests. Until then, he vowed to continue fighting the congressional officials who crafted local policy, the white business and community groups that enforced the racial inequalities that stemmed from those policies, and the black leaders who were complicit in their enforcement.

MARION BARRY COMES TO WASHINGTON

Hobson was not the only activist to use confrontational politics to push Washington's local movement in new directions. Marion Barry, a prominent leader in the Student Nonviolent Coordinating Committee, did so too. Unlike Hobson, Barry came to Washington to undertake national work. But when he took over the local SNCC office in May 1965, he saw new opportunities for political organizing and chose to stay in town to help force the federal government to loosen its grip over the capital.

Born in Itta Bena, Mississippi, in 1936, Barry was the third of ten children. When he was four years old, his father died and his mother moved the family to Memphis, Tennessee. There his mother found work in a slaughterhouse, and he took on a variety of jobs, including picking cotton, delivering newspapers, and bagging groceries. Barry's industrious spirit shone brightly from a young age. He attended choir practice at a church that he did not belong to because he had heard that the choirmaster gave out carfare to all attendees. The young entrepreneur would pocket the money and walk home. Barry graduated from nearby LeMoyne College in 1958 and, two years later, earned a master's of science in organic chemistry from Fisk University, in Nashville, Tennessee. While at Fisk, Barry joined the local NAACP chapter and began participating in local demonstrations. In 1960, after four black students tried to integrate a Woolworth's in Greensboro, North Carolina, Barry joined Nashville lunch counter sit-ins staged in support of their efforts. His first political victory came that same year when students met in Raleigh, North Carolina, to organize SNCC.[48]

Martin Luther King's Southern Christian Leadership Conference had given Director Ella Baker an eight-hundred-dollar grant to hold a student conference for black sit-in leaders in the South. Baker held the April 1960 conference at Shaw University, where she encouraged the over two hundred participants to articulate their own vision for the organization. Baker had hoped that the students would realize a more collectivist model of leadership than the more established organizations had adopted, and she encouraged them to distance themselves from groups like the NAACP and SCLC. Thanks to Baker's guidance, the students created an independent organization that would become known for its sit-ins at racially segregated lunch counters, public libraries, parks, swimming pools, and movie theaters.[49]

Barry was not the obvious choice to become SNCC's first chairman. He was not even the leader of the larger Nashville contingent attending the Shaw conference—that honor belonged to an activist named Diane Nash, who was out of the room at the time the key vote was held. Barry was, instead, the compromise pick, "in the right place at the right time," according to one journalist. And, just one year later, he quit SNCC to pursue a doctoral program in chemistry. But SNCC's multifaceted civil rights portfolio, along with its meteoric rise into the nation's consciousness, seduced Barry back into the fold.[50]

In May 1965, SNCC executive secretary James Forman dispatched Barry to Washington, D.C., to raise funds for the organization, lobby for national civil rights legislation, and serve as a liaison with federal officials. On his arrival, Barry outlined to SNCC a dire situation. According to Barry, local residents did not do "much of anything in terms of sit-ins at lunch counters, or rent strikes, or school construction site marches, school boycotts, store boycotts, or any kind of boycott over a sustained time." In addition, he reported, they regularly witnessed outside activists use their city to wage national demonstrations. "[Washingtonians] have psychologically grown accustomed to people who come in and do things and go out," the activist reported to SNCC officials. Based on Barry's reporting, SNCC leaders agreed to let him stay to gain organizing experience in the capital and lead the organization's first major experiment in urban reform.[51]

Barry's observations undersold Washington's decades-long history of civil rights activism, particularly the protests led by black women during the 1940s and 1950s.[52] But his comments also pointed to the real challenges leaders faced fighting for racial justice in the shadow of the national civil rights movement. Julius Hobson had confessed his own failings to incite action. According to the agitator, "Nobody has moved Washington. You could take a little black girl, dress her in organdy, take her downtown, pour gas over her, and it wouldn't move the community." As fellow SNCC activist Lester McKinnie pointed out, the fact that so many African Americans worked for the government created a "formidable hindrance to organizing protest."[53] Liberal white businessman and future city council leader John Hechinger pointed to another barrier to activism. "The idea of trying to inject the hope of effective democracy on a people who have been pistol-whipped into lethargy by an unresponsive, sometimes malicious House of Representatives committee is, indeed, a difficult one," he said.[54]

Reverend Walter Fauntroy could empathize. Born in D.C. in 1933, Fauntroy had graduated from the city's prestigious Dunbar High School in 1951. He attended Virginia Union University before completing his studies at Yale University's Divinity School. In 1958, he returned to the District to serve as a pastor of the New Bethel Baptist Church, located in the historically black Shaw neighborhood. In 1961, Martin Luther King asked him to head SCLC's Washington chapter, a position from which he oversaw local arrangements for the 1963 March on Washington and coordinated national voting rights marches in 1965. That same year, after helping stage a march to win welfare reforms, Fauntroy admitted that it took a lot of energy to convince residents just to show up. But that was all starting to change.[55]

Journalist Hayes Johnson observed firsthand the growing disconnect between the black working class and underclass and the city's more established civil rights leaders in the early 1960s. According to Johnson, the "slum dwellers" were isolated from the black middle class, the city's clerical leadership, and the "old-line, well-established" civil rights organizations like the Urban League and NAACP. By the mid-1960s, the strong intraracial class divisions in Washington helped pave the way for militant activists who challenged the more moderate civil rights leadership for power. When Barry arrived in the District, he quickly picked up on this sense of alienation among the city's black low-income residents and focused on building his constituency around them.[56]

Eight months after relocating to the District, Barry had converted the local office from a national money-raising operation for the organization's southern campaigns to a storefront for local organizing. In January 1966, he made his mark on the city by launching a protest against its privately owned bus company, D.C. Transit, for its proposed 25 percent fare increase. To execute the one-day boycott, Barry relied on SNCC members, many of whom were women, to make direct appeals to the city's mostly poor black bus riders and employed volunteers to chauffeur passengers to their places of employment. With only three weeks to prepare, Barry meticulously mapped out all of the details of the boycott. SNCC estimated that D.C. Transit lost 150,000 fares that day as over 75,000 people braved the blustery weather and stayed off the buses. Two days after the boycott, the Metropolitan Area Transit Commission rejected D.C. Transit's proposed fare hike, and the boycotters declared victory.[57]

Although SNCC executed a successful boycott, Barry knew that it did not change the District's governing structure. The activist recognized that protests could only accomplish so much in a town absent of local control. Barry's choice to advocate for home rule originated from a few different sources. First, it derived from the expressions of Black Power circulating throughout the national discourse during the mid-1960s. It also stemmed from political opportunism. Barry, a savvy and charismatic leader, saw firsthand the power vacuum that congressional rule had created in D.C. He assumed that if he lobbied successfully for home rule, there would be a political seat for which he could then campaign.

As it was, Barry's successful January 1966 boycott of D.C. Transit had elevated his status in the District and provided him with the latitude to launch Free D.C., a new campaign dedicated to self-government. His goal was to breathe new life into the campaign for home rule, which had been led for two decades by the Washington Home Rule Committee, a largely ineffective interracial organization. Barry persuaded the NAACP's Washington chapter, local SCLC leader Walter Fauntroy, and other more moderate activists to join. On February 24, flanked by local ministers, Barry boldly declared, "We want to free D.C. from our enemies: the people who make it impossible for us to do anything about lousy schools, brutal cops, slumlords, welfare investigators who go on midnight raids, employers who discriminate in hiring, and a host of other ills that run rampant through our city."[58] Barry then called for a boycott of downtown businesses owned by Board of Trade members and other "moneylord merchants" who had opposed home rule for decades. In accordance with Barry's plan, activists and residents alike went door to door requesting that store owners sign petitions supporting home rule, display bright orange stickers with the Free D.C. emblem, and contribute to a $100,000 campaign for nationwide newspaper advertisements promoting self-government for the nation's capital.[59]

While historians traditionally focus on Free D.C.'s financial solicitations of white business owners, Barry also believed the campaign had to empower black residents to view home rule as a political imperative. "They do want to vote," Barry told the *Washington Post*'s William Raspberry, "they just don't respond to the name 'home rule!'"[60] His work with SNCC suggested to him that the issue was not simply one of semantics. Barry observed that much like black citizens across the South, black residents in D.C. had internalized the blame for their disenfranchisement. But unlike other black southerners, black Washingtonians did not have an army of volunteers there to demand that the government protect their right to vote and then subsequently assist them in registering to do so. In this regard, their disenfranchisement differed from that of other black citizens in the lead-up to and aftermath of the 1965 Voting Rights Act. Barry's hope was that a sustained campaign focused on self-determination would help move the needle locally not just with businesspeople but also with black residents. And, in fact, after a community meeting leading up the campaign, dozens of residents walked around the targeted area chanting "Freedom, freedom!" and singing adapted civil rights staples like "This little light of mine, I'm gonna let it shine all up and down H Street" and "We shall overcome the Board of Trade."[61]

Barry's primary goal was to shame the local white stakeholders and racist legislators who opposed home rule. Free D.C. aggressively targeted downtown merchants with two objectives: first, to solicit financial contributions to their campaign; and second, to pressure them to lobby Congress for meaningful home rule legislation. But Free D.C. participants' confrontational tactics triggered accusations of blackmail and extortion. The charges forced Free D.C. to redirect its appeals to white merchants in predominantly black commercial districts like 8th and H Streets NE, and 14th and U Streets NW. The downside of relocating its home rule campaign soon became clear: merchants in black commercial districts wielded less influence over the Board of Trade's lobbying efforts than merchants in the city's white commercial districts did. Even so, within just one week of canvassing, volunteers managed to convince 150 of 300 stores along a thirteen-block section of H Street NE between 2nd and 15th Streets to display its orange and black window sticker and sign its petition for home rule.[62]

Marion Barry delivers a statement to reporters about the Free D.C. campaign on the steps of the District building on August 26, 1966. (Star Collection, D.C. Public Library © *Washington Post*)

Barry refused to leave unsympathetic merchants alone. Those who declined to affix the window sticker or sign the petition received a letter warning them that they would be picketed. On March 5, at the end of their first week canvassing H Street, Barry cruised down the corridor in a sedan with speakers mounted on its roof. From inside the vehicle, he encouraged shoppers to exclusively patronize stores sporting Free D.C. stickers and threatened a boycott of merchants who did not participate. The scare tactic worked. On March 12, Free D.C. wrapped up its campaign on H Street with a one-hour celebratory march. Of the 260 merchants Free D.C. contacted, 225 had agreed to display its stickers.[63]

By shaming or, as white businesspeople argued, threatening local businesses into supporting home rule, Barry's Free D.C. campaign marked a distinct challenge to existing civil rights tactics. From Barry's perspective, the campaign proved that black residents were primed to take the next step in the fight for self-determination. Perhaps more importantly, what the campaign revealed was that residents were ready to protest in ways that the city's black middle class had traditionally found unacceptable.[64]

Free D.C.'s confrontational politics alarmed the *Washington Post*, which called it "a free-swinging band of pro–home rule militants."[65] Barry's tactics, including his unilateral call for a boycott and the strong-arming of merchants for financial donations, caused local civil rights and business groups to denounce him as well. Barry lost, for example, the support of the Washington NAACP branch, which voted unanimously to quit the campaign and reverse its endorsement. He also lost the support of some of SNCC's black and white female organizers, including longtime participants like Tina Smith, Sharlene Kranz, and Betty Garman, who left the organization in 1966 following concerns over Barry's leadership style.[66]

Unsurprisingly, the Board of Trade did not mince words, calling Free D.C.'s tactics "immoral, un-American, and unjust."[67] The Federation of Citizens Associations, Washington's all-white neighborhood association umbrella group, agreed. Reflecting on the campaign's tactics, and cautioning white residents about the dangers of Black Power, its president warned, "If they can do it for home rule, they can do it for the Democrats or for the XYZ welfare program or any cause they choose to back."[68] But the Federation missed the point. Residents did not want to participate in piecemeal campaigns. Instead they wanted wholesale changes to the city's political structure.

Obstinate white business and real estate groups were not Free D.C.'s only obstacles to achieving elected municipal representation. On the federal level, the House District Committee presented the most direct challenge to home rule legislation. Chairman John McMillan called the campaign a "communist plot" and formed a committee to investigate whether Barry had violated federal antiracketeering law. The threat of black self-determination continued to captivate the House District Committee's attention throughout the year's legislative session. In fact, fearing that he would lose a floor vote, McMillan fought to keep a home rule bill off the agenda until the committee ran out of time for debate during the Eighty-Ninth Congress.[69]

After the end of the legislative session that fall, Free D.C. fizzled out. Barry's enthusiasm for shaping the District's political future, however, had not. Since arriving in the District, Barry could not resist getting involved in local issues. Barry's boycott of D.C. Transit had successfully mobilized the city's low-income black residents around grassroots politics. That same year, Free D.C. had the opposite effect, mobilizing white stakeholders and southern members of Congress to shut down his campaign for home rule, thereby preserving their influence over the city. This only fueled Barry's push for local municipal elections. Eleven months after he launched Free D.C., he resigned as the head of the Washington SNCC office to devote himself fully to solving black Washingtonian's problems. "The civil rights direction of protest is dead," he announced. "Now we must concentrate on control—economic and political power."[70]

WASHINGTON'S WAR ON POVERTY

Even before President Johnson issued his War on Poverty, neighborhood centers, settlement houses, churches, and other reform agencies provided spaces for low-income black residents to address their economic demands. One such organization was the United Planning Organization, created in December 1962 by the Ford and Meyer Foundations as part of President Kennedy's efforts to address juvenile delinquency and the need for effective employment strategies. It eventually coordinated human resource programs throughout Washington. According to UPO executive director Wiley Branton, the Ford Foundation's funds gave black Washingtonians rare authority over the city's resources. They liberated the organization and allowed local groups and their boards to create innovative programming that dealt with poverty, blight, employment, and crime free from congressional control. "When this money came in, in an unrestricted fashion and in a city like Washington where there was no Home Rule, it gave to the leadership of the UPO a certain independence so that they were free to do and act as they saw fit," Branton explained. But the Johnson administration's War on Poverty would complicate this plan.[71]

In August 1964, as the White House launched its War on Poverty to help

America's chronically poor citizens, it passed the Equal Opportunity Act. Drafted by former Peace Corps founding director Sargent Shriver, the legislation created the Office of Economic Opportunity (OEO) to administer funds for local initiatives. It also established the Community Action Program, the centerpiece of the early War on Poverty effort and one of the highest-profile Great Society programs. CAP had two guiding principles: first, to deliver federal aid to the poor and provide them with the skills to improve their economic standing, develop employment opportunities, and better the conditions under which they lived; and second, to deliver social services in a manner that emphasized decentralization and local control. A controversial feature of this was the requirement for "maximum feasible participation" of the people directly affected by poverty in the administration of federal funds in their communities—a prospect that angered some local government officials used to running their cities without such community input. In Washington, where the local government already had limited controls, this was yet another example of the federal government shaping the parameters of local control.[72]

In poor areas across the nation, local nonprofit Community Action Agencies (CAA) were established as clearinghouses to administer and coordinate social service, education, job training, and legal service programs—everything from birth control clinics, law clinics, and educational programs—with oversight by boards of residents in the targeted neighborhoods being served. Designated as the city's CAA, the UPO administered the OEO's federal grant dollars locally. Ironically, by accepting federal money intended to increase citizen participation, the UPO lost the freedom it had enjoyed under the Ford Foundation's largesse. For some grassroots organizers, it became another organization that undermined black self-determination. "I don't think they put forth much of an effort to try and work out a cooperative arrangement with the traditional church leadership, neighborhood groups, civic groups and fraternal groups which had been sponsoring, say, day care programs, some welfare information, seminars and things like that," Branton said of these administrators. Disappointed, Branton admitted, "They just sort of left them out in the cold. . . . I thought it was a terrible mistake to bypass these people."[73]

In 1967, on the president's request, Branton made a seamless transition from the Department of Justice (DOJ), where he had served as Johnson's personal representative, to the UPO, where he supervised over one thousand employees and managed a $21 million budget. Branton, an Arkansas native, had dedicated his life to civil rights. He had filed a lawsuit against the Little Rock School Board for failing to integrate the city's public schools, led a voter registration drive among African Americans in the South, and served as executive director of the Johnson administration's Council on Equal Opportunity. Branton had also helped coordinate the implementation of the 1964 Civil Rights Act and, at the Justice Department, worked on the Voting Rights Act of 1965.[74]

In his new leadership position at the UPO, Branton provided low-income minority residents with resources and administrative power, funding black women in particular to participate in the UPO and other CAPs. He remained optimistic that citizen participation would force the government to listen and respond to District residents. However, several factors prohibited the organization from building significant influence in the community. Johnson's reorganization plan had failed to provide local agencies with unfettered control of District resources. On top of that, the UPO had to contend with the heightened scrutiny of overzealous southern Democrats. For example, Representative Joel Broyhill (R-Va.) warned members of Congress that UPO "had been for many months in the hands of men with long records of agitation for left-wing and black power causes," a comment intended to stoke anti–home rule flames.[75]

Meanwhile, the UPO's very location helped magnify its missteps. Having the dubious honor of operating in the capital "was like living in a glass house," Branton explained. Its close proximity to federal power also thwarted creativity. According to Branton, Congress allocated 95 percent of the UPO's federal funds for government programs with strict guidelines and restrictions. "It is extremely difficult for you to come up with any innovative priorities," he lamented. This particularly frustrated Branton and local antipoverty activists, who knew that the Johnson administration had intended for CAPs to provide more, not less, creativity and freedom.[76]

The UPO's close working relationship with the federal government occasionally bolstered the organization's programming efforts. "If we had good programs, it meant that they could be made visible to the members of Congress, who, after all, appropriate the money," Branton explained. In fact, Branton admitted that they probably received more money per capita than other cities for congressional pet projects like methadone treatment centers, studies on narcotics addiction, and juvenile delinquency programs. "We might get a dozen or more congressmen calling some government agency encouraging them to give us a grant, when only the home congressman would be interested in the project going into his own district," he admitted, alluding to the historic role the District played as a laboratory for programs politicians sought to implement across the country.[77]

By the late 1960s, the UPO and other community action programs employed more than fifteen hundred low-income residents in administrative and advisory positions. Through its financial support of their direct action strategies and emphasis on participatory democracy, Johnson's War on Poverty particularly benefited welfare rights activists. It helped finance local community centers, whose female members came together in 1966 to create the Washington Welfare Alliance (later renamed the Citywide Welfare Alliance). Headed by Annie McLean and comprising black women who received Aid to Families with Dependent Children (AFDC), the alliance fought for "more money, more dignity, and more justice." The group took aim at policies they believed disproportionally harmed poor black mothers and their families and lobbied Congress to increase welfare funds.[78]

The Southeast Neighborhood House was one of the most successful beneficiaries of War on Poverty funds. Founded in 1929 by black physician Dorothy Boulding Ferebee, Southeast House was a neighborhood agency that offered a variety of social services, including recreation programs and health clinics. In the mid-1960s, it became a central place for radical organizing thanks, in large part, to a $133,000 grant from the UPO that went to paying community organizers, including ten neighboring unemployed residents, most of whom lived in public housing. Settlement House employees included Lois Wilson, who had served as president of the tenants' council in her housing project and local Planned Parenthood clinic volunteer, and Theresa Jones, who had helped organize tenants in her apartment complex to protest the National Capital Housing Authority's (NCHA) decision to install wooden rather than metal doors. Southeast House's early initiatives were so successful that it hired a second team of organizers to focus on initiatives in Barry Farms, a public housing complex that housed twenty-six hundred of the city's lowest-income residents in Anacostia. The Barry Farm Band of Angels tenants' group, for example, was formed to combat the NCHA's refurbishment plans.[79]

Southeast House is also where local resident Etta Mae Horn got her start as a community organizer. Horn, a black single mother of seven children with an eighth-grade education and disabilities that forced her to accept ADFC payments and subsidized housing, had initially focused her public activism on the PTA and her church. After seeing how welfare rights activism enhanced rather than took away from her work as a mother, she began to take a leading role in local welfare rights campaigns to improve the lives of her children, as well as the lives of poor women and children throughout D.C. In 1967, members of the National Welfare Rights Organization elected Horn to serve as the national organization's vice chairman, though she never lessened her engagement with the community or her emphasis on local control by the poor over programs that affected their lives. In fact, through her stubborn independent streak and flair for the dramatic—she notoriously disrupted a welfare department celebration by spearing the cake with a picket sign—Horn's approach rivaled Julius Hobson's. During the 1960s, she became one of the city's most recognizable welfare advocates, one of the hundreds of black women who put their bodies on the line to press for needed reforms as they negotiated with federal officials and local authorities.[80]

Through his efforts organizing the 1966 bus boycott and Free D.C. campaign, Marion Barry had also forged links between economic empowerment and political activism. In 1967, Barry again made these connections as he, too, capitalized on funds from Johnson's War on Poverty to create Pride, Inc., a summer job-training program for Washington youth, with the help of D.C. SNCC fund-raising committee chair Mary Treadwell. Treadwell had run into Barry, a former classmate at Fisk University, while he was picketing for home rule and, thanks to that encounter, had decided to throw her energy into the local movement. She helped Barry found Pride with a $250,000 grant from the Department of Labor to employ five hundred men for five weeks to work on civic improvement projects. Following its initial success, the Department of Labor gave Pride a $1.2 million grant to extend its programming for another forty weeks. From 1967 to 1970, with Treadwell serving as codirector, Pride received nearly $9 million from the federal government for job-training and related business development programs. At the height of its power, the organization, along with its subsidiary Youth Pride Economic Enterprises, operated gas stations, a landscaping company, a printing company, an apartment complex, and other service-related companies. Its success demonstrated the innovation and evolution of the civil rights movement as it tackled a broader portfolio of issues in the 1960s.[81]

The infusion of federal funds into local advocacy work gave black women formal opportunities to play a role in the city's activism. As they advocated for welfare rights and affordable housing, and increasingly employed the politics of self-determination in their own advocacy, they charted a new course for D.C. Their work was, however, hampered by several factors. First, they lived with the fear that their political activity would compromise their already-precarious economic status. Horn and other welfare recipients specifically worried that their activism would jeopardize their AFDC checks. Moreover, they were limited by stipulations set by the funding agencies. As scholar Anne Valk has illustrated, the employment programs backed by the UPO implemented a family wage model that ignored single women; were not open to citizen input; were often male-centered; and deprived women of the job skills necessary to secure financial independence. Nevertheless, for many black women, the UPO-funded projects offered a better opportunity to develop leadership among residents than local civil rights organizations like CORE and SNCC did.[82]

Yet in pursuing paid opportunities to serve as community organizers, dedicating their lives to neighborhood-level work, and being forced to defend their reputations as mothers, low-income black women were marginalized from the fight for home rule. Instead, it was black men like Barry who were given greater opportunities to bridge the divide between grassroots politics and mainstream establishment politics. As racial tensions mounted in Washington and feelings of futility intensified following nearly thirty-five years of civil rights crusades, many wondered whether Barry would help loosen the government's grip over the capital.

LIMITED HOME RULE COMES TO WASHINGTON

The House District Committee, controlled by white southern segregationists like Chairman John McMillan and member Joel Broyhill, did the most to constrain black Washingtonians' political freedom. Born in rural South Carolina in 1889, McMillan was elected to Congress in 1938. After advancing to chairmanship of the House District Committee in 1945, he refused to hold hearings on bills or proposals for self-government. Between 1949 and 1965, the Senate passed six home rule measures, five of which McMillan killed in committee despite repeated requests by both Republican and Democratic administrations to pass them.[83] Like McMillan, Broyhill, the Virginia Republican, was an unrelenting and outspoken opponent of home rule for the District. The Republican congressman maintained that the U.S. Constitution placed ultimate responsibility for the nation's capital with Congress and battled for years with McMillan against measures to increase D.C. residents' sovereignty.[84]

Although activists did not anticipate getting a home rule bill through McMillan's committee, they did hold out hope of persuading President Johnson, who had passed monumental national civil rights legislation in 1964 and 1965. Since taking office, Johnson had expressed interest in granting the city self-government. First, he was genuinely fond of the capital, which he had called home for most of his life. Second, he viewed the passage of a home rule charter as an important piece of his broader civil rights agenda. Third, he worried about racial violence in the District and believed that locally elected representatives might better prevent crime in the city. So during the summer of 1965 he threw his political weight behind a home rule bill.

To help secure the bill's passage, Johnson knew he would need to circumvent the House District Committee. The masterful tactician invoked an arcane procedure that allowed all House members to vote on a bill provided a majority successfully petitioned to discharge the committee of it. Johnson poured all of his energy into a legislative victory, but it remained a risky proposition. During the summer, he warned White House Aide Joseph Califano, "If they beat us on this one, they'll know they can win. It only takes one for them to see they can cut us and make us bleed. Then they'll bleed us to death on our other legislation." Timing was not on the president's side. The combination of the Watts riots, a nationwide lobbying effort against the bill by the Board of Trade, and a particularly grueling legislative session pushed House members to vote for a shrewd substitute bill put forth by House District Committee members to further delay home rule. For its part, *Congressional Quarterly* blamed the bill's defeat on bipartisan fears that the black majority would dominate local elections and, in turn, the local government.[85]

Johnson was furious. His defeat at the hands of Congress, followed by Barry's notorious Free D.C. campaign in 1966 and increasing civil disturbances in cities across the country, convinced the president to reintroduce home rule legislation in 1967. The 1965 Watts riots, which began just a few days after the president signed the Voting Rights Act, had particularly rattled Johnson. The uprising in Watts lasted for five days and had left thirty-four people killed, hundreds injured, and $35 million in property damage. As Califano noted, it "sharpened the President's concern that the poverty of predominately black Washington was fertile soil for violent outburst." Johnson's fear of urban unrest, combined with what Califano described as "an almost religious faith in the right to vote," helped turn D.C. home rule into a legislative obsession.[86]

Speaking to Congress in February 1967, Johnson laid out a three-part plan to improve the District by focusing on better government, the war on crime, and capital improvements. He made an impassioned appeal to secure D.C. citizens basic rights, including the right to "elect the government which serves them; efficient and effective government machinery, representation in the Congress if the United States, and streets and homes that are free from crime and the fear of crime."[87] When he promoted home rule throughout the spring and early summer, Johnson underscored the fact that crime in D.C. was a major factor in his decision. He had good reason to do so. Crime across the country was on the rise. According to statistics reported by the Federal Bureau of Investigation (FBI), the rate of property crime, which included burglary, larceny, and auto theft, increased 73 percent, while the rate of violent crime, which included murder, robbery, forcible rape, and aggregated assault, rose 57 percent between 1960 and 1967. By 1965, Washington had the fastest-growing crime rate in the nation. The rising crime rate created panic across the nation fed into conservatives' powerful law-and-order narrative.[88]

Johnson wisely factored this into his appeals for home rule. "The city government cannot effectively deal with crime, which cuts across virtually every function of government—from police and corrections to housing, education, health and employment," the president told Congress in June.[89] As he outlined the deficiencies of the D.C. government's current configuration, he framed self-determination as a preventative measure against crime. "Of all the benefits," he said, "one stands out in particular—the strong leadership it provides as the cornerstone of support for any effective attack against crime."[90]

Tired of losing out to unwilling political opponents and powerful local stakeholders, the president tasked Califano with crafting a new plan for the nation's capital. The assignment, the White House aide admitted, plunged him "into the racially charged atmosphere of the capital's local politics." In order to set the stage for home rule, Califano proposed using the presidential reorganization authority to change the structure of the District's government. Reorganization Plan No. 3 would offer limited self-government to District residents by replacing the city's three commissioners with a single mayor-commissioner and a nine-member council appointed by the president. The plan conceded significant terrain to Congress, which would continue to oversee the city's budget and have veto power over its laws. Johnson acknowledged that the reorganization plan was a poor substitute for elected city government. But while the concessions made the reorganization plan only a partial measure of political independence, they also increased its likelihood of passing at a time when the prospects of getting a home rule bill through Congress appeared particularly bleak. With a suitable plan in hand, Johnson once again sidestepped the House District Committee, which fervently opposed any step toward home rule. He shrewdly sent his bill to the House and Senate Government Operations committees, which were more amenable to the idea of self-determination.[91]

Although he crafted a plan that conceded ultimate decision-making power to Congress, Johnson still faced strong opposition from members of the House District Committee. Unsurprisingly, McMillan and Broyhill testified against the plan. "The problems of crime, housing, schools, urban renewal, cannot be solved by this reorganization plan because other agencies of Government with which there is constant conflict prevent an orderly and proper solution," Broyhill stated. For his part, McMillan contested Johnson's promise that his reorganization plan would solve the crime problem. "If there is anything in this proposal then I fail to see it where there would be any assistance in solving crime," he added. McMillan even accused the White House of inflating crime statistics. "They have tried to make it look as bad as possible in order to get this plan into effect," he said—a position he would abandon as soon as the implications of Richard Nixon's law-and-order campaign rhetoric became clear.[92]

Other members of Congress rallied against the reorganization plan. Opponents warned against the possibility of local corruption and expressed dismay at the way Johnson's plan transferred power from Congress to the White House. Representative Thomas Abernethy (D-Miss.) accused the White House of obstructing good governance in D.C. and suggested that it instead cede the northern parts of the District to Maryland. Representative Clarence "Bud" Brown (R-Ohio) suggested that the plan was an executive power grab at a time when the White House had bigger issues, like Vietnam and race riots, to address. Opponents' concerns that the president had intentionally crafted a plan that would remove local governance from Congress's authority and place it in the hands of the executive branch were striking. Evidence suggests that this is far from what Johnson had in mind. But due to its design, the president's limited home rule bill set up a larger fight for control of District affairs.[93]

Despite strong support from over fifty organizations and one hundred city leaders, the Board of Trade zealously fought Johnson's reorganization plan. It cited an unduly oppressive tax burden on Washington's residents as its official reason for opposing the proposal. Yet it was no secret that the group feared power shifting to the city's black population. This time, though, Johnson had secured the support he needed. According to the *Washington Post*, the president had executed a savvier campaign. "It was unlike 1965's home rule fight (in which President Johnson was defeated), in that this appeal was pitched by him on good government and efficiency and crime fighting," the *Post* reported. In August 1967, Johnson's plan passed over the opposition in a vote of 160–244. In what the *Post* called "a surprisingly strong vote," the plan granted Washingtonians a greater degree of political power.[94]

Pressure from local white stakeholders initially persuaded Johnson to search for a white leader to run the city's government. The *Washington Post* exerted a particularly strong influence at the start of the process. One year earlier, the president had met with publisher Katharine Graham and executive editor James "Russ" Wiggins to solicit advice about appointing a black resident as president of the D.C. Board of Commissioners. They pushed back, citing their discomfort with a black official in charge of the police, strong resistance from the business community, and the threat of white flight from the District as their rationale for preserving a white-led commission. Frustrated, Johnson sent Califano back to the drawing board.[95]

In 1967, as Johnson's reorganization plan began to crystallize, Graham and managing editor Ben Bradlee met with White House aides to craft a short list of possible candidates for mayor. At the top of their list was former New York governor and future vice president Nelson Rockefeller, former secretary of state Dean Acheson, and Office of Economic Opportunity director Sargent Shriver. Roger Wilkins, a black DOJ aide and nephew of longtime NAACP leader Roy Wilkins, saw the folly of this strategy. As he explained to Attorney General Ramsey Clark, it would be unwise to pass legislation to grant the majority-black city political independence only to appoint a white mayor. The president agreed and allegedly made a surprise offer to Wilkins, who demurred. Instead Johnson set his eyes on Walter Washington, a fifty-two-year-old politically moderate African American man and veteran housing expert with D.C. connections, for the top post.[96]

Born in Dawson, Georgia, in 1915, Washington was raised in upstate New York after his family moved north during the Great Migration. By 1934, he had saved enough money to move to D.C. to attend Howard University, where he earned his bachelor's and law degrees. It was there that he met Washingtonian educator Bennetta Bullock, the daughter of a prominent pastor and the descendant of one of the city's Le Droit Park black dynasties. After graduating from law school in 1948, Washington threw himself into public service and built a successful career as a civil servant. For over a decade, he worked as a supervisor for D.C.'s Alley Dwelling Authority. In 1961, President Kennedy appointed him to run the National Capital Housing Authority, the congressionally administered housing department for the District. Five years later, Washington moved to New York City to head the city's Housing Authority under Republican mayor John Lindsay.[97]

Washington was already familiar with the president. One year earlier, Johnson had entertained making him the president of the D.C. Board of Commissioners. Racial anxieties over the police issue were initially too much for federal officials to overcome, and negotiations had fallen apart. Johnson continued to try to toe the line between granting black self-determination and preserving white control. Although he clashed with local white stakeholders over the appointment of a black mayor, he felt strongly that a black mayor should not have control over the city's police department. Walter Washington stood his ground. Just as he had the year before, he refused to accept the job without jurisdiction over the police. Because he wanted to make a quick announcement, Johnson relented. In September 1967, he swore Washington in as mayor-commissioner, the official title hyphenated as a concession to the plan's congressional opponents. The occasion was historic. Washington, along with Richard Hatcher of Gary, Indiana, and Carl Stokes of Cleveland, Ohio—

who were both elected to office—became part of the first cohort of black mayors chosen to lead major cities that year.[98]

Shortly after Johnson passed his reorganization plan, he announced that he would welcome local suggestions for the nine city council positions. Inspired by his call for names, a coalition—comprising, according to the *Washington Post*, "Washington poverty fighters, Black Power advocates, civil rights workers and freeway opponents"—scheduled a "Peoples' Convention" to give District residents an opportunity to nominate members. The Washington Committee on Black Power, an ad hoc group, even sent "vote-mobiles," armed with ballot boxes and ballots, throughout D.C.'s main black thoroughfares to solicit public statements on candidates. The mock election was designed to show Johnson who black residents wanted on the council. As C. Sumner "Chuck" Stone Jr., public relations director of the National Conference on Black Power, told the *Post*, "The President should have some indication of grassroots sentiment in the Capital of this democracy which is two thirds black."[99]

When the votes were tallied, Julius Hobson won the straw vote with 11,614 votes. Marion Barry, one of the convention coordinators, received 416 votes as a write-in candidate, good enough for eleventh place. Though the coalition submitted the results to the White House, the short list of names the Johnson administration gave the FBI for vetting purposes suggested that it paid them no attention. Hobson complained that Johnson had gone out of his way to ask for names only to ignore them. "I never entertained the idea he'd appoint anybody of my stripe," the militant activist said, "but there are a lot of people between me and the Urban League that he could consider."[100]

For the Peoples' Convention organizers, many of whom were employed by the United Planning Organization, one man on the White House's list, former Republican District Commissioner Mark Sullivan, was a particularly flawed choice. Sullivan had been a vocal opponent of the city's antipoverty agency, going so far as to call it "a failure, a waste of money, and a deception." On learning that Sullivan was being considered for the D.C. Council, Barry responded with characteristic bluster: "Either President Johnson can't read or is stupid." Some wondered how Barry, who worked for the government-underwritten agency, could criticize Johnson so freely. The charismatic leader responded, "I get paid by the UPO three days a week, and today's my day off."[101]

On November 4, Johnson swore in a new city council. At the ceremony, the president issued a strongly worded warning on crime, urging the new council members to help make the capital the safest city in the country. White House officials viewed the appointed council as a stepping-stone to elected government and thus demanded that appointees have unimpeachable qualifications.

Julius Hobson (*right seat*) and colleague drive throughout the District to conduct informal straw votes on behalf of the Washington Committee for Black Power for prospective nominees for leadership posts in the city's newly reorganized government. (Star Collection, D.C. Public Library © *Washington Post*)

They avoided appointing more controversial figures likes Hobson and Barry. Instead they selected a majority-black council that included Reverend Walter Fauntroy as vice chair. To balance the appointment of a black mayor, Johnson selected John Hechinger, a liberal white businessman, to serve as city council chairman. The implementation of the president's partial home rule measure, and the accompanying opening of new bureaucratic positions, left the city's black leaders at a crossroads: join Mayor Washington as part of D.C.'s political establishment or opt out of a system over which the federal government still had ultimate control. For those who had fought tirelessly for civil rights, the opportunity to shape local policy was too enticing, and many of them readily accepted roles in the city's new government.[102]

The appointment of a black mayor and majority-black city council in a majority-black city that demanded self-government was a leap forward for the city's home rule advocates. But it was also a mimetic reform. By transitioning some of the most prominent members of the city's black community into bureaucratic roles, Johnson had hoped to eliminate a powerful justification for violent protest, curb local confrontational politics, and minimize black residents' demands on the federal government, all while allowing Congress final say over the city's municipal government.[103]

Johnson had also hoped that Walter Washington's wealth of experience in public housing management, roots in the District's black upper-class community, and Howard University pedigree would satisfy D.C. residents, as well as national legislators who had not been keen on the reorganization. But placating local civil rights groups, white powerbrokers, and federal legislators proved to be a nearly impossible task. As the city's black governing body settled into office, an assortment of black stakeholders pushed back. When asked how he felt about Johnson's reorganization plan, Reverend Channing Phillips said, "I just see [it] as being a more efficient form of colonialism."[104] Meanwhile, at a September 1967 press conference, Marion Barry did not mince words. Speaking out about the president's city council appointments, Barry announced, "Johnson's setting himself up a dictator role with this list. They should be people who could get elected if there were an election. These men couldn't make it for a dog catcher." While his comments were representative of the bombast residents had come to expect from Barry, they still pointed to the fractured movement left in the wake of Johnson's reorganization plan.[105]

In October, Chuck Stone also lashed out, calling the new council "the most unbelievably motley collection of white racists, Uncle Toms, 'house Negroes' and white patronizers." The Washington Committee on Black Power added that it was "a cruel charade that had victimized the voiceless, poverty-stricken, powerless black people." To the group, the appointed council proved that Johnson did not have the wishes of Washington's black community at heart. Dismayed, it threatened to convene a "Black People's Convention" to elect the people's mayor and city council, begin a massive civil disobedience program to "paralyze" the District until home rule was won, and hold a "Day of Mourning" for the "death of democracy" in the city.[106]

A NEW FORCE TO BE RECKONED WITH

Looking to shape the direction of a civil rights movement in limbo, Black Power activist Stokely Carmichael helped create a new umbrella organization called the Black United Front in January 1968. Carmichael was not new to D.C. politics or to grassroots organizing. Born in Port of Spain, Trinidad, in 1941, he moved to New York when he was eleven years old and later attended the selective Bronx High School of Science. In April 1960, as a high school senior, he participated in the founding of SNCC at the Shaw University conference Ella Baker had organized. That fall, Carmichael enrolled at Howard University, where he majored in philosophy. While at Howard, Carmichael joined the Nonviolent Action Group (NAG), the SNCC Howard campus affiliate determined to "nag the conscience of Washington." Organized by Howard students in 1960, NAG succeeded in desegregating twenty-five facilities in the city, including lunch counters, restaurants, a movie theater, and the District's only amusement park. By 1962, many members had moved on, leaving only twenty-five to thirty dedicated students still involved. As one NAG member admitted, "Picket lines and demonstrators were not considered glamorous activities anymore."[107] Perhaps because of that, the organization performed an important function in the District. Whenever local civil rights groups needed picketers, they could count on NAG to send volunteers.[108]

Carmichael also threw himself into the national civil rights movement. During the summer after his freshman year, he participated in CORE's Freedom Rides challenging the enforcement of segregated interstate travel laws. At the age of nineteen, Carmichael served forty-nine days at Parchman Farm, Mississippi's maximum-security prison, after trying to integrate the white section of a train from New Orleans, Louisiana, to Jackson, Mississippi. With Carmichael's help, SNCC became a leader in southern voter registration drives and a key organizer in the CORE-led Freedom Rides, and he was instrumental in building community-based political organizations led by the rural poor.[109]

In the mid-1960s, the lanky, charismatic activist changed the face of both the local and national civil rights movements as the controversial chairman of SNCC from 1966 to 1967. Following his election as chairman of the organization, Carmichael quickly popularized the Black Power slogan, shorthand for what he described as "a call for black people in this country to unite, to recognize their heritage, to build a sense of community . . . to define their own goals, to lead their own organizations."[110] Under his leadership, SNCC underwent a radical transformation. Members voted to expel white volunteers from the organization and renounced nonviolence as a pragmatic tactic. But following an internal disagreement over Carmichael's leadership style and unilateral decision-making, the activist stepped down as chairman in late 1967 and embarked on a global tour of Europe, Asia, and North Vietnam. While acquiring an international following and attempting to globalize the black struggle, Carmichael became, according to white *Washington Post* editor Ben Gilbert, "the personification of the 'outside agitator' who moved from place to place creating trouble."[111]

In December 1967, Carmichael returned to the states and made Washington, D.C., his home base. Wasting no time, he assembled a January meeting of one hundred local black leaders to assess the city's movement for racial justice. Under Carmichael's leadership, BUF sought to accomplish several ambitious goals. First, it wanted to bring black activists, civil rights leaders, and politicians together at a time when Johnson's reorganization plan had fractured the city's local movement. As evidence of this, it had on its steering committee ex-SNCC leader and Free D.C. leader Marion Barry, ACT's Julius Hobson, and local SCLC leader and newly appointed city council vice chairman Walter Fauntroy. According to BUF leader Charles Cassell, an architect-turned–grassroots organizer deeply committed to D.C. transportation issues, racial solidarity would have to serve as BUF's fundamental unifying principle in order to keep political infighting at bay. In Cassell's view, members had to stop squabbling and "realize that all black people have this one thing in common—that is prejudice and discrimination and deprivation." Second, BUF hoped to convert the promises of home rule into permanent institution building and "to provide for black people a real and meaningful share in the fruits of this so-called democracy."[112]

Building off of the work of activists such as Hobson, Barry, and Carmichael, BUF also provided a platform for leaders to articulate a new, more radical organizing philosophy to effect change in the District. Tying together various strands of activism, Reverend Channing Phillips, director of the Housing Development Corporation and pastor of Lincoln Temple, explained BUF's philosophy as "the ability to effect the changes that one wants, whether he's exercising it in economic strength or whether he's exercising sheer weight of the people." Phillips added, "Whatever he's exercising, if he can effect the change, then take that to be the exercise of power."[113] When asked whether BUF acted as the political arm of the community, Charles Cassell objected. BUF, he clarified, was an educational organization that worked with black residents rather than the so-called establishment. With limited home rule in effect, BUF sought to empower residents to demand greater accountability from those who governed them.[114]

Willie Hardy and D.C. CORE's Roena Rand also joined BUF, two of the few black women who became members. During the 1950s, Hardy worked for the U.S. Department of the Treasury while attending night school in order to qualify for a promotion. In 1960, she volunteered for Hubert Humphrey's presidential campaign and, later, served on the inaugural committee for John Kennedy. Hardy also threw herself into community organizing, "quietly waging her own war on poverty," according to the *Washington Post*'s William Raspberry.[115] By the mid-1960s, Hardy served as the secretary for the Far East Democratic Organization, a local organization that helped poor families navigate welfare applications; volunteered with the Metropolitan Community Aid Council, Inc., to help the homeless find food, shelter, jobs, and clothing; was elected the head of the University Neighborhood Council to help residents in

Black United Front member C. Sumner Stone addresses fellow members on July 31, 1968. Listening, from left, are the Reverend Walter Fauntroy, Stokely Carmichael, and Tony Cox. (Star Collection, D.C. Public Library © *Washington Post*)

need in D.C.'s Cardozo neighborhood; and had organized Operation Checkmate, an initiative for teens to report police violations. Hardy quickly became a leader in BUF, where she fought for "power to participate."[116]

Consciously distancing themselves from the political elite, members of BUF conducted grassroots organizing efforts around freeway construction, police brutality, and community control—issues that were important to the city's black residents at a time when, it argued, both local and national leaders had abandoned them. Echoing Marion Barry's earlier sentiments, Cassell argued that politically ambitious black leaders in the District had become "pretty well absorbed in the establishment activities to the point that they're not really effective in making changes in the interest of black people." Conversely, Cassell boasted that BUF members remained undeterred by Washington's power structure.[117]

The fact that the current city council vice chairman sat on BUF's steering committee was not lost on its members. If anything, Fauntroy's presence added legitimacy to the new style of confrontational politics that activists had ushered into the District over the past decade. But not all black residents found BUF's mission or leadership acceptable. In particular, Stokely Carmichael's renewed participation in local affairs fueled controversy among the city's black middle-class residents.

Less than one year before the formation of BUF, Lincoln Temple congregation members forced Reverend Channing Phillips to defend his decision to allow Carmichael to speak from the pulpit of the respected church. Situated in the heart of Washington's historically black Shaw neighborhood, Lincoln Temple housed a vocal group of conservative Church of Christ members. They frequently criticized Phillips for opening the facility to militants and, in May 1967, tried to oust him. While the charismatic minister skillfully defeated his critics, the confrontation signaled the growing rift within the black community over confrontational politics.[118] Reverend Phillips expressed dismay at his congregation's unfaithful faction. "The Stokely issue was simply something for people who disagreed with the basic concept of the church as being an open and accepting community," he said. "They saw this as a peg on which they could hang their hats and incite some support based, really, on fear." One year later, Phillips defied his congregation yet again by agreeing to serve on BUF's steering committee.[119]

Although Phillips joined BUF, black business groups and conservative organizations like the Committee of 100 Ministers refused to get involved. BUF's highly visible profile also caught the attention of the Union League and NAACP. These more moderate civil rights groups targeted Sterling Tucker and H. Carl Moultrie, their respective D.C. representatives, for associating with the militant organization. Ultimately Moultrie, a lawyer and president of the NAACP Washington branch, declined a position on BUF's steering committee. But according to the *Washington Post*, Moultrie did not make the decision independently; instead, the paper suggested, the NAACP's national office pressured the local leader to "stay clear of an organization bearing Carmichael's stamp."[120]

Like Moultrie, Tucker faced national pressure to disassociate the local Urban League chapter from Carmichael's name. National Urban League chairman Whitney Young said his organization would not "hold still" for a coalition led by the radical SNCC leader. Following Young's directive, the Washington Urban League's board of directors also expressed misgivings about BUF. However, it voted to defer a decision on Tucker's involvement with the coalition until BUF had more fully articulated its structure and policies. In a small act of autonomy against the national organization, its board authorized Tucker to continue exploring connections with BUF. Together Moultrie and Tucker's trials reveal the ways that national and local civil rights organizations continued to collide in the capital. As BUF outlined its fight for self-determination, it recognized that the relationship between the federal government and District residents was not the only one it needed to redefine.[121]

Local leaders like Tucker and Moultrie not only posed problems for national civil rights organizations. Even BUF's more militant members had wavered on whether to include them. According to BUF member and antifreeway crusader Reginald Booker, it was not clear that they could be trusted. "These so-called established Negroes began to pull back. Because, you see, then the white man through his propaganda machine began to ask questions of how could these so-called established Negroes sit in a room with Stokely Carmichael." For Booker, the answer was simple. "Whether you're Roy Wilkins or Stokely Carmichael, you're still black," he explained, bringing the conflict back to racial solidarity, BUF's chief organizing principle.[122]

From the time he graduated high school until the army drafted him, Reginald Booker worked for the D.C. CORE chapter under the tutelage of Julius Hobson. Prior to the formation of BUF, Booker described CORE as "the only organization that was doing anything in Washington" and Hobson as "the only black person in Washington at that time who had the courage to do anything public and take what was then considered a radical or revolutionary position." After Hobson's expulsion from CORE by national leadership, Booker believed that CORE's influence in the District decreased dramatically. Though Booker had not been in Washington to witness CORE's shakeup for himself, he allied himself with Hobson and the city's other more militant activists. On his return to D.C., he joined BUF and spearheaded a challenge to Congress's racially and economically charged transportation policies.[123]

BUF's goals mirrored those of other more confrontational black groups elsewhere. Black activists on both the local and national level had grown disillusioned with traditional civil rights organizations like SCLC that continued to work for legislative victories, remained tethered to integrationist beliefs, and outwardly criticized violence even when they privately accepted it. With mounting opposition from white citizens and growing resistance from the federal government to civil rights demonstrations, black activists across the country saw the utility of aligning themselves along racial lines. In fact, BUF's work actually duplicated similar efforts in Los Angeles and Detroit, though both L.A.'s Black Congress and Detroit's Citywide Action Community formed after major racial violence had devastated their respective cities. In Washington, racial confrontations had not yet sparked civil disorders of that magnitude.[124]

The mere existence of an umbrella group of black leaders, politicians, private citizens, conservatives, and radicals confounded the city's press corps. For its critics, the fact that Carmichael spearheaded BUF made it an even bigger lightning rod. WTOP radio host Jack Jurey did not hide his astonishment that the city's more moderate black leaders would attend a conference arranged by Carmichael knowing his "well-deserved reputation for acute extremism." The white commentator called BUF a "racist coalition" and chastised Carmichael for his bitter assessment about the state of D.C.'s race relations. Speaking on behalf of white residents who were uncomfortable with the local shift toward black political power, Jurey explained that he would "feel a lot better about BUF if the word 'black' weren't so prominent—and if Carmichael wasn't the moving force." If the advent of limited home rule did not already scare whites, it was clear that the Black United Front would.[125]

BUF faced additional opposition from those troubled by the local government's tolerance of it. The Federation of Citizens Associations, speaking on behalf of its thirty-four neighborhood groups, rebuked the municipal government for its alleged tolerance for officials who participated in radical groups or who antagonized the police. "We believe that such members of the Council are doing a disservice to their community by not opposing the activities of groups of this sort," it argued. "We believe that one of the most important steps in improving law enforcement at this time is support by the local government of their police departments and police officers."[126]

The Federation's views illustrated the wide ideological chasm between black and white Washingtonians. After almost a decade fighting for self-determination, black residents did not want to cater to the needs of white police officers or improve relations with white residents in communities that the Federation helped keep segregated. On a larger level, they no longer wanted to live in a city whose terms were dictated by white stakeholders, federal officials, and unelected representatives. Instead, as BUF leaderr Charles Cassell explained, they wanted to remove "every manifestation of white power from the black community." "The people," he said, "simply don't submit to arbitrary and harsh controls as we once did." With a wide sector of the city's black leadership committed to self-determination, BUF had revolutionary momentum on its side. However, the riots following Martin Luther King's assassination were about to alter the city's landscape in ways they could not have imagined.[127]

2

THEY JUST WON'T LET IT HAPPEN HERE

THE 1968 RIOTS

There is legitimate fear among many that one or more of the area's pockets of despair may simply explode if something isn't done soon to relieve conditions. People don't explode when they have legitimate reason to believe that help is coming.
—Reverend Walter Fauntroy, April 1966

Washington is different during crisis. It's quiet, eerie, and unreal.
—National Guardsman Thomas Oliver, April 1968

In the spring of 1967, federal officials anxiously awaited the Student Nonviolent Coordinating Committee's next move. Fresh from chairman Stokely Carmichael's coinage of the Black Power slogan and his subsequent trips to China, North Vietnam, and Cuba, the organization had entered a new, more militant stage in its seven-year history. When White House Aide Stephen Pollak learned that the group might concentrate on Washington that summer, he nervously alerted the president. Hearing that the Howard University graduate had plans to return to the District could not have assuaged the president's concerns about the fragile state of race relations in the nation's capital. However, Pollak promised the president that he would work with FBI, the DOJ, and local police to keep potentially disruptive activities at bay.[1]

Carmichael did come to Washington that summer, but only to kick off a national campaign against a bevy of racial justice issues, including the Vietnam War. His peaceful visit did not stop the Johnson administration from keeping tabs on his and other activists' whereabouts as police confrontations in cities like Newark, New Jersey, and Detroit, Michigan, catalyzed large-scale rebellions during the summer of 1967. Inside and outside the beltway, many could not help but wonder: Would Washington also burn? If so, when?[2]

White House Advisor Harry McPherson found hope from an unexpected source. Over the summer, the Johnson cabinet member encountered three black teens who reassured him that the District was riot-proof. When McPherson asked them about the chances for a major riot in Washington, one said, "There'll be a lot of little riots, but nothing like Newark or Detroit." When pressed, the teens explained, "It's the capital. They won't let it happen here. . . . It's not just the troops—they just won't let it happen here. Negro people know that." The teens' comments revealed an acute awareness of the city's federal presence and mindfulness of the government's surveillance over their city. However, the Johnson administration knew that the government's strong oversight would not be enough to deter an uprising from erupting in the capital—and, in fact, White House officials worried that a heavy hand in District affairs could spur further violence.[3]

To eliminate a powerful justification for violent protest and to create a path to full electoral representation, the president issued Reorganization Plan No. 3 in August 1967, granting Washingtonians partial home rule. The appointment of a black mayor and majority-black city council was a means for the Johnson administration to placate local activists and an attempt to safeguard the city from riots. But on April 4, 1968, one of his worst fears came true. That night, after Martin Luther King was assassinated, D.C. residents took to the streets. While allowing Washingtonians limited self-government may have helped buffer the blow of civil violence, it did not resolve the systemic problems that fueled that violence.

The uprising, the first test of the city's new government, complicated the question of who could and should govern the city. The civil violence revealed both interracial and intraracial fault lines among the federal government, the white growth machine, law enforcement, an emerging black majority electorate, and the recently appointed local government. On the one hand, the riots gave black residents an unexpected platform from which to express their grievances, and they called for better housing, elected representation, and protection against police brutality. On the other hand, their demands for political and economic control, combined with the violence that erupted throughout the city's black neighborhoods, provided fuel for critics of home rule—including members of the previously supportive Johnson administration.

Local white stakeholders and national lawmakers had long feared that the rise of black political power would weaken their influence over local affairs. Following King's assassination, groups like the Washington Board of Trade and Federation of Citizens Associations used the rebellion as a means to challenge the prudence of home rule legislation and pose questions about the viability of black self-determination. Their efforts were aided by several mechanisms set in place by the Johnson administration. The president's reorganization plan—a measure Johnson had compromised on for the sake of political expediency—had not transferred real power or redistributed significant resources to black residents. Instead, it gave Congress the final say over the city's budget and laws. Thanks to the selective incorporation of upper- and middle-class African Americans into the local political system, it had also further politically fractured black Washington. By exploiting the weaknesses in Johnson's reorganization plan and capitalizing on the city's civil violence, white stakeholders fought to retain control over District affairs.

The president helped conservative lawmakers and white business and real estate groups in another way as well. From 1965 to 1967, Johnson dedicated significant resources to staving off further urban rebellion throughout the country. But as he searched for answers through crime commissions, conferences, and special reports, his conservative opponents waged a rhetorical assault against his administration and forced punitive adaptions to his anticrime legislation. The 1967 D.C. crime bill, which included an antiriot provision, demonstrated their ability to capitalize on the already-repressive tactics honed by the Johnson administration to maintain power. Johnson's riot prevention and control measures—and particularly the ways in which they were implemented in the District—reordered the government around the problem of crime, challenged the local black government's authority, and laid the groundwork for the conservative ascendance.[4]

Stokely Carmichael, more than any other activist, was at the center of debates about law and order, black political power, and self-determination. Although his influence on the uprising was subject to contrasting interpretations, his impact in Washington during and after the riots was undeniable. The federal government and conservative politicians' surveillance and repression of the militant activist highlights, on a national scale, the force of law-and-order campaigns in limiting the work of Black Power activists. The story resonated on the local level. As the reactions to the D.C. riots illustrate, the federal government and white stakeholders shaped the parameters of the local black government's response to the crisis. They then used the civil violence to justify narrowing the possibilities of meaningful home rule for all Washingtonians.

PREVENTATIVE MEASURES

While federal officials surveilled Stokely Carmichael during the summer of 1967, tensions between local police and black residents continued to escalate. Although the Johnson administration's national focus was on crime control and riot prevention, the D.C. case forced it to take a closer look at Washington's Metropolitan Police Department. Activists had long pointed to the MPD as an example of a local institution that failed to protect black residents. One key reason for this failure was discrimination within the police department. In 1957, the NAACP had launched a discrimination suit against the institution. Although the court sided with the MPD, the NAACP shed light on a clear pattern of discrimination in hiring and promotions. That year, African Americans represented only 11 percent of the force, and none held positions higher than corporal. A decade later, that number had only climbed to 20 percent.[5]

John Layton, the city's powerful police chief, kept this number low. Layton, a Washington native, had joined the police force in 1936. He moved through the department's ranks in narcotics and internal investigations and served as chief of detectives before becoming chief of police in 1964. During his almost three decades on the force, he had cultivated relationships with the southern representatives who controlled the House District Committee. As a result, he had been given the green light to rule the department as he saw fit. When Layton became chief, the MPD was already a polarizing force in the District. His presence did not mitigate the situation. Under his supervision, black officers remained 20 percent of the force.[6]

Layton worked with the House District Committee to oversee the MPD. According to John Hechinger, Washington's first city council chairman, Representatives McMillan and Broyhill "watched over District Affairs with the tenderness of a plantation overseer with a bullwhip in hand." Every year, they attached a rider to the District Appropriations Act allowing policemen to live outside the District. As Hechinger explained, the MPD "attracted white southern police recruits who settled in the suburbs and infused the police force with the callous cracker attitudes of Georgia, Alabama, and Tennessee." The MPD also disproportionally targeted black residents. Police records in 1962 revealed that 85 percent of those arrested for serious offenses were black. On occasion Hechinger observed that the police even valued property rights more highly than human rights and appeared more responsive to southern members of Congress than to disenfranchised Washington residents.[7] The relationship between police and black residents had become so fraught that in 1967, the *Wall*

Street Journal observed that the "slum-dweller" regarded the D.C. police force as an "army of occupation," staffed by "racist cops who hate Negroes."[8]

Public confrontations between police and city residents, the principal trigger of uprisings throughout the country, were not uncommon in Washington. But in the aftermath of the Watts riots, the frequency of local conflicts attracted additional scrutiny from the White House. In April 1967, as the White House lobbied for its reorganization plan, Stephen Pollack, presidential assistant for District Affairs, told Johnson that work was needed to increase black residents' confidence in the police. "Hostility appears to exist on both sides," he explained. Pollack recommended recruiting African Americans to fill three hundred vacancies in the force and proposed desegregating squad cars. He also suggested meaningful discussions between the police and community residents and stressed the importance of improvements in law enforcement, corrections, and police-community relations to the District's safety. The White House aide even accompanied a patrol team to observe, firsthand, the city's racial climate. Afterward he warned the president about escalating racial tensions caused by an 80 percent white police force patrolling black neighborhoods.[9]

Washington was not the only city where a police incident could catalyze urban unrest. On July 12, a minor incident involving the arrest of a taxi driver in Newark triggered five days of riots as city residents protested what they perceived as another instance of police brutality. The uprising left 26 people dead, over 1,000 injured, 1,400 arrested, and more than $10 million in property damage. Less than one week later, riots broke out six hundred miles away, when another routine arrest escalated into days of unrest in Detroit. The riots here were even more costly. Forty-three people died, 7,200 were arrested, and property damage was estimated at $40 million. President Johnson found the riots in Newark and Detroit extremely discouraging. He had backed civil rights legislation and fought a War on Poverty, but he still could not subdue the anger boiling over in America's cities.[10]

The uprisings left Johnson with relatively few options that would satisfy both black and white citizens. On July 27, 1967, as the Detroit riots ended, the president announced, in a televised address, the formation of a National Advisory Commission on Civil Disorders. Johnson had stacked the commission with political moderates, including its chairman, Illinois governor Otto Kerner (D), and New York mayor John Lindsay (R). The president ordered the commission to examine the origins of the recent disorders and make recommendations to prevent or contain future riots. He formed the commission in part to preempt a congressional investigation that could attack his policies from the right as well as the left. He also hoped the investigation would give the appearance of taking concrete solutions without immediately committing to anything specific.[11]

The July disturbances in Newark and Detroit threw the capital into turmoil. Rumors swirled: the National Guard had been deployed; bridges were burning; black police officers were refusing to report for duty; and federal offices had closed. Although these reports were false, a disturbance did erupt on the night of July 31 that threatened to turn D.C. into another damning statistic. Shortly before midnight, a fire broke out in a used furniture store on 7th Street NW, in one of the city's black neighborhoods. By the time the police and fire department arrived, a few hundred young residents had already gathered. Some hurled bottles and stones at them. Soon after the police broke up the crowd, reports of smashed store windows, cars set on fire, and looted liquor stores drew them back to the scene. By five in the morning, they had arrested thirty-four residents, including thirteen juveniles, and restored order. The MPD reported the incident to the Kerner Commission, which categorized it as a "minor disorder." Even so, the *Washington Post* reported that the incident was far from trivial. "The event demonstrated, not for the first time in Washington, the danger of wild outbursts that is always present in large cities," it said. But large-scale violence had been averted. The *Post* praised the MPD for having learned from the mistakes of police departments in "less fortunate" areas. Instead of exercising force, it claimed, officers had used restraint. While most news sources corroborated the *Post*'s reporting, some activists complained that the police had demonstrated excessive force, especially when it came to their treatment of the juveniles.[12]

As the Kerner commission conducted interviews, held hearings, and collected information for its report, the president demanded that federal agencies make preparations for the possibility of another round of riots the following summer. He assigned his attorney general, Ramsey Clark, to supervise the broad project. Clark, a Texas Democrat and son of Supreme Court Justice Tom Clark, had begun work at the Department of Justice in 1961. He served as assistant attorney general, then as deputy attorney general, and, in 1967, was appointed by Johnson to the highest post in the DOJ. During his years at the DOJ, Clark made strides toward securing black citizens their civil rights. He supervised the federal presence at the University of Mississippi during the week following James Meredith's historic enrollment and subsequent white protests; managed federal enforcement of the court order protecting civil rights activists' march from Selma, Alabama, to Montgomery; oversaw the drafting and passage of the Voting Rights Act of 1965; and headed the Presidential Task

Force following the 1965 riots in Watts. His extensive work in the DOJ and on civil rights issues made him uniquely qualified for the work at hand.[13]

Clark's first step was to hold a series of conferences on riot prevention and control with the mayors and police chiefs of over one hundred cities. Speaking at a closed-door panel in advance of the conferences, Clark admitted that the unrest that plagued the nation had created uneasiness and considerable fear among the general public. However, Clark maintained a sensitivity to the plight of the country's black citizens consistent with the Johnson administration's views on civil rights. He believed that conservatives' allegations that rioters wanted "death and destruction and guerilla warfare" were just examples of conservative fearmongering. When four hundred police officials, including the police chiefs of the largest U.S. cities, attended the conferences, he cautioned them to exercise no more force than necessary to keep incidents contained on the local level.[14]

The Johnson administration could not preach restraint and cooperation to police chiefs across the country without reckoning with the controversial man holding court in its backyard. Johnson had deeply resented the D.C. Board of Commissioners' decision to appoint John Layton as police chief in 1964. Prior to the commissioners' announcement, the administration had requested that the board's president, Walter Tobriner, consult with the White House and the Justice Department to select a new chief. When Tobriner refused, Johnson unleashed his fury. Two weeks after Layton's appointment, Charles Horskey, White House advisor on National Capital affairs, met with Tobriner. Horskey told him that Johnson's concern over crime in the District necessitated federal oversight over changes or appointments within the MPD.[15]

The next year, Johnson established a President's Commission on Crime in the District of Columbia to investigate the causes of crime and delinquency, research preventative measures, and examine "the organization and adequacy" of local law enforcement. Johnson intended for the crime commission to diffuse local tensions, quiet conservatives who challenged his law-and-order credentials, and, importantly, further cement his control over D.C.'s crime control efforts—a preview of what would come after the riots. In July 1966, the commission took an unconventional step. "Based on the urgent needs disclosed by its review of the Metropolitan Police Department," it submitted a single-issue one-hundred-page report on the MPD five months before it published the rest of its findings.[16]

The D.C. Crime Commission's research confirmed much of what black residents had articulated for decades. It found that "some elements of the community see the police not as protectors but as part of an oppressive social order."

Moreover, it observed, "a substantial segment of the community believes that Negroes in the custody of the police are physically mistreated." Verbal abuse further heightened police-community tensions. Police departments in other cities had begun to ban the use of trigger words like "boy" and "nigger." Layton, however, had dug in his heels, insisting that there was no need to forbid his policemen to use offensive language. The commission disagreed. It suggested that resorting to this demeaning language compromised officers' ability to do their job effectively. It also took Layton to task for the absence of a firm policy on police-community relations and for his "general and imprecise" statements on the subject. To improve the MPD, the commission placed a high priority on efforts to strengthen police-community relations. Its recommendations all hinged on actions Layton had failed to take, including prohibiting the use of racial trigger words by policemen, issuing an order outlining appropriate uses of force by the police, and increasing the number of black officers on the force.[17]

Although the president was dead set on removing Layton, he had signed control of the police over to the new mayor. Mayor Washington quickly understood the limits of local power under Johnson's reorganization plan. In November 1967, the municipal government faced its first test when residents in the predominantly black Southeast neighborhood of Congress Heights complained about their abuse at the hands of a white Eleventh Precinct policeman. The city council moved swiftly to conduct hearings on the matter. When Layton and his congressional allies caught word of what was happening, they immediately forced the mayor's hand. In a closed-door meeting with the police chief, Washington told the council members to drop their inquiry and allow the MPD to conduct its own internal investigation—a proposition that residents found unsatisfactory considering that, in the civilian review board's history, only one complaint had resulted in disciplinary action against an officer.[18]

The White House staff worked closely with Mayor Washington to "solve" the Layton problem. In December 1967, Washington addressed the issue indirectly by creating the position of public safety director and giving the post jurisdiction over the MPD. It was a calculating but controversial move. It helped the mayor circumvent the regulations that barred the selection of an outsider as police chief. This allowed him to bring in Patrick V. Murphy, a reform-minded law enforcement official nationally known for trying to defuse tensions between police and inner-city residents. Murphy received enthusiastic support throughout the Johnson administration, from the attorney general to the president. But District officers bristled at the mayor's meddling. They did not like the idea of their police chief becoming subordinate to an outsider—especially one who would go on to attack their boss.[19]

Murphy got his start in New York as a cop before serving as chief of police in Syracuse, New York. He had helped cities across the country implement community relations programs and directed the Justice Department's Office of Law Enforcement Assistance, an agency that Johnson had created to help fight crime. It appeared that Murphy was the perfect candidate to help solve D.C.'s crime problem without committing further harm to the city's black residents. Murphy, who had been stationed in D.C. for his DOJ post, had already had ample time to consider the strengths and weaknesses of the city's police force. He did not think Washington was unique for its strained relations between officers and black residents. But, according to Murphy, "to permit the local police force, operating in the shadow of the White House, to remain in such a circumstance was . . . risk taking at its worst."[20]

When Murphy was appointed, he quickly moved to address the pervasive culture of racism and abuse that the police chief had cultivated. After Layton failed to disclose to him that white officers who had been drinking heavily fired off gunshots as they drove past the president of Howard University's home, Murphy unleashed his fury. The generally cool-headed leader publicly accused Layton of trying to cover up the incident and called his actions a "big inexcusable error." Privately Murphy reminded Layton that he was his boss—an accurate statement, though one complicated by both the amorphous nature of Murphy's position and the fact that the federal government still had ultimate control over the MPD's budget.[21]

To further marginalize Layton, Murphy appointed Jerry Wilson, a talented young commander, as assistant chief of field operations. Within the year, he promoted Wilson to run the MPD's day-to-day affairs. Murphy claimed that Wilson emphasized restraint in planning for riot prevention and control, a critical skill that he feared Layton lacked. Even so, Layton kept his title and many of his duties. He remained a destructive presence to black citizens and was, according to city council chairman John Hechinger, "an irritant for Murphy, the mayor, and the City Council" until his retirement in August 1969.[22]

Authorizing the Kerner Commission, deputizing Clark to coordinate federal efforts, and reorganizing the District's government exemplified the president's indirect approach to riot prevention and control in 1967. As the winter months advanced, Congress confronted the president with a more direct—and punitive—crime bill for the city. The local crime bill, the first major anticrime law enacted during the 1960s, was the result of a long and protracted fight that began in 1965. It was largely the work of the House District Committee, which was simultaneously waging a war against home rule legislation. The controversial bill permitted police officers to question suspects prior to their arraignment, introduced increased mandatory-minimum sentencing penalties for certain crimes, and allowed warrantless arrests for misdemeanors. It also included an antiriot provision for the District, which would give penalties of up to five years imprisonment and fines of up to $10,000 for engaging in, inciting, or encouraging others to participate in a riot. Meanwhile, the House and Senate District Committees erased more progressive provisions related to gun control, drug treatment, and rehabilitation. The president first vetoed the bill in November 1966, citing excessive police questioning rules, unjust mandatory minimum sentences, and no increase in police funding. The next year, Congress reintroduced the D.C. crime bill with provisions that were, as Johnson lamented, "virtually unchanged."[23]

The bill divided the Johnson administration. Attorney General Clark, along with White House Aides Joseph Califano and Harry McPherson, believed the bill did not address the root causes of crime. Moreover, they worried that announcing an antiriot law for Washington in the immediate aftermath of the rebellions in Newark and Detroit begged for trouble. The optics would certainly be questionable. Not only would it suggest that the president was predicting riots. It would also imply that he did not have confidence in the local officials he had appointed. Yet other aides believed the bill embodied the Johnson administration's desire for "quick and effective prosecution." For select members of the Justice Department, the bill even constituted "a model local law."[24]

Internal debate only mattered so much. When the bill was sent to Johnson for his signature, he was politically vulnerable, preoccupied with the Vietnam War, and losing popularity. In December 1967, he signed the bill. In doing so, he presented an increasingly punitive template for crime prevention designed by his conservative opponents. Reordering the government around the problem of crime helped him manage the city's municipal government but also fueled Republicans' powerful law-and-order narrative and paved the way for Richard Nixon's national presidential campaign.

As the city's local government settled into office, the Johnson administration continued to take more aggressive measures to shape its response to future disturbances. With the White House's consent, Attorney General Clark established the Interdivisional Information Unit, a secret intelligence unit within the Justice Department, to collect information on black activists and to better coordinate responses with state and local officials. It also allowed the U.S. Army to conduct its own surveillance operation and commissioned the Office of the Secretary of Defense to issue riot-control plans. Led by Under Secretary of the Army David McGiffert, a special task force designed an operation, code-named "Cabin Guard," during the tail end of the Detroit riots in July 1967. The plan it hatched called for "maximum application of manpower and minimum application of force."[25]

The army's plan relied on well-prepared, racially integrated military units trained in riot control techniques that emphasized restraint instead of physical force. The units were assigned to specific police precincts. In February and March 1968, officers toured their assigned precincts and met with local police officials. Some scholars have pointed to the close coordination between the National Guard, local police, and U.S. Army as the reason that local police and government officials understood the roles and responsibilities of federalized forces going into the uprising. That may be true. But for D.C. residents, the presence of troops provided an oppressive atmosphere at a moment when racial tensions were already high.[26]

As soldiers familiarized themselves with the city, the Kerner Commission finalized its much-anticipated report. It published its findings on February 29, 1968. The commission's report immediately angered conservative lawmakers by blaming riots on white racism and offering criticism of law enforcement. The commissioners' trips to riot areas and hearing testimony convinced them of the deep sense of alienation and anger felt by African Americans due to institutional neglect. Their report emphasized the systemic causes of the disorders that continued to plague the country each summer and the inherent danger in the use of "indiscriminate and excessive" force to curb future riots. The report received nationwide attention for its prediction that the country was "moving towards two societies, one black, one white—separate and unequal." Its call for dramatic and expensive reforms of the nation's programmatic efforts on behalf of welfare, housing, and education particularly infuriated the president. Livid at the perceived attacks on his Great Society programming, Johnson chose not to accept the commission's final report.[27] City council vice chairman Walter Fauntroy, on the other hand, celebrated the fact that the commission identified white racism at the heart of the problem and was hopeful that "this will be the occasion for serious soul-searching on the part of individual Americans."[28]

In March 1968, President Johnson reflected on the achievements of his District reorganization plan in a message to Congress. He had created the city's first municipal government in nearly one hundred years. The black mayor that he had appointed stood proudly in city hall. Furthermore, a city council chaired by Hechinger and vice chaired by Fauntroy provided Washingtonians with expanded municipal representation. Instead of serving as a progressive benchmark, however, Johnson's message served as a pessimistic warning about crime. "The long shadow of crime falls over the streets of the nation's capital, mocking its proud institutions," he said. Johnson then outlined a massive plan to curb local crime, including recommendations to further strengthen the city's police department; implement a strong gun control law; and reorganize the courts, all buttressed by calls for increased surveillance and repressive measures. Before either the federal or local government could respond to his recommendations, Martin Luther King was assassinated.[29]

THE RIOTS

On April 4, within half an hour of hearing the news of King's assassination, a crowd congregated on 14th and U Streets NW, in the vicinity of the Southern Christian Leadership Conference's Washington headquarters, to mourn the loss of the great civil rights leader. Reporters arriving on the scene found residents distraught. Local police decided not to disperse the group. A few hours later, the police detected a shift in the crowd's mood from grief to anger.[30]

That evening, Stokely Carmichael mingled with hundreds of D.C. residents outside SNCC's 14th Street headquarters before leading a group of demonstrators up and down the commercial avenue to encourage stores to shut down for the night. Eaton's Barber Shop closed first. YanKee Restaurant and Wings 'N' Things followed suit. The crowd stopped at both Republic Theater and Lincoln Theater to usher audiences out of the venues.[31] Carmichael acknowledged that he did not stop followers from breaking store windows. Instead he encouraged them to arm themselves. "If they don't have guns, we are not going to let them throw bricks and bottles at guns, but when they get guns we'll be on the streets," he told reporters. The fact that police teargassed the local SNCC office that night went unreported.[32]

Officers first heard the sound of windows shattering at People's Drug Store. By 10:30 P.M., reports of looting blared from police radios. Rioters broke into Sam's Pawnbrokers and Rhodes Five-and-Ten, both on 14th Street. Shortly thereafter, the first fire call brought news of a vehicle aflame at Barry-Pate-Addison Chevrolet. By then, the crowd on 14th Street stretched over an entire block, from U Street to V Street. Police backup arrived on the scene, and officers jostled with rioters for over forty-five minutes. A fire blazed in the midst of their dispute. When firefighters arrived, residents threw stones at them. The police encroached on the crowd, hurling tear gas canisters their way. Rioting quickly spread in African American neighborhoods throughout the city, including the 7th Street NW and H Street NE corridors. Then it began to rain.[33]

Police officer stands next to a damaged storefront at People's Drug Store during the D.C. riots. (Star Collection, D.C. Public Library © *Washington Post*)

The violence ebbed in the early morning. At dawn, hundreds of police officers still lined the sidewalks. 14th Street had finally quieted down. One man had died. A quick survey of the area revealed broken glass and debris strewn throughout the streets. Tear gas still hung in the air. Alarms reverberated against the empty storefronts. Traffic lights flashed on and off. Burned-out buildings collapsed. The only people one reporter saw along the nine-block stretch from the Lincoln Memorial to Washington Circle were police officers and a single nurse getting off her shift. According to one soldier, "It looks like a city in one of those horror movies where everybody gets out."[34]

By midmorning Friday, the MPD confidently predicted that the worst was over. News of incidents had dropped sharply, looting had dissipated, and fires remained only in scattered locations. In fact, police officials indicated that they were more concerned about a nearby rally that Carmichael was holding than the situation out on the streets. Based on their reporting, they released the officers who had been placed on extended duty the day before, thereby reducing the force's street presence to almost normal capacity.[35]

Based on predawn reports, the mayor opened the city's schools on Friday. After learning that those in attendance were ditching school throughout the morning, he officially dismissed students at 1:30 P.M. Schoolchildren abandoned classrooms and headed toward 14h Street. That afternoon, stores that looters had broken into the night before were set ablaze. Firefighters could not get through the streets to put out the flames dotting 14th Street. Down on 7th Street, a major black shopping area, looters continued to dart in and out of shops with various items in hand. It was on the corner of 7th and Q Streets that teenagers set a fire inside Quality Clothing. Clarence James tried to stop them. His mother, obese and bedridden, lived above store. But his cries fell on deaf ears. Mrs. James inhaled too much smoke and died en route to the hospital, the eighth person killed in the riot, and the fifth fire victim.[36]

The rioters vandalized liquor stores, pawnshops, jewelry shops, clothing boutiques, salons, and hardware stores. All of the main commercial arteries of black Washington had been hit. Police tossed tear gas canisters at rioters across the city. Fire reports on 14th Street alone averaged twenty to thirty an hour. Meanwhile, tens of thousands of downtown workers fled the city. The city's police chief, John Layton, notified his superior, Public Safety Director Patrick Murphy, that the MPD could no longer control the uprising on its own.[37]

Federal and local government officials, including Murphy, Mayor Washington, Deputy Attorney General Warren Christopher, White House Aide Califano, and Under Secretary of the Army McGiffert, debated the use of federal troops to contain the crisis. With Attorney General Clark already dispatched to Memphis, where King had been assassinated, it fell to Christopher to provide a recommendation to the president about the need to deploy troops. White House officials feared that requesting soldiers would draw attention to the federal government's inability to control a disorder within miles of the White House and would likely exacerbate tensions between local law enforcement and black Washingtonians. But further delaying the decision could prove costly.[38]

Borrowing Chief Layton's car, Christopher surveyed the riot areas and quickly provided Johnson with the executive order and proclamation necessary to authorize the use of federal troops and federalize the District National Guard. He also collected signatures from Washington, Murphy, and Layton to ensure that none of the top local officials could deny giving their consent after the fact. At 4:02 P.M. on Friday, April 5, less than twenty-four hours after King's death, the president authorized the military to restore order to the nation's capital. An hour and a half later, Mayor Washington declared a state of emergency; prohibited the sale of alcoholic beverages, firearms, and portable quantities of gasoline; and ordered a curfew effective until 6:30 A.M. on Saturday, April 6.[39]

The city's black leaders and political appointees reacted quickly. Expressing grief over the slain civil rights hero, local SCLC leader and city council vice chairman Walter Fauntroy told reporters, "There is no one in the city whose heart is more crushed and broken than mine." Fauntroy, along with Mayor Washington, then sped from one television and radio station to the next to broadcast appeals to District residents to exercise restraint, remain calm, and resist violence. Others channeled their grief into political commentary. Edward MacClane, president of the Federation of Civic Associations, the black middle-class counterpart to the city's white neighborhood association group, rationalized the disorders. "You just can't expect people not to react this way," he said. "The city has been heading this way for a long time," he added, suggesting that the civil violence stemmed from more than King's assassination.[40]

Some of Washington's black activists inscribed racial meaning onto the moment. Lester McKinnie, of the local SNCC chapter, had strong words for the federal government. "The white racist government of the United States let Dr. Martin Luther King be shot down on the streets of Tennessee," he explained. Overcome with anger and fear, he added, "Dr. King was a man of peace. We can see by this act of aggression what is in store for all of us—the African people in America."[41] Willie Hardy and Julius Hobson had more suggestive messages. As Hardy explained, "When white America killed the father of nonviolence, it killed all hope of settling our problems by peaceful means."[42] Meanwhile, Hobson threatened, "the next white man that comes into the black community preaching non-violence should be dealt with violently." Hardy and Hobson almost certainly did not intend for their comments to be taken literally. Rather, they likely meant to distance themselves from some of the more tepid responses coming from D.C.'s black establishment, like local NAACP branch president H. Carl Moultrie, who suggested that Congress was in part to blame "in its refusal to pass the gun control and crime bills."[43]

For SNCC, King's death demanded action. McKinnie called for a nationwide strike of black people everywhere to mourn the SCLC leader's death. Meanwhile, Stokely Carmichael said that it "made it a lot easier for a lot of Negroes—they know it's time to get guns now." When asked whether he feared for his life, Carmichael told white newsmen, "The hell with my life—you should fear for yours. I know I'm going to die." He added, "We're going to die on our feet—we're tired of living on our stomachs." Unlike Hobson's comments, which officials knew to take with a grain of salt, Carmichael's words garnered national attention. His appeals to African Americans to arm themselves and take to the streets in retaliation for King's assassination prompted the Justice Department to keep even closer tabs on him.[44]

At the White House's insistence, Mayor Washington invited Cyrus Vance, former deputy secretary of defense and Johnson's personal representative during the 1967 Detroit riots, to coordinate strategy and manage the response of the National Guard, army, and local police. Vance arrived in Washington on Friday, April 5. By Saturday morning, incidents of looting and arson had greatly diminished. The mayor, along with Vance and city council chairman John Hechinger, used the interim peace as an opportunity to tour the riot areas. On witnessing the devastation, the trio immediately established plans to distribute food and provide temporary shelter for the dispossessed. Exercising caution, Mayor Washington imposed an additional curfew for Saturday afternoon. By early Saturday evening, the city returned to a reasonable calm, but the effects of the riots wreaked havoc on Washington for another week.[45]

By the end of the riots, the commercial districts lined with mostly white-owned movie theaters, car dealerships, department stores, and restaurants looked unrecognizable. Smoke had enveloped the city. The sound of gunshots rang out throughout the District for days. Most of those killed during the riots died tragically in buildings set on fire by looters themselves. To ensure order, troops continued to move into the city. By noon on Monday, April 8, the National Guard had stationed 13,450 troops at key points throughout Washington. On Wednesday, April 10, five days after Johnson ordered troops into the District, they finally began to withdraw—though the last 3,758 troops continued to patrol the city's troubled neighborhoods for another week.[46]

By the time the civil disturbance ceased and troops departed the capital, 13 residents had died, 2 from police gunfire, and 1,201 people has been injured, including 54 police officers, 21 firefighters, and 16 soldiers. Over fifteen thousand federal and National Guard troops assisted local police, and suburban fire companies helped control the widespread blazes. An estimated twenty thousand people participated in the riots—roughly one out of eight residents of the riot areas, but less than 4 percent of the District's total black population. Police arrested 7,640 participants, 1,082 for looting and 4,464 for violating curfew. Direct and indirect property losses, the cost of troop deployment, and other city expenditures rose to over $27 million. The National Capital Planning Commission, the central planning agency for the federal government, reported that 1,352 private businesses, 645 buildings, and 403 housing units were damaged or destroyed, leaving over two thousand residents homeless. Of the local businesses harmed, more than 40 percent either never reopened or relocated elsewhere. As a result, the city lost almost five thousand jobs.[47] The

Acting police chief Jerry V. Wilson (*left*) and Mayor Walter Washington (*center*) stand at the intersection of 14th and V Streets NW during the D.C. riots. (Star Collection, D.C. Public Library © *Washington Post*)

Washington Board of Trade conducted its own extensive study of the damage. It found that Washington's retail and service establishments suffered staggering losses, ranging from $17 million to $29 million. Additional losses accumulated on both the local and the federal level: the city's tax revenue losses aggregated over $2 million, the federal government's direct military outlays reached at least $2.2 million, and though the Board of Trade conservatively estimated the total value of damaged property at $15.3 million, the group believed it exceeded $40 million.[48]

The Johnson administration closely monitored the city's new government during the riots. The president had trouble delegating responsibility, in part because his home rule measure had not yet been tested, certainly not by such extensive civil violence. The White House had intended to scale back its involvement in the District. But it knew that all eyes were on the capital as one of the country's first black mayors navigated the racial landmine precipitated by King's assassination. At best, the initial interactions between federal and local officials suggested the ease with which the Johnson administration could work with its black municipal appointees. At worst, however, they revealed the ease with which the White House could still intervene in local affairs under its weak home rule bill.[49]

The House and Senate District Committees, which historically governed Washington with paternalistic flair, did not disappoint during the disorders. Senator Robert Byrd (D-W.Va.), whose position as chair of the U.S. Senate Appropriations Subcommittee on the District of Columbia gave him a vested interest in local affairs, personally phoned White House Aide Califano immediately after King's assassination to express his opinion about a citywide curfew. Byrd did not hesitate to let Califano know that the curfew "should be reinforced immediately, that the looters should be shot, if they are adults (but not killed, just shot in the leg); [and] that the time for restraint has ended."[50]

Black Washingtonians did not take news of the curfew well. Some residents accused black attorney and city employee Charles Duncan of discriminatorily enforcing the curfew, which extended beyond the duration of the riots, only in black neighborhoods. Duncan did not disagree. Speaking candidly, he admitted, "The attitude of the police department in this jurisdiction at this time is such that a white person would be less apt to be arrested on a curfew violation than the Negro. That's unfortunate and it probably would be disputed, but that's true." Mediating between the police and the black community took its toll on Duncan. "We are more often than not put in a position of defending police conduct," he said, "and this naturally puts me on the other side of the table from my friends . . . upholding a system that is suspect."[51]

Duncan's impression that he had been pitted against the black community to uphold a suspect system revealed the larger problem black officials confronted: their ascendance to public office gave the impression that they had meaningful power to make decisions about the city's governance. But in reality, power resided indirectly with other constituents. Meanwhile, the selective incorporation of African Americans like Duncan into the city's municipal government divided Washington's black community and hampered collective protest. The mechanisms put in place by the Johnson administration took a toll on the city. Throughout the crisis and in its aftermath, federal officials and white stakeholders capitalized on the limits of the president's home rule measure to shape black officials' response to the riots.

THE HEARINGS

As the dust settled in the riot-torn areas and the Johnson administration scaled back federal support, the District's majority-black city council tried to pick up the pieces of the shattered city. In the weeks following the riots, it held public hearings on the rebuilding and recovery of Washington. On May 10, the council released a lengthy report based on its findings. "The disturbance which struck Washington with little notice following the death of Dr. King was a great shock to those of us who live in and love this city," white city council chairman John Hechinger remarked. "This disturbance was a strong setback for the democratic process," he said, hinting at the trouble the uprising would cause for those seeking self-determination.[52]

The city council had a difficult task. Not only did it bear responsibility for rebuilding the city under the nation's watchful eye; it also had to balance a growing number of black voices, an uptick in militant demands, and rising congressional skepticism about its authority. Likewise, the council's post-riot recommendations had to assuage national concerns about disorderly conduct and fears about rising crime rates while remaining sensitive to community concerns. To balance this assortment of considerations, the council emphasized the need for special measures to improve the economic and social opportunities for the city's black residents—measures that tied their fate to the success of Lyndon Johnson's Great Society programming.[53]

Crowds lined up for the public hearings, held at four different venues over five days in May 1968. Ninety-three residents registered to testify, and over fifteen hundred people attended the sessions. News stations televised the hearings, and the press extensively reported on them. Witnesses, many of whom had participated in or had been personally affected by the uprising, spent days preparing for the hearings. Prior to them, many met with members of the Black United Front, which took a special interest in "addressing itself to the destiny of the 'rebuilding' of the Black communities" after the riots.[54] In addition to witnesses' oral testimony, the council received numerous written communications from organizations and groups that wished to represent their perspective on the recovery process.[55]

At the hearings, the council sought residents' input on the District's reconstruction. While offering constructive feedback, participants refused to withhold judgment about some of the basic factors—including the lack of housing, employment, and other opportunities for black residents—that contributed to the disturbances. In fact, many witnesses expressed hostility and bitterness toward the city council itself. Despite the modicum of control Johnson had provided the city government, residents had not elected its council members. Just weeks before the riots, on Congress's approval, Johnson had signed a bill allowing District residents to elect their own eleven-member Board of Education for the first time in almost a century. But that did not placate those who felt excluded from the democratic process. Participants were still determined to make their misgivings clear and their demands heard.[56]

The council graciously accepted their feedback. "Many presentations were forceful and challenging—often eloquent and moving," it said. In the end, it expressed its gratitude to the large number of "public-spirited citizens" who stayed long into the night to offer their recommendations. Overall, the council took pains to ensure that the hearings, one of its first post-riot undertakings, were inclusive of all black residents, especially those who felt they lacked the political channels necessary to articulate their grievances.[57]

The council's strong emphasis on community control was a notable feature of the hearings. The council maintained that the city's black community should have a central role in both planning and implementing rebuilding and recovery policies. Furthermore, it argued that those policies ought to recognize the black community's need for economic and political power. Council members reported that the black separatists' voices had startled them, but they recognized that those ideas did not dramatically diverge from the views of the vast majority of witnesses. Ultimately, the council observed, "what came through was the universal demand for the right of self-determination for the neighborhoods that need rebuilding," a sentiment that members could likely empathize with in light of their limited governing powers in the nation's capital.[58]

In its broad-based conclusions, the city council straddled the line between supporting the Johnson administration and aligning itself with a more conservative law-and-order contingent. On the one hand, its report indicated that members sided with the president. In addition to its general support for Johnson's domestic policies, the council concurred with the basic findings of the 1967 Kerner Commission, "that the systematic unequal treatment of Negroes by the institutions created by white society has created the ghetto." D.C. Council president John Hechinger went out of his way to mention the need for "a sharp and large scale reappraisal of the attitudes and actions of the white community, especially business, financial and investment sectors." In doing so, Hechinger, a prominent white businessman himself, hoped to use his influence to persuade members of the white growth machine to let black political power coexist with their development plans and financial goals.[59]

On the other hand, the council quickly condemned the rioters' turn to violence and advocated for the maintenance of law and order. "The pursuit of violence and lawlessness can only lead to the destruction of our city, not to its regeneration," it said. The council expressed little tolerance for the "no-white policy" championed by some of the hearing's more militant witnesses and refused to seriously consider their threat that another rebellion would occur unless officials halted all planning and rebuilding efforts by white residents. Since many city council members hewed closely to the pro-integration attitudes of the civil rights movement's older guard, their positions on these matters were unsurprising. If anything, they reaffirmed Johnson's decision to appoint uncontroversial upper- and middle-class African Americans and white liberals, rather than militant firebrands, to the city's appointed council.[60]

The city council could not discuss the disorders without addressing the role of Washington's police department. For those who believed that the riots stemmed from the police's long-standing tension with and animosity toward the black community, the MPD's seven thousand arrests and its rigid enforcement of the curfew during the riots indicated the use of inappropriate force. The council viewed it differently. It stated that the MPD's strong use of force accelerated the restoration and maintenance of order. Regardless of their private views, it is clear that they sought to project a balanced view of the riots. In doing so, they gave residents on both sides of the racial divide something to champion.[61]

To the credit of the various police officers and military officials that joined together to stop the rebellion and curb further violence, few witnesses levied specific criticism against police officers or troops during the riots. Officers' restraint played a large part in this. "To indiscriminately shoot would have cost lives, aggravated the situation, and led to more incidents," the council reported as it commended the MPD, the army, the marines, and the D.C. National Guard.[62] The National Capital Area Civil Liberties Union agreed. The organization, which generally considered the MPD a "deeply troubled government agency," praised it for performing "magnificently" during the disorders. "The men of the MPD can be proud of the restraint and the coolness which they showed in the face of one of the most difficult situations that any Police Department has ever faced," it concluded.[63]

Police officers and troops deliberately exercised restraint. Federal officials had observed the bloody lessons that killed thirty-four in Watts, forty-three in Detroit, and twenty-three in Newark during those cities' respective riots. Training following the 1967 uprisings emphasized minimal necessary force, the maintenance of a professional demeanor, and the use of tear gas instead of gunfire. The results reaffirmed this strategy: despite more than seventy-five hundred arrests made and over fifteen thousand troops called in, only thirteen citizens died. Of the thirteen deaths in Washington, only two were at the hands of police. No soldiers shot residents, and no policemen, firemen, or soldiers died. Most victims died trapped in fires. This differed drastically from the death tolls in other big-city riots, where city and state police and guardsmen bore responsibility for most of the deaths.[64]

Yet for all the instructive lessons local police and national troops factored into their performance during the riots, their actions did not please everyone. According to one Maryland resident, law and order had not been maintained "for fear of having the police accused of brutality or some other nonsense by the irresponsible minority leadership."[65] *U.S. News and World Report* founder David Lawrence echoed this sentiment. "Efforts to apply vigorously the weapons of the law have been met with cries of 'police brutality,'" the conservative columnist observed. Lawrence derided the timidity expressed by local officials in Washington and cautioned that the minority-led government was not fit to manage the crisis.[66]

Evidence from District police officers indicated that they, too, believed this to be true. Weeks after the riots, local white officers revealed to Senator Robert Byrd in a series of closed interviews that they had followed orders they did not support—especially Public Safety Director Patrick Murphy's policy not to shoot looters. "I was not very proud to be a policeman," admitted one thirty-three-year-old officer who had served on the force for seven years. "I felt as though I had handcuffs on myself. I really couldn't do anything. I felt as though the department did not want me to do anything out there," he elaborated. While that may have been true, the MPD's restraint helped prevent the police force from becoming the chief focal point of the city council's post-riot hearings.[67]

During the hearings, witnesses discussed a variety of issues that negatively impacted the city's black community, including poor police-community relations, overcrowded courts, and inadequate housing. The council's report did not offer concrete policy solutions, but it did instruct the mayor to address many of the issues residents mentioned. Specific suggestions included finding a means for effective citizen and youth participation in the policing of troubled areas, implementing strong weapons licensing regulations, and improving juvenile court procedures. Overall the message it reiterated was clear: "The black community of Washington should have a central and powerful role in the planning and implementation of policies for the rebuilding and recovery."[68]

The council's report successfully captured a wide range of voices on systemic problems, racial tensions, and civil rights in the late 1960s. Reflecting on the seeming futility of the civil rights movement, one witness explained, "Singing won't get it. Prayer marches won't get it. Running down to the White House and sipping tea with Johnson, that won't get it no more. The only thing that this city and the nation seem to recognize is fire and flames and gasoline." Another witness lamented the limited self-government Johnson granted the District, suggesting, "We don't want any plantationships, we want partnerships." The term "plantationship" signified more than a political compromise between the local and federal government. It suggested the limits of Johnson's home rule measure and the nation's unwillingness to hand major cities over to minority-controlled municipal governments. The creation of the D.C. City Council was in and of itself a mimetic reform, passed in part to respond to demands for self-determination and fears of black insurgency.[69]

As the riots unfolded, it became clear that the council had to compete with the White House, members of Congress, and powerful local white stakeholders for control of vital resources and over the response to the crisis. Take Senator Byrd's closed-door interviews in May 1968, for example. Mere miles from the city council's offices, where it was conducting public hearings on the riots, the chairman of the Senate Appropriations Subcommittee on the District of Columbia met with police officers and firefighters and also with local business owners. To protect the identity of those participating, Byrd held his interviews in his office after hours. He collected almost fifteen hundred pages of testimony, which, he claimed, revealed "a story of fear and frustration and anger."[70]

Washington's business owners were eager to voice their resentment toward local and federal officials for not doing enough to protect their property. Many had suffered significant losses during the riots. C. D. Kaufmann, the president of Kay Jewelers Stores, could not believe officials' celebratory spirit for the restraint exercised when the business community had lost millions of dollars. Other merchants, like Albert Schindler, the co-owner of a dry-cleaning business on 14th Street, and Irving King, the operator of a menswear shop on U Street, watched their dreams crumble as looters ruined machinery, stole clothing, and burned their stores. Byrd inserted transcripts of interviews with riot zone merchants like Kaufmann, Schindler, and King into the *Congressional Record*. The House District Committee then used them as the basis for its attacks on the city government in hearings held later that month.[71]

THE BACKLASH

The Johnson administration relied on the assistance of Attorney General Ramsey Clark, recently appointed mayor Walter Washington, the Metropolitan Police Department, the National Guard, and federal troops to contain the civil violence. But none of these actors could stop members of the media, elected officials, white residents, and black activists from projecting the city's tumultuous events onto the national stage. Once concealed by the placid veneer of the Capitol, Washington's racial fractures, black residents' frustration over the conditions of their lives in the shadow of the White House, and the efficacy of Johnson's 1967 reorganization plan all became part of the local and national conversation about race, violence, and self-government in the aftermath of King's assassination.

The city's white business and civic groups responded quickly, though not in unison. "On the whole," Board of Trade president William Calomiris reported, "the job of containing the disorders and restoring normal patterns was well done." Calomiris went out of his way to compliment local officers and national troops for their discipline. He even praised Mayor Washington for his leadership and decisiveness. Calomiris did not, however, let the city's local officials off the hook. "Looting, arson, property destruction, and threats to life and limb cannot be condoned under any circumstances," he said with reproach, "so I hope very much that those proved responsible for leading and encouraging such activities are appropriately punished." His message was clear: the Board of Trade demanded law-and-order measures from local black officials.[72]

Despite the Board of Trade's public praise for aspects of the local and national responses to the riots, dissent permeated the organization. In a letter to the organization, businessman Joseph Deckman expressed his frustration with its public stance. Deckman had served as president and general manager of a successful building and supply company before heading the Federation of Citizens Associations in the 1940s. During that time, he testified on slum clearance policies, squarely placing the blame for slum conditions "on the shoulders of the owners of slum properties, the poor housekeeping methods of slum-tenants and the municipal authorities who allow unsanitary slum conditions to exist." Two decades later, the riots reaffirmed his views.[73]

Deckman strongly believed that the Board of Trade could not effectively represent the interests of the business community if it did not call out local officials for their shortcomings during the riots. If Washington's city council did not look out for the business community then, he reasoned, it would be difficult for the Board of Trade to support its liberal policies and provisions for the "so-called Ghetto residents." His comments offer an intimate look at how white merchants viewed the city's black leadership and their own political power after the implementation of Johnson's reorganization plan. Deckman's desired warning to the city council would serve, to his mind, as a reminder of the group's influence over local policy. Other D.C. business owners were also eager to deliver this message in light of the mayor's hesitance to send in troops immediately after King's assassination, even if the federal government rarely called in troops as a purely preventative measure.[74]

In Deckman's predominantly white home of Prince George's County, Maryland, police, he argued, met nonviolence with nonviolence and violence with violence. Deckman lauded the policy as "a language understood by all factions of our society as attested to by the absence of looting and burning [there]." Casting the issue of law and order in explicitly racial terms, he implored even "the most naïve liberal" on the Board of Trade to understand the work of the "hoodlums, teenage delinquents, Black Power advocates of violence and criminal elements" as "the willful pillaging of properties under the guise of lamenting the death of Dr. Martin Luther King Jr." Deckman, like many of Washington's business owners, refused to view the civil violence as anything but willful destruction. This belief fueled merchants' calls for repression and surveillance and encouraged them to flex their authority at the very moment that the White House had given local black officials a modicum of power over local affairs.[75]

Washington's powerful white stakeholders grappled with how to reassert their authority and who to blame for the riots. While the Board of Trade focused its attention on the city's black government, the Association of the Oldest Inhabitants of the District of Columbia (AOI), Washington's oldest white civic organization founded in 1865, directed its anger toward white liberals on the federal level. In a letter to Attorney General Clark, AOI president Burton Langhenry expressed the organization's concern regarding Clark's "ineffective leadership" during the "sacking of Washington, D.C." Among Langhenry's grievances against the attorney general was the time Clark allowed to elapse before calling in the military and his privileging of rioters' lives at the expense of property damage. "This might never have happened," Langhenry accused Clark, "if instead of adopting a position of weakness and of permissiveness, you had moved to uphold the law by whatever means were necessary under the circumstances." Langhenry also noted his open support of civic leaders in cities like Chicago, where, he believed, "shoot to kill" orders kept the situation under control. Finally, he attacked the liberal tenor of the Clark-run Justice Department. "You were placed in office to enforce the law not to circumvent it . . . or is social work more important to you than law enforcement work?" he asked with disdain. By focusing its opprobrium on federal officials, the organization explicitly attacked liberals' weaknesses on law and order while indirectly challenging the scope of the local black government's authority.[76]

The Eighteenth and Columbia Road Business Association had grown equally disappointed with government inaction. In a letter to Lyndon Johnson, its president, John Jarboe, expressed the organization's growing disillusionment with Johnson's domestic policies. As Jarboe explained, the president had been one of the most vocal opponents of crime. However, he chided, "these forceful and moving words of yours have not been translated into action in the Nation's Capital." In filing its grievance, the group added itself to the lengthy list of local white stakeholders both disenchanted with Johnson's law-and-order policies and dissatisfied with his reorganization plan. Their view of the riots, the local government's response to the disorders, and the federal reaction to both encouraged them to reassert their influence over local black officials and fight to establish parameters on the city's government.[77]

Local organizations were not the only voices to disapprove of the riots' handling by black municipal officials and liberal white lawmakers. Disturbed by the black mayor's newfound local powers, Senator Bourke Hickenlooper (R-Iowa) took his concerns over Walter Washington's desire to withdraw troops from the District straight to Johnson's Senate liaison Mike Manatos. As chairman of the Republican Policy Committee, Hickenlooper had positioned himself as one of the most powerful, and most conservative, Republicans in Congress. He had made a name for himself by routinely opposing civil rights legislation. This time the senator warned the president to "stop this foolishness" and block local officials from calling the shots. Hickenlooper also conflated international warfare with the national civil disorders. He indicated to Manatos that local thugs anxiously waited troop removal and were "particularly hopeful it will happen over Easter so that they may have their own Tet Holiday by bombing individual homes in the Chevy Chase area."[78]

The senator's message reveals how Congress perceived local governance in the capital. First, Hickenlooper's remarks manifested the broad criminal strokes with which Congress painted rioters in general and the capital's black residents in specific. By comparing the citizens of Washington, D.C., to the Viet Cong, he indicated the extent to which race factored into lawmaker's fears about riots and self-government. Second, Hickenlooper's comments exemplified Congress's persistent preoccupation with District affairs. The Iowa senator did not serve on any District committees, but, like many members of Congress, he expressed a clear concern over the question of the capital's governance. Third, his remarks suggest that critics of the administration of justice during the disorders felt free to bypass the city's black officials and express their displeasure directly to federal officials. In doing so, Hickenlooper and other members of Congress reinforced the idea that the District's municipal government could easily be marginalized and that order could be maintained through indirect rule. Their concerns over the fitness of the city's black governance fed directly into Republicans' law-and-order platform during the 1968 presidential campaign.[79]

Despite congressional pressure to keep troops in Washington, Attorney General Clark hesitated to rely too heavily on federal forces. In an address to the American Society of Newspaper Editors twelve days after the riots, Clark explained that the army can suppress, has suppressed, and will continue to suppress riots, but "to prevent a riot or to control a riot before it is widespread, we must rely on the police." Not all of Clark's remarks accurately reflected the situation in the District. His belief that police-community relations measured "the difference between an authoritarian government acting by fiat for people it does not serve and a democratic government of the people, by the people and for the people" rang hollow in Washington, where self-government had yet to arrive and the police force remained over 75 percent white.[80]

The riots quickly became a wedge issue between federal officials who questioned the fitness of black leaders to govern and black residents who had decades of pent-up grievances that the civil violence allowed them to air. The riots were also fodder for those who believed that white liberals had become too lenient on law and order. In a telegram to Ramsey Clark, Representative Joe L. Evins (D-Tenn.) levied a national critique against the attorney general for his work in Washington. "This nation needs an attorney general who will not only stand for law and order but who will act to uphold the law—both in advance of anticipated violence and to retard a recurrence of lawlessness," he told the Johnson appointee. Evins, a fellow Democrat, also recommended that Clark resign from office and "give the president a free hand to appoint a strong and fearless attorney general with the will to prosecute agitators who are committed to destroying our country."[81]

Evins was not alone in wondering whether the federal government had exercised too much restraint during the riots. While maintaining a more objective tone, *Meet the Press* commentator Carl Stern asked Clark if allowing looters to "festively clean out one store after another" while police followed orders to do nothing seemed like the right strategy for America's cities. Left unsaid was the assumption that the federal government ought to exert control over U.S. cities, at least in moments of crisis.[82]

For some conservatives, neither the liberal White House nor the municipal government could suppress the city's rising militancy. Thomas Lane of *Public Affairs* accused Johnson's "improvised city council" of spiraling out of control. "The council bows to the arrogant and contemptuous verbal brickbats of black militants," he remarked. Continuing his screed, Lane said, "The federal government is helpless. It has surrendered control of public order by allowing the militant revolutionaries to install a responsive rabble in the capital city." Furthermore, he predicted, "President Johnson and the city government will be as ineffectual as King Louis XVI on the eve of the French Revolution."[83]

For Lane and other opponents of black self-determination, the riots underscored the pitfalls of transferring power to local black officials. With the specter of home rule looming, white stakeholders leveraged the riots as evidence of the need to limit local black politicians' oversight over the city and as justification to establish parameters on self-government so that Black Power organizers did not seize control of the city. To achieve this, they tried to control the narrative about the riots even as they were still under way, weaving a cautionary tale of a city overrun by black militants and municipal appointees incapable of controlling public order. Because they believed the Johnson administration had opened the floodgates to black political power, the necessity to hold powerful liberal Democrats accountable was a crucial component of their story.

Not only did local white stakeholders and conservative lawmakers accuse the city government and the Johnson administration of failing to curb civil violence in Washington during the uprising; they also questioned both parties' command of the local police. Even before the riots, conservatives had advocated for increasing the size and scope of the city's police force, an idea counter to the D.C. Crime Commission's advice. The commission had refrained from recommending a police force expansion because, among other reasons, the department was already "one of the largest and most costly police forces in the Nation." To conservatives, this was irrelevant. The riots only reinforced their belief that the MPD's current configuration was inadequate.[84]

Washington Star reporter Richard Wilson argued that during the uprising, the police were powerless to curb the wide-scale looting that occurred. Therefore he supported more and better-trained police—something, he noted, "cities with high crime rates and unruly populations will have to face sooner or later regardless of cost and rising tax rates." By painting a picture of powerless police officers battling an "unruly population," Wilson furthered the narrative of a city out of control. In couching his argument in racially coded language, he helped create a way for critics of black political power to address the issue in more oblique terms.[85]

For some black residents, the recommendation to expand the police force was a frightening prospect. The memory of fifteen thousand federal troops descending on the city, combined with the lingering image of deserted streets still heavily patrolled, already conjured feelings of living in a surveillance-heavy state—so much so that Mayor Washington had privately told associates that he wanted "to eliminate the aura of a federal occupation of the city as quickly as possible."[86] But Wilson preemptively dismissed these concerns. "The creation of a police state is not even remotely involved," he argued. "What is involved," he explained, "is the creation of effective and large police departments equipped and trained to handle civil disorders without resort to [Chicago Mayor Richard] Daley's shoot-to-kill doctrine." Perhaps Wilson was right. But national lawmakers and local white stakeholders found that law-and-order measures were a powerful mechanism by which to manage the city's black government and limit its powers over local affairs. As Washingtonians would discover, the depth and breadth of repression and surveillance measures that some, including presidential candidate Richard Nixon, proposed so as to enforce order in the capital hewed closely to the image of a police state.[87]

"RIOT FEVER"

While the nation mourned King's death, no one could predict with certainty the impact of the uprisings on the civil rights and Black Power movements. Among African Americans, the results were mixed. Senator Edward Brooke (R-Mass.) condemned the uprising, noting that "riots and violence are the mortal enemies, not the servants, of the civil rights movement."[88] City council vice chairman Walter Fauntroy had a different perspective. He viewed the riots as an evolutionary step to expand the movement into something broader. "The riots," he said, "were a reflection of a transition that inevitably had to come of the Civil Rights Movement into a Human Rights Movement." According to Fauntroy, protestors did not dive into the riots thoughtlessly. Instead, he argued, they were fueled by demands for the basic rights of which they had been deprived for decades.[89] But others expressed uncertainty as to whether rioters had such political motives. As Michael Harris, the president of Howard University's freshman class, explained, "Nobody knew anything, all they knew is that they were mad."[90]

Speaking on *Meet the Press* just days after King's assassination, Attorney General Clark echoed the conclusions of the Kerner report and reinforced the Johnson administration's message on civil violence. He indicated that the disorders manifested citizens' beliefs that they lacked channels through which to make effective claims on the state. "We must give them a stake in this country," Clark told NBC's Lawrence Spivak. On the one hand, Clark hinted at White House officials' frustration following the riots. They had, after all, initiated steps toward self-government in Washington the year earlier, opening channels of political access to the District's black residents. On the other hand, they knew the uprising could have been worse. The fact that they had established a local municipal government filled with respected black leaders who outwardly condoned the riots as counterproductive was not lost on them. But Clark's observation that black Washingtonians still did not have a stake in the country can be read as an admission that Johnson's reorganization plan did not go far enough.[91]

In stark contrast to Clark's liberal assessment of the underlying issues that had motivated rioters, the city's papers did not generally depict participants with sympathy. In the immediate aftermath of the riots, the *Washington Post* reported, "The assassination of [King], monstrous as that crime was, cannot in any way excuse or explain the massive wave of looting, burning and killing which followed in Washington." Initially the *Post* wrote disparagingly of the black residents who desecrated the nation's capital by stealing, looting, and setting fire to private property during the riots. The paper clarified that the rioters were not motivated by grief or anguish but were, instead, in a "festive" mood.[92] The *Star* concurred. It suggested that the general mood of the riot participants was not anger but joy. "Some militants spoke gleefully of the fire bombings as 'instant urban renewal,'" it reported, unintentionally foreshadowing the sad irony that urban renewal in black riot-torn neighborhoods would take almost a half century.[93]

Yet local media outlets typically attributed the disorders to a small group of militants. In its broadcast the week of April 14, WMAL implied that national hysteria concealed the truth about the local disorder. "Huge doses of common sense are prescribed as Washington recovers from riot fever," the station cautioned listeners. According to the station, "The terrorism of this one or two percent of the local Negro population must not indict the Negro race. Thousands of Negro police, firemen and soldiers worked valiantly to stop the riot."[94]

Even though rioters represented a larger and more diverse segment of the community than reported, reporters took pains to emphasize that the majority of black Washingtonians did not participate in the riots. The local press maintained that "a relatively small band of black hoodlums" had "sacked and burned" the capital.[95] In fact, in an op-ed following the weekend's events, the *Washington Daily News* described the idea that the riots represented a black uprising against King's assassination as "a gross libel on the predominantly Negro Washington."[96]

Local outlets offered a competing narrative to that propagated by opponents of self-determination. They did so by praising those who came together to pitch in. The *Washington Star*, for example, focused on area churches and community members who had rushed food and clothing to victims and had arranged temporary shelter for those displaced by the riots. Reflecting on District politics, the paper mused, "In a city accustomed to disorganization, slow-paced planning and even slower action, this was a remarkable performance." Underlying the *Star*'s vivid account of how the city came together in a time of need was the desire to prove that residents did not need continual federal oversight.[97]

The *Star* took the experiences of the National Guard as a testament to Washington's upright citizens. One white solider, the paper reported, was "struck by something no one had suggested was possible during all our civil disturbance training—the friendly attitude of people living under what almost amounted to a military occupation."[98] Meanwhile, Captain Thomas S. Connell Jr., a black commander of the D.C. National Guard's 171st Guard Military Police Battalion, downplayed reports of physical abuse. "The people on the street heckled our Negro troops, especially with stuff about why they were there, soul brothers, guarding the white man's property," he told the *Star*. In collecting the positive experiences of out-of-town National Guardsmen, the paper also belabored the civility of Washington's black residents, especially during a time of crisis.[99]

Despite the fact that Stokely Carmichael called D.C. home, many media outlets characterized him as an outside agitator and blamed him for inciting Washington residents to riot. WMAL unfavorably compared the SNCC activist to Mayor Walter Washington, the consummate political bureaucrat, who had "worked around the clock for public order." Offering several comparisons between reactions to the riots, WMAL explained, "Looters used Dr. Martin Luther King's death as an excuse to steal, but the Reverend Walter Fauntroy pleaded for nonviolence that was Dr. King's hallmark. Black power militants cry for the destruction of America. But Negro entertainer James Brown offered one of the most stirring defenses of America we have heard"—a reference to the rousing performance by the "Godfather of Soul" in Boston the night after King was killed. Left unmentioned was the fact that local black talk show host Ralph Waldo "Petey" Greene Jr. had performed a similar service right in D.C. Greene, who had been convicted of armed robbery in 1960, landed a job at Washington's popular R&B station WOL 1450 AM on his release from Lorton Reformatory in 1965. There Greene practiced his patented blend of humor and social awareness, connecting with members of the black community. When King died, the radio personality and community activist shared his anger with listeners and urged peace for hours over the airwaves.[100]

In pitting looters and Black Power militants against respectable black leaders, local and otherwise, the station made several race-conscious comments

Military police officers drive down the street during the D.C. riots.
(Star Collection, D.C. Public Library © *Washington Post*)

on the state of political affairs in the capital and around the country. First, it reminded its audience that moderate civil rights leaders, in the vein of King rather than Carmichael, ran Washington's local government. Second, it intimated that these leaders would not condone violence. Third, it implied that Black Power militants could not in good conscience justify violent protest when other African Americans were giving rousing defenses of America.

In addition to efforts to marginalize black militants and present a positive view of the city's black residents, the *Washington Post* even offered a redemptive narrative about those who did riot. According to the *Post*, which reported the most widely circulated account of the riots, even looters exercised restraint, targeting white-owned shops while sparing those bearing the "Soul Brother" insignia.[101] Clarence Mitchell, head of the NAACP's Washington Bureau, questioned the paper's reporting. Mitchell believed that the rioters had not differentiated between white and black establishments in seeking vengeance, as the press argued. As he explained, "The best evidence of that is to go up and down U Street and see various shops that had soul brother written on them.

You can see how they were looted just like the others." Mitchell's admission spoke to the general chaos of the riots. Yet the *Post*'s account was intended to help persuade outsiders that the city could manage its own crisis.[102]

While the media marginalized the rioters as the city's "riff-raff," the D.C. Bail Agency's data told a different story. Its data was slightly skewed because it omitted the 15 percent of people under the age eighteen arrested and because it underestimated female participation, which was higher than the number of women arrested. Yet it still provided valuable information. According to its data, the typical participant was twenty-nine years old, had attended some high school, held a job, had a firm home address, and had never been in trouble with the law prior to the disturbances. Four out of five had called Washington home for at least five years, while one out of three had been born there. According to one Bail Agency employee, "This is an amazingly respectable crowd, compared with the people we usually get here." In fact, more than half of the adult rioters were or had been married, and a number of them worked for the federal government, a point that agitated many legislators who believed that government employees should have abstained from protesting.[103]

In a report to the president, the U.S. Civil Service Commission claimed that only twenty federal government employees, all low-grade, had been charged with serious offenses. As Civil Service Commission chairman John Macy complained, national media reports grossly exaggerated the number of federal employees arrested for serious crimes during the riots. "While some additional federal employees involved in the disturbances are bound to be uncovered, I am gratified at what I consider, in view of our large work force, a very limited involvement of federal employees," he told President Johnson, dismissing concerns over what he viewed as a nonissue.[104]

Local newspaper outlets, radio stations, and select government agencies cast the riots as an aberration in D.C.'s racial history and as atypical behavior for the city's black residents. They marginalized rioters, emphasized the black civil servants who abstained from violence or rose above the fray and quelled it, and distanced moderate black officials like Mayor Washington and city council vice chairman Walter Fauntroy from allegedly militant Black Power activists like Stokely Carmichael. In doing so, they worked to shelter the city from claims that it could not handle its own affairs.

THE SAGA OF STOKELY CARMICHAEL

No single person bore the brunt of the attacks on Black Power more than Stokely Carmichael. His whereabouts during the riots attracted unparalleled national attention and lent the uprising a greater spotlight than the other hundred disorders that took place across the country. Nothing drew more attention to him than the press conference he held the day after King's death at the New School for Afro-American Thought's 14th Street headquarters. Less than twenty-four hours after King was assassinated, many looked to Carmichael for wisdom. Rumors that he had caused the riots made his first public appearance an even more powerful draw. On that Friday, dozens of reporters, photographers, and TV news crews showed up at the press conference. Flanked by several SNCC officials, including local SNCC activist Lester McKinnie, Carmichael opened the conference. He had originally come to discuss the arrest and detention of his successor, SNCC chairman H. Rap Brown, for inciting to riot in Cambridge, Maryland, in June 1967. However, the discussion quickly turned to King's death and the subsequent riots.[105]

The press conference provided Carmichael with a national platform to discuss the meaning of King's assassination to the local and national civil rights movements. According to Carmichael, King had been the only black man of the older generation to whom the black masses, including militants and revolutionaries, still listened. Speaking on behalf of other young activists, Carmichael explained that while they did not always agree with the SCLC leader, they still respected him. King was, according to the SNCC activist, "the one man in our race who was trying to teach our people to have love, compassion and mercy for what white people had done." Carmichael's appreciation for the slain leader stood in marked contrast to the way the media continually depicted their relationship. Instead of calling King his enemy, Carmichael called him his brother, "flesh of my flesh and blood of my blood."[106]

Carmichael's political agenda edged out his eulogy for King. Shifting gears, he channeled his frustrations about the country's systemic issues toward revenge. "The rebellions that have been occurring around the country is just light stuff to what is about to happen," the SNCC leader warned. "We have to retaliate for the death of our leaders. The execution of those debts will not be in the courtrooms, they are going to be in the streets of the United States of America," Carmichael went on. His comments contributed to the tense atmosphere in D.C., especially among white conservatives, who chaffed at his violent tone.[107]

For black citizens, Carmichael's press conference raised a key question: Would they accept the SNCC activist as their de facto leader on issues of civil rights? A Kerner Commission study of civil rights attitudes completed prior to King's death suggested that Carmichael had his work cut out for him if he wanted to become the new "face" of the black freedom movement. Black residents in Washington and fourteen other cities overwhelmingly preferred the stances of moderates over extremists. In fact, only one out of seven black citizens polled had approved of Black Power advocates like Carmichael and H. Rap Brown. Time would tell whether or not King's assassination would change those results.[108]

At twenty-seven years old, Carmichael had captured the hearts of a segment of the black community dissatisfied with the pace of the civil rights movement and disenchanted with the nonviolent tactics its leaders continued to preach. He had also captivated the attention and imagination of the federal government. Carmichael likely knew that he was under federal investigation; just that month, a DOJ spokesman had told the *Washington Post* as much. Moreover, Carmichael likely recognized FBI agents in attendance at his New School press conference, as he habitually watched for surveillance during public appearances. Nevertheless, in light of King's assassination, Carmichael did not mince words. On the mortality of black Americans, Carmichael commented soberly, "We die in your jails, we die in your ghettos, we die in your rat-infested homes, we die a thousand deaths every day, so we're not afraid to die." Throughout his speech, he took pains to draw attention to the country's racial hypocrisy and the impending consequences of losing the leading proponent of a nonviolent framework for American protest.[109]

After the press conference, Carmichael made his way to Howard University. When he arrived on campus Friday afternoon, he met an enthusiastic crowd and anxious DOJ officials. Returning to the campus where he had made a name for himself as a young activist with the student-led NAG, Carmichael felt at home—even if the school's administration did not welcome him with open arms.[110] At the conclusion of Carmichael's brief speech at the university, he allegedly pulled out a gun and said, "We will go out tonight. Don't loot—shoot." Immediately afterward, Deputy Attorney General Christopher called the speech "very ugly," and Mayor Washington described it as "inflammatory."[111]

John Anderson, who covered the event for the *Washington Post*, had a different perspective. The reporter, who never sensed that his life was in danger, explained, "The hostility was directed at an abstraction that was white, and powerful, and downtown; it was not toward a specific white man standing in the crowd in the middle of the Howard campus." Yet in painting Carmichael as the face of violence during the riots, and distancing the militant firebrand from the city's black residents, federal and local officials tried to control the narrative about the riots even as they were still underway.[112]

As soon as the riots ended, the DOJ, in conjunction with the FBI, conducted a thorough investigation of Carmichael's participation in them to determine whether he had instigated violence. Carmichael had driven to Baltimore the night before the riots to meet with local black leaders. The FBI claimed that they had met to plan the uprising and publicly speculated that Carmichael directly incited not only the D.C. riots but also the Baltimore riots. However, its evidence remained unsubstantiated. It was clear that the main intent of the investigation was to find justifiable cause to persecute the renowned agitator. The federal government's constant surveillance of the SNCC leader during the riots and conservative politicians' calls to imprison him in their aftermath underscore the force of law-and-order campaigns in alienating black militants from the mainstream political scene. Not only did this hamper Carmichael's influence on local politics at a time when residents sought out someone to help channel their dissatisfaction with political, economic, and social marginalization into action. It also helped safeguard the new municipal government from conservative attacks. The repressive measures used by federal officials to sideline Carmichael helped improve moderate black politicians' status among white stakeholders as they responded to the crisis.[113]

The Carmichael investigation comprised one piece of a larger inquiry into violent uprisings in the aftermath of King's assassination. Police in several cities, including Chicago; Gainesville, Florida; and Hartford, Connecticut, had arrested militants in April 1968. According to the FBI, there appeared to have been interstate communication among "militant leaders" to proceed to Atlanta immediately after King died. However, based on a tip that Washington's local SNCC group would "take the lid off Tuesday night," and on longer-term suspicions that militants planned to disrupt SCLC's upcoming Poor People's Campaign, the FBI and DOJ continued to monitor SNCC's general actions and Carmichael's specific movements in the nation's capital.[114]

Impatient with the Justice Department's proceedings, Congressman Robert Dole (R-Kan.) urged Attorney General Clark to closely survey the activities and "inflammatory utterances" of Carmichael and other Black Power advocates for violations of the country's new 1968 Civil Rights Act. Johnson had signed the act, best known for its fair housing provisions, on April 11, 1968, to honor Martin Luther King. However, Congress had attached an antiriot rider to it, similar to the one passed in D.C. in December 1967, making it a felony to incite, organize, promote, encourage, or participate in a riot. "All citizens deserve to be apprised of your plans regarding those who openly advocate racial war," Dole warned Clark, demanding information on how the DOJ intended to enforce the new provision. The Kansas Republican criticized liberal government officials for their lack of "genuine desire to prosecute the hate mongers for their utterances advocating violence and murder," adding that "citizens expect and demand these tools shall be used to the fullest extent." By blaming African Americans for inciting racial warfare, and by upholding the 1968 Civil Rights Act's antiriot rider, Dole made law-and-order measures the focal point of a campaign designed to curb black political power.[115]

Members of Congress typically opposed to Johnson's civil rights platform joined Dole in his dogged determination to "throw the books at racial extremists like Stokely Carmichael."[116] Representative Joe Evins believed that Congress ought to prosecute black radicals without delay. The Tennessee Democrat was specifically concerned with Carmichael's influence in the capital. He thought that Carmichael's "incendiary statements and call for the slaughter of America poured fuel on the flames of violence and lawlessness in Washington." "Our cities lie in rubble as a monument to Carmichael's strength and your inaction," Evins told the attorney general in frustration. Together, Dole and Evins's reactions to the riots illustrate the ease with which federal officials could deploy repressive measures to marginalize black radicals, the pervasive power of indirect rule in the capital, and conservative lawmakers' ability to use the uprising as a means to levy larger criticisms of the Johnson administration's law-and-order policies.[117]

Some members of the Johnson administration agreed with Evins and Dole. Privately, White House officials called Clark "Ramsey the Marshmallow" for his moderate positions on law and order. Johnson aides feared both a Republican backlash and an escalation of militant activities if the Justice Department did not find an appropriate punishment for agitators like Carmichael. During a post-riot planning session, one official went so far as to suggest, "We must be prepared for guerilla-type warfare, incidents in the suburbs, use of children, Castro-trained commandos, and various other possibilities, however remote they may seem now." Memoranda between White House officials suggest that even before the riots, they were willing to shift governance away from local black officials to the nexus of multiple federal agencies—a move most easily executed under the pretext of law and order.[118]

As the story of the Washington riots and of Carmichael's involvement catapulted into the national conversation, NBC *Meet the Press* moderator Lawrence Spivak inquired into the DOJ's investigation of the notorious activist. In response, Clark deflected responsibility. "The decision will be for the proper law enforcement authorities within the city of Washington," he said. If Carmichael committed a federal crime, the DOJ would prosecute him fully, Clark assured. But the blurred line between local and national jurisdictional duties pointed to the unique problems of administering justice in the nation's capital. Due to the structural limits of Johnson's home rule measure, legislators' fears of black self-determination, and pushback from white stakeholders, national lawmakers questioned the degree of autonomy they were willing to grant District residents. While home rule forced the question in D.C., lawmakers held the same concerns about black citizens in cities across the country. Stokely Carmichael, then, became a proxy for larger debates about self-determination, black political power, and law and order.[119]

As the April riots made way for May's Poor People's Campaign, the DOJ dropped its case against Carmichael. Undeterred by their pursuit of him, Carmichael adjusted to life post-riots. That summer, the SNCC leader married South African singer Miriam Makeba; moved to Washington's "Gold Coast" neighborhood, an affluent black neighborhood on upper 16th Street NW; and became an honorary prime minister of the Black Panther Party. Though he tried to maintain a low profile in the District, Carmichael came under fire for steering the Black United Front in a more militant direction, selling out his base by leaving the ghetto, and engaging in an internal power struggle with SNCC officials. SNCC expelled him from the organization in late August. In September, Carmichael left the country for Senegal to fight more global race struggles in self-imposed exile.[120]

It is not certain whether Carmichael had a vested interest in staying in Washington and throwing himself into local politics. But it is clear that the federal government did not want the militant to participate in the District's governance in any capacity. His story offers important lessons about local black political power and national politics. The Johnson administration designed a reorganization plan that officially yielded authority to municipal government appointees. But in practice, the president's home rule measure was no more than a mimetic reform. While Johnson appointed prominent black leaders to office, those who broke the mold were pushed to the margins of city politics. This encouraged the more militant activists, like Carmichael, to move from the sidelines to the sidewalks during the riots. But when it came to issues of law and order, Johnson even bypassed the local black politicians who paid lip service to him when it proved politically expedient to do so.

Those who participated in the riots did not do so to explicitly protest their lack of electoral representation. However, the lack of permanent political infrastructure necessary to protect their interests lay at the heart of the uprising. Without direct political channels to express their grievances, some residents found in the riots an unexpected platform from which to expand on their frustrations about the city's conditions. But they faced off against local and national opponents of black self-determination who launched an explicitly racialized campaign for law and order in the District—a campaign intended to limit the work of black political operatives and narrow the scope of black self-government.

For local government officials, the rebellion illustrated the supremacy of federal power in the District and the need for legislation to expand their powers. Eleven days after the disturbance began, and one day before the last troops left town, the mayor, deputy mayor, and public safety director met with White House, DOJ, and military officials to discuss the lessons learned from the riots. There the local officials complained about their inability to make informed decisions during the crisis. Walter Washington pointed out that the intelligence he received was inadequate. He argued that if he had known of Stokely Carmichael's activities, the rally at Howard, or the number of students who ditched school on April 5, he "could have made a better assessment" of the situation and need for federal troops. His curfew also exemplified his limited powers under Johnson's reorganization plan. To put the April 5 curfew into effect, the mayor had to rely on arcane and legally questionable statutes because a direct law did not exist, and he lacked the authority to create one.[121]

The mayor's legal struggle to implement a citywide curfew epitomized the more general problems that the D.C. government confronted in the wake of Johnson's reorganization plan. Washington, along with the city's council members, served as ambassadors to both District residents and the federal government. The burden fell on them to find ways to communicate with members of Congress, who determined not only whether the District would have adequate funds to run city services but also whether or not they would even entertain their budgetary appeals, and with the White House, to which they had to convey the urgency of the city's problems without appearing incompetent. The *Washington Post* articulated this burden well. According to the paper, "The list of people Mayor Washington needs to please is awesome—from Lyndon B. Johnson in the White House to John McMillan of the House District Committee, from Julius W. Hobson to GOP National Committeeman Carl L. Shipley, from the ghetto poor to the Georgetown rich."[122]

From the beginning of their tenure, black politicians like Walter Washington specifically sought—and received—the support of the powerful white-run Board of Trade. In doing so, they created tensions within the black community that only grew deeper after the riots. Prior to his September exile, for example, Stokely Carmichael accused city council vice chairman Walter Fauntroy of selling out the black community. Locally, Fauntroy had taken up the cause of revitalizing the inner city. After the Southwest Redevelopment Project had displaced over twenty thousand low-income black residents, Fauntroy had become particularly wary of government-directed urban renewal efforts that excluded citizen participation. In response to these federal initiatives, he spearheaded the creation of a coalition of 150 community organizations, churches, and civic groups called the Model Inner City Community Organization (MICCO) in 1966. The following year, Fauntroy pressured federal officials to designate MICCO as an authorized planning group for urban renewal projects in the District's Shaw neighborhood; received $1.8 million from the Department of Housing and Urban Development (HUD) to help planners integrate local residents' input and ideas into its plans; and encouraged residents to take charge of the physical and spiritual renewal of the area. As a result of his efforts, MICCO employed black architects, city planners, and construction engineers to design and build homes, schools, stores, and other projects in urban Washington.[123]

Yet following his 1967 appointment to the D.C. City Council, he faced increasing pressure from black activists who believed he cared more about serving the city's business interests than the needs of Shaw's residents. The Black United Front had originally organized around a specific idea: that the disparate organizations would work together "in a solid coalition against the power structure." But less than a year after the Johnson administration implemented its reorganization plan, the so-called power structure had quickly become the landing place for black leaders like Fauntroy. This upset Carmichael, who told the vice chairman, "You should defend to us why you are a member of the City Council which does not speak for us and which we did not elect." Although BUF ultimately gave Fauntroy a vote of confidence, the confrontation was further evidence that the creation of the appointed municipal government had divided Washington's black community.[124]

In the midst of all of this, SCLC prepared to descend on the city for its Poor People's Campaign. Although SCLC had lost its revered leader and the capital was struggling to recover from the riots, the organization decided to forge ahead with its national campaign. Scheduled to start in May 1968, the campaign inspired new fears of black violence in the minds of local white business groups and conservative lawmakers. The event, the details of which SCLC kept shrouded in secrecy, gave the federal government little time to fortify the city against what it saw as yet another insurrection. It did know one thing, however: as Ramsey Clark told FBI director J. Edgar Hoover, "The protection of the interests of the City" would depend on the fragile state of local and federal cooperation.[125]

3

SCLC GOES TO WASHINGTON

THE 1968 POOR PEOPLE'S CAMPAIGN

We are not coming to Washington to engage in any
histrionic action, nor are we coming to tear up Washington.
I don't like to predict violence, but if nothing is done between
now and June to raise ghetto hope, I feel this summer
will not only be as bad, but worse than last year.
—Martin Luther King Jr., March 1968

This country is not going to be very happy if somebody
comes in and makes a shambles out of Washington. . . .
We have to be ready for big trouble.
—Senator Karl Mundt (R-S.D.), May 1968

Five years after the Reverend Dr. Martin Luther King delivered his renowned "I Have a Dream" speech at the 1963 March on Washington, Reverend Ralph Abernathy made his way to a lectern in front of the Lincoln Memorial. The new leader of the Southern Christian Leadership Conference had big shoes to fill. He had fought to ensure that SCLC proceeded with its Poor People's Campaign even though members of the organization, residents of Washington, D.C., and American citizens at large were still reeling from King's assassination two months earlier. Now, on June 19, 1968, more than fifty thousand people listened as he gave his own speech on Solidarity Day, the campaign's capstone event.[1]

Originally scheduled for April 1968, the Poor People's Campaign was the first nationally oriented civil rights demonstration to take place in the nation's capital since the March on Washington. It marked King's desire to broaden the black freedom struggle into a larger human rights struggle. Inviting a wide cross section of citizens to participate—including American Indians, Puerto Ricans, and people of Mexican descent—SCLC reached beyond the traditional civil rights coalition to train the spotlight on conditions in America's ghettos and the systemic poverty that plagued the nation. Moreover, in building and living in Resurrection City, a shantytown on the National Mall and in view of the Lincoln Memorial, SCLC pushed the imaginative boundaries of African American protest.

Yet in the months prior to King's April assassination, the unique and unpredictable format of SCLC's campaign, combined with the violent backdrop of urban rebellion, made members of President Johnson's cabinet, the Department of Justice, and Washington residents nervous. The fact that SCLC finished building Resurrection City, a shantytown in view of the Lincoln Memorial, just one month after the D.C. riots devastated the District's black neighborhoods and left two thousand residents homeless added insult to injury. As citizens from across the country arrived in Washington to set up temporary living quarters on the National Mall, federal and local opposition grew sharper. When Abernathy took the stage on June 19, Solidarity Day, it seemed like almost everyone in the capital wanted the camp's three thousand residents to pack up and go home.

The enduring impression of the Poor People's Campaign is one of failure. But using the PPC as a bookend to the 1963 March on Washington and depicting it as a national event executed by a well-known organization and contextualized as part of the tumultuous decline of the civil rights movement is severely limiting. While scholars have begun to shed light on the internal workings of SCLC's campaign, the coalition that participated in it, and the opposition that it faced, they still fail to situate the PPC within the context of a city fighting for self-determination, fraught with racial tension, and in the midst of bearing witness to law-and-order measures that undermined grassroots activism.[2]

By ignoring Washington's radical voices, racial tensions, and local organizations in planning the PPC, SCLC made its campaign irrelevant to the needs of black Washington. Its overdependence on white organizers left many black residents feeling alienated from the movement. Its exclusion of the city's main antipoverty agencies in the planning of an antipoverty campaign staged in Washington also upset black activists. Many of the city's black residents struggle to find meaning in SCLC's national campaign. In addition, when participants left the city in June, just six weeks after they had arrived, District residents were left to handle the campaign's remnants and repercussions—including increased tensions with the local police department and a presidential candidate eager to make the city's lawlessness a focal point of his campaign—without the support of national civil rights organizations. From this perspective, the PPC represents an important rupture between the local and national civil rights movements.

SCLC's Poor People's Campaign is a litmus test as much of the split between the local and national civil rights movements as of the federal government and white growth machine's battle for law and order and against meaningful self-determination in the District. As white business and real estate groups became aware of SCLC's plans for another march on Washington in early 1968, they grew anxious about the potential for violence. Leaders of these groups, along with conservative national lawmakers, demanded that the federal government use its powers to contain the Poor People's Campaign. They insisted on measures that would continue to undermine the local black government's authority and that would become the backbone of Richard Nixon's law-and-order platform. These calls grew deafening after the devastating civil disturbances triggered by King's assassination.

The president, Department of Justice, and local government faced a difficult decision. None wanted to appear weak in the face of potentially chaotic and violent demonstrations. However, the use of troops, surveillance tactics, and, on occasion, retaliatory violence deeply divided federal and local officials. After being roundly criticized for its handling of the April riots, the Johnson administration responded aggressively to the Poor People's Campaign. Without coordinating with local officials, the White House directed the Justice Department to implement repression and surveillance measures to keep control over the PPC. And they did so with little concern over the possible effects on the city. The formidable federal reaction to the PPC shows how SCLC's campaign did not reflect the rapid decline of the civil rights movement so much as the ascendance of law-and-order measures intended to curb black self-determination in D.C. and around the country.

On the surface, the Poor People's Campaign appears to have existed remotely on the National Mall, in isolation from the District of Columbia's neighborhoods, including those burned down during the April riots. But the campaign was profoundly shaped by the political and social milieu of Washington, D.C., a city deeply affected by both the long hot summer of 1967 and the 1968 riots following King's assassination. The decision to locate the campaign on the National Mall; the unprecedented coordination between local business and civic groups and federal officials to stifle it; and the riots, which provided fuel for opponents of home rule, reveal how the Poor People's Campaign was at the center of local and national debates about self-determination, law and order, and black political power in the late 1960s.

LAUNCHING THE POOR PEOPLE'S CAMPAIGN

Martin Luther King had been interested in staging an antipoverty demonstration ever since two thousand welfare rights activists conducted a one-day march on the capital in October 1966. King continued to envision a march to protest cuts in poverty programs throughout the next year, though it was Marian Wright, a young black NAACP Legal Defense Fund attorney and Child Development Group of Mississippi board member, who helped give the idea shape. In March 1967, Wright testified before the Senate Labor Committee's subcommittee on poverty, imploring senators to witness for themselves the effects of poverty and hunger in Mississippi. Outraged by what he saw, and frustrated that the Johnson administration had not sufficiently responded to the issue of poverty, Senator Robert Kennedy (D-N.Y.) told Wright to tell King to "bring the poor people to Washington." Wright did so at a September SCLC retreat, noting that King "instinctively felt that that was right and treated me as if I was an emissary of grace."[3]

Under King's direction, SCLC continued to outline the contours of the Poor People's Campaign during a five-day retreat in November 1967. Originally called the Washington Spring Project, the event—part mass demonstration and part lobbying program—was designed to draw attention to American poverty in all its diversity. It would, King said in December, bring "waves of the nation's poor and disinherited to Washington, D.C. . . . to demand redress of their grievances by the United States government and to secure at least jobs or income for all." King and his aides envisioned placing on the National Mall a shantytown dubbed "Resurrection City," much like the one constructed by World War I veterans during the 1932 Bonus Army March. Located in the federal government's front yard, Resurrection City would showcase unity among a multiethnic coalition of poor people and would serve as a strategic launch pad for protests, marches, and civil disobedience. In the capital, in front of the nation's starkest symbols of power, the poor would demand to be heard and would, King suggested, "stay until America responds."[4]

SCLC chose the capital for its campaign knowing that it had been the perfect stage for the 1963 March on Washington. The capital had provided a national platform for King and his fellow civil rights leaders, visibility for racial justice issues, and support for then-pending civil rights legislation. The interracial marchers had conducted themselves peacefully and won widespread approval. Much to the consternation of some black activists, however, SCLC organizers had exercised tight control over the 1963 demonstration in order to avoid embarrassing the supportive Kennedy administration. Shortly before

SNCC leader John Lewis took the stage, for example, the march's chairmen demanded that he excise "militant language" from his speech. The Justice Department was prepared to cut power to the microphone if Lewis did not comply. Lewis eventually agreed to tone down his rhetoric, and the government did not obstruct his speech. Ultimately the government's strict control over the closely scripted event, as well as the coordination between civil rights leaders and the Kennedy administration, helped ensure a peaceful, nonmilitant march that cemented the National Mall as a symbolic—and even safe—site for civil rights activism.[5]

Much had changed between 1963 and 1968. King had not necessarily been out of step with the ongoing shifts in the civil rights movement. He had, in fact, been focusing increasingly on economic inequality. In January 1965, King had announced the Chicago Freedom Movement, a campaign that took SCLC to Chicago to address a wide range of issues, including open housing, education, transportation, employment, and the criminal justice system. However, the ambitious campaign was roundly criticized as a failure, thanks in part to the violence it engendered. During a march through an all-white neighborhood on August 5, 1966, for example, black demonstrators, including King himself, encountered white protestors who threw bottles and bricks. Afterward King observed, "I have seen many demonstrations in the South but I have never seen anything so hostile and so hateful as I've seen here today."[6]

The same year he launched the Chicago Freedom Movement, King traveled to D.C. at the invitation of local SCLC head Walter Fauntroy to help petition Congress for home rule. King had scheduled his three-day August visit to correspond with President Johnson's signing of the Voting Rights Act. While he was there, he made several community appearances. In the midst of his trip, he even dined at the Capitol to plead residents' case with members of the House and Senate Committees that governed the District. He then spoke at a home rule rally and marched with five thousand demonstrators to Lafayette Park, across the street from the White House, to show support for self-determination. King returned in March 1967, this time to help Fauntroy protest the relocation of low-income residents away from the city's Shaw neighborhood, located just north of downtown Washington, and to participate in a ten-thousand-spectator-strong parade in support of community-led urban renewal efforts.[7]

King was also among a growing group of critics who believed that the Vietnam War took resources away from civil rights issues at home. He chastised President Johnson for abandoning the War on Poverty and pressed him to end the destructive war abroad. King's linkage between the cause of economic justice and the Vietnam War became a central tenet of his late career. It also set the stage for the Poor People's Campaign and alienated him from many former allies.[8]

In the face of increasing militancy in local communities and national organizations, King remained committed to nonviolence. SCLC intended for the Poor People's Campaign to restore the credibility of nonviolent action. However, its leadership recognized that the crises of the late 1960s demanded a different kind of campaign. "Our cities are literally burning down, our people are literally dying of hunger and joblessness and mental disorder," said SCLC's Reverend Andrew Young early in the planning process, "and it may be necessary for us to run through certain little 'traffic laws' to dramatize the fact that there is an emergency." Thus when SCLC came to Washington, organizers vowed not to simply support federally mandated legislation, remain confined in a narrow racial binary, or blindly do what the Johnson administration asked of them. Yet in organizing a campaign under conditions that differed so drastically from those under which it had planned the 1963 March on Washington, SCLC opened the doors to a dangerous backlash.[9]

Young, the group's executive vice president, took charge of planning the PPC. Born in 1932, the Louisiana native graduated from Washington, D.C.'s Howard University and Connecticut's Hartford Theological Seminary before heading to Marion, Alabama, in 1955 to become a pastor. Young traveled north to New York in 1957 to work for the National Council of Churches before settling in Atlanta in 1961. Affable, soft-spoken, and even-tempered, the thirty-six-year-old Young, who would later become mayor of Atlanta and U.S. representative from Georgia, had risen through SCLC's ranks. He skillfully represented SCLC in meetings with an increasingly crowded field of civil rights organizations. He remained one of just a few SCLC leaders who did not alienate officials from the younger SNCC or the more established NAACP. He could also comfortably negotiate with white stakeholders—so much so that SCLC leaders jokingly referred to him as their "resident Uncle Tom." Thus Young became the obvious choice to sell SCLC's embryonic campaign to a diverse group of constituents.[10]

Speaking on behalf of SCLC, Young approached religious and civic groups across the country to win support for its national antipoverty campaign. In a meeting with the National Council of Churches of Christ held in Washington, D.C., Young explained the group's decision to mount another national campaign in the capital. "We decided that the poor, the ones who are now catching the hell, had to be involved in a movement which we were sponsoring," he said in March 1968, "and we decided that we would bring some of those who suffered to the nation's capital where they could be very visible." The irony of importing poor people into Washington to gain visibility when the District's poorest black residents remained invisible in their own city was lost on SCLC.[11]

In an interview with *Christianity and Crisis* in late January, Young reveled in discussing an aggressive strategy for occupying the District. He demonstrated little concern for whatever imposition this might create for Washington residents. If SCLC assembled a few hundred marchers on the heavily traveled bridges that connected the capital to its suburbs, Young reasoned that they could create a high-profile rush-hour nightmare. If they wanted to create an even greater disruption, Young suggested that they could target the city's institutions. "A thousand people in need of health and medical attention sitting in around the Bethesda Naval Hospital, so that nobody could get in or out until they get treated . . . would dramatize the fact that there were thousands of people in our nation in need of medical services," he stated. By plotting a campaign in Washington that focused solely on influencing a national audience, SCLC displayed a striking indifference to local conditions. The organization also overlooked an important opportunity to draw attention to the struggles of the District's disfranchised residents. Its indifference to local conditions frustrated local activists and created logistical problems as the campaign went forward.[12]

Despite Young's boastful rhetoric about occupying the District, SCLC had not lost faith in the power of nonviolence. If anything, the rising demands for Black Power, articulated most famously by SNCC leader Stokely Carmichael; the more widespread militance in local communities and national organizations; and the increase in urban rebellions across the country strengthened SCLC members' resolve to plan a nonviolent mass demonstration to influence public policy. Consequently, SCLC had a fine line to toe. On the one hand, its success depended in part on the approval of a wide range of mainstream institutions and organizations dissatisfied with the rise of Black Power rhetoric. On the other hand, it still wanted to execute a campaign radical in design and ambitious in scope. Thus, when Young met with Washington's Interreligious Committee on Race Relations in March, he rightly predicted that their support for the upcoming campaign would hinge on assurances of stability, peace, and cooperation. "It is not our intention to come to Washington, D.C., to eject Congress or to immobilize the Capital," Young said reassuringly. Instead, SCLC wanted to come "educate the nation," a vague statement that helped persuade them to lend their support to the campaign without holding SCLC to any concrete promises.[13]

SCLC also fielded questions about where the nation's more militant activists stood in relation to its campaign. During Young's meeting with Washington's Interreligious Committee on Race Relations, George Butler of the Catholic Interracial Council asked Young if SCLC believed it could handle those who might not share its philosophy of nonviolence. The question was not unwarranted. SCLC had traditionally focused on large-scale campaigns to advocate for legislative victories. Yet youth-led organizations like SNCC had disavowed the philosophy of nonviolence, voted to expel its white volunteers, and focused on community organizing to build political power on the local level. In the rapidly changing milieu of the late 1960s, the latter organizations had become more vocal, with militant activists like Carmichael accusing SCLC of becoming ineffective.[14]

Even before the 1968 riots, Carmichael's figure loomed large over the Poor People's Campaign. When confronted with Butler's question about militants and the PPC, Andrew Young acknowledged the larger movement's fractures but dismissed Butler's fears that violence would cloak the demonstration and compromise SCLC's peaceful goals. "In my estimation H. Rap Brown and Stokely Carmichael are mostly creatures of the Press. I want to take nothing away from them and the leadership that they provide and yet for them to take something away from us they would have to be better staffed and better organized than they are now," he replied.[15] Elsewhere, Billy Hollins, a Chicago-based SCLC regional coordinator, predicted behind-the-scenes support from outwardly militant activists. "Stokely Carmichael will publicly disavow this approach of the SCLC to the problem of poverty but privately will give support," he forecasted.[16] Together Young and Hollins's comments pointed to SCLC's cautious optimism toward national figures like Carmichael. In fact, SCLC representatives had met with militant activists around the country and had found them willing to give their campaign a chance. According to Young, "We have discovered that they respect our right to fight for freedom by nonviolent means." "We understand this to mean that they will help furnish food, housing, etc., and that they will stay out of the way," he explained.[17]

Yet members of SCLC had their doubts about nonviolence. Through extralegal surveillance tactics, officials from the DOJ learned that SCLC leader Ralph Abernathy believed Carmichael would attempt to take over the PPC and turn it into a force for violent disorder. They also learned that Billy Hollins did not even believe unequivocally in SCLC's public stance on nonviolence. Speaking privately about the campaign in March 1968, Hollins had forewarned, "SCLC will publicly disavow violence but many of us feel self-defense is essential. The official stance of the SCLC is one of nonviolence but SCLC can't police everyone." By the late 1960s, Hollins's views on nonviolence were not uncommon among activists. But to the federal government they forecasted grave problems with SCLC's upcoming demonstration.[18]

SCLC organizers knew all too well that the consequences of a violent outbreak during the campaign were great. "If such a thing happened it would deal a death blow to SCLC and the doctrine of non-violence," Abernathy reportedly told SCLC officials at a mid-April meeting held at the Atlanta church where he preached. In fact, Abernathy was so concerned about militants infiltrating planning for the PPC that he proposed relocating their upcoming retreat from Atlanta to Stone Mountain, Georgia, to prevent SNCC staff from learning their plans. Nevertheless, the organization shielded its doubts from plain view.[19]

THE FEDERAL GOVERNMENT PREPARES

Immediately after Martin Luther King announced the vague contours for SCLC's antipoverty campaign, the FBI and DOJ launched a proactive law-and-order campaign. Assistant Attorney General Fred Vinson Jr. led the charge. In December 1967, he suggested to Deputy Attorney General Christopher that early planning, including "possible preventative action," be enacted. To prepare for the demonstration, the DOJ created a task force to supervise the campaign. Meanwhile FBI Director J. Edgar Hoover demanded exceptional interdepartmental cooperation, requiring that agents secure direct lines to key information-sharing sources in the local police, state police intelligence units, and regional military intelligence groups. Throughout the winter and spring, Hoover and Vinson made the Poor People's Campaign a focal point of their frontal assault on the rising tide of black militancy throughout the country.[20]

SCLC organizers had applied to the National Park Service for permits for fifteen hundred marchers to camp on the National Mall. However, they quickly discovered that the DOJ's increased supervision led to tedious bureaucratic negotiations that made securing a permit time consuming and laborious. Andrew Young suspected that the government was essentially trying to run out the clock. "We do not want to get into lengthy negotiations about obtaining permits. All of the time between now and the beginning of the PPC could be preoccupied with that one single matter," Young forecasted in March. His prediction came true. In the month leading up to the campaign's anticipated start, SCLC became enmeshed in an uphill bureaucratic battle against the federal government.[21]

The permit issue did not preoccupy SCLC alone. It also preoccupied the DOJ-led task force, which could not fathom granting permission for civil rights activists to camp on the National Mall. Thus, with less than two months before the campaign's launch, members of the task force advised Justice Department officials to reject the organization's proposal for encampment sites on the grounds of "impracticality." Tired of negotiating with SCLC, Fred Vinson went so far as to suggest that they create a firm policy against the issuance of campsite permits for the demonstration. The long, hot summer of 1967 loomed large in Vinson's mind. It convinced him and other federal officials that not even the capital could be kept safe from violence. The riots that followed in April, just one month after they had considered SCLC's proposal, confirmed their suspicions and signaled to them that they should not acquiesce on the permit issue.[22]

The D.C. riots reinforced the Johnson administration's already-negative opinion of the Poor People's Campaign. The April disorders had jarred them, and the possibility of another uprising remained a great source of anxiety for White House officials. It undoubtedly shaded how they viewed SCLC's impending campaign. Two weeks after King's assassination, for example, President Johnson's assistant, Matthew Nimetz, told Deputy Attorney General Christopher that King's absence only increased the White House's belief that militants would take over the campaign. The disturbances "have charged the air with new tensions," Nimetz told Christopher. "We know that large collections of people on the street, the possibility of a real or imagined incident, the presence in Washington of groups eager to promote discord, and fear and hate in various sectors of the community all combine to make a new outbreak of violence during the march more likely than we had originally thought," he cautioned. Although inaccurate intelligence and racially motivated suspicions informed his comments, the White House aide did indicate a sensitivity to the ways in which Washington residents and protestors from around the country could unexpectedly collide—something the SCLC seemed to have overlooked in the lead-up to its campaign.[23]

The Johnson administration's dealings with SCLC over the details of the PPC differed dramatically from the Kennedy administration's participation in the 1963 March on Washington and even from its own involvement in the city's uprising the month before. Despite cabinet members' increased concerns over violence, they recognized that denying SCLC a permit for its demonstration would only heighten racial animosity, especially so soon after African Americans around the country had protested their lack of agency and the conditions in the cities in which they lived by burning them to the ground. But between the unraveling of Johnson's national agenda and the escalation of the war in

Vietnam, the president's administration never offered a clear or consistent policy on the Poor People's Campaign. As a result, Attorney General Clark and the Justice Department were left in charge of overseeing it.[24]

Ramsey Clark had made enemies across party lines thanks to his perceived leniency when it came to law and order during the April riots. Unwilling to pander to his critics, Clark refused to preemptively condemn activists in the lead-up to the Poor People's Campaign. In fact, after King's assassination, the attorney general remained cautiously optimistic about it. Clark reasoned that demonstrators, if denied legal means to express their grievances, would resort to extralegal, disruptive measures. Therefore, he believed, the administration ought to allow the country to pay tribute to Martin Luther King through SCLC's campaign, provided they did so within proper legal bounds. As Clark told *Meet the Press* moderator Lawrence Spivak in April 1968, "We can show reverence, we have to show reverence, but we have to do this within the rule of law." Yet as the Johnson administration, DOJ, and FBI enacted crime prevention measures during the lead-up to the Poor People's Campaign, the rule of law narrowed dramatically.[25]

Meanwhile, as organizers arrived in Washington in late April, the Justice Department could only speculate about SCLC's tightly wrapped plans. DOJ officials admitted to the president's aides that they knew "very little about what the militants are doing" and worried about how active they appeared. The DOJ's focus on militant activity in the wake of the D.C. riots led them down fruitless rabbit holes in search of potential radicals. But SCLC also contributed to the uncertainty that enveloped its upcoming campaign. As late as April 25, SCLC leaders had managed to keep the size of the PPC, the location of Resurrection City, and the date of its planned mass demonstration concealed.[26]

As the campaign began to materialize in May, Clark toured the Sunday morning press circuit yet again to discuss SCLC's activity. Prior to King's assassination, journalists had covered the Poor People's Campaign with perfunctory spirit. But as calls for law and order rose across the country, reporters refocused their coverage to emphasize the PPC's potential for violence. On ABC's *Issues and Answers*, hosts Bob Clark and Irv Chapman grilled the attorney general. Bob Clark told Ramsey Clark, "This is a rather jittery capital today, as I am sure you know, with the arrival of the first units of the Poor People's March." The moderator continued, "There is every hope that this march is going to be conducted peacefully, but there is considerable concern in Washington that it could provoke more violence of the sort that erupted in the city last month." The attorney general tried to debunk this notion, explaining to

Clark and Chapman that neither SCLC leadership, city officials, nor the federal government wanted violence. However, civil rights leaders, the D.C. government, and federal officials differed radically on the measure of force necessary to curb potential violence—a difference that illustrated the wide ideological gulf between proponents of civil rights and law and order.[27]

Voicing further unease over the Poor People's Campaign, the ABC hosts pressed Clark for details on the government's plans. Moderator Bob Clark asked the attorney general about Reverend Ralph Abernathy's "ultimatum" to disrupt the government with civil disobedience. "Are you going to have to go to mass arrests or something to deal immediately with civil disobedience?" he asked. In response, the attorney general reiterated that SCLC had launched its campaign in the spirit of nonviolence and with the noble goal of spotlighting one of the country's ugliest problems. "To dwell now on the riot potential and on law enforcement capabilities and on the use of gas and mass arrests is to miss the major point and that is that we have problems in this country that must be resolved," he declared. Clark feared that both government officials and citizens would overlook these problems as the contours of the PPC took shape. He was correct. As the federal government and citizens across the nation fixated on civil violence, black militance, and law and order in the wake of King's assassination, SCLC's interracial message about the nation's poverty epidemic took a backseat.[28]

Yet even Clark reflected the changing discourse on law and order in the late 1960s. The attorney general, who had been the target of congressional opprobrium for his reluctance to use force during the riots, did not miss an opportunity to highlight the large police apparatus in place. "We have a fine city police department here, we have the police of the National Park Service; we have a variety of federal civilian law enforcement personnel, we have a good National Guard unit and, if necessary, federal troops," Clark said reflecting on the unique range of local and national officials primed to enforce law and order should violence occur in the capital.[29]

To ensure Clark's promise that violence would not disrupt SCLC's campaign, the Justice Department initiated increased surveillance measures—in coordination with its riot prevention operation—during the lead-up to the PPC. Privately, DOJ officials worried that SCLC's campaign would impose "a heavy and intense burden" on them. Thus, they monitored all rumors of allegedly suspicious activity. The DOJ received word that a number of large groups—up to seven thousand additional participants—were headed to Washington. As one official warned Attorney General Clark, unlike the three thousand demonstrators scheduled to camp at Resurrection City, "these people will arrive without the benefit of non-violent schools and without any real preparation for their lodging or feeding." Even worse, they feared, was the likely possibility that SCLC would not take responsibility for demonstrators outside of those officially sanctioned to camp in Resurrection City. This would leave thousands of African American agitators to mill about the capital. While the bulk of their suspicions were unfounded, DOJ officials made a discerning point about SCLC's attitude toward the demonstration's impact on Washington, D.C. As the campaign unfolded, protestors did engage with life outside the camp. The demonstration undeniably became enmeshed with the fabric of life in the capital city—with lasting consequences for District residents.[30]

The DOJ did not limit its surveillance to SCLC's local activity. Instead it continued to monitor intelligence of militant action brewing in other locales. Working closely with the FBI, it kept tabs on black militants who said they were traveling to Washington for the demonstration. Rumors abounded: black activists in Alabama were planning to take over the Poor People's Campaign and foment unrest when they arrived in the District. Local leaders down south were conspiring with noted militant and D.C. resident Stokely Carmichael. Southern youth were carrying weapons in order to loot Washington stores. The FBI found the rumors baseless. For example, one of Carmichael's suspected allies, Reverend Charles Boone, did not support his agenda. Quite the opposite, Boone had refused to allow Carmichael to speak at his Montgomery, Alabama, church as the campaign neared. Moreover, the Montgomery Improvement Association, in charge of coordinating local plans for the PPC, had already excluded high school students from participating. Nonetheless, such stories stoked officials' fears about the potential for violence.[31]

The DOJ and FBI tracked rumors like these in part because this time, unlike in 1963, SCLC did not communicate its plans to the agencies. SCLC's reticence spoke not only to its internal disorganization but also to its best weapon: its ability to be flexible, nimble, and creative. As late as April 25, less than three weeks before Ralph Abernathy would drive the first stake into Resurrection City, SCLC leaders had managed to keep the size of the campaign, the location of Resurrection City, and the date of its planned mass demonstration concealed.[32] "So far as we know they have no real plans," White House Aide Matthew Nimetz admitted in an internal memo, "it is thus hard for us to have a definite plan for dealing with them."[33] In fact, all White House officials knew for sure was that "in the middle of May, 3,000 or more poor people plan to arrive in the city from various parts of the country."[34]

Lacking firm information and fearing disorder, jittery federal officials cooperated closely with the Metropolitan Police Department to prepare for SCLC's upcoming protest. The April riots had prompted the Justice Department to expand its intelligence capabilities to yield more accurate information about the activities of the city's own militant groups as well as those heading to Washington for the Poor People's Campaign. In the month between the riots and the campaign, Attorney General Clark worked to improve coordination between District, Maryland, and Virginia officials on curfews, traffic control, and the sale of guns, gas, and liquor. Meanwhile, Under Secretary of the Army David McGiffert refined plans to better facilitate troop deployment into the District. Deputy Attorney General Christopher pressured the FBI to share information with the MPD. The White House also helped establish a central command post in the police department's Municipal Building to increase communication between entities. City government officials had complained that they could not get in touch with the White House during the riots, something officials sought to rectify with the creation of a command center. Finally, the Department of the Army allocated $150,000 to the local government to upgrade the city's intelligence networks, one of Public Safety Director Patrick Murphy's chief concerns. Taken together, these measures illustrate the ways in which a variety of federal and local actors and agencies implemented mechanisms intended to repress and survey black citizens under the pretense of thwarting potential violent outbreaks. Their coordinated campaign worked to suppress grassroots organizing and narrow the possibilities for black self-determination in the capital.[35]

CONSERVATIVES RESPOND

As the federal government plotted its response to the Poor People's Campaign, critics from around the country voiced their concerns about the failures of the liberal Johnson administration and its local black government to curb civil violence in Washington during the riots. Moreover, they warned of the potential for further disorder during the upcoming demonstration. "The nation's capital, crime-ridden and riot-sacked, now faces a new crisis," observed *U.S. News and World Report*. According to the magazine, "Thousands of 'poor people's marchers' are descending on Washington. Members of Congress, businessmen and residents are demanding official action to protect the city. Shopkeepers and homeowners are arming to defend themselves. New riots are feared." In drawing these conclusions, the magazine bolstered the narrative of a city out of control. It ominously suggested that individuals were primed to take matters into their own hands if stronger law-and-order measures were not passed.[36]

Lawmakers readily exploited the capital city's anxiety to their own political advantage. Some of the most vocal advocates of law and order, southern Democrats with poor civil rights records, scheduled hearings on more than seventy-five bills designed to block the PPC. Prior to King's assassination, Senator Robert Byrd, chair of the U.S. Senate Appropriations Subcommittee on the District of Columbia, spoke out against the SCLC leader and the dangers of civil rights activism in the capital city. He called King a "self-seeking rabble-rouser" and described his work on behalf of sanitation workers in Memphis as "a preview of what may be in store" in the nation's capital. In doing so, Byrd alluded ominously to King's troublesome hand in local demonstrations.[37]

Byrd deliberately referenced King's time in Memphis, where the leader had assisted local sanitation workers in a strike against the city's government. Inspired by the community's dedication to the strike, King had agreed to return to lead a march on March 28. The march ended in disarray as younger demonstrators smashed storefronts and, in return, local police wielded wooden batons and sprayed mace indiscriminately on participants. At the end of the long day, the police had killed 1 black teenager and arrested 125 citizens. King's inability to keep tight control over the local march provided ammunition for those, like Byrd, who viewed Memphis as a precedent for the trouble that would ensue during SCLC's upcoming campaign. By forecasting disorder in Washington, Byrd proactively laid the groundwork for the implementation of law-and-order measures to counteract "dangerous" civil rights activity.[38]

Not only did Byrd use the upcoming Poor People's Campaign as an opportunity to attack SCLC. He and other lawmakers also used it as a vehicle to attack the Johnson administration for its record on law and order and demonstrators for their potential to incite violence. Speaking on King's involvement in the PPC just days before his assassination, Byrd said, "It is time for our federal government—which in recent years has shown itself to be virtually spineless when it comes to standing up against the lawbreakers, the hoodlums, and the Marxist demonstrators—at least to let the nation know . . . that it will not allow this Nobel Peace Prize winner to create another Memphis."[39]

Southern Democrats eagerly voiced their displeasure at the federal government for allowing SCLC to go forward with its demonstration. They remained intent on coupling civil rights activism on behalf of poor people with black militance and violent activity. Following King's assassination, Senator John McClellan (D-Ark.) echoed Byrd's concerns and made a prediction for Washington, D.C.: "militant advocates of violence" would infiltrate the campaign and turn the capital into a "Mecca" for migrants.[40] "They are bragging that they will not leave Washington without new wardrobes which they will acquire when the looting starts," the Arkansas Democrat cautioned.[41] Similarly, Maryland

Representative Harvey Machen (D-Md.) predicted that the PPC would be "the trigger for another round of violence" and admitted that he could "see nothing that this march can accomplish, except to create more chaos."[42] Through comments like these, southern Democrats tethered civil rights activity and violence to the nation's capital, pointed to weak federal governance in Washington, and crafted early forecasts about urban rebellion. In doing so, they paved the way for strong federal intervention to curb civil rights activity.

Despite their contempt, congressional leaders indicated that they would not bring a bill to the floor to prohibit all camping on federal land in the District—provided that the Department of Justice could negotiate a satisfactory permit with SCLC.[43] For the District's local white business and real estate groups, however, a satisfactory permit simply did not exist. Immediately following King's death, Association of Oldest Inhabitants of the District of Columbia president Burton Langhenry called on the federal government to suspend SCLC's campaign. White House domestic policy aide Frederick Bohen tried to reassure the white civic leader that the administration was prepared for the upcoming demonstration. "Working closely with District officials, the federal government has been working for some months to ensure that law and order are maintained in the District of Columbia in connection with the proposed march. Violations of the law will be handled promptly, firmly and justly," the aide told Langhenry. "We hope that this careful planning conducted by the many Departments and Agencies which have responsibility for law enforcement and order will constitute the ounce of prevention that you call for," he added.[44]

This exchange highlights several important themes. First, despite the admission that the White House was working closely with D.C. officials, the White House aide willingly discussed the matter with the civic group president. In doing so, he underscored the mimetic nature of the president's home rule measure and the importance of the city's white growth machine to the running of Washington. Second, Bohen adopted the law-and-order rhetoric about which the city's white stakeholders had been increasingly vocal since the riots. Third, in revealing the coordinated efforts by government agencies and departments to ensure law and order in Washington, the domestic policy staffer demonstrated the ease with which the White House applied surveillance measures in the city. While the level of coordination was not unprecedented, it did illustrate the Johnson administration's heightened efforts to maintain control of the city in lieu of having direct access to the demonstration—a far cry from when those in the Kennedy administration had asserted their authority over the 1963 March on Washington.

Other civic groups echoed the AOI's concerns about the PPC. On April 25, the Federation of Citizens Associations, Washington's white neighborhood association umbrella group, passed a resolution against the Poor People's Campaign. "The planned march of the poor people and live-in to and in Washington is a definite threat and menace to the peace and order of the District of Columbia," Delegate Phelps wrote. "In view of the constitutional responsibility of the president, the attorney general, and local authorities to preserve order at all times," he concluded, "the [Federation] recommends that the president instruct the attorney general immediately to seek a permanent injunction enjoining the march leaders from furthering or carrying out their contemplated plans and conspiracy." The group did not only argue that the PPC was a direct threat to Washington's tenuous peace. It also challenged the Johnson administration and the local black government to execute their alleged constitutional responsibility. The Federation fanned the flames against the liberal administration, called into question the local government's judgment, and further bolstered its support for law and order.[45]

As the white growth machine confronted the first mass demonstration in Washington not only since the April riots, but also since the long, hot summer of 1967 and anti–Vietnam War protests in October 1967, it threw its weight behind preventative federal action. John Jarboe, president of the Eighteenth and Columbia Road Business Association, urged Johnson to dispense with partisan politics and preemptively reinforce the city with federal troops. "Despite your warning of further disorders," Jarboe wrote, "federal troops have not been returned to the streets of our city, even in token numbers. We request that be returned NOW without further delay and equivocation."[46]

The Washington Board of Trade agreed. Toward the end of May, the city's powerful white booster group asked Johnson to provide additional troops to bolster the local police force. While the riots had certainly provided white Washingtonians with ammunition in their fight for law and order, the Poor People's Campaign provided them with a concrete event around which to strengthen support for it.[47]

In part to demonstrate his toughness on crime and help restore confidence in local government, Mayor Washington sided with the Board of Trade and advocated for pre-positioning U.S. Army units around Resurrection City. Washington had another compelling reason for his recommendation: the city's police force had worked overtime since the April riots. "The fatigue factor is a real problem for them," he explained to White House and DOJ officials one month after the riots. DOJ officials were not convinced. They sided with Deputy Attorney General Christopher, who argued that pre-positioning troops would make for bad optics. "It is bad for the city to have troops moving in and out, giving Washington a crisis atmosphere," Christopher said. In ignoring Mayor Washington's recommendation, the Justice Department once again asserted its authority over law-and-order decisions in the capital.[48]

The Poor People's Campaign was a perfect illustration of the federal government's ability to marginalize the municipal government in issues of law and order. On the one hand, the DOJ counted on District officials to help coordinate local and national security in the months prior to the PPC. Mayor Washington offered the federal government intimate knowledge of local conditions and remained a welcomed presence in biweekly meetings with the White House and DOJ. Yet federal officials freely overruled local counsel as they saw fit. When it came to managing the PPC, the D.C. government had no financial resources or decision-making powers. As Mayor Washington reminded officials, it could not even make independent decisions about SCLC's permit request.[49]

Despite their marginalization by the federal government, local black officials remained integral to the execution of the Poor People's Campaign. For example, local officials helped broker a deal between SCLC and the federal agencies in charge of issuing the organization a permit for its demonstration. Walter Fauntroy, the leader of Washington's local SCLC chapter and vice chairman of the D.C. City Council, had used his political connections to lobby the Departments of Justice and Interior on the issue. Even before King's assassination, Fauntroy had made a compelling case for an encampment on the National Mall, where it would be isolated from homes, businesses, and other areas of dense population. The local official could not have known that King's death would trigger the city's worst civil violence. However, he had a realistic and indispensable knowledge of local racial tensions and could better predict how to preserve peace in the city.[50]

By advocating on behalf of SCLC, Fauntroy revealed one of the pitfalls of Johnson's reorganization plan. Since taking a seat on the president's appointed city council, Fauntroy continued to wear several hats. But planning for SCLC's arrival brushed up against the city's civil violence following King's assassination. Fauntroy's dual role, "as a member of the local government and as a director of the organization whose campaign might well include disruption of that government," according to the *Washington Post*'s William Raspberry, had been thrown into sharp relief. Fauntroy had tried to steer a course down the middle. By visiting the Department of Interior in early April, he made his position clear: he would prioritize his advocacy on behalf of SCLC.[51]

King's death and the subsequent riots persuaded Attorney General Clark that Fauntroy's argument was sound. The Mall, he agreed, was, in fact, the safest place for such a demonstration. Clark overruled Assistant Attorney General Fred Vinson, as well as Secretary of the Interior Stewart Udall, and recommended that the National Park Service issue SCLC a permit to stage its campaign and encampment. Moreover, he instructed the Park Service to reject alternative locations for campers, such as Southeast D.C.'s less centrally located Anacostia Park or other areas "near the ghetto and less accessible to law enforcement," in favor of the National Mall.[52] On May 10, in response to Clark's orders, the Park Service approved a permit for fifteen acres alongside the Reflecting Pool and at the foot of the Lincoln Memorial, just next to the National Mall. Within federal parkland and in plain view of tourists and commuters, SCLC believed they had secured an ideal site for a national campaign.[53]

Not everyone believed it was the ideal location to mount a campaign. Although the majority of citizens were not concerned about D.C. residents' welfare, per se, the capital's symbolism struck a chord in people's hearts. On returning from South Carolina after a week of campaigning for reelection, Representative and House Committee on the District of Columbia chairman John McMillan told President Johnson, "The people in my district and the entire United States are very much distressed over the fact that a permit was granted for the so-called poor people to build tents on government property." Speaking on the floor of Congress, McMillan explained, "The chief topic of discussion with practically every person I talked to was the lack of law enforcement in Washington." Much like his fellow congressional opponents, McMillan laid the groundwork for repressive measures to counteract civil rights protest. And he used his constituents, who lived five hundred miles away, to bolster his point.[54]

The Park Service permit held SCLC accountable for basic municipal functions, prohibited firearms, required organizers to remove garbage properly, and demanded that sanitary conditions be maintained. It also gave SCLC leaders unprecedented powers. The Park Police, which had jurisdiction in all federal parkland, agreed not to enter the camp unless invited. Instead, SCLC implemented one of its most radical ideas: the recruitment of young men to serve as marshals and maintain order in Resurrection City. Under the supervision of James Orange, a large, bearded man with a penchant for wearing bib overalls, street gang members from several cities—including men such as twenty-nine-year-old Sweet William Wine, a member of the Invaders gang from Memphis—served industriously, at least at the start, as the camp's internal police force. "These gang members have always lived outside the system," Orange told a *Washington Post* reporter at the time. "Our idea was to bring them into the system, let them have a role in the functioning of Resurrection City."[55] In granting power to these young men, SCLC purposefully demonstrated its homespun version of community policing. It explicitly countered the law-and-order measures championed by politicians following the April riots and demonstrated black self-determination, even as it overlooked local Washingtonians' own challenges.[56]

The permit was a double-edged sword. On the one hand, it was critical for SCLC to be able to control law and order in the camp at a time when the black community's distrust of the police had reached a crescendo. On the other hand, however, the six-page permit included dozens of conditions that would grow increasingly difficult for the group to meet. The SCLC leadership wanted to provide national visibility for Resurrection City, but its very location would sow the seeds of the campaign's demise. As the group began making preparations for Resurrection City, DOJ officials worked to fortify the capital, calling for additional "Special Duty Officers" ready to familiarize themselves with both the campaign and the city and, borrowing a page from the National Guard's April response, fan out throughout the District rather than only in "dangerous" areas to watch for problems. Then in late May, a DOJ official instructed Attorney General Clark to "proceed with the formation of confrontation squads," indicating its more aggressive approach to law and order following the riots.[57]

BLACK WASHINGTONIANS RESPOND

Despite a rich history of mobilizing on behalf of civil rights causes, few local African Americans were involved in the Poor People's Campaign prior to the April 4 assassination of King. Indeed, at a packed mid-February planning session, white SCLC organizer Kay Shannon spotted only two black attendees. This lack of enthusiasm was, in part, because the city's black middle class had trouble relating to the experiences of poorer black Washingtonians. Black campaign administrator James Peterson went so far as to question the motivations of those who did turn out. They "always wanted their name to be on the program," he said, indicating that appearances were of utmost importance to black middle-class volunteers.[58]

The black community's apathy toward the Poor People's Campaign did not faze some local activists. Robert Rippley, a United Planning Organization employee and self-described "firebrand ghetto worker," was not surprised. He noticed the same barriers at work in the Metropolitan Police Department's civilian complaint review board. The board, instituted to incorporate local feedback before the riots, lacked what Rippley called "grassroots people." "Just lawyers, doctors, people never in the community," he said.[59] His observations bolster urban historian Michael Katz's theory of selective incorporation: in Washington, the integration of elite African Americans into city functions by the federal government came at the expense of grassroots activists. As Johnson created his presidentially appointed local government and selected prominent black leaders like Walter Washington and SCLC's own Walter Fauntroy to lead the city, the trend became even more pronounced. As local activists and federal officials forged an uneasy partnership, poor black Washingtonians grew further disillusioned.[60]

The fear of unrest and police retaliation were also barriers to local black participation. As police-community relations deteriorated during the mid- to late 1960s, many black activists had called for a massive overhaul of the city's criminal justice system. So, too, did President Johnson's 1966 Crime Commission. But change was slow to come by. Frustrated, the Black United Front had taken on issues of police brutality, high incarceration rates, and racially motivated crime policies since its founding in January 1968. Its more militant members dismissed ideas of integration and demanded neighborhood control of the police and the termination Police Chief John Layton. Relations were so tense that in March, local activist and BUF member Julius Hobson predicted that "trigger happy" police would "slaughter" demonstrators during the Poor People's Campaign.[61]

Finally, many black Washingtonians stayed on the sidelines prior to King's assassination because white liberals had dominated the early local planning period. White volunteers had a variety of reasons for joining the campaign. For some white women, organizing simply felt like second nature in a city like D.C. According to *Washington Post* reporter Judith Martin, "Some Washington women can tell you to the penny how much can be extracted for a charity ball from any pocket you name. . . . Other women apply the same tactics to marches and demonstrations." "It takes someone who is a good housewife to plan a march," added SCLC organizer Kay Shannon. "You have to be practical—able to set things in order."[62] James Peterson speculated that for others, guilt loomed large: "They are beginning to feel that the world they are living in and the world of the poor people are quite different. They feel they have neglected their brothers and sisters and this campaign has given them the opportunity to assist the poor."[63]

While many upper-class white women had the necessary experience and desire to get involved, their assistance came at the exclusion of black residents. William Moyer, a white Philadelphian who headed SCLC's local operations, admitted as much. Moyer had built his career with the Chicago branch of the Quaker-based American Friends Service Committee and served as a principal organizer in the 1966 Chicago Open Housing Movement. There Moyer connected with James Bevel, Martin Luther King, and other SCLC leaders. Two years later, SCLC selected him to serve as the point person for the PPC's local operations. Moyer believed that the District perfectly embodied the nation's poverty problems. Yet despite holding committee meetings at 14th and U Streets NW—then the heart of black Washington—he and other white volunteers had trouble recruiting African Americans. "It was basically a white group that met which was supposed to be doing this thing for poor black people," Moyer observed. "This upset a lot of people. I was concerned about it. I think there should be more black involvement, but I understand why there wasn't more black involvement."[64]

Despite these overtures to the black community, SCLC did not even reach out to the United Planning Organization, the District's de facto antipoverty organization, in planning the Poor People's Campaign. Instead it continued to emphasize the national scope of SCLC's antipoverty program over local issues like police brutality and self-determination and downplayed the fact that the capital's black neighborhoods, just steps away from the Mall, remained in disrepair. While SCLC was forward looking in its desire to coalition build and focus on poverty, its campaign revealed a deep rupture between the national and local civil rights movements in the wake of urban rebellion. A large demonstration on behalf of poor Americans seemed incongruous with the grassroots organizing that local activists believed would help achieve black self-determination in the face of mimetic reforms, selective incorporation, indirect rule, and repression and surveillance.[65]

Though King's assassination did not change the growing divide between the local and national movements, it did spur diverse groups to join the Poor People's Campaign. In the spirit of cooperation, even militant black organizations were willing to join what had taken on the mantle of King's final action. Carmichael had not originally endorsed the campaign, but King's assassination caused him to reconsider. Like other militants, Carmichael believed that SCLC was ineffective, but he was willing to give the Poor People's Campaign a chance. At a SNCC-sponsored press conference the day after King's death, Carmichael mourned the slain hero and pledged his support to SCLC, prompting many of his allies around the country to follow suit.[66]

After King's death and Carmichael's blessing, members of the Black Panther Party reversed their opposition and traveled to D.C. in caravans from the West Coast. Milwaukee's NAACP Youth Council, a radical proponent of open housing initiatives, voted to participate. Meanwhile, in California, the Los Angeles Black Congress, a Black United Front–type umbrella group for the city, endorsed the campaign and sent volunteers. By deferring to SCLC, Carmichael and his supporters demonstrated their ability to traverse the tactical lines between violence and nonviolence, as well as their desire to honor King's legacy.[67]

Despite Carmichael's peripheral role in the PPC, members of the media kept him at the center of its news coverage, in large part because they maintained a one-dimensional rendering of the movement's violent/nonviolent dichotomy. After a February summit between Carmichael and King, for example, the black-run *Pittsburgh Courier* published a headline blaring "King, Carmichael in Strategy Clash" rather than focusing on the historic significance of their meeting.[68] SCLC deputy coordinator Tony Henry expressed his frustrations with the media's coverage of Carmichael and the upcoming PPC. "Stokely, to my knowledge, was never asked to agree not to interfere," he said. Yet, Henry explained, "I was quoted as having said that in a newspaper article, that he had agreed not to interfere, but that was misinterpreted by an overzealous reporter who was trying to make the campaign respectable."[69]

Ultimately, Carmichael did visit the camp at the end of May. According to surveillance teams, he was widely recognized, though he did not receive any special treatment while there. But the persistent spotlight on Carmichael frustrated SCLC, both for having been pitted against Carmichael in a false binary and in having its campaign sanitized for a general public uncomfortable with the upcoming demonstration.[70]

For their part, local militant groups acted supportive but aloof. SNCC's Washington chapter supported the campaign, but Director Lester McKinnie offered only a tepid endorsement. "We hope that the Poor People's Campaign accomplishes its goals, because it will make our work unnecessary," McKinnie said.[71] Even that statement was misleading. SCLC had set its eyes on national objectives and continued to place faith in both the persuasive power of the large-scale demonstration and in federal legislation. But McKinnie's group, not to mention national SNCC members, had poured its resources into grassroots organizing. "There was a real reluctance among the black militant groups to become too involved," acknowledged Tony Henry, deputy coordinator for the Poor People's Campaign. "They were skeptical about its ability to achieve any meaningful results and also skeptical of the massive involvement of white people." Thus they remained largely disinterested in SCLC's spectacle on the Mall.[72]

The Black United Front also grew disenchanted over the planning period. In February 1968, BUF leaders had initiated meetings with SCLC to discuss how the campaign would directly benefit poor Washingtonians. After King's assassination, BUF voted unanimously to lend its support to the campaign. However, those members who chose to get involved in the campaign—like member Roena Rand, who had implored fellow members to take in two demonstrators each for meals and showers—did so as Washington residents and not as representatives of the organization.[73]

Wealthy black Washingtonians also remained ambivalent. On the one hand, many believed they had an obligation to pitch in. At the same time, they were torn on whether to prioritize the national struggle or lend support locally. Writing checks to help the Poor People's Campaign was easy, and many did so; more personal involvement was difficult to solicit. The campaign needed housing, food, and transportation—logistical assistance that the city's black elites were not accustomed to giving. When one black woman suggested that her social club make sandwiches to hand out when the caravans arrived, she was told, "If they can bring thousands of poor here, they ought to know where to feed them." Her comments again pointed to the intraracial class politics at play in Washington—politics that SCLC overlooked in planning its campaign in the capital.[74]

Many Howard University students had hoped to connect with black demonstrators during the Poor People's Campaign. Living in the District, at the intersection of local and national politics, they had long been involved in civil rights efforts. As Clyde Aveilhe, a student and director of the university's student activities, boasted in 1968, "Anywhere from 65 to 80 percent of the most 'militant' students on our campus have working involvements with off-campus organizations and individuals who are in the revolution."[75] That year alone, Howard students had protested administrative policies, demanded a stronger voice in academic affairs, and emphasized the relevance and necessity of a black university to the black community. Freshman Michael Harris was among those who had protested Howard administrators' "Uncle Tom" attitude. They had been particularly frustrated with the university's decision to deny SCLC use of its classrooms and dormitories for its upcoming campaign. Imploring the university to "come off the Hill," and help erase the divisions between "so-called intellectuals and the people, college students and block boys," Harris joined a number of Howard students who made the short trip from campus to the National Mall to participate in the Poor People's Campaign.[76]

Howard students' involvement did not reflect their support for SCLC per se. Like many younger activists, a lot of them preferred SNCC's militant rhetoric, local organizing tactics, and black solidarity over SCLC's more traditional style. But they felt a responsibility to help politicize the community. According to Ewart Brown, president of Howard's student assembly, "Black people in the

District of Columbia are still disenfranchised. Howard should put pressure on the powers that be using the people in the community as the mass force to move towards Home Rule."[77] For Harris, the campaign's meaning could be found in on-the-ground interactions. "The great thing about the Poor People's Campaign," he told an interviewer, "was the fact that, in my opinion, the two groups in the black community that could cause and sustain revolution were the black college students and the black gangs. The white man tries to divide us, but we liberated ourselves from that." What he appreciated most was how Resurrection City inhabitants accepted Howard students.[78] Accepted, perhaps, but as Clyde Aveilhe observed with frustration, "Some people there didn't take [us] seriously."[79] Even so, Howard students found different ways to get involved. The school's Delta Sigma Theta sorority, for example, serenaded Resurrection City residents every Friday afternoon. Other students offered workshops on various topics through the encampment's Poor People's University.[80]

But while white volunteers officially took charge of organizing the PPC, and Howard students searched for ways to get involved, some black women became its unofficial champions. This mirrored national trends. As historian Michael Honey notes, in cities across the country, "women were the backbone of much of the organizing for the PPC."[81] In D.C., they fought to make the demonstration meaningful on the local level. "We are trying to organize the mass of Washington's black middle-class community and get them integrated into the Poor People's Campaign," June Fowler told the *Washington Post*. That spring, Fowler, the wife of an attorney and mother of two teenage sons, gathered seven other women in her home to strategize regarding how to support SCLC's upcoming campaign. "People are always criticizing Washington's Negro society for not doing enough," she said. "But what has been done has largely been done individually or in small groups and those involved haven't had what they've accomplished publicized." This time the women sought to draw attention to their efforts. "Move over Lady Bountiful," Fowler exclaimed, "soul sister is here!"[82]

Although only a small group had assembled at Fowler's house, the forty clubs and organizations to which the women belonged represented thousands of potential middle-class African American volunteers. The friends had a variety of reasons for participating. A sense of justice compelled Mrs. Alvin Robinson, president of Girl Friends, a social organization best known for its sponsorship of cotillions. "If a small group of half-senile, bigoted old men on Capitol Hill think they can get out of making changes by claiming they are sought only by a small minority within a minority, we're here to tell them they're wrong." Meanwhile, Mrs. John F. Clark, president of Washington's local Jack & Jill chapter, had been motivated by the "burning in American cities" which "shattered the myth of the contented slum dweller for all Americans." Mrs. Waddell Thomas added, "I am a grandmother and too old to be a militant. But I'm not too old to be good old-fashioned angry." Mrs. Claude Cowan, who recruited volunteers on the neighborhood level, best summarized their dedication to the cause. "My daughter is getting married next month and two of my children are graduating from college, but preparation for that will have to wait," she said. "The Campaign is more important."[83]

Despite their best intentions, some of the District's middle-class black women had a difficult time relating to residents of Resurrection City. In May the National Council of Negro Women opened a rare dialogue between the two groups at a poverty workshop it organized. The *Washington Post* described the result as "a confrontation both painful and illuminating." While participants generally agreed on the problems they faced—including welfare, lack of consumer protection, access to child care, and unemployment—they differed on how to solve them. The D.C. women believed in working within the system, while the female demonstrators accused the government and the middle class of "turning their backs on the poor." In fact, one protester directly challenged the black middle-class women in the room, including Mayor Walter Washington's wife, Bennetta Washington. "Some of the Negro people here are in places where they can change things for the poor," she pointedly noted. "It's time they stopped sitting on their furs and realize we're all black sisters."[84]

The National Welfare Rights Organization had a better time relating to poor black women. On May 12, Mother's Day, the organization, led in part by D.C. resident and NWRO vice chair Etta Horn, marched over three thousand people down 14th Street toward the White House. Carrying signs that called for "Mother Power" and "Income, Dignity, Justice, Democracy," the protesters walked alongside Coretta Scott King, Martin Luther King's widow. Together they demanded a repeal of amendments to the 1967 Social Security Act, which raised eligibility standards and reduced welfare benefits to low-income mothers and their children. Perhaps recognizing the way that women's rights took a backseat to more general calls to end poverty by SCLC, NWRO officials insisted on organizing their march outside the umbrella of the Poor People's Campaign. In a moving speech in front of more than seven thousand people at the end of the march, King emphasized the importance of women's roles in spreading the gospel of nonviolence and helping the poor.[85]

Unlike the NWRO, SCLC overlooked D.C.'s poor women of color, who had been battling the government over antipoverty funds since Johnson announced his War on Poverty in 1964. Thanks to its role as the city's de facto antipoverty agency, the United Planning Organization should have been a natural partner for SCLC. However, it was the DOJ, rather than SCLC, that had the foresight to discuss plans for the group to join the campaign. In March 1968, Department of Justice Community Relations Division official Roger Wilkins alerted Ramsey Clark to the issue. "One local government policy issue to which the Mayor should give special priority attention is the role that he would deem it appropriate for the UPO to take in the campaign," Wilkins told Clark. "We know already that a number of the UPO and Neighborhood Development Program community organizers are individually wrestling with the issue of what role is appropriate for them to undertake. It would be desirable if overall policy and strategy could be work[ed] out," he explained. The lack of overall policy toward the UPO underscores SCLC's focus on national issues at the expense of Washington's own antipoverty movement.[86]

The mayor never did work out an overall strategy for the UPO. By the time demonstrators arrived in Washington, the organization had its own controversies to attend to. On April 18, 1968, less than two weeks after the D.C. riots had erupted, three hundred UPO employees engaged in a four-hour work stoppage at the organization's headquarters to protest the UPO's detachment from black residents living in poor neighborhoods. The next day, Branton fired nine employees for taking part in the stoppage. According to the dismissed workers, "The United Planning Organization is a Greek Revival–style plantation mansion run for the benefit of the white establishment by Uncle Toms." They claimed they were fired "because we identified with the struggle of black people and acted out of our commitment to black people."[87]

The protests shrouding the UPO point to the complicated relationship that both the federal government and grassroots organizers had with local black government officials in the wake of Johnson's limited home rule measure. Due to the selective incorporation of prominent black Washingtonians into local office, many UPO staff members felt alienated and undermined. Yet to members of Congress, the mere fact that African Americans were in charge at all allowed them to accuse the organization of being "militant." The consequences were striking. By forcing the UPO to narrowly tailor its agenda, halt cooperation with local activists, and shy away from innovation, the Johnson administration effectively defanged the District's antipoverty agency. Meanwhile, internal and external criticism rendered it powerless. If SCLC's leaders had worked with UPO employees and other community organizers, they could have provided a national platform for these issues. But in choosing to bypass the city's antipoverty agencies, SCLC continued to fail Washington residents by ignoring local issues taking place just blocks beyond the monumental core.

SCLC's refusal to shine a light on local problems, while simultaneously

Protestors demonstrate outside the United Planning Organization headquarters. (Star Collection, D.C. Public Library © *Washington Post*)

asking for assistance from D.C. politicians, activists, and residents, drove a deep wedge between the local and national movements. Not only did SCLC's snubbing of black residents leave them to fend for themselves when it came to issues of poverty in the capital. It also forced them to navigate increased surveillance and repressive measures—measures enacted in large part because of SCLC's campaign—alone. Regardless, all eyes turned to the National Mall as the Poor People's Campaign commenced.

RESURRECTION CITY

On May 13, Ralph Abernathy, sporting a Levi's jacket and carpenter's apron, drove the first stake into Resurrection City. To the SCLC leader's great delight, the crowd chanted "Freedom! Freedom!" in time with his blows. But shortages in funds caused immediate problems for the PPC. Four days after its ceremonious beginnings, SCLC had built shelters for only seven hundred residents.

Eight hundred additional participants were temporarily forced to stay elsewhere, with another fifteen hundred scheduled to arrive within days. In light of this critical housing shortage, SCLC leaders held an impromptu press conference announcing the need for more than $3 million in additional funds.[88]

Mayor Walter Washington nervously watched the news unfold from his District office. The mayor presided over a city still reeling from the King assassination, as well as a local government and police department already stretched thin. In October 1967, his police department presided over antiwar demonstrations that brought one hundred thousand protestors to the city and led to almost seven hundred arrests. Fearful that a disorganized campaign could bring further disorder, he brought together all city department heads to expedite aid and speed the construction of the encampment. He and other city officials quietly began aiding the campaign in early May, making plans to feed demonstrators, provide emergency housing, health services, blankets, and raincoats.[89]

Two weeks after Abernathy drove the first stake into Resurrection City, a city of A-frame huts made of plywood and canvas filled the six city blocks along Constitution Avenue NW, between the white marble of the Lincoln Memorial and the National Mall. Nine caravans, including ones from the Deep South, Midwest, and Appalachia, delivered more than two thousand demonstrators to the capital. They quickly adjusted to life in Resurrection City. Residents created streets out of the grassy space between tents and gave them names like Love Lane and Abernathy Avenue. They also took good care of their own homes and used the three hundred gallons of paint donated to the campaign to personalize their tents. Some honored their hometowns by naming their huts "Cleveland's Rat Patrol," "Motown," and "Beale Street Baptists," among others. The makeshift streets were lined with larger wood structures for the city's governing council, health and dental clinic, cafeteria, freedom school, and cultural exchange center. Inside the camp, barbers, marshals, doctors, and teachers all kept busy. Meanwhile demonstrators participated in daily protests at the Capitol and the Departments of Labor, Interior, Education and Agriculture, learning advocacy techniques and how to confront their political representatives.[90]

While the early days of Resurrection City were peaceful, accounts of violence within and outside the camp soon emerged. Reports of rapes, muggings, and theft heightened the perception among D.C. officials that SCLC leadership was losing control of its campaign. Meanwhile, local hospitals carried the burden of treating out-of-towners, from those with mild complaints to others such as South Carolina resident James Walter, who was shot in the leg in the

Mayor Walter Washington during a visit to Resurrection City.
(Star Collection, D.C. Public Library © *Washington Post*)

encampment. Food provisions also proved a strain as demonstrators turned for help to local private organizations, church groups, and the D.C. Health and Welfare Council. An ad hoc committee led by Joseph Danzansky, president of Giant Foods, Inc., had agreed to contribute meals for Resurrection City since mid-May. By the end of the campaign, Danzansky estimated that the group had provided 185,000 meals, using roughly $75,000 in manpower and supplies from local grocery store chains and the Washington Hotel Association.[91]

The heaviest strain on participants and planners was one for which they could not have reasonably prepared: exceedingly wet weather. For more than half of Resurrection City's lifespan, it poured, including two inches of rain in a twenty-four-hour period in mid-June. "The site is literally a sea of mud, which is about five inches deep and about the consistency of a thick milk shake," wrote National Park Service Director Nash Castro, who visited Resurrection City at the end of May. "I . . . was appalled to find that the conditions there are even worse than I had expected," he admitted to DOJ officials.[92]

The mud, combined with massive puddles of water pooling across the Mall, slowed the demonstrators' momentum and hurt morale. It also hindered volunteers' ability to provide meals and basic sewage functions. Camp doctors worried that the contaminated water and limited shelter posed serious health risks. The media focused on these visible problems in unsympathetic articles with headlines such as "For the 'Poor March': Detours," "Turmoil in Shantytown," and "Poverty: Courting Trouble." Ultimately the press emphasized the unraveling of the campaign and disorder of the camp rather than the problem of poverty that drew so many to Resurrection City in the first place.[93]

Despite conditions at Resurrection City, the government's disapproval of the campaign's day-to-day activities, and the media's largely negative coverage, SCLC leaders continued to organize the campaign's capstone event, Solidarity Day, a rally at the Lincoln Memorial on June 19. Leaders chose the date, also known as Juneteenth, because it commemorated the anniversary of when the last slaves in Texas learned of their freedom following the end of the Civil War in 1865. In late May, longtime King associate Bayard Rustin, initially a critic of the Poor People's Campaign, volunteered to replicate the organizing work he did for the 1963 March on Washington. SCLC readily accepted his offer. The media praised Rustin's credentials, and government officials breathed a sigh of relief knowing that the pacifist had taken charge.[94]

However, not everyone approved of Rustin's leadership. Representative Joe Pool (D-Tex.) led the political opposition against the civil rights leader. "Under Rustin's leadership," Pool told Attorney General Clark, the demonstration "is part of an organized effort to undermine established government and orderly society in America." Pool urged Clark to issue a court injunction against the PPC. If an injunction was not issued, he warned, "the city of Washington may again be sacked as it was in April." Although his premonition did not come true, Pool believed that "professional agitators" had already corrupted the "shantytown organization." Their "increasingly rowdy" activities in the camp suggested to him that Solidarity Day was a colossal mistake.[95]

Rustin ultimately did not fare much better within SCLC. He quickly alienated leadership by releasing to the press a list of specific demands titled "Call to Americans of Goodwill," which Rustin believed contained more immediate and realistic demands than Ralph Abernathy's vague organizing statement. Outraged that Rustin acted without consulting SCLC leadership, Abernathy and other SCLC officials dismissed Rustin after only two weeks of service. After SCLC and Rustin parted ways, many people, including the stunned press, turned against the campaign. "In rejecting Mr. Rustin and his program, the divided Southern Christian Leadership Conference has thrown away its best chance to rally broad national backing for a worthy but faltering crusade," the *New York Times* scolded.[96]

Following Rustin's departure, SCLC assigned D.C. Urban League Director Sterling Tucker to finalize plans for Solidarity Day. Born in Akron, Ohio, in

1923, Tucker ran the Canton Urban League before relocating to Washington in 1956 to head the D.C. Urban League. The lean and bespectacled Tucker caught the eye of New York mayor John Lindsay, who tried to recruit him to direct New York's antipoverty efforts in 1966. Tucker had declined, claiming that his job in Washington was not complete.[97]

Tucker's work was not unilaterally admired. Speaking out after a 1967 Black Power Conference in Newark, New Jersey, D.C. activist Julius Hobson had strong words for Tucker and other local leaders of moderate civil rights organizations. He called them "black prostitutes" for leveraging the uprising to raise funds for their organizations. Other Washington delegates railed against Tucker, too, emphasizing that the city's black masses desperately sought new leadership. "Just as no single white man speaks or attempts to speak for the entire white community, we wish to warn that no single black man in D.C., least of all Sterling Tucker, speaks for the black community of this city," they cautioned.[98] Despite these critiques of Tucker, the *Washington Post* hailed him as a "veteran organizer, noted for his broad access to both white 'establishment' and the world of the black 'militant.'" The paper noted approvingly that he was "a frequent guest at the White House and the District Building" and, during the riots, had "equal access to police headquarters and the SNCC office on U Street, N.W."[99]

SCLC's decision to tap Tucker reflected a stronger understanding of the way that local conditions helped shape national campaigns. By harnessing Tucker's knowledge of the District, as well as his wide range of local and federal contacts, SCLC steered Solidarity Day back on track and executed a flawless event. On June 19, fifty thousand protesters, including residents from the Washington area, demonstrators living in Resurrection City, and others who caravanned by bus and car, marched from the Washington Monument to the Lincoln Memorial, where Ralph Abernathy gave a stirring, albeit long-winded, speech. "We have shown this government that the poor are there, that the poor can make themselves heard, that the poor are silent no more," he proclaimed.[100]

More inspiring was the rousing speech Coretta Scott King gave the same day. In a speech that rivaled her husband's forceful rhetoric, she connected poverty, policy neglect, and systemic violence. Rather than focusing on violence committed *by* oppressed people, King argued, society should pay attention to the economic violence done *to* them. "Poverty can produce a most deadly kind of violence," she said, explaining that starving a child, punishing a mother, offering substandard housing, and ignoring medical needs all exemplified the routine violence committed against poor people and minority groups. Other women, including National Council of Negro Women president

Dorothy Height, American Indian activist Martha Grass, white welfare rights organizer Peggy Terry, and black singer Eartha Kitt, also captivated the audience with empowering speeches that demonstrated the importance of women, particularly women of color, to the fight against poverty.[101]

SCLC organizers rejoiced over the demonstration's results: the marchers, ten thousand more than campaign leaders had predicted, represented all ages, races, and classes and had remained orderly and peaceful throughout the day. However, their celebration was short-lived. On June 20, one day after Solidarity Day, police clashed with demonstrators who had headed to the Department of Agriculture to renew demands for an expanded surplus-food program for the poor. When the demonstrators turned to mass civil disobedience, blocking the Department's doorways and rush hour traffic on 12th Street NW, police arrested seventy-seven of them. Most of those arrested went limp and allowed police to drag them to buses that would then take them to police headquarters. Others proved more resistant, confronting those officers who had chosen to use their nightsticks to restore order. News of the protest gone awry traveled quickly through the camp. Waves of demonstrators—upwards of five hundred at peak strength—arrived on the scene to see what had happened. With clubs swinging, police dragged onlookers out of the street and onto the sidewalk.[102]

As the remaining three hundred demonstrators crossed the Washington monument grounds on their way back to camp, they scuffled with a lone Park policeman, who immediately called for backup. One hundred fifty officers from Park and Metropolitan Police units arrived on the scene. The situation quickly escalated as demonstrators hurled bottles, rocks, and baton sticks at the policemen. Policemen responded by throwing fifteen tear gas canisters into the crowd and several more over the fence into Resurrection City. Police finally retreated after campaign marshals shepherded the demonstrators back into Resurrection City.[103]

Three days later the peace was shattered again when a few youths—reported to be from Milwaukee's NAACP Youth Council—threw rocks at Park Police officers stationed outside the camp. Howard University's Michael Harris observed the incident firsthand. As he recalled, "[They] were going to move in on us with their guns and billy clubs. We didn't have any—I realized what a real position we were in." Instead of billy clubs, though, the officers fired several rounds of tear gas into the encampment. Thick clouds of gas rolled through the campgrounds, and hundreds of residents ran out of their tents, choking, vomiting, and screaming. After that, Harris knew that the demonstration was "no plaything"—it was "a life and death struggle," he said somberly. Though peace was soon restored, the damage had been done.[104]

SCLC and DOJ leaders disagreed over whether the police response was warranted. The gassing was "worse than anything I ever saw in Mississippi or Alabama," Andrew Young fumed. "You don't shoot tear gas into an entire city because two or three hoodlums are throwing rocks."[105] Resurrection City 's leaders were left shaken. Yet internal Justice Department memoranda indicate that officials were satisfied with how Park Police and local officers had controlled skirmishes, found police officer morale high, and charged that SCLC's failure to impose proper sanctions for the June 20 uprising had created a general lack of discipline within the camp. Based on those intelligence reports, National Park Service officials denied SCLC a permit extension and told the organization to be out of Resurrection City first thing on Monday, June 24.[106]

National politicians across the political spectrum, from Democratic presidential hopeful Senator Eugene McCarthy (Minn.) to Republican governor Ronald Reagan (Calif.), spoke in favor of the decision to close Resurrection City. By June, Mayor Washington, who had reluctantly made arrangements for participants to feel at home in the District, regarded the continued occupation of Resurrection City as counterproductive and, "quite simply, menacing."[107] D.C. Corporation counsel Charles Duncan, a black official who sympathized with the campaign, agreed. "The situation had gotten quite out of hand in terms of who the residents were," Duncan recalled that December. "It was obvious that leadership, in my opinion at least, had failed." Duncan lamented the fact that the camp's day-to-day problems overshadowed "a very beautiful opportunity for concrete achievement and symbolism which the city represented."[108]

Some District white organizations, such as the Kalorama Citizens Association, expressed vindication for having opposed Resurrection City from the beginning. The group had vehemently disagreed with the National Park Service's decision to grant camp residents a permit with such unprecedented freedoms. Furthermore, it could not believe that the Park Police and Metropolitan Police Department had agreed, in their view, to refrain from enforcing the law. In their stead, the group rather hyperbolically charged, self-appointed rangers ruled in "a reign of lawlessness such as has been without parallel in our history" with "rapes, beating, burglaries, and other crimes" taking place "every hour of the day."[109]

The Park Police estimated that about one hundred assaults and other violent incidents had occurred inside the camp since its mid-May opening and reported that at least twenty visitors had been robbed, beaten, or stabbed by residents outside the encampment. Campaign officials acknowledged that media reports about camp violence were largely true. However, they objected to the exaggerated frequency of the reports, the omission of details about police provocation, and the almost singular focus on violence and turmoil in the camp. When *Washington Post* reporters interviewed Alvin Jackson, a local TV repairman and self-proclaimed chief security marshal at Resurrection City, he requested that they not just report the bad news. "Put in all the good, too," he urged. Nevertheless, Jackson acknowledged disappointment with the changing tenor of the camp: "Men are getting tired of coming home from a day's picketing to find their belongings stolen or their wives raped," he said. Jackson had used two weeks of vacation and all of his nights off, as well as a week's leave of absence, to help. Now he lamented that SCLC leadership "just won't allow any kind of discipline in the camp."[110]

For many Resurrection City residents, June 19's Solidarity Day was the Poor People's Campaign's natural endpoint. The majority left after the day's events, leaving about five or six hundred people in the camp, according to DOJ estimates. Roughly half of those left by bus and car following the violent events of June 20 and 23 and the announcement of Resurrection City's closure.[111] Despite Ralph Abernathy's promise that they would stay indefinitely, SCLC leaders admitted that they, too, were ready for the campaign to end. The campaign "has become a noose around our neck," one SCLC official told a reporter.[112] Hosea Williams, King's chief field lieutenant, had been hesitant to go forward with the campaign after King died and exhaled a little more deeply when the government ordered them "out of that mud hole."[113] Even Poor People's Campaign architect Andrew Young acknowledged that "whoever cleared us out may have done us a favor." However, Abernathy did not leave without one last protest; while he agreed to allow police to close down Resurrection City, he arranged for the remaining residents to march to Capitol Hill and allow police to arrest them as a symbol of their protest against Congress.[114]

The task of clearing out Resurrection City fell to the Park Police, which had jurisdiction over the area but had only a tenth of the manpower of the D.C. Metropolitan Police Department. Roger Wilkins, head of the Justice Department's Community Relations Service Division, anticipated problems with this arrangement. Reflecting on the situation in his 1982 memoir, Wilkins wrote, Park Police officers "just didn't like niggers" and, at the time, he had suspected they would be itching for revenge.[115] So he deftly arranged for the District's local police to be standing ready and waiting at Resurrection City's gates on the morning SCLC's permit expired. Dressed in military flak jackets and riot helmets, and armed with riot sticks, tear gas canisters, launchers, revolvers, and shotguns, the 1,000 policemen easily arrested the remaining 123 tent city inhabitants, whom they had found inside the camp singing freedom songs.

The District's Civil Disorder Unit sweeps through Resurrection City.
(Star Collection, D.C. Public Library © *Washington Post*)

The rest of the camp's residents had followed Abernathy to the Capitol, where police arrested 235 compliant demonstrators, including Abernathy, on charges of unlawful assembly.[116]

Following the mass arrests they made at both Resurrection City and the Capitol that morning, local police officers collided once more with national demonstrators in the afternoon; those whom they had not immediately arrested had migrated to 14th and U Streets NW, the epicenter of April's riots. When demonstrators began breaking windows and hurling rocks at the police, officers blanketed the area with tear gas. Mayor Washington quickly declared a state of emergency and ordered a citywide curfew. Between the morning of June 24 and the morning of June 26, officers arrested another 286 people around 14th and U Streets and elsewhere in the city—roughly half of which were for curfew violations. "It became very much a D.C. problem again," city attorney Charles Duncan said.[117]

Abernathy had hoped that returning to mass arrests, the protest strategy that had originally put SCLC on the map, would generate sympathetic media coverage. However, by the end of June, fears of lawlessness had swept the nation. That summer, Republican candidates stumped across the country on the platform of law and order. The media followed suit. Instead of sympathizing with the arrestees, local and national news outlets commended the police, Justice Department, federal troops, and even Mayor Washington for their tough stance on crime during the Poor People's Campaign.[118] Senator Byrd, who was notoriously resistant to black self-determination in the capital, was sure to contrast this action with what happened in April. "Had the same firm and prompt action been manifested in the April riot, the city and Washington's business community would have been spared the looting, the arson, and the destruction it suffered," he chastised.[119]

FROM RESURRECTION CITY TO CRIME CAPITAL

Before the mud had hardened on the National Mall, SCLC organizers began to evaluate the Poor People's Campaign. They generally deemed the effort a success. Not only did it help dramatize the plight of impoverished citizens across the country; it also proved that the organization could carry on without Martin Luther King. Beyond quantifiably measurable successes—three thousand Resurrection City residents, fifty thousand attendees at Solidarity Day, extensive news coverage—it broke ground in uniting the poor across demographic divides. "It was in our wallowing together in the mud of Resurrection City that we were allowed to hear, to feel and to see each other for the first time in our American experience," SCLC leader and future Democratic presidential nominee Jesse Jackson said. "This vast task of acculturation, of pulling the poor together as a way of amassing economic, political, and labor power, was the great vision of Dr. King," he added.[120] Similarly, for local white organizer Kay Shannon, the campaign succeeded "because it radicalized an awful lot of people." The Poor People's Campaign "was an extremely valuable educational tool for the whole society," she explained. "It was a national demonstration; it was a great, great, sit-in, sleep-in, stay-in and demonstrate-in, and it came to Washington."[121]

Behind the scenes, SCLC's Marian Wright lobbied bureaucrats in several federal agencies to push for policy changes, including $100 million for free and reduced-price lunches for schoolchildren; $25 million for Office of Economic Opportunity and Head Start programs in Alabama and Mississippi; the hiring of over thirteen hundred poor people by OEO agencies; a small expansion of the federal food stamp program; and changes to federal welfare guidelines that punished female welfare recipients. Etta Horn and the NWRO also forged relationships with members of Congress and officials in the Health, Education, and Welfare Department over the course of the Poor People's Campaign to improve local black women's conditions. In fact, after SCLC left town, the number of local NWRO affiliates grew. In January 1968, the national office had recognized five D.C. chapters, each averaging twenty-five members. By August 1969, it counted nineteen local groups, with roughly 850 members, and by July 1970, D.C. membership in various groups rose to thirteen hundred people, all from diverse neighborhoods and housing complexes throughout the District. Throughout the late 1960s and early 1970s, low-income black Washington women fought for control over their sexual behavior, protested practices that restricted their reproductive rights, and pressed for better health care options.[122]

Due in large part to King's assassination, the PPC did include African Americans who might not have otherwise supported it. Despite rumors that Stokely Carmichael would disrupt the campaign, his public support ultimately encouraged other militants to join the effort. Howard students, who had been turned off by SCLC's continued insistence on nonviolence, found their experiences down on the Mall empowering. And local black government officials and activists like Walter Fauntroy and Sterling Tucker worked behind the scenes on behalf of SCLC. But the Poor People's Campaign's success came at a price.[123]

The campaign had asked a lot of Washington residents. In addition to SCLC's requests for local organizers, participants, and general hospitality, the campaign tied up the city's resources and sidetracked the local government for much of the summer. Even though federal officials were primarily responsible for Resurrection City itself, the problems of health, sanitation, police, and to a lesser extent, transportation and fire all fell on the District. To reduce the prospects of another uprising, local officials and businesspeople worked to ensure that participants were properly cared for. According to Deputy Coordinator Tony Henry, "People in business and government here were concerned at first to see that the people who came here were well-fed and well-cared for on the theory that that would lessen the frustrations of the camp and lessen the likelihood of rioting, or things getting out of hand." But when demonstrators wanted to leave, Henry admitted, "there was the immediate influx of people needing various services"—services that SCLC failed to provide.[124]

On the local level, one of SCLC's biggest missteps, aside from bypassing the city's United Planning Organization, was ignoring the city's Black United Front. When SCLC proved unwilling to take BUF's inquiries seriously, it condemned the organization in a sprawling manifesto that accused SCLC of exploiting the District for national gain: "SCLC failed to honor the commitment made by our late and beloved brother, Reverend Martin Luther King Jr., to involve the D.C. black community in its planning and to keep D.C. black people abreast of its plans." "Honkie cops didn't go down against SCLC. They went down against the entire black community of Washington, D.C.," BUF members charged. BUF criticized Solidarity Day as a "white-conceived exercise to divide the black community" and claimed that SCLC had not invited the city's all-black organizations to participate or apprised them of their plans. "How could any Solidarity Day be achieved," BUF asked, "when any segment of Black People is deliberately excluded?"[125]

BUF refused to absolve SCLC for descending on its city to push a civil rights agenda that overlooked Washington's own poor people, devastated neighborhoods, and colonial rule. After the campaign, BUF warned that "no organization is going to come into this city, program a protest and then expect D.C. black people to sit back and get put in a white racist trick bag." The group also offered an ultimatum to the national civil rights community. "Unless such organizations are prepared to join with D.C. black people in helping to build a strong and viable black community," it cautioned, "then we sternly warn against further protests which do not involve BUF." By juxtaposing SCLC's national campaign with the failure to administer justice on the local level, BUF emphasized the fragile ties between federal and municipal government, civil rights and Black Power, and between national demonstrations and local grassroots organizing.[126]

The PPC also exposed black Washington's intraracial class tensions. The city's black middle class was reluctant to help the nation's poor. In the early planning stages of the campaign, SCLC's Hosea Williams had speculated that "in order to move Congress, we had to move the Washington community" and advocated for spreading the poor people throughout the homes of sympathetic Washingtonians. When Williams's idea met with local resistance, he dropped it. But the underlying truth, that SCLC had trouble moving District residents, spoke to the deep divide between D.C.'s black lower- and middle-class residents. Johnson's home rule measure exacerbated these tensions. With the selective incorporation of black middle-class residents into local office, poor black Washingtonians became even more alienated.[127]

In the aftermath of SCLC's antipoverty campaign, many observers questioned the strength of the national civil rights movement. In contrast to how it lauded the 1963 March on Washington, the press painted Solidarity Day, and the Poor People's Campaign overall, as a failure. According to William Raspberry, a black columnist for the *Washington Post*, "What [Solidarity Day] taught us, perhaps, is that the day of the demonstration as an effective civil rights tool is over, that there can never be another Aug. 28, 1963."[128] Another black *Post* reporter agreed, calling the campaign "a story about a symbol that turned into a near disaster."[129]

Resurrection City was a risky endeavor, but one that reflected the necessity of flexibility and inventiveness within the civil rights movement at a time when activists were focused on firmly entrenched barriers to upward mobility, job security, and economic opportunity. At the center of SCLC's innovative campaign lay Washington, D.C., where organizers brought together a multiethnic coalition to draw visibility to those who suffered from poverty. And they succeeded. "The poor couldn't be missed," reported journalist John Neary in *Life*. "Go to the Lincoln Memorial and you could hear their guitars. Climb the Washington Monument and look over toward the Potomac and there below was this sprawling muddy mess of a shantytown, and you knew these were people who just plain didn't have the dime to take the elevator to the top," he wrote. The poor, Neary concluded, "never intend to be invisible again."[130]

But the campaign SCLC planned in the District depended heavily on local support while simultaneously overlooking the city's own poor residents and its specific racial, economic, and political problems—especially those heightened by the April riots just one month earlier. In this respect, SCLC failed spectacularly. It lost an opportunity to emphasize the supreme irony of the District: that the ultimate representation of federal power stood just blocks from where the city's black neighborhoods sat devastated from the April riots, decades of neglect, and a century of local disfranchisement. It was clear that the group's leaders paid attention to local Washington only when it was in their interest to do so.

Meanwhile, the nation had turned to different issues. In May 1968, *U.S. News and World Report*'s headline read, "Washington's fears go beyond riots and marches. The big and growing problem is crime." According to the magazine, "White residents are fleeing to suburbs as Negroes increase to nearly two thirds of the city's population; Washington's crime rate is one of the highest in any major city." Senator Byrd described the District as "a paradise for animalistic hoodlums where women cower in fear behind locked doors." "People are afraid to venture out on the streets at night," he said, and "law-abiding citizens are no longer assured that their Government will act to protect their lives and their properties."[131]

SCLC's Poor People's Campaign played right into these fears. The coordinated efforts between the White House, Department of Justice, and local government to manage lawlessness during the campaign signaled the growing concern in the District—and the nation at large—over a variety of issues that politicians broadly lumped into the category of law and order. As a result, Washington, D.C., became the focal point of the 1968 presidential campaign.

Stumping in Chattanooga, Tennessee, in September, Republican presidential candidate Richard Nixon told his audience not to trust Vice President Hubert Humphrey's promise to turn the District into a model city of law enforcement. "Death-bed conversions are always welcome—but where has Mr. Humphrey been these last four years while Washington, D.C., was becoming one of the crime capitals of the world?" he asked. As Nixon assumed the presidency, SCLC's hopes for a federal shift toward antipoverty programs spiraled into jeopardy. Meanwhile, Washingtonians waited to see what the new president had in store for them.[132]

4

D.C. SHOULD NOT STAND FOR DISORDER AND CRIME

RICHARD NIXON'S LAW-AND-ORDER CAMPAIGN

On May 1, 1967, Private William Rull shot nineteen-year-old Clarence Brooker in a scuffle outside a grocery store in Northeast D.C. Brooker died an hour later of massive internal hemorrhaging. He was one of four black citizens fatally shot by policemen that year. A coroner ruled his death a "justifiable homicide." Representatives from the Metropolitan Youth Council, a neighborhood youth group, wrote to the city's police commissioner to express their dismay at the verdict, one increasingly made in the cases of black deaths by white officers in the District of Columbia. "We feel that it was just another example of the sad state of affairs in law enforcement and justice in the District," they bemoaned.[1] Meanwhile, protestors assembled in front of the Fourteenth Precinct's police department to call for the immediate suspension of Private Rull and a complete investigation into Brooker's death. In response to community concerns, the District Attorney's office launched a grand jury investigation, in which a jury affirmed the coroner's decision and refused to indict Rull. Surveying the local racial landscape in the aftermath of the Brooker affair, a black employee in the D.C. Commissioners' office lamented that police-community tensions had increased substantially and worried that Washington had "all the ingredients" to spark a riot—a familiar admission in D.C. and one that came to fruition eleven months later.[2]

The responses to Clarence Brooker's death foreshadowed the larger debate over law and order brewing in the capital city. On the one hand, national officials sided with local police. Senator Robert Byrd and Representative Joel Broyhill, members of the House and Senate Committees on District affairs, even cautioned President Johnson against caving to the demands of black Washingtonians. Heading into the summer of 1967, Broyhill warned residents that their calls for community control would "engulf the city in a wave of lawlessness" and "destroy police morale" if left unchecked. Broyhill and Byrd's actions were telling. In the months leading up to the passage of Johnson's reorganization plan, they forcefully intervened in local affairs. They pitted black residents against white police officers and challenged White House officials to defy them.[3]

On the other hand, Brooker's death added to the growing antipolice sentiment within the city's black community. Black residents used the teen's death as a rallying cry against police misconduct. In fact, the Black United Front named police brutality as one of its main concerns when it formed in January 1968. Following the April riots, it raised the issue in a more formal setting, conducting public hearings on police-community relations. Its investigation led to a public airing of grievances against the local police force; renewed calls for the department's white chief of police, John Layton, to resign; and demands for neighborhood control of the police. But by the summer, residents' calls for community control were met with national calls for federal legislation to combat crime in Washington.[4]

Patrick Buchanan, Nixon's chief campaign strategist, seized on national anxieties, media attention, and racialized rhetoric to craft a D.C.-centric law-and-order platform during the lead-up to the 1968 election. Buchanan focused particular scrutiny on President Johnson's perceived failures in the capital and the racial anxieties they had inspired. Over the course of the campaign, Buchanan instructed Nixon's campaign staff to expose the city's "exorbitant" crime rate and craft speeches that reflected a desire to make the nation's capital "*the* model city." Through this strategy, they created high expectations to achieve visible results in the nation at large and in D.C. specifically. But once in office, they found themselves engaged in a prolonged political battle over control of the nation's capital.[5]

No president used law-and-order measures to curb Washingtonians' autonomy as did Nixon. As his administration embarked on its anticrime crusade, it dismantled community initiatives, reassigned local oversight from the mayor to the chief of police, and provided conditional monetary support of District policies. The cornerstone of the White House's anticrime initiative was the District of Columbia Court Reform and Criminal Procedure Act. The D.C. Crime Bill was a massive crime-control measure that would reorganize the city's courts and criminal procedure codes. The most controversial provisions of the legislation would allow the preventative detention of dangerous suspects before trial and the use of no-knock search warrants, which granted police the authority to search premises with a warrant but without first announcing their presence. While the constitutionally questionable provisions were hotly debated inside Congress, Washingtonians themselves had limited ways to protest them.

Johnson's 1967 reorganization plan had left local black municipal appointees —especially Mayor Walter Washington—in a precarious position vis-à-vis the federal government. They felt immense pressure to reduce crime. But they also recognized that Nixon's agenda would disproportionally target the constituents they were appointed to represent. Moreover, they knew that black residents deeply distrusted the local police department. Thus, they searched for alternatives to the White House's legislation. For years, community leaders had recommended citizen-participation with the police. The Johnson administration responded to these recommendations by approving the Pilot Precinct Project, an ambitious program funded by the federal government and coopted by local activists to improve police-community relations in the inner city. But as the Nixon administration embarked on its law-and-order crusade, it dismissed community efforts and demanded a quick and punitive federal response. In doing so, the White House undermined grassroots activism, forced the city's appointed government into a compromised position on the crime issue, and allowed the community's solution to crime to die a slow death.

Nixon's War on Crime presented Washington's white stakeholders with a tantalizing opportunity. Many were displeased with the ascendance of Washington's black leaders to municipal office following the implementation of Johnson's limited home rule measure. And they still blamed the city's poor black residents for the April riots following Martin Luther King's assassination and the tensions surrounding the summer's Poor People's Campaign. Whereas the riots had provided black residents with a platform from which to express their grievances, Nixon's anticrime crusade offered groups like the Washington Board of Trade and Federation of Citizens Associations their own platform to fight back.

As the city's municipal government tried to move out of the shadow of the riots, local white stakeholders partnered with national lawmakers and the Nixon administration to criminalize black Washingtonians and federalize policing efforts. Together, they used the crime issue to weaken black political influence in the city. Their efforts, combined with political compromises made by black municipal appointees and power struggles among black leaders, paved the way for the passage of punitive federal crime policy and the failure of community-based crime policy in the District. The former allowed the Nixon administration to declare victory in its political war against crime before handing control of the city back to the local black government it had spent over three years undermining.

LAW AND ORDER DURING THE 1968 CAMPAIGN SEASON

For Richard Nixon, no city better symbolized the dangers of the Democratic administration's liberal racial policies than the country's capital, to which President Johnson had recently granted new political autonomy. Following the April riots, which had devastated the District's black neighborhoods, Nixon positioned the city at the center of his presidential campaign. In a glossy pamphlet distributed to voters, with a picture of D.C.'s U Street neighborhood burning in view of the Washington Monument on the cover, the Nixon campaign argued that local criminals committed one thousand felonies each week, a rate of more than fifty thousand major crimes a year in a city of eight hundred thousand people. "The nation's capital has become one of the crime capitals of the nation. The disorders and the crime and the violence that are now commonplace in Washington are more than a national disgrace; they are cause for grave national concern," the pamphlet read. Even the slogan adopted in campaign materials marked a deliberate decision to shift the city away from its earlier aspirational moniker, the "capital of democracy," to the more dystopian "D.C. Disorder and Crime." In doing so, the Nixon campaign depicted the city as a symbol of urban decay.[6]

Statistics bolstered the campaign's narrative. Between 1964 and 1968, the city's crime rate increased over 200 percent, from 3,754 to 7,868 incidents per 100,000 people and from 30,334 to 63,653 total incidents. Incidents of violent crime more than doubled, from 5,112 to 12,180. By 1968, Washington's crime rate had risen to more than twice the national crime rate of 3,370 incidents per 100,000 people, making it the highest crime rate per capita in the country. California, which had the next highest crime rate, reported 5,721 incidents per 100,000 people, almost 30 percent lower than the District's. But still D.C. ranked twenty-seventh of fifty-two large cities on crime, trailing far behind Denver, Chicago, and New York, a figure that the Nixon campaign did not mention.[7]

President Johnson had intended to tackle the District's increasing crime rate during the fall of 1967. As he told newly appointed Mayor Walter Washington in October, the solution lay in passing legislation to provide better training for the city's police officers, build new precinct houses and jails, equip the police department with the latest technology, and control the circulation of arms in the city. In addition, he listed the court's backlogs, the correctional system's inefficiencies, and poor police-community relations as major concerns to address.[8] But Johnson's political capital had greatly diminished, thanks in large part to the crime issue. In November 1967, for example, members of a House Republican Task Force on Crime claimed that the president's "get tough" statements about the capital amounted to too little too late. "We are persuaded that this is nothing more than talk, born more of the realization that he couldn't ignore the problem forever than of any particular interest in ridding the District of crime," the task force asserted, paving the way for both his signing of the conservative-driven D.C. crime bill in December and for a Republican challenger to address the crime problem more aggressively.[9]

Between the unraveling of his domestic agenda and the escalation of the war in Vietnam, Johnson was not sure whether he could defeat a challenger from either party. For months he vacillated between running for reelection and stepping down. Johnson's March 1968 polling numbers told the story. A 36 percent approval and 52 percent disapproval rating for his overall performance, coupled with a 26 percent approval and 63 percent disapproval rating of his actions in Vietnam, helped persuade him not to run. On March 31, a week prior to Martin Luther King's assassination, the president announced that he would not seek or accept his party's nomination for another term.[10]

After withdrawing from the election, Johnson continued to lobby for safer streets with legislation to assist local law enforcement through federal grants to municipalities. His grant-in-aid program would empower Attorney General Clark to underwrite direct grants to local governments and to finance capital construction and research projects to deal with local crime problems. By the summer of 1968, the bill differed drastically from what the president had proposed. Conservatives had amended the legislation, distorting the president's original intentions and tacking on twenty-five amendments to make the bill unrecognizable. The coalition of Republicans and southern Democrats opposed to Johnson's proposal cited its threat to state's rights and the authority it granted the attorney general to dictate local policy among its chief objections.[11]

The Omnibus Crime Control and Safe Streets Act replaced municipal grants with federally funded block grants to states, thereby reassigning control of funds from Attorney General Clark to state governors. Unlike municipal grants, the block grants lacked specific federal mandates on how to allocate funds. The bill also created the Law Enforcement Assistance Administration, which strengthened ties between local police and the federal government and channeled more federal dollars into local police departments. In addition, conservative politicians had added provisions to Johnson's legislation that overturned three major Supreme Court rulings relating to defendants' rights, removed the federal courts' ability to review state court rulings on voluntary confessions, dramatically expanded the legal use of electronic surveillance, stripped the bill of its gun-control provisions, and disqualified from federal employment any person convicted of a felony committed during a riot.[12]

Johnson debated rejecting the bill. But given the political climate, the ease with which it sailed through both chambers of Congress, and the harmful effect of a veto on Vice President Hubert Humphrey's presidential aspirations, he reluctantly signed it in June, stating that it contained "more good than bad." The conservative takeover of his Safe Streets legislation upset Johnson. Unlike conservatives, the president believed that crime fed on issues of poverty, ignorance, thwarted opportunities, and unemployment. He sought to pair proposals to intensify the attack against crime with the benchmarks of his Great Society program: jobs, education, and fair housing, all issues that conservatives tried to decouple from crime prevention measures.[13]

Like Nixon, Johnson wanted to make Washington "a showcase of safety and security for all the people."[14] Yet throughout his presidency he wrestled with how much emphasis he should give to the nation's capital. As Johnson's attorney general, Nicholas Katzenbach, told him in December 1965, "We do not favor a comprehensive crime bill which pledges to make the District a model city and leads the public to expect immediate and drastic reductions in crime." White House aides feared that unrealistic promises to restore order and control crime in Washington would jeopardize their credibility, as well as the reputation of law enforcement officials. Even so, by signing the 1967 D.C. Crime Bill and the 1968 Safe Streets Act, Johnson created the largest crime-fighting apparatus that the nation had ever seen and set the stage for Nixon's national presidential campaign.[15]

On the campaign trail, Nixon continued to craft stories about Washington's rampant lawlessness that conflated race and crime and drew negative attention to the capital. His stump speeches included portraits of roving gangs that extorted downtown business owners with threats of looting and arson, Marine Corps officers shot midday in wealthy Georgetown, and a bus system targeted by armed thugs. Nixon also generalized from the D.C. example to offer a cautionary tale intended to appeal to the nation's white business and property owners. Under Johnson's watch, he argued, the crime crisis had thrown tens of millions of dollars in business, revenue, and private property into jeopardy.[16]

With Johnson out of the race, Nixon turned his attention toward his Democratic challenger, Vice President Humphrey. "A few days ago," Nixon told a rapt crowd in Chattanooga, Tennessee, on a warm September day, "my opponent made the great promise to turn Washington, D.C., into a model city of law enforcement. Death bed conversions are always welcome—but where has Mr. Humphrey been these last four years while Washington, D.C., was becoming one of the crime capitals of the world?"[17] Two weeks before the general election, Nixon continued his assault on the vice president. "Mr. Humphrey is the do-nothing candidate on law and order. While he has been at the center of power and responsibility, the worst crime wave in history has swept the nation and crime has risen nine times as rapidly as the population," Nixon told onlookers in Cincinnati, Ohio. Zeroing in on the capital, the candidate described the District as an "occupied city," once again conflating race and crime in a coded message to voters about the majority-black city.[18]

In Dayton, Ohio, the Republican challenger made his own pledge. "If I am elected President in November the war on crime in this country will begin in January. Crime in America will receive the Federal attention, resources and priority it deserves," Nixon promised. "My friends," he concluded, "we are going to wage an all-out war against crime in this country, and we are going to win it." The candidate's message was clear: social programs were a distraction, Democrats were ineffective, and, in a Nixon White House, the federal government would intervene directly in District affairs to win the war on crime.[19]

The first thing Nixon intended to do was replace Johnson's attorney general, Ramsey Clark, who had come under fire during the summer of 1968. Republicans negatively characterized Clark as "more social worker than cop" and accused him of permitting the Justice Department's criminal division to languish. Despite Clark's work in the field of civil rights, Nixon called his efforts to curb the nation's crime rate "indifferent, lame, and ineffectual." As Nixon's campaign gained steam, Clark's response to the 1968 riots, his sympathy for SCLC's Poor People's Campaign, and the perception that he was "soft on crime" made him vulnerable to conservative attacks.[20]

In Nixon's August acceptance speech at the Republican National Convention in Miami, Florida, the presidential nominee devoted considerable time to the question of the attorney general's fitness to run the DOJ. Following the Republican Party's official nomination, Nixon intensified his criticisms of the attorney general. According to the *Washington Post*, "Clark himself seems somewhat surprised to find himself in the eye of the storm raging over law enforcement, charged with coddling criminals and fiddling as the lawless roam the streets with murder, rape, and arson daily occurrences in every city." But the attorney general did not waiver on his belief that law-and-order measures had to be coupled with Johnson's Great Society programming—a connection that Nixon actively sought to sever. Through the construction of a presidential campaign that conflated race and crime, stoked fears of lawlessness, and targeted Johnson's top man in the Justice Department, Nixon strategists made a calculated appeal to white voters.[21]

Over the summer, the city's white merchants welcomed Nixon's targeted appeals. During Johnson's presidency, they too had taken up the mantle of law and order. In June 1968, Board of Trade president William Calomiris expressed reservations over Johnson's performance during the summer of alleged lawlessness. "The business community and I believe all District residents—in fact all Americans—are deeply concerned about the maintenance of law and order here in the National Capital," Calomiris told Johnson in an open letter. He praised the president for advocating for an increase in law enforcement personnel to handle the "inner-city problems" that undermined the group's success and to a larger extent hindered the city's economy. Nonetheless, he maintained that Johnson's inability to restore order to the District following the April riots spelled disaster.[22]

For Washington's white stakeholders, Johnson's reorganization plan had compounded the crime problem. In July, the Federation of Citizens Associations chafed at the local government's allegedly militant body. Speaking on behalf of its nearly fifty thousand white members, the Federation said, "we continue to be disturbed by the apparent tolerance in the District government, and particularly by some members in the District City Council, who continue to participate in radical groups which have taken and are endeavoring to promote positions which harass the police adversely, affect their morale and subject already poor community relations to further deterioration." According to the Federation, black council members who did not speak out against the city's radical groups or in favor of its police department actively harmed their community. By accusing black officials of participating in "radical" groups and implying that their involvement in those groups disqualified them from local office, the Federation used the crime issue to discredit progressive local representatives.[23]

July events had particularly aggravated racial tensions in the community. Since its January 1968 founding, the Black United Front had called attention to the issue of police brutality. In early July, it raised its critique of the police into a defense of black defendants when it termed the killing of a white police officer at the hands of three black residents "justifiable homicide." BUF's statement infuriated Mayor Washington, who called it "inflammatory, irresponsible, and unfortunate." Walter Fauntroy, vice chairman of the city council and BUF steering committee member, was not present when BUF's resolution passed. He joined Washington in denouncing the rhetoric as "wrong."

Fauntroy, who remained silent for almost a week, had come under congressional pressure to resign either from his city council post or from the Black United Front. Fauntroy refused. Renouncing his membership in BUF would be akin to renouncing his citizenship, he explained, since he did not agree with all federal policies. But that did not stop Representative Mendel L. Rivers (D-S.C.) and Senator Daniel Brewster (D-Md.) from calling on President Johnson to reconsider Fauntroy's local appointment, a move the *Washington Post* called "an inexpensive ploy for publicity."[24]

When asked whether he condoned the statement, Reverend Channing Phillips, BUF member and newly elected leader of the D.C. delegate to the Democratic National Convention, said, "Well I was there and the vote was unanimous." Phillips, who was widely respected in D.C., also emphasized that it was the unjust system that precipitated violence rather than individuals that deserved the blame and implored Washingtonians to focus on the intentions of BUF's message. "The attempt to police the community from the outside produces hostility from the person policed," he added, alluding to the growing enthusiasm for community-based solutions in the capital.[25]

Two weeks after the controversy, and ten weeks after the riots, two white policemen shot a young black man to death while he was carrying groceries out of a Safeway Supermarket. Though the larger black community had spurned BUF for its "justifiable homicide" comments, the *Washington Afro-American* acknowledged the legitimacy of the underlining sentiment. "If there is anything redemptive about the Black United Front's controversial resolution two weeks ago, it is that no matter how much cruelty exists in the black community, it has roots in wrongs inflicted by the white community in the past and present and those which we may expect in the future." While D.C. residents still considered BUF extreme in its views, the city council invited the group to make a more formal presentation in the fall.[26]

According to many white residents, including those in the Kalorama Citizens Association, one of the Federation's thirty-four neighborhood groups located in Northwest D.C., the Metropolitan Police Department needed to be given more, not less, power. They felt this even more strongly after witnessing the unprecedented powers that the Johnson administration granted SCLC during the summer's Poor People's Campaign, when neither Park Police nor MPD officers were permitted to enter Resurrection City. Instead Poor People's Campaign participants created their own internal police force. "The result," the Kalorama group said with disgust, "was a reign of lawlessness such as has been without parallel in our history, with rapes, beatings, burglaries, and other crimes taking place every hour of the day." Due in part to their accounting of the summer's events, the group demanded a reversal of the trend toward citizen participation.[27]

While the city's white neighborhood groups largely aligned themselves with the Nixon campaign and in support of increased punitive measures to curb crime, some white groups did criticize the MPD. In August 1968, the National Capital Area Civil Liberties Union issued a damning report on the city's police force. "A Police Department in Trouble" focused on the general racial discrimination and misconduct rampant in the D.C. police department and on the specific military occupation of the city during the summer's Poor People's Campaign. For the District's American Civil Liberties Union branch, police officers simply were not doing their job. "Unless the city is prepared to face the prospect of continuing military occupation, order can be maintained only if the police department is made to reduce drastically the number of physical attacks and other abuses directed at Negro citizens," the organization warned.[28]

The Black United Front also spoke out on behalf of the city's most vulnerable residents. In July and August, it conducted its own public hearings on police-community relations. Then, in September, it announced: "The Black community has now decided to turn to itself and either create a meaningful change in the police or eliminate the police—as they exist—from our community entirely. The Front declares that without justice—Black justice—there will be no law and order." At a time when the local and national spotlight was on black citizens' propensity for crime, BUF shifted attention toward the city's police force. BUF had many questions. Why, when the city was majority black, was the police force over 80 percent white? Why, it wondered, were officers recruited from outside the city? By 1968, the statistics were bleak. Ninety-five percent of the city's 2,199 white police officers lived in the Maryland or Virginia suburbs. To put it more bluntly, the group asked, "Why are there low-educated southern racists on the D.C. police force?" To address this issue, BUF recommended that the MPD implement a residence requirement for officers. "Anyone who feels he is too good to live in the Black community is not qualified to serve in that community," the group explained.[29]

In addition to the residency requirement, BUF called for the immediate prohibition of all-white police patrols in the black community, an end to an MPD rule that barred those with police records from being hired, and the election of precinct-level and citywide citizen boards to set standards for police conduct, recruit new officers, and review citizen complaints against officers. In some respects, BUF offered a more militant critique of the police than would traditionally resonate with the District's black middle-class residents. However, the overabundance of white policemen in black neighborhoods remained a sticking point for many, and the addition of black officers was seen as a popular solution to the problem of police-community relations. Black councilman William Thompson even gave BUF mild praise when he said that its platform had "many good aspects."[30]

BUF also demanded the termination of the city's police chief, John Layton. After over three decades with the MPD, Layton had cemented a culture of racism within the force. Even after Mayor Washington stripped him of some of his powers, he retained his title and remained a pernicious reminder of the force's brutality. According to his critics, the problem was that he lacked the training, experience, and personality to improve police-community relations. Even worse, he had come to symbolize, according to *Washington Post* columnist William Raspberry, "all that was wrong with the Metropolitan Police Department." Thus, it was not a surprise to see BUF seize on the hot-button issue.[31]

BUF's call for Layton's termination angered the Randle Highlands Citizens Association, a white neighborhood group that represented Southeast D.C. residents in Anacostia. The group had witnessed white flight from its neighborhood to the surrounding suburbs during the 1950s and 1960s. By 1968, the group's leaders presided over a diminished power base. For them, BUF's motivations reeked of "reverse racism." "How utterly ridiculous these statements are," the group's presidents, Joseph Mosesso and Morris Clark, said dismissively. "The real truth," the duo suggested, "is they do not want a white Chief of Police, nor to be policed by a white policeman." "Thank goodness this is not the feeling of the good non-white citizen; they are grateful to see a policeman when needed regardless of their color," they added. In making this claim, the group refused to allow BUF to speak for black Washingtonians but freely did so itself. But even more damning than the group's decision to bifurcate the black community into good and bad segments was its inability to understand what BUF continued to underscore: that Layton's police force had taken a physical and psychic toll on members of the black community.[32]

Without explicitly mentioning race, the Federation, to which the Randle Highlands Citizens Association belonged, painted black residents in broad criminal strokes. In an August statement to the D.C. City Council regarding public safety, the group explained that one of the city's greatest problems was the growing disrespect residents had for the law. It instructed the city government to offer its support to the police "from the top of the government down" and give "short shrift" to those who attempted to downgrade the police in effort to satisfy ulterior political goals. In addition, it demanded that the local government devise and initiate programs that would "promote respect for the law in those segments of our citizenry who do not now have it." But the Federation feared that the city's black-majority government would not accomplish its agenda. "It is a fact that the worst outbreak of lawlessness in the history of Washington occurred under the new City Government," it said pointedly. Thus, while it gave unsolicited counsel to local officials, it also worked methodically to erode trust in them.[33]

As for local black activists' alternative crime prevention proposals, the Federation sharply objected. "We believe that these proposals spring from a false premise, namely that the people regard the police as their enemy," it said, adding that black demands to replace Layton with a black candidate constituted "extreme racism." In fact, it argued, attacks against Layton could only be ascribed to groups "bent on destroying our Police Department to create anarchy in the District." By undermining both black government officials and community activists during the fall of 1968, the Federation hoped to curry favor with Nixon, whose path to the White House had been built on promises to restore law and order to the capital. But it remained to be seen how the incoming president's anticrime efforts would intersect with struggles for black self-determination.[34]

RICHARD NIXON COMES TO WASHINGTON

District residents found themselves in the unique position of having voted overwhelmingly against the man who, in January 1969, became their newest neighbor and chief executive. Eighty-two percent of Washingtonians had voted for Hubert Humphrey in this election, only the second time they had been able to vote in a presidential contest. Since Nixon campaigned so stridently on the crime issue, many suspected he would have a strong hand in local policy. BUF was skeptical that he would embrace any racially progressive measures. "What we expect from Richard Nixon is concentration camps, but we will allow him a chance to fulfill the theme of his campaign—forward together," one member said.[35]

Washington residents tuned in to Nixon's first presidential address for insight into how he planned to govern the city. In his speech, the president committed to giving the District greater power over local affairs. However, his plan followed a more ambiguous timeline than home rule advocates preferred. "I continue to support home rule, but I consider the timing of that effort the key, as is proven by its past history of failure," he said, referring to the House District Committee's decades-long refusal to pass a bill. Instead, Nixon explained,

"I will seek within the present system to strengthen the role of the local government in the solution of local problems."[36]

BUF was not persuaded. The group denounced the president's intentionally vague statements and accused him of being complicit in Congress's decades-long racist agenda. "We are united in our opposition to President Nixon's perfumed colonialism for D.C. that denies people the right to vote for their own local government. In a democracy there is no such thing as 'eventual home rule,'" it said. With home rule again delayed, and crime declared as a national problem, residents and local officials were left to speculate about their role in local policy.[37]

The president wasted little time outlining his agenda to combat Washington's crime problem. "The rapidly mounting urgency of the crime crisis in the District makes immediate, direct anticrime measures the first priority task," Nixon said just eleven days after taking office.[38] His plan hinged on the control of crime and the more efficient administration of justice, both of which would strip local officials of significant powers. To implement his program, the president assembled a small team of trusted advisers, including John Ehrlichman, Egil "Bud" Krogh, and Daniel Patrick "Pat" Moynihan. Perhaps most detrimental to the city's autonomy, Nixon appointed Donald "Don" Santarelli, his crime policy adviser during the 1968 campaign, to a special D.C. post in the Department of Justice and unofficially assigned John Mitchell, his campaign manager, close friend, and newly appointed attorney general, greater supervision over the city's governance.[39]

Don Santarelli, a twenty-nine-year-old lawyer who had drafted many of the position papers on crime for the campaign, was in the process of joining the DOJ when he first met with the president and his top advisers to discuss possible law-and-order initiatives in January 1969. Santarelli knew they had to find a way to make good on the many promises made during the campaign and do something dramatic in the area of law enforcement. In his view, the capital was the perfect staging ground to test new weapons and tactics, first because it was the only place where the federal government had the authority to address crime, and second because it allowed them to "exercise vigorous symbolic leadership." "With the president and attorney general as spokesmen, we could elevate the issue of crime to the level of the president," he stated. Over the next six months, Santarelli evaluated the plausibility—and legality—of law-and-order actions and helped outline a wide-ranging anticrime program for the nation's capital.[40]

The White House's program, which served as the blueprint for its D.C.

Crime Bill, contained reforms of the bail system, including the recommendation that dangerous criminals be held without bail while awaiting trial; new juvenile codes, including the elimination of jury trials for juveniles; more effective police recruitment policies; and no-knock provisions that would allow police officers to more easily search suspects' premises by entering without announcing themselves. To modernize the city's courts, the president also called for the appointment of ten additional judges for the D.C. courts, forty additional assistant U.S. attorneys, and the addition of one thousand policemen.[41]

For the white residents in Washington's numerous neighborhood groups, the high crime rate was an incentive to lobby for federal intervention over local sovereignty. Fear of black crime had already become a rallying cry for change. "One cannot meet with friends in their daily lives in our City without the subject of crime coming up, whether you are on the streets, homes, churches, banks, theater, grocery stores, gas stations, etc.," Joseph Mosesso and Morris Clark, copresidents of the Randle Highlands Citizens Association, said in January 1969. But the city's white civic group had faith that the new president would restore the city's reputation. This was more than they could say about local black appointees, whom they accused of spending more time tearing down the city's police department than prosecuting criminals.[42]

The Randle Highlands Citizens Association, like many neighborhood groups in the Federation of Citizens Associations, opposed home rule and sought a more limited role for the city's black government. One reason it supported Nixon's War on Crime was to help counterbalance the black influence on local government. "What words of assurance has the Mayor given that our city will be maintained as an integrated city? So far I have not heard any. . . . Can't the powers to be in Congress see the hand writing on the wall of what is going to happen to the Nation's Capital?" Mosesso and Clark asked, revealing their deep-seated fears of the black majority's growing political power.[43]

Much as they had done in the aftermath of the riots, local white stakeholders used Nixon's War on Crime as an opportunity to challenge the prudence of home rule legislation and pose questions about the viability of black self-determination. They also lent strong support to the new administration. George Brady, president of the Federation of Citizens Associations, offered Nixon the group's assistance in solving the problems that afflicted the District. Similarly, Osby L. Weir, president of the Board of Trade, expressed the organization's gratitude for the steps Nixon was taking to reduce lawlessness in the city. "The positive policies you have adopted, are implementing, and have voiced to the public, have tremendously boosted the morale of our people, and in my opinion, of law abiding citizens throughout the Nation," Weir fawningly wrote the president in early February.[44]

To win a quick symbolic victory with Washington's vocal white stakeholders, the White House initially focused on increasing the size of the city's police force by one thousand officers. The Federation of Citizens Associations supported Nixon's recommendation to enlarge the department and suggested that it relax its standards for police recruiting. But the proposal was not without its critics. The Northwest Citizens on the Urban Crisis, a majority white residents' group that formed to aid the Poor People's Campaign, wrote to the city council to protest the proposal. "In our view the call for 1,000 additional policemen is not an intelligent response to present conditions in the District of Columbia but rather an automatic and unthinking reaction," stated David Rein, chairman of the group's Committee on Police-Community Relations. Instead, he argued, "the remedies for the present critical situation in the District lie in other directions." But increasingly loud demands for punitive measures drowned out calls for social safety nets.[45]

The *Washington Daily News* spoke excitedly about the president's dedication to curbing the city's crime rate. "It is plain that the President, having committed himself to attempt to make this city a model for the nation, is not going to settle for token gestures," the paper reasoned. "That his concern about the crime situation here is coupled with his concern for those streets still bearing all the depressing wounds and scars of the April rioting—that he sees the interrelationship between urban crime and urban blight—is also impressive," it added admiringly.[46] In using the riots as a backdrop for its praise, and by insisting on racially coding urban crime and blight, the paper turned a blind eye to the needs of those who actually lived in the riot-torn neighborhoods. Nevertheless, in early February, the president returned the paper's compliment. He commended *Washington Daily News* editor Richard Hollander on the paper's front-page coverage of the city's crime problem and assured him that he was "cracking the whip" on the Justice Department to reduce crime in the District.[47]

While Nixon appreciated the front-page coverage, it also served as a nagging reminder of the need for early and attention-getting action on the crime problem. "I feel we need to do something more dramatic than simply repeating the need for more police, more courts, more public defenders, etc.," he complained to Attorney General John Mitchell. Thinking outside the box, Nixon proposed bringing in law enforcement officials from other areas of government, including, possibly, U.S. Marshals, Secret Service, or FBI agents. In doing so,

Nixon underscored his refusal to take activists' quest for self-determination seriously.[48]

LAUNCHING THE WAR ON CRIME

During the first half of the year, Nixon outlined the broad contours of his D.C. Crime Bill. Then, in July 1969, Attorney General John Mitchell sent Congress its anticrime legislation intended to modernize local court management, streamline the administration of justice in the District, and reduce the city's crime rate. The White House argued that its crime program would create "bold and basic reforms in civil and criminal practice" and turn the city into a showcase for what it wanted to see implemented throughout the country.[49] But in September, Deputy Counselor Bud Krogh admitted to Nixon's inner circle that the administration had not done an effective job selling its crime package. In particular, it had underestimated congressional opposition from the House and Senate committees that supervised District affairs. It had also received an unexpected backlash from municipal government officials.[50]

That fall, as Congress deliberated over the D.C. Crime Bill, the situation on the ground took a turn for the worse. New crime data drew added scrutiny to the White House's efforts. The city's 1969 crime rate rose 32 percent, resulting in a rate 23 percent higher than the national average. As the crime rate climbed, journalists and politicians questioned whether Nixon would accomplish his campaign pledge. The president and his staff knew that the stakes were extraordinary. As one reporter observed, crime rates were high in cities across the nation, but "the horrible local mess is more significant, for it was here that President Nixon had been most intent on restoring law and order."[51]

In September, Nixon's Domestic Council, which oversaw the bulk of District operations, reassigned responsibility for official crime briefings from the mayor's office to the Metropolitan Police Department. One month earlier, Police Chief John Layton had stepped down amid growing civic tensions. His retirement paved the way for Jerry Wilson, a white navy veteran with twenty years on the force, to assume the top post. The Domestic Council's September reassignment positioned the chief of police as a key authority in the District. While residents held Wilson in greater esteem than Layton, the White House's move was an affront to the city's autonomy and a reminder of the limits of Johnson's home rule measure.[52]

Yet not even the police chief thought he could slow the city's rising crime rate. As Wilson cautioned White House staff, none of the measures they adopted would prevent crime from continuing to increase. Pessimistic predictions notwithstanding, Wilson was a powerful local resource and important national symbol. By bringing the white police chief into the president's inner circle, the Nixon administration elevated the MPD to the center of the District's governance and, more generally, raised policing to the center of its national agenda.[53]

The White House's interference in local crime matters was part of a larger assault on the city's autonomy. *D.C. Gazette* editor Sam Smith was among those infuriated by the Nixon administration's meddling in District affairs. For Smith, 1969 marked a turning point in the city's quest for self-determination. "From that point," he argued, "the D.C. administration pulled back. No longer was it the style for Walter Washington to walk the streets. He knew he had to deal with an occupying government." According to Smith, "The Nixon Administration treated the District as another federal agency—a colony."[54]

Looking at the bigger picture, one would have little trouble finding evidence of Smith's charges. Earlier that year, with limited input from Mayor Washington, Nixon made a key decision about local affairs. That February, the president had asserted partisan control over the nine-member city council by appointing local Republican Party chairman Gilbert Hahn to replace John Hechinger, the well-respected Democrat, as chairman. In his capacity as local party chair, Hahn had suggested to Nixon that he replace the mayor with a Republican candidate. Due to the poor optics of replacing the city's first black mayor with a white appointee, Nixon refrained. Instead he elevated Hahn to the top council position, along with local Urban League Director Sterling Tucker as city council vice chairman. The moves infuriated the Black United Front. According to BUF, Hahn's principal qualification for the chairmanship "appears to be his public statements on law and order, that tired euphemism for the right of white racist cops to whip niggers' heads indiscriminately." It was no more pleased with Tucker, whom it had expelled in December 1968 for "deliberate nonparticipation."[55]

By the fall of 1969, Hahn, a Washington native and Ivy League–educated Republican, had ingratiated himself with the Nixon administration. Flexing his political connections, Hahn even lobbied Attorney General John Mitchell to try to secure himself a seat in the Domestic Council's meetings on District affairs and in Mayor Washington's regular meetings with the president. While White House officials wished to include Hahn, they knew that doing so would risk an outcry from black activists who already believed their autonomy had been jeopardized. Instead White House Deputy Counselor Bud Krogh told Associate Deputy Attorney General Donald Santarelli to send Hahn to rally the city's white stakeholders around its anticrime legislation. Krogh deftly cashed in Hahn's desire for greater exposure for communitywide support of the administration's crime measures—something he doubted Mayor Washington could provide them.[56]

In November, the Nixon administration made another partisan appointment when it selected Graham Watt as deputy mayor. Watt, a city manager from Dayton, Ohio, replaced the well-liked Thomas Fletcher, who President Johnson had appointed alongside Walter Washington back in 1967. Slowly chipping away at the mayor's responsibilities, the Nixon administration assigned Watt operational responsibilities for the police force. In doing so, the White House further marginalized the city's black municipal government in the name of law and order.[57]

In its final assault on self-determination that fall, Nixon issued a directive to remove "certain unacceptable personnel" in the D.C. government. White House officials worked with the Department of Justice to fulfill the president's order. Under Bud Krogh's instruction, White House District Liaison Richard Blumenthal identified two of the city's most prominent black employees for removal from their posts within "the D.C. hierarchy": Charles Duncan, the mayor's trusted counsel and amiable staff member, who had skillfully handled the dismantling of the Poor People's Campaign the year before, and Julian Dugas, the city's director of economic development. "How this should be done and if it can be done without impossible political reaction are the questions I leave to you," Krogh told Blumenthal. The White House ultimately stopped short of removing Mayor Washington's confidants. However, in threatening the employment of black city officials, the Nixon administration underscored the ease with which it could upend the city's governing body under Johnson's weak home rule measure. Taken together, the Nixon administration's personnel decisions revealed its eagerness to exert federal control over local autonomy as it prioritized its war on crime in the majority-black city.[58]

Aside from the support of its new municipal appointees, the White House still wanted local approval for its anticrime program. Following a directive from Bud Krogh to aggressively sell its crime bill to District residents, the White House switched tactics.[59] In October, Nixon aides attempted to orchestrate a presidential visit to one of the city's riot-torn neighborhoods to emphasize his concern for black residents. "It would hearten responsible members of the black community in Washington, D.C. (and of black communities in other cities) who must resist the urgings of militants to abandon hope and turn to more extreme tactics," White House District Liaison Richard Blumenthal proposed. But in suggesting that militants would corrupt "responsible" black Washingtonians, White House officials committed the same error as the city's white stakeholders, who refused to admit that the public outcry against Nixon's repressive measures was anything but extreme radicalism.[60]

Meanwhile, Pat Moynihan, Counselor to the President for Urban Affairs, had what he initially believed was an easier task. The same month that White House officials debated staging a highly symbolic photo op with black residents, Moynihan met with a group of powerful white Washingtonians to discuss the president's crime program. The District represented just one piece of the White House counselor's portfolio. But as long as the federal government still had oversight over the city, and the administration prioritized fulfilling its campaign pledge and passing its crime bill as a model law for other cities, D.C. affairs would occupy a significant portion of his time.

The meeting featured some of the city's leading stakeholders, including Robert Baker, president of the American Security and Trust Company; Katharine Graham, publisher of the *Washington Post*; Edward Bennett Williams, a defense lawyer and Redskins owner; and S. Dillon Ripley, secretary of the Smithsonian Institution. But while Moynihan had arranged the meeting to garner support from the powerful individuals for Nixon's War on Crime, he was confronted by residents who believed the District had deteriorated "to a point near disaster," and he became enmeshed in debates about racial politics. With local crime rates on the rise, the economy spiraling downward, and businesses relocating to the suburbs, the group was none too pleased with the city's municipal government. At the meeting, participants revealed to Moynihan that they thought the District government was incompetent to deal with the city's urban crisis. In fact, Robert Baker disclosed that Walter Washington had told him privately that he did not know what to do about the city's crime problem, an admission that prompted Baker's involvement in the White House meeting in the first place. There Baker, along with the rest of the group, told Moynihan that the president had a responsibility to seize control of District affairs. Moynihan was taken aback. What he believed would be a fairly benign summit about Nixon's anticrime proposals turned into a heated exchange with some of Washington's white stakeholders over the state of District affairs under the city's majority-black government.[61]

Moynihan was deeply frustrated. Despite expressing their support for federal intervention, he did not believe that the well-connected attendees had made any attempts to learn anything about the administration's crime proposals. Nor did he think that they demonstrated a willingness to mobilize local or national support for them. Moynihan's hands were tied. The only thing he felt like he could do was educate the group on the legislation's merits and urge them to pressure legislators to pass its crime bill. But their lack of public support, especially when Nixon aides had trouble garnering any from the black community, angered him.[62]

Privately Moynihan bemoaned the attendees for their alleged hypocrisy. "They have let Richard Nixon do the dirty work of proposing and fighting for crime control measures while they have given credence to black leaders who extol riots as rebellion and describe police as pigs," Moynihan said in disgust. "They have called for Home Rule," he added, "while complaining that the present District Government, headed by a black Mayor, is incapable of running the city and should be fully programmed by the White House."[63]

On the one hand, Moynihan's observations pointed to the thorny racial politics surrounding the District's governance and, specifically, the city's quest for self-determination. While the Board of Trade and Federation of Citizens Associations were willing to openly criticize the city's black officials, other prominent white stakeholders did not want to do so publicly. On the other hand, Moynihan's comments revealed a continued effort to distort black officials' motives. The black leaders whom the Johnson administration had incorporated into local government had not advocated for militant measures during or after the riots. But both white stakeholders and federal officials continued to contribute to this narrative in order to undermine their authority. Black activists saw through their efforts. Reverend Douglas Moore, chairman of the Black United Front, described Moynihan, who had served in both the Kennedy and Johnson administrations, as a "plantation boss for black people throughout the country" and "a functional, outright racist."[64]

Toward the end of its first year in office, the Nixon administration found itself in a bind. White stakeholders' public and private support gave White House officials tacit permission to continue to marginalize black municipal officials and cast doubt on the mayor's ability to govern. At the same time, they believed that earning Mayor Washington's support would help them pass a District-level crime bill. Thus, following Moynihan's October meeting, the White House scheduled a summit between the president and mayor-commissioner to force Washington to get on board with its anticrime program.[65]

Relations between the White House and the D.C. government had been so fraught that the mayor had not seen the president in over nine months. It was only two years earlier that Washington had demanded that the appointed mayor-commissioner post include jurisdiction over the police department. During the riots, the Johnson administration demonstrated its willingness to overrule him, creating friction that carried over to the Nixon White House. Washington's divergent positions on law and order and White House officials' unwillingness to give them serious consideration exacerbated tensions between them. In the months after the election but before Nixon took office, for example, Washington boldly outlined the contours of a federally funded community policing project antithetical to Nixon's proposals in hopes of creating a model of cooperation between police offers and citizens in the District. But when the mayor took such a stand, White House officials merely dismissed his actions as politicking.[66]

The same thing happened when Washington testified against the White House's proposal to deny bond to suspected criminals. Rather than acknowledge their differing views, the president's Domestic Council simply maintained that the mayor must have been embarrassed for having taken the position he did. As White House Advisor John Ehrlichman explained to the president prior to his summit with Washington, "He was under very heavy pressure from civil rights and black groups" to do so. Perhaps he was. But in their summary dismissal of the mayor's actions on issues like preventative detention as the product of lobbying by "black groups," Nixon officials deeply misjudged the situation. Not only did they refuse to acknowledge that the blowback against their crime bill was more widespread than they cared to admit. They also underestimated the fact that the D.C. government was mounting its own opposition to their punitive proposals.[67]

In its desire to secure local support for its anticrime legislation, White House officials refused to accept that "reasonable" black residents would oppose their programs. They were therefore furious that the mayor had not yet articulated a tougher stance on crime. As D.C. liaison Richard Blumenthal bluntly pointed out to Bud Krogh before the arranged November 1969 summit, "The Mayor does not seem to place a sufficiently high priority on solving the crime problem and he has been reluctant to support the President's legislative proposals." As black officials around the country turned toward more punitive solutions to local crime problems, the District's appointed mayor remained a holdout. In the nation's capital, the crime issue was too intimately intertwined with the struggle for black self-determination for the mayor to embrace Nixon's "get tough" solutions.[68]

Initially Mayor Washington held firm. He made it clear to officials that they could not simply steamroll the D.C. government. To earn his support, Krogh knew that the administration would have to meet certain demands. "He needs to feel that we back him up, that he is instrumental in the crime war we have declared on the District," Krogh explained. "Occasionally, he has felt as if he is out on a limb by himself [and] I am told that this will work wonders for us in the future," Krogh speculated. Krogh's comments pointed yet again to the thorny racial politics surrounding limited home rule. To win local black support for the bill, the Nixon team needed the mayor's endorsement. The relationship was reciprocal. Without an electoral mandate, and especially as white stakeholders publicly and privately called for his removal, the mayor also needed the president's backing. Yet for either side to get anything out of the upcoming summit, their positions would have to converge more than they had thus far into Nixon's presidency.[69]

During their meeting, the president's concern over short-term reductions to the city's crime rate undercut his confidence in local governance. Nixon did give the mayor a show of support. He acknowledged that Washington's job was "one of the toughest in the Nation." "I appreciate your problems, and I want to do everything I can to help you," he told the mayor.[70] At the same time, he assigned Attorney General John Mitchell responsibility for coordinating the Metropolitan Police Department, National Guard, and federal troops and urged the mayor to consult frequently with the Justice Department. In doing so, Nixon once again restricted the mayor's authority over the city's police force and outlined a much more limited role for local government than Johnson had initially envisioned.[71]

While the administration offered its tepid support of Mayor Washington, it expressed great pleasure with one particular black government appointee. "It has been very distressing to us all that the black leadership has not spoken out against the crime wave in the District of Columbia. Now Sterling Tucker at least has done so—and very eloquently," an aide told Bud Krogh.[72] Tucker had been handpicked by Nixon to serve as city council vice chairman. Nine months into his appointment, Tucker outlined his views on the city's crime problem at the 19th Street Baptist Church in Northwest D.C. There, at the historic church, the moderate political leader explained that crime's true victims were not the ones who cried loudest for law and order but the country's poor black citizens.[73]

Tucker situated his feelings about the District's crime epidemic within a larger critique of the city's black leadership. "What disturbs me is the failure of black leadership to speak out against crime itself," he said, echoing the administration's frustrations. Tucker, who had explored connections with the Black United Front less than two years earlier, criticized the city's black activists for placing undue attention on police brutality at the expense of crime. "I do not hear their voices raised against the robbery and burglary and rape that is perpetrated on our people, against the gun toting that turns out streets into alleys of fear," he continued, chastising them for their silence. His statements animated the Nixon administration, which believed that securing the support of a black moderate like Tucker would lend credibility to its agenda.[74]

By January 1970, the tide began to turn in the White House's favor. That month, Bud Krogh observed that the mayor had heard Tucker's message and had begun to make a concerted effort to develop support among the black community for stronger anticrime proposals. "You will remember that we had discussed the problem of the black community thinking that to be against crime was also to be racist," he told a White House staffer. "However," he said, "that strong middle-class conservative black community is finally raising itself and deciding to do something about it." Tucker's statements certainly lent credence to the idea that black residents cared about crime. But just because Tucker admonished black activists for their silence on the crime issue did not mean he supported Nixon's anticrime agenda, an important distinction that White House officials overlooked in their excitement. Instead, Tucker would go on to advocate for community-based solutions brewing in the capital.[75]

As Nixon's anticrime package made its way through Congress, it still did not carry the local government's stamp of approval. One reporter reasoned, "The mayor could not offer any strong support of the bill without isolating a huge segment of his constituency."[76] Moreover, the White House still faced a barrage of criticism from neighborhood and community activists. Following yet another unproductive town hall meeting in January 1970, White House Deputy Counselor Bud Krogh admitted that he was not sure Nixon should be involved in community-level lobbying on behalf of his crime measures. As Krogh explained, they always ended in "some form of noisy, disruptive altercation in which no one wins." Perhaps if White House officials had solicited local input rather than mere support, they would not have been in this bind. But instead they had crafted local anticrime legislation intended to serve as a model bill for the nation against the wishes of much of the city's black residents and with little evidence of coordination between the bill's drafters in the Justice Department and District government officials. What became increasingly clear was that local autonomy mattered little in their larger War on Crime.[77]

The White House's marginalization of black municipal leaders prevented it from winning much-needed local support and contributed to its mismanagement of the D.C. Crime Bill. The bungling of its crime bill shook White House aides. In January 1970, Urban Affairs Counselor Pat Moynihan lamented that his morale was at an all-time low.[78] Unlike the rest of Nixon's inner circle, Moynihan directed the blame inward. "I do wish to make one thing perfectly clear," he admonished his White House colleagues. "If there were any other area of high, public Presidential commitment in which we have failed as badly as we have done in the matter of crime in the District of Columbia, you would be looking around for someone to fire."[79]

Without a victory in sight, White House aides formulated a more aggressive plan to promote the administration's D.C. crime legislation in the new year. Nixon commissioned media analyst and speechwriter Patrick Buchanan, his chief anticrime strategist in the White House, to gin up anger at the previous administration's permissiveness on crime. He also asked White House Advisor John Ehrlichman to "ride hard" on the attorney general and to keep the press on the offensive. As part of its new public relations strategy, the White House deflected responsibility for the crime bill's stalled progress. Instead it blamed Congress for failing to enact its legislation.[80]

The Nixon administration, which was in the midst of stripping the city's municipal government of local powers, still placed high expectations on it to succeed. In a January meeting, Nixon turned up the pressure on Mayor Washington for failing to reduce the city's crime rate. The president even warned the mayor that if they did not receive good statistical results by the end of May, then he would "get a new city government."[81] White House officials suspected that the mayor had finally heard them loud and clear. "As I view it politically," Krogh reflected, "it is a now or never proposition, and the District Government, while it is still blowing smoke in my face, has gotten the message," he said. The White House's approach revealed yet again its willingness to treat local black officials as pawns in its larger War on Crime.[82]

Under the Nixon administration, local black politicians found themselves in a compromised position. Vocalizing broad support for the heavy-handed Republican administration infuriated local activists, who still wielded sizable power in the community. But opposition to the president's policies proved risky at a time when Nixon controlled local political appointments. In January, Mayor Washington caved. In response to administrative pressure, he held a January press conference to announce new goals for the crime effort, to take personal responsibility for increasing the police department's capacity, and to call for early action in the House District Committee on the administration's legislative package. According to Nixon aides, the mayor's press conference—his first "major anti-crime declaration"—"reflected a changed mood in the city." After the mayor's speech, White House staff professed that fighting crime was no longer a racial or partisan cause. "To be anti-crime is not to be anti-black or anti-poor; it is to be in favor of the safety of all the District's citizens," one aide declared confidently.[83]

Yet the mayor's endorsement did not reflect black Washingtonians' widespread support. Instead it revealed the compromises that the District's black government appointees were forced to make as they negotiated their roles as intermediaries between the federal government and D.C. residents, black and white, in the shadow of a home rule measure that did not give them real power. The *Los Angeles Times* foreshadowed this dilemma a year earlier when it reported, "The white population seems satisfied with Mayor Washington's ability to run the city but it is not yet clear whether or not Negroes support him with any degree of commitment. . . . There is a growing feeling among many Negroes that he is becoming known as a white man's mayor."[84] Black United Front member Reginald Booker confirmed militant black activists' disillusionment with Washington when he said in 1970, "The only reason you have black mayors is to act as a political buffer against the black masses."[85] Even Sam Smith noted a change in Washington's demeanor when Nixon came into office. Washington, he said, once was the "walking mayor, spreading word of the Great Society among the people." However, Smith argued, "when Nixon took over, Walter Washington took off his shoes, stayed in his office, and shut his mouth."[86] Thus, while black officials across the country turned to more punitive crime measures in response to community demands, evidence suggests that Mayor Washington's public condemnation of crime was in large part a result of pressure from the White House and white stakeholders.

Despite Washington's public change of heart, rumors swirled that the White House wanted to replace him. In late January, the *Jackson Daily News* even reported that the mayor was "sadly inadequate to cope with the increasing explosive problems in the federal city." Krogh was happy to see support from the Mississippi paper, but he worried about what the local press would say if the White House forced Washington out of office. As the deputy counselor told White House staff, "Washington is an honest, scholarly, and sincere gentleman, but these personal attributes do not dampen the long list of complaints about his ineffectiveness as an administrator." Due to the mayor's continuing popularity among black residents, Krogh reluctantly argued against replacing him. But he stressed that the Nixon administration should continue to flex its federal authority over D.C.'s municipal officials.[87]

Fortunately for the mayor's job security, the first half of 1970 marked a turning point for the city. For the first time since taking office, the White House touted a declining crime rate. In May it announced the fifth consecutive month with a decrease in major reported crimes. The decline represented the confluence of several factors. First, it accounted for measures implemented by Mayor Washington, including the employment of several hundred police officers on overtime since February, the establishment of a narcotics treatment agency to handle the city's growing heroin problem, and a new street lighting program. But it was also the result of the Nixon administration's purposefully misleading reporting. As scholar Vesla Weaver has explained, "One tactic used to make it seem like crime was decreasing and was much worse during the Johnson years was accomplished by using rate of increase instead of the crime rate." So, for example, the Uniform Crime Reports documented a 13 percent increase in crime from January to March 1970 compared to the same time period in 1969.[88]

Attorney General Mitchell spun these statistics into a positive narrative to make it appear like crime had decreased. As his office reported, "The rate of increase of violent crimes in the first three months of 1970 slowed by 7 percent in the major cities of the nation—and by 3 percent in the nation as a whole." In order to report this, Mitchell exploited a weakness of Johnson's 1968 Omnibus Crime Control and Safe Streets Act, which had stipulated that the attorney general was "to collect, evaluate, publish and disseminate statistics." Johnson had intended for the research-intensive provision to help the DOJ address issues of crime. Mitchell instead used the provision to manipulate publicly shared data, once again demonstrating the limits of Johnson's legislation to protect and serve D.C. residents.[89]

Regardless, the results earned the mayor high praise from Nixon. But some federal officials still harbored ill will toward Washington. At the end of May, Associate Deputy Attorney General Donald Santarelli wrote to Bud Krogh to express his displeasure with the mayor for his allegedly callous disregard of the department. The DOJ official listed the mayor's silence following recent antipolice statements from black leaders and his "cavalier" opposition to pretrial detention among his grievances. "As long as the White House continues to praise the Mayor for his 'silent war on crime' and as long as the Justice Department continues to appear to the mayor 'out in right field,' the mayor's posture cannot be expected to change," Santarelli concluded pessimistically.[90]

White House staff tried to assuage Santarelli's fears by dismissing the mayor's positions once again as politicking. Krogh even defended the mayor's decision not to endorse pretrial detention or no-knock legislation and abstain from "get tough" rhetoric. According to the Nixon aide, Washington's actions were merely an effort to maintain the support of the black community. That was no comfort to Santarelli, who believed he had been unfairly tasked with waging a war on crime in a city where the appointed mayor did not always toe the party line. His frustrations pointed to the larger political battle playing out in the capital in the aftermath of Johnson's limited home rule measure. As the White House was learning, it was impossible to untangle its war on crime from local issues of self-determination.[91]

THE D.C. CRIME BILL GOES TO THE HILL

After submitting its anticrime package to Congress in July 1969, White House officials found themselves locked in a territorial battle with the House and Senate committees on the District of Columbia. The leaders of D.C.'s congressional committees, Senator Joseph Tydings (D-Md.) and Representative Brock Adams (D-Wash.), placed the blame for the legislative delays in the D.C. crime fight squarely with the administration. Frustrated, Budd Krogh admitted to John Ehrlichman that D.C.'s congressional committees had substantial power over District affairs—far more than they had assumed. In underestimating Congress's jurisdiction over capital affairs, Nixon officials made another misstep in their fight to pass their crime bill.[92]

The D.C. crime bill followed two different trajectories in Congress. On the Senate side, the District Committee deliberated over bills to ensure pretrial detention, to reorganize the District's court system and revise its criminal code, to create a public defender system, and to revise the District's juvenile code. The Senate District Committee reported out revised bills that stayed true to Nixon's vision, and the larger Senate approved, with amendments, all but one of Nixon's D.C. crime proposals by early 1970. The remaining proposal, on preventive detention, remained a hot-button issue and did not immediately pass the Senate.[93]

On the House side, the District Committee consolidated the White House's crime measures for the capital into an omnibus bill and added to it a number of provisions. Its massive bill differed from the more moderate Senate-approved bills in more than 170 items, including several highly contentious provisions that authorized the pretrial detention of persons accused of certain crimes; allowed no-knock search and arrest warrants enabling the police to more easily search suspects' premises; transferred the District's Lorton Reformatory to federal jurisdiction; lowered the age at which a juvenile charged with a felony could be tried as an adult to fifteen; and authorized mandatory sentences for repeat offenders, including life sentences for those convicted of a third felony.[94]

Of the twenty-member House District Committee, four Democrats remained opposed to many of the House bill's provisions—including pretrial detention, no-knock entries, and wiretapping and electronic surveillance—calling them "dangerous and repressive."[95] They accused its supporters of foolishly assuming that giving police officers and prosecutors authority to wiretap, knock down doors, or detain and imprison citizens before trial would reduce crime. Moreover, they questioned the wisdom of minimizing the jurisdiction of the juvenile court and handing local correctional institutions over to the federal government. But in March 1970, after lengthy debate, the House District Committee reported out its omnibus crime bill and urged the larger House to swiftly pass it in order "to give to the people in Washington, its citizens, and those temporarily sojourning here, as well as the millions of visitors who come here annually, some measure of surcease from the ever-growing criminal element."[96]

After the committee reported out the bill, the House overwhelmingly approved it. It did so thanks in large part to House District Committee chairman John McMillan's persuasive efforts and despite the opposition of a small group of liberal representatives who tried to narrow the broad sweep of the bill's more drastic provisions. From there, the bill went to conference along with the Senate's version, which had been consolidated from various bills into one measure. On account of the controversial nature of the House bill's provisions, the House-Senate conference on legislation met twenty-four times between April and June to resolve the almost two hundred differences between the two bills.[97]

As Nixon's crime bill moved through Congress in the spring of 1970, Washington's white civic groups shifted their lobbying efforts into high gear. In April, George Brady, president of the Federation of Citizens Associations, called on Senator Joseph Tydings and Representative John McMillan to pass the omnibus crime bill. "As citizens of the District we are sick and tired of the increase in crimes of all categories, particularly street crime; of delays in prosecution and trial even where the criminal is caught red-handed; of the release of dangerous persons who are awaiting trial; and of the apparent growth of organized crime in drug traffic," Brady complained. Brady made the Federation's position clear: they would remain on the side of punitive measures.[98]

Tydings, chairman of the Senate District Committee and manager of the bill, did not let them down. The senator received support from local white groups, like the Federation of Citizens Associations, as well as his white suburban constituents, many of whom worked in the capital. Emboldened by their strong backing, he argued that the bill was "a sound, effective, constitutional and fully safeguarded response to this crime crisis." He dismissed black residents' fears that the administration had not considered their interests in crafting the anticrime legislation, declaring that the fear of unchecked crime trumped community concerns. "To those who say this bill is anti-black, I say crime in this 70% black city is anti-black," he affirmed as he defended the legislation. But the Maryland senator also added several racially coded provisions to the bill, including a measure that would require plaintiffs to pay policemen's attorney fees in all false arrest suits, regardless of the outcome.[99]

D.C.'s black officials were particularly frustrated by white suburban senators, like Tydings, who voted against local black interests, as well as legislators representing far away states, like Majority Leader Mike Mansfield (D-Mont.), who advocated for the bill despite confessing ignorance of its legal implications. The D.C. City Council's frustration reached a boiling point over one particular stipulation in the House bill: the transfer of the Lorton Correctional Complex from the D.C. Department of Corrections to federal authority. Introduced by local suburban representatives Joel Broyhill and William L. Scott from Virginia, the provision provided local government officials with glaring evidence of how they had become collateral damage in a larger War on Crime that devalued black self-determination.[100]

Members of the D.C. city council were furious. Of the two thousand men and women incarcerated in the Lorton Correctional Complex, 95 percent were District residents. If the transfer went through, council members cautioned that the majority of them would be forced to relocate to prisons across the country. In addition, the council maintained that its correctional programs were some of the most progressive in the country. It had one of the lowest recidivism rates for youth and adults, in large part because it emphasized the importance of providing treatment programs that involved the community in the area of work release and education programs, community correctional centers, and parole supervision by officers who maintained positive relationships with young offenders. The council worried that it stood to lose many of its gains in the area of corrections, including the trust of the wider black community, if it was forced to federalize the city's correctional system. Furthermore, as city council chairman Hahn, Nixon's own appointee, pointed out, the transfer was entirely inconsistent with the principle of home rule. Rather than unify the city government under greater local authority, the transfer would serve to further fragment it.[101]

Why, *Washington Post* columnist William Raspberry wondered, would conservatives advocate for more, rather than less, federal control? Raspberry speculated that racial politics drove their insistence on a federal takeover. The head of the Department of Corrections, Kenneth Hardy, was black, while most of his subordinates were white Virginia residents represented by the suburban members of Congress. "These Virginia gentlemen, it seems clear, do not like the idea of black men being in charge," Raspberry observed wryly. Their push to federalize Lorton was not the only evidence of their intent to undermine the city's majority-black government. Broyhill and Scott also wished to transfer control of the local police department to Congress and were outspoken in their personal attacks on Mayor Washington. Thus, the white southern legislators who controlled the House and Senate District Committees exploited their powers under limited home rule, attempting once again to use the War on Crime to curb Washingtonians' autonomy.[102]

The Nixon administration had hoped not to get involved in the local-suburban conflict. But suburban officials' outspoken support of the transfer forced it to weigh in. The White House elected not to support the Lorton transfer. "We have been strongly opposed to the transfer because it is completely out of step with the Administration's general program to place local functions under D.C. government control," White House staff said. But given that the administration had presided over a crime bill that systematically undermined local governance, the excuse of self-determination rang hollow.[103]

In Congress, liberal senator Edward Kennedy (D-Mass.) and conservative senator Sam Ervin (D-N.C.) came together to spearhead the opposition to the House version of the bill. Ervin, a strong supporter of states' rights and a leader in punitive crime policies, called the bill "a blueprint for a police state." He criticized the Department of Justice for trying "to put a fast one over on the Senate and the American people." According to him and Kennedy, the pending legislation contained dangerous threats to personal liberty and a flagrant disregard of the Constitution. Moreover, they complained that conservatives' law-and-order sloganeering had replaced realistic solutions to the crime problem.[104]

Some members of Congress who supported the crime bill's less contentious aspects still could not let go of its more controversial provisions. Senator Thomas Eagleton (D-Mo.), for example, supported the crime bill's interventions in the areas of court reform and regulation, juvenile reform, and public defender services. But he believed that the bill's preventive detention measures, mandatory minimum sentences, and wiretap provisions represented unsound public policy and threatened to open the door to broadened invasions of privacy. Other opponents joined Eagleton to argue that the no-knock, wiretapping, and search warrant provisions came close to violating the Fourth Amendment against unreasonable searches and seizures. Concerns about constitutionality were not unwarranted. In fact, the Supreme Court invalidated one of the bill's provisions, allowing juveniles to be found delinquent by a "preponderance of the evidence," on March 31, less than two weeks after its House passage.[105]

Inside and outside Congress, the no-knock provisions generated some of the most heated debate. On the local level, they threatened to upend police-community relations. Samuel C. Jackson, assistant secretary of Housing and Urban Development, warned President Nixon that they could even provoke violent confrontations between local officers and black residents. Jackson, a black Republican from Kansas, had served as one of the five original commissioners of Lyndon Johnson's U.S. Equal Employment Opportunity Commission from 1965 to 1968. In 1969, Nixon made him the third-ranking official in HUD, where he helped develop and implement policies for the federal government's housing and planning programs. His position gave him access to the city's low-income black residents as well as to its municipal leaders. "Respected black leaders, including ministers of our leading churches, are calling on their fellow citizens to shoot police officers entering their home under the no knock provisions," he warned the president in May 1970.[106]

Jackson was referring to comments that Reverend David Eaton had made earlier that month. In one of Eaton's first sermons at All Souls Unitarian Church, at 16th and Harvard Streets NW, he had warned the primarily white congregation that Nixon's crime bill was an oppressive piece of legislation, akin to something one would have found in Hitler's Germany. There, in front of the pulpit, he had suggested, "Any time persons break into your homes unannounced, shoot them." All Souls had been a hub of activism during the civil rights movement and had installed Eaton as the first black senior minister to serve in a large Unitarian church. Under Eaton's direction, the church established low- and middle-income housing along the 14th Street corridor after the riots. Although he caught flack for his comments on the president's crime bill, the majority of the board of trustees and congregation stood with him.[107]

While Jackson exaggerated the extent to which respected leaders called for retaliatory violence, even Mayor Washington cautioned that no-knock could lead to harm against local police officers. The crime bill's no-knock provisions specifically put Washington in a difficult position. If the mayor had to support police activity conducted under them, then his credibility with black activists would be seriously impaired. Yet if he did not uphold them, he risked losing support from the Nixon administration as well as local white business and homeowners groups that had backed the bill.[108]

In aggressively lobbying for its no-knock provisions, White House officials likely knew they would alienate black activists who had long been critics of the city's police force. But they seriously underestimated the fact that they also risked jeopardizing the little goodwill local law enforcement had established with more moderate black residents. According to the *Washington Post*'s Raspberry, by 1970 many black residents had become "reluctant allies of the police in the fight against crime."[109] Jackson agreed. "Although the police are still regarded in many parts of the city as enemies, more and more citizens, on all levels, have come to view the police officers as a protector," he told the president. Jackson warned that punitive programs like no-knock would diminish any cooperative efforts already underway.[110]

Concerned about the backlash to its no-knock legislation, the White House discussed restricting its provisions to narcotics cases or eliminating it altogether. Attorney General John Mitchell expressed strong opposition to any such action. To do so, he cautioned, would undermine the administration's relationship with House members who had overwhelmingly supported no-knock. Bud Krogh remained on the fence. He wondered whether it would be best to reverse their position, thereby reducing local pressure but also undermining their overall strength while the bill was in conference. The issue as I see it," Krogh told John Ehrlichman in May, "is whether relief of local pressure on no knock by a letter reneging from our position is worth the risk of undermining our Conferees' strength in the Conference on other issues." Ultimately the White House decided not to capitulate to local pressure. Instead it continued to pursue repressive measures that antagonized the city's black community and undermined all residents' sovereignty.[111]

Over local objections and after lengthy congressional debate, the House adopted the conference report on July 15 by a 332–64 roll call vote. Thirteen days later, the Senate voted 54–33 to accept the conference report. "After more than three months of spirited debate, after 24 sessions of conference and compromise, the best in these disparate measures was at last brought together in a single omnibus crime bill for the District of Columbia," Representative Gerald Ford (R-Mich.) told the House in July 1970. "The bill is not a panacea for every problem in this crime-beleaguered capital," he added, "but it is a reasoned response to rampant lawlessness—an immediate response to immediate problems."[112]

Ford's comments did not do justice to the drastic scope of the D.C. Crime Bill. While the final bill watered down many of the House bill's features, it still included provisions that closely resembled it. The final version dramatically diminished the D.C. Circuit Court's liberal tendencies by weakening its criminal law precedent and stripping it of its local jurisdiction over criminal appeals. In addition to dramatically restructuring the District's judiciary system, the bill allowed no-knock police searches, extended broad wiretapping authority, and granted police new rights to detain criminal suspects in lieu of bail for an unprecedented sixty days before conviction. Moreover, it authorized five-year sentences for those convicted of a second armed offense, permitted life sentences for third-time felony offenders, allowed juveniles to be tried as adults, and eliminated juvenile jury trials altogether. "It is an unprecedented measure, a very strong measure, but it deals with an unprecedented problem," President Nixon said as he signed District of Columbia Court Reform and Criminal Procedure Act into law on July 29, 1970.[113]

In July 1972, one month after the Washington Metropolitan Police Department arrested five men for breaking and entering into the Democratic National Committee's headquarters at the Watergate Hotel, the White House declared victory in the president's War on Crime. Not only did Congress pass the White House's signature crime bill. The administration also pressured the local government into implementing its own repression and surveillance measures, including a one-thousand-man special squad for riots and disturbances, more uniformed officers on the streets, an increase in streetlights, and cameras to record violations. "In Washington, D.C., our Nation's Capital, where the Federal Government has the responsibility and the authority to deal with local crime, the programs of the Nixon Administration have been implemented fully," declared White House Aide Edwin Harper.[114]

The Nixon administration provided statistical evidence to bolster its victory. Ernst and Ernst, a major contributor to the Nixon campaign, conducted an audit that found a 50 percent decrease in crime. The White House celebrated the fact that D.C.'s serious crime rate was reduced to half of its all-time high in the first quarter of 1972. But, as political scientist Vesla Weaver has documented, the Brookings Institution determined that these decreases were the result of a change in how stolen goods were classified. Nevertheless, the White House attributed the changes to its harsh policies, pointing in particular to its D.C. crime bill as the cause of the capital's crime drop.[115] As the president campaigned for reelection, he further credited these developments in part to a new, less permissive public attitude toward crime and criminals and a renewed climate of respect for law and law enforcement. "The day of the criminal is past in America, and the day of the citizen is here," Nixon said triumphantly.[116]

WASHINGTON'S OTHER ANTICRIME EFFORT

In the shadow of Nixon's overly punitive anticrime efforts, another effort unfolding in the District revealed how the limits of Johnson's partial home rule measure and increasing demands for self-determination hamstrung local anticrime efforts. The Pilot Precinct Project ran on a parallel timeline to the D.C. Crime Bill. In fact, the same month that Nixon assumed the presidency in 1968, Mayor Walter Washington addressed the Washington Home Rule Committee, an organization that lobbied the federal government for local municipal elections. There the mayor outlined the contours of an ambitious new project: a government-initiated experiment financed by a $1.4 million grant from the Office of Economic Opportunity, with additional funds from the Law Enforcement Assistance Administration, the federal agency created by Johnson's 1968 Omnibus Crime Control and Safe Streets Act, to develop a project that would serve as a model of cooperation between police offers and citizens.[117]

Under the Johnson administration's supervision, Robert Shellow, a white psychologist in the OEO, designed the Pilot Precinct Project. It was intended to encourage participation of residents traditionally outside the scope of federal initiatives. The project called for local citizens' advisory committees, decentralized police substations in neighborhood storefronts manned by both police and social service agencies, day care centers within the storefronts, patrols comprising salaried black youth, clerical assistance from civilians, and sensitivity training for officers. Shellow, a liberal bureaucrat, had designed a progressive-minded, research-heavy, social science–oriented plan that on paper seemed like it would have citywide appeal.[118]

Genuine fears of crime within the black community, coupled with an increase in black deaths at the hands of white officers, which doubled from 1967 to 1968, and the implementation of limited home rule had led activists to demand more control over law and order within the city. As scholar Michael Fortner has documented, black fears of crime intensified across the nation during the 1960s. In a representative 1969 survey conducted in Baltimore, black respondents reported being more afraid than whites of a variety of crimes, including being beaten up, raped, robbed, and murdered.[119] That year the Black United Front went so far as to announce a war on black crime in order to combat "the whole pattern of criminalization that is sucking the life-blood out of the black community." But while BUF searched for the root causes of and remedies for black participation in crime, its focus on law enforcement for giving preferential treatment to whites, for perpetuating criminality among blacks, and for its aggressive surveillance measures never subsided.[120]

After years of listening to BUF's antipolice rhetoric, the *Washington Post* took pleasure in hearing it talk about "a rarely discussed feeling," "that blacks have a keener interest in erasing crime than do whites because Negroes are the principal victims of crime in this city." The *Post* attributed black residents' silence on the crime issue to their fears of aligning with racist white residents and policy makers, their long-standing distrust of white police officers, and their larger concern for reducing racial discrimination than crime. The paper was glad to see the militant organization give voice to the larger black community's concerns and express a desire to curb crime by black offenders. But it also understood that BUF was not shifting priorities away from police brutality as much as it was simply examining the crime issue from a different perspective. Thus, BUF's demand for "self-police and self-protection" was not a request for more punitive policies but a call for the decentralization of the police.[121]

In the hands of the federal government, white bureaucrats refashioned BUF's plea into a program that inner-city residents rebuffed. The United Planning Organization, the OEO's local Community Action Agency in Washington, led the early opposition to the Pilot District Project. Much like when SCLC came to Washington to stage its Poor People's Campaign, the OEO overlooked its own antipoverty organization when it designed its local anticrime program. It was a tone-deaf move at a time when residents demanded more autonomy, especially around the issue of policing. Wiley Branton, the UPO's director, accused the OEO of designing a project without sufficient citizen participation. The UPO's board was offended that it had been asked to sign off on the federal plan without its input. Branton specifically worried that the OEO's funding for the pilot project, coupled with budget cuts to his organization, would be interpreted around the city as the UPO losing its "political muscle." For these reasons, the UPO rejected the plan. Even so, OEO officials pushed forward, funding a Community Action Program that the local CAA opposed.[122]

Mayor Washington selected thirty-nine community representatives, including black activists and Board of Trade and Federation of Citizens Associations members, to help choose a suitable precinct to launch the project. In response to their feedback, officials selected the city's Thirteenth Precinct as the project site in January 1969. In some respects, it was a worthy choice. The Thirteenth Precinct had the city's second-highest crime rate and was home to much of the riot-torn areas along 14th and 7th Streets. But residents of the racially and economically mixed 106,000-person precinct had not shown enthusiasm for the project—certainly not along the lines of what planners had hoped—and the project languished.[123]

In early 1970, as the D.C. Crime Bill stalled in Congress, Sterling Tucker, city council vice chairman and longtime director of the local chapter of the Urban League, revived the idea of the Pilot Precinct Project as a solution to the city's crime problem. Instead of promoting more traditional "get tough" approaches—like stricter punishment for criminals, the reorganization of the courts, or the expansion of police powers—Tucker advocated for the Pilot Precinct Program's community-oriented approach to reducing crime in Washington. Tucker believed that the OEO-funded program offered citizens a chance to play a specific role in crime prevention and neighborhood policing.[124]

Despite Tucker's endorsement, two issues had made the program unacceptable to black activists. First, to improve police operations and management,

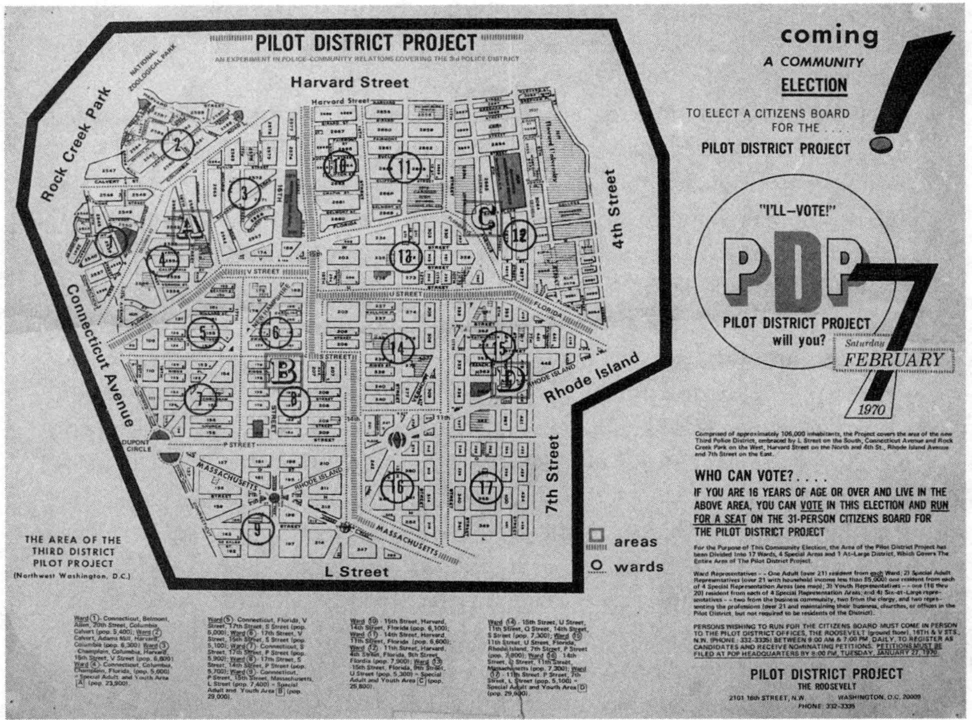

Map and voting information for the Pilot District Project. (Thomas L. Lalley Pilot District Project files [MS 0885], Historical Society of Washington, D.C.)

the city council had voted in July 1969 to consolidate the city's police precincts into larger police districts. As a result, the council incorporated the Thirteenth Police Precinct, the site for the Pilot Precinct Program, into a new Third Police District that accounted for twice the territory and a significantly larger and wealthier white population. It then expanded the Pilot Precinct Program into the Pilot District Project to cover the new territory and population accounted for in the Third Police District. Activists perceived these actions as the municipal government's desire to weaken black involvement in the project by dispersing their power throughout the Third Police District.[125]

Second, in the eighteen months since the Office of Economic Opportunity had funded the project, officials had only implemented the police training aspect of the program. The elements of the program that residents had prioritized, including the delivery of social services and the development of a youth patrol, continued to be held up by the election of a Citizens' Board. As deliberations continued, William Raspberry wondered whether the proposal would ever take off. "Is the game worth the candle?" he asked. "Police aren't hated in the ghettos because of their inefficiency in delivering social services," the columnist reminded the *Post*'s readers. "They are hated because of their actions and their attitudes, current and remembered."[126]

Black activist Marion Barry, former SNCC leader and head of Pride, Inc., a youth self-help organization located in the original Thirteenth Precinct, revealed mixed feelings about the program. On the one hand, police-community relations had become so fraught that perhaps the situation demanded new cooperation between the two groups. As Barry explained, many black residents looked at the police as an "alien occupying army" rather than a force to protect them. Yet Barry had joined the initial opposition to the Pilot District Project. According to the activist, bringing in a program that was thought to be good for the community but that the community did not really control was an insult to black residents. For these reasons he threatened lawsuits, held mock trials to indict officials, and filibustered planning sessions, all to torpedo the federal project.[127]

Recognizing that the project was going to be implemented over community objections, Barry moderated his position over the year. He even carved out a role for himself in the program by running for chairman of its Citizens' Board. He also modified his demands. Rather than require absolute control, the activist merely insisted that the elected Citizens' Board have authority over project money and staffing decisions. Barry's political calculations paid off. After nearly eighteen months of opposition, residents successfully elected him to chair a Citizens' Board along with a slate of his supporters. His victory signaled that once again federal initiatives were entwined with debates about self-determination in the nation's capital.[128]

Despite Barry's competent leadership, the program faced seemingly insurmountable challenges. The Police District Project "had more narrow escapes than Dick Tracy," one reporter observed in 1971. In addition to withstanding federal control, the project had survived demonstrations by young African Americans against its presence in the black neighborhoods of Shaw and Cardozo in Northwest D.C., community protests against its white director, and strong opposition to "repressive" OEO stipulations. Then, in September 1971, Barry stepped down from his post as Citizens' Board chairman and declared his candidacy for the upcoming D.C. school board elections. According to one observer, when Barry left the project, "the place sort of lost its authenticity."[129]

The Pilot District Project could not weather the diverse assortment of obstacles hurled its way. As *D.C. Gazette* editor Sam Smith observed, community

Marion Barry speaks to the press about the Pilot Police Precinct at the project's headquarters on June 24, 1969. (Matthew Lewis/The *Washington Post* via Getty Images)

control was "spurned as a radical plot" in Washington because it signified to its opponents "more black power."[130] The project faced annual threats of increased oversight by the OEO; criticisms from legislators, led by House District Committee chairman John McMillan, that the project served as a vehicle for community control of the police; allegations that black militants manipulated the program for financial gain; accusations by black militants, including Barry himself, that the program was part of a spy network monitoring inner-city residents; severe limits to the Citizens' Board's authority; and continual financial crises. In November 1973, the project finally folded after five unsteady years, "the victim of federal starvation," according to the *Washington Post*.[131]

The failure of community-based crime policy took a backseat to the flashier passage and implementation of punitive federal crime policy in the District. The latter grabbed the attention of *U.S. News and World Report*, a news outlet that regularly reported on law and order and routinely ginned up racialized fears of crime in the capital. According to the news magazine, "The progress that Washington, D.C., has made in its war on lawbreakers offers hope—and perhaps a blueprint—for other crime-ridden cities."[132]

Others had a different take on the Nixon White House's local accomplishments. On the one hand, journalist Simpson Lawson argued, it had implemented policies that significantly deterred crime while securing for the city substantial federal aid. On a less optimistic reading, however, he compared federal rule in Washington to Soviet rule in Hungary during the mid-1950s. The comparison was certainly hyperbolic. But when it came to law and order, District residents bore witness to repressive federal measures that they themselves had limited ways to protest or influence. Under limited home rule, the federal government even controlled community programs.[133]

As the Nixon administration declared a legislative victory in its campaign against crime in the capital, local problems continued to fester. A year after the implementation of the crime bill, D.C. city council chairman Hahn worried about three problems that lingered: the correctional problem, the drug problem, and the juvenile problem. The increase in the number of people entering correctional institutions posed challenges to the city's prison system. "We cannot escape the consequences of the course on which we embarked three years ago," he said. The plan, developed under President Johnson's supervision, had called for a larger number of police, judges, and prosecutors and speedier fair trials. But when it was implemented under President Nixon's guidance, it overburdened the city's correctional facilities. With over 50 percent of the city's crime committed by those eighteen and younger, juvenile delinquency was an even more pressing issue, and one for which Hahn confessed to having "no plan at all . . . not even a bad plan." The city's increasing narcotics problem created an even greater dilemma for the District. In fact, local officials admitted they knew very little about the problem of drug addiction, the cure, or ways to control it. But as Hahn drew urgent attention to these issues, the White House reconsidered his appointment to the city council. In April 1972, the president dispensed with Hahn and named a new appointee to chair the D.C. city council.[134]

Meanwhile, although Nixon had declared his War on Crime victorious, black Washingtonians' concerns about crime were on the rise. A March 1972 survey of inner-city residents conducted in neighborhoods like Shaw, Stanton Park, Trinidad, and Ivy City, with crime rates among the city's highest, suggested that they were more likely than residents in other parts of the capital or the neighboring suburbs to list crime as the most serious issue facing the nation. A staggering 40 percent of inner-city residents polled believed that the police were not tough enough, while 52 percent believed that the courts were not severe enough. By December 1972, the *Washington Afro-American* was fed up, not with Nixon but with black residents. "It is also time that we stop blaming everybody else for the criminal acts which occur in the neighborhoods. . . . The vast majority of these acts are caused by black people, and in the end, the whole city, which prides itself on being a Black City . . . suffers."[135]

While this suggests that black residents were genuinely concerned with crime, they did not have a favorable view of Nixon's crime program. If anything, the White House's crime legislation overlooked local factors to produce a highly symbolic bill that was demonstrably punitive to black citizens. In Washington, rising black fears pointed to the failure not just of the D.C. Crime Bill but also of the Pilot Precinct Project. However, in the absence of self-determination, appointed black officials could only do so much. Federal oversight hamstrung their efforts and continued to shape the parameters of their responses to the crime problem. As the 1976 Bicentennial celebration approached, it remained to be seen how the city's local officials would respond to other challenges confronting the black community.

5

THE SPIRIT OF '76

THE BATTLE OVER SELF-DETERMINATION AND URBAN DEVELOPMENT DURING THE BICENTENNIAL

Six months after the Nixon administration passed its sweeping omnibus crime bill for the District, White House Counselor John Dean insisted that the administration achieve national recognition for its work in the capital. The 1976 Bicentennial celebration appeared to be the perfect occasion. The White House could commemorate the positive effects of its anti-crime efforts and, it reasoned, pair its law-and-order program with a further gilding of the city's downtown core to showcase the capital.[1]

The previous administration had already set in motion plans to commemorate the nation's two hundredth anniversary. On July 4, 1966, President Johnson had established the American Revolution Bicentennial Commission (ARBC) to shape the contours and schedule of the historic event. The ARBC's governing body, which included members of Congress, the executive branch, and private citizens appointed by the president, initially envisioned the Bicentennial as a great national celebration. It enthusiastically discussed plans for an international exposition that would hark back to the 1893 World's Columbian Exposition and in the style of the more recent world's fairs held in Seattle, New York, and Montreal during the 1960s. The city assigned to anchor the Bicentennial would preside over the spectacle and receive federal funds for urban renewal efforts, an emphasis that was in line with Johnson's Great Society programming.[2]

When President Nixon took over, he narrowed the size and scope of the national celebration but still promised Washingtonians meaningful incentives. In 1969, for example, the president pledged District residents millions in federal funds, a national platform to showcase the city, and substantive local social and economic development projects. However, as the celebration neared, the White House withdrew funds, decentralized Bicentennial programming, and minimized the importance of urban renewal to the overall celebration. When the country's largest national project for the Bicentennial celebration, the Freedom Train, headed toward Washington in 1976, it was anyone's guess whether the local Bicentennial Commission would even welcome it into the District.

In the 1970s, the ongoing Vietnam War, the 1973–74 oil crisis, and Nixon's August 1974 resignation made the idea of an ostentatious Bicentennial celebration unpalatable to many Americans. For these reasons, the ARBC handed control of local events over to residents across the country and positioned many of its national festivities under the jurisdiction of corporate America.[3] In Washington, however, Bicentennial plans could not be delegated so easily. Much like law-and-order measures and civil rights protests, the urban development plans crafted during the Bicentennial planning period called into question the role of the federal government in local governance, shaped the parameters of Washingtonians' lives, and revealed the limits of attempting community-driven projects under congressional oversight.

The Bicentennial, more than any other event, crystallized the divisions that urban development sowed locally. The national shifts in its programming provided an opening for the District's white booster organizations. Established groups like the Washington Board of Trade and newer booster organizations like Downtown Progress wanted to change the city's national image as the country's crime capital. They viewed the Bicentennial as a short window within which they could shape the direction of downtown development in what they worried were their waning moments of power. While they lobbied for a comprehensive highway system and the construction of the Washington Metro, they recognized that big development projects were growing increasingly less economically feasible in the early 1970s. Thus, they turned to other projects to spur economic growth. In collaboration with both the Nixon administration and congressional representatives, the city's white boosters planned to use the national celebration as a platform for the redevelopment of downtown Washington. As they would discover, they had an ally in the city's black municipal leaders.

Thanks to Johnson's reorganization plan, Washington's political order promised black leaders a louder voice in local affairs. But the mimetic reforms ushered in during the late 1960s—including the selective incorporation of upper- and middle-class African Americans into the local political system—further politically fractured black Washington, undermined grassroots activism, and prompted the city's appointed government officials to take compromised positions on urban issues in order to garner funds and secure municipal appointments. As activists fought for self-determination, many of the city's black leaders sided with the federal government and white developers in favor of the development of the city's downtown core. Studies of the Pennsylvania Avenue redevelopment project and the Eisenhower Convention Center illustrate how, after decades of playing host to other groups, festivities, and protests, a new coalition of stakeholders tried to cash the Bicentennial's promissory note for permanent development.

Black residents tried to use the Bicentennial as a platform to reflect on the state of the city's urban problems, including its deteriorating inner city, housing shortage, fraught police-community relations, and struggling school system. They viewed the celebration as a crucial opportunity to channel funds toward long-range social and economic programs. Yet they remained wary of development. For them, the memory of devastating urban renewal efforts in the 1940s and 1950s continued to loom large. The Southwest Redevelopment Project, which Congress had authorized in 1945, particularly influenced black Washingtonians' outlook on present-day development. The project, which was in the final stages of turning Southwest D.C. into a high-income residential center, had relocated over twenty thousand poor black residents to housing projects across the city. In the process, the area's racial composition changed dramatically, shifting from 70 percent black to 70 percent white by the 1970s. As the city planned for the Bicentennial, black activists fought to keep this long history of neglect at the forefront of debates over urban development.

While the city attempted to rebuild after the riots, the issue of home rule fell from view. As the interracial coalition of local politicians and business groups strengthened, Washington's more militant black activists found themselves pushed even further to the margins of traditional political power. During this time, more mainstream leaders and groups returned to the fight for home rule, opening up new, but gradualist, political possibilities during the Bicentennial planning period. In 1970, the Nixon administration allowed for the election of a nonvoting congressional delegate. Then, in 1973, Congress passed the D.C. Home Rule Act and scheduled mayoral and city council elections for the following year. Much like the 1968 riots, the Poor People's Campaign, and the D.C. Crime Bill, the Bicentennial became a battle not only over urban development but also over the leadership and direction of the city.

THE ORIGINS OF THE BICENTENNIAL CELEBRATION

Established in 1966, the American Revolution Bicentennial Commission operated in a period of political turmoil. During the decade, the nation witnessed the assassinations of President John Kennedy, his brother Robert Kennedy, and civil rights leader Martin Luther King Jr.; polarization over the Vietnam War; and increased racial upheaval. Thus, the government gave the organization's financial and staffing needs low priority. Throughout this time, Congress sat on the ARBC's funding request. In 1968, it finally appropriated a paltry $150,000 to the commission. During the tense aftermath of the 1968 riots, District residents also paid little attention to the Bicentennial. Instead, local problems like affordable housing, police brutality, a broken school system, haphazard urban renewal plans, and contentious debates regarding freeways took precedence over the national celebration—until, that is, they learned that the commission would designate one city as the official host of the Bicentennial ceremonies, a title that would come with federal funds to address systemic issues.[4]

On April 14, eight days after the riots began, the *Washington Post*'s influential architectural critic Wolf Von Eckardt cynically questioned whether the Bicentennial would function as a benchmark for racial progress and urban renewal or whether it would be "business as usual as we rebuild the shambles and shame of our ravaged Capital." Skeptical of the ARBC's intentions, the critic asked if the organization planned to ignore Washington's urban areas in favor of beautifying the tourist city or seize the challenge of the crisis as a turning point to build one city, "the true Capital of America's aspiration." The journalist's deliberate pairing of local issues with the ARBC's national aspirations for the Bicentennial did not represent a new approach; Philadelphia's civic leaders had deployed the same strategy in their bid for federal funds. But the pairing provided a more complicated crucible for understanding the narratives of Washington that circulated within and outside the city. Since the city's federal identity deeply resonated with citizens across the country, Von Eckardt used his platform to increase awareness of the problems that plagued local Washington. And he urged city officials to leverage the District's symbolic capital for local improvements.[5]

In 1968, the *Post* advanced its own proposal, which it dubbed "Mission '76," for the celebration. The paper suggested that the American Dream ought to guide planners in making the District a model city of livable homes, good schools, and meaningful jobs in time for the Bicentennial. The *Post*'s plan included the requisite hyperbole it believe the ARBC desired, combined with a Great Society mission still in vogue. Furthermore, the paper strategically used its national influence to focus the Bicentennial's heretofore fuzzy agenda on urban renewal efforts in the District. What would be better, the paper reasoned, "than a National Capital that has demonstrated to its own people and the world that the United States is capable of solving the foremost problem of our time?" Rallying an army of architects, planners, artists, technicians, and behavioral scientists, the paper called for the development of a more creative city, one that never stopped improving itself.[6]

The *Post* had been a major backer of urban renewal in recent decades. The paper's co-owner and publisher Philip Graham's involvement in the founding of the Federal City Council, as well as the *Post*'s perennial role in covering and commenting on local politics and urban development, meant that the paper would serve as a central player in debates over the Bicentennial. It requested projects that would cease alienating residents, encouraged planners to avoid superblock projects, and suggested that developers build fewer structures like the recently built FBI building, whose "hostile Pennsylvania Avenue face," according to one architect, symbolized government power and local disenfranchisement.[7] The paper had an even more ambitious idea: major industries could underwrite Bicentennial housing, education, and transportation projects that would remain afterward as permanent features of the capital city—a provocative idea on the heels of SCLC's Resurrection City. In addition, the *Post*'s editorial staff promoted a utopian idea of a "Georgetown for everyone," calling for the democratization of the racially and economically segregated neighborhood.[8]

Even as the country's financial realities threatened the feasibility of a big fair, and the White House revaluated the Bicentennial's initiatives, the ARBC continued to search for a city that could exemplify the event's main themes. By early April 1969, it had narrowed down its choices to Philadelphia, Boston, Washington, and Miami. The winner would receive over $1 billion for the local economy, forty thousand jobs, millions of dollars in additional property taxes, and the promise of social and economic improvements.[9] Washington's proponents had their work cut out for them. One year after the riots, the *Post*'s Von Eckardt lamented that the city could not compete with the "political and theatrical clout" that Boston and Philadelphia presented to the commission. All D.C. had, he said, was an idea that had "no official endorsement, no organization, no specific plan, no attempt at community support—not even a modest brochure."[10]

The promise of a national showcase enticed the District's boosters. Historically, the Board of Trade had spent a considerable amount of resources investing in the District's cultural infrastructure. The organization was founded in

1889 as part of the city's push to win a congressional bid to host an international festival commemorating the four hundredth anniversary of Columbus's "discovery" of America. Again from 1929 to 1965, the BOT devoted significant efforts into attempting to become a host for a World's Fair. Thus, the idea of hosting the Bicentennial greatly appealed to its members. Downtown Progress was also excited about the prospect of hosting the Bicentennial celebration. Like the BOT, the organization advocated for large-scale projects like highway and subway construction. But as federal funds for massive infrastructure development rapidly dwindled in the early 1970s, Downtown Progress sought to use the Bicentennial as a vehicle to lobby for alternative projects that would stimulate the economy.[11]

In August 1969, a group of local stakeholders launched a campaign to host the celebration. Members of the city's leading white-run business and trade groups formed the D.C. Bicentennial Commission (DCBC). The DCBC made a calculated appeal to the ARBC, paying deference to the capital's symbolism while also demonstrating its role as a thriving metropolitan center. The local commission's list of projects already underway in Washington emphasized the blurred line between local and national imperatives. In the same breath as the John F. Kennedy Center for the Performing Arts, the National Visitor Center at Union Station, and new galleries on the Mall, the DCBC referenced local projects like the rebuilding of riot corridors; the development of a new mixed-income town at Fort Lincoln, a former military post located in Northeast D.C.; and Metro construction. By linking these projects, the DCBC hoped to demonstrate the city's ability to merge tourism with permanent civic development. The city could be, it argued, at once a shining example of federal experimentation and a model for municipal development. Of course, none of this would matter unless the city became the official host of the Bicentennial.[12]

To ensure proper consideration from the ARBC, the DCBC also implemented a regional strategy to bring the Bicentennial to the area. It joined forces with local commissions in Maryland and Virginia to form the National Capital Historic Region Bicentennial Committee (NCHRBC). The regional committee coordinated the bid to make the capital region the focal area for the Bicentennial. The NCHRBC's proposal still played up the capital's uniqueness, claiming D.C. was "the only city which all Americans share, which belongs to no one jurisdiction but to all." It also continued to center its plan on Washington's downtown core, with a wide array of activities and exhibits scheduled to take place on the National Mall. Moreover, it capitalized on the ARBC's early mission, challenging the commission to select the Washington area in order to prove that it could solve the problems of the American city. "If we cannot undertake this task in the Nation's Capital, in our showcase to the world, then perhaps we cannot truly confront the urban crisis anywhere in this nation," it boldly suggested.[13]

In fashioning a bid to host the Bicentennial, the NCHRBC even alluded to Washington's historic role as a laboratory for urban experimentation. For these reasons, it insisted on the inclusion of urban renewal proposals within the Bicentennial's programmatic scheme. It was not alone. The White House received hundreds of letters from citizens across the country urging it to tether the Bicentennial to capital improvements. In 1970, for example, as Congress considered proposals for the Bicentennial and the president's crime bill, two Pennsylvania residents outlined their vision for the capital city's role in the upcoming celebration. "We feel that the capital of the United States of America should be a clean and safe place to live and visit in. If we can clean up our capital, it will be a challenge and an example to the people and the state and city governments of America to do the same," they said in a letter to the Nixon White House. As with issues of crime, they believed the responsibility fell to the federal government, not ordinary citizens, to tackle the monumental project.[14]

To further sell the Capital area to the ARBC, the NCHRBC emphasized its regional connections and highlighted a variety of historic locations right outside the District, like Jamestown, Williamsburg, and Mount Vernon, Virginia, and Annapolis, Maryland. In addition, its coordinated activities centered on transportation projects—like Metro construction, freeways, and airports—that would benefit the entire metropolitan region and for which boosters needed financial support regardless of the Bicentennial. The proposal certainly made the most of the greater capital region's assets. However, by partnering with Bicentennial commissions in neighboring states, and by focusing on the capital's national appeal, the DCBC's actions suggested that the potential for local improvements would take a backseat to more regional—and perhaps national—considerations.[15]

As local proponents anxiously awaited the ARBC's decision, the Nixon administration held its own deliberations. According to White House staff members, the Bicentennial was one of the most important ongoing efforts under their supervision. But it could serve as the administration's capstone project only if Nixon won reelection. Thus, political calculations persuaded the administration to favor other cities over Washington. Just one month before the ARBC's announcement, White House Aide Charlie McWhorter told White House Special Consultant Leonard Garment, "I think it is extremely important from a political standpoint that the Administration give the impression of being strongly in favor of anything which would make the people of Pennsylvania more favorably disposed to the President." In addition, McWhorter argued that a grandiose scheme to rebuild Washington would overshadow Bicentennial projects in other cities across the country and risk drawing local capital and attention away from homegrown programming. So he did not favor Bicentennial proposals that shifted a disproportionate balance of funds or focus onto Washington's celebration.[16]

REBUILDING DURING THE BICENTENNIAL PLANNING PERIOD

In July 1970, the same month Nixon signed his D.C. Crime Bill into law, the ARBC deferred to the White House and selected Philadelphia as the official host city. Then, as a result of the turbulent political climate, it decided to eliminate the exposition component altogether. The ARBC's new thematic focus encouraged citizens to examine the nation's past, share America's attractions and diversity, and look ahead to the future.[17] The organization still favored Philadelphia, the host city, as the focal point for international participation. However, as a consolation prize, and a nod to the NCHRBC's proposal, the ARBC recommended that Washington serve as the symbol of its proposed Festival of Freedom. Washington could be, it suggested, "an outstanding example of the kinds of creative solutions possible to the challenges which now beset our nation's urban areas."[18] Perhaps it could. But that summer, a White House aide confided to Garment that he "seriously doubt[ed] whether the Congress could be persuaded to put the necessary funds into a rebuilding of Washington, D.C."—even, he admitted, for the Bicentennial.[19]

Uncertainty enveloped the city's Bicentennial plans. On reviewing the ARBC's 1970 draft report, Arthur Kallen expressed little optimism about the Bicentennial's ability to address urban renewal efforts. As Kallen, a government bureaucrat in the Treasury Department, told the ARBC, "While the passages of rhetoric in the section on Washington are inspiring, they are far removed from the realities with respect to the District's financial resources." According to Kallen, Congress's refusal to provide adequate revenue streams for local urban renewal efforts made the completion of its inspiring goals by 1976 "dubious in the extreme." Though he lauded the ARBC's vision, Kallen believed the plan would require a dismantling of the city's political and economic structures to achieve it. Thus, the Treasury Department recommended that the ARBC temper its language and goals, a preview of the greater compromises the commission—and Washington residents—would be forced to make as plans went forward.[20]

In Washington, the Bicentennial's early focus on urban renewal dovetailed with rebuilding efforts following the 1968 riots. Two years after the riots, the city's riot zones had not been restored. The Redevelopment Land Agency, the federal commission tasked with eliminating blight and modernizing the city, once again played an integral role in the efforts. It funneled funds from the Department of Housing and Urban Development into the purchase of vacant lots and run-down buildings to eventually be sold to private developers. But in April 1970, it could only account for the construction of three stores in the new buildings on 14th Street NW and six stores on a block of 7th Street NW, which had been home to thirty-two stores, theaters, and restaurants. The commercial strip on H Street NE had not fared any better. Potential investors proved too hesitant to build in the riot-torn neighborhoods, especially as white middle-class families continued to move to the suburbs. The RLA did an even worse job with the residential properties it owned. HUD had given the agency funds to house thirteen thousand people, whom the RLA forced into substandard housing. Mayor Walter Washington expressed concern about the RLA's approach to rebuilding and promised residents that he would try to accelerate the pace of urban renewal to help the families living in shameful conditions. But without control over its own budget, the city had to depend on congressional beneficence to rebuild following the riots.[21]

In the aftermath of the riots, local political issues—especially housing and freeways—were matters of increasingly intense controversy, ones where racial and class cleavages became even more visible. Residents had contended with freeway development since the 1930s. Following the passage of the National Interstate and Defense Highways Act of 1956, Congress pledged federal funding for the initiative. In the 1950s and 1960s, a coalition of powerful Board of Trade business owners, construction companies, city planners, newspaper editors, and members of Congress backed freeway development. Freeway construction faced little opposition until residents saw plans designed by the National Capital Planning Commission, which oversaw the city's planning and urban development. The original plans included concentric circles of multilane freeways, including an Outer Loop, Intermediate Loop, and Inner Loop that cut through city neighborhoods and its downtown core. The neighborhood relocations required to build the freeway would displace up to twenty thousand residents, including white professionals and even federal legislators. Some wealthy white residents successfully mobilized against freeway construction in their neighborhoods. Residents in predominantly black and poor neighborhoods had less luck and bore witness to massive demolition efforts.[22]

During the 1960s, freeway advocates remained determined to link the Inner

Loop to the Outer Loop. In 1964, city planners proposed a ten-lane freeway that would cut through predominantly black neighborhoods in Northeast D.C. and the white suburbs of Takoma Park and Silver Spring, Maryland. They also recommended an eight-lane bridge across the Potomac River at Three Sisters Island near Georgetown University, designed to shuttle tens of thousands of Virginians into downtown Washington every day. This time opponents were better prepared. Sammie Abbott, a white community organizer and founder of the Emergency Committee on the Transportation Crisis (ECTC), joined forces with white lawyer Peter Craig and BUF member Reginald Booker. Booker, who worked in the federal General Services Administration and whose family had relocated from Southwest during the prior decade's urban renewal efforts, took over as chair of the ECTC in February 1968. The ever-present Marion Barry and BUF member Charles Cassell served as vice chairs. Together the leaders waged a campaign that explicitly attacked the racism underpinning freeway construction.[23]

In addition to testifying, picketing, and talking to the media, the ECTC persuaded the appointed city council to endorse a rapid transit plan. But despite well-organized community opposition, Congress continued to flex its political muscle. Kentucky Democrat William Natcher, unfavorably known as "the dean of this city's congressional overseers" since his appointment to the House Subcommittee on D.C. Appropriations in 1961, notoriously withheld federal funding for a subway system until the city agreed to the freeway construction. Opponents accused him of blackmailing the city council into approving the Three Sisters Bridge and North Central Freeway, which it did behind closed doors in August 1969. Following increasingly vocal protests that involved an expanding coalition of citizens and protracted court battles spanning several years, the antifreeway movement finally won.[24]

In December 1969, the House of Representatives ended Natcher's blockade of subway funds. That month, the Washington Metropolitan Area Transit Authority (WMATA) broke ground on an expansive Metro project, a rapid transit system serving the District of Columbia and its Maryland and Virginia suburbs. As with other federal relocation efforts, the WMATA employed a heavy-handed approach to renewal. It relied on its power of eminent domain to condemn properties, relocated small businesses and families, and left streets and sidewalks in disarray. In 1970, the Nixon administration made continued financial support for Metro construction contingent on the WMATA's ability to meet federal standards for minority hiring. Subsequently, the WMATA established a successful affirmative action program to employ blacks as apprentices in skilled jobs like carpenter, operating engineer, and surveyor. By 1971, it boasted a 57 percent minority employment rate in the construction workforce. Because the project promised to connect black neighborhoods to the downtown core and employed black residents, it did not generate the same community opposition as freeway construction. However, the proposed "Mid-City" subway line, which would run through the riot areas of Shaw and the 14th Street corridor, took a backseat to downtown and suburban Metro routes.[25]

In 1971, Joseph Danzansky, Board of Trade president and chairman of the mayor's Economic Development Committee, explained the city's predicament to members of Congress. "We live in one of the nation's most beleaguered cities," the Giant Food president told the House District Committee. "Whole city blocks of gutted homes and shops still stand, wholly unreconstructed reminders of the 'civil disorders' of 1968." Danzansky had worked with Marion Barry to establish food distribution centers during the riots. He had also received high marks from city council vice chairman Walter Fauntroy for his aide during SCLC's Poor People's Campaign. Three years later, he played an instrumental role in efforts to revive the neighborhoods that had burned following the D.C. riots. But without Congress's help, the white booster warned, the city would continue to deteriorate. The government agreed. While official hosting responsibilities and the bulk of federal Bicentennial funds still poured into Philadelphia, Congress tentatively earmarked $500 million in urban renewal funds for Washington.[26]

Not everyone trusted the federal government to allocate these funds equitably. As the city entered its third year of planning for the reconstruction of the riot corridors, boarded-up buildings and barricaded stores still overwhelmingly marked the riot zones' commercial districts. Moreover, what had been constructed did not match the needs of the city's poorest residents. According to city council vice chairman Sterling Tucker, "The primary benefits of this building activity are bestowed on white collar workers and suburbanites." He lamented, "As a city, we appear to respond solely to pressures which are external to our own needs. Often priorities are imposed by interests which have not in the past been responsive to the aspirations of the residential city of Washington." Tucker's complaint pointed to a historic pattern that haunted the Poor People's Campaign, the D.C. Crime Bill, and now the Bicentennial. Tucker, who had been an early advocate of community policing initiatives, fought for local control of the urban renewal process. Despite early signs that he wanted to rebuild black neighborhoods, it remained to be seen what he and other black leaders would do under the auspices of the Bicentennial.[27]

RACE AND SELF-DETERMINATION DURING THE BICENTENNIAL PLANNING PERIOD

Just as the Southern Christian Leadership Conference overlooked the needs of poor black Washingtonians when it came to town for the Poor People's Campaign, Bicentennial officials ignored local racial tensions in their singular focus on staging a national celebration in the District. In December 1970, Vincent DeForest spoke out against the whitewashing of the Bicentennial. That month DeForest established the Afro-American Bicentennial Corporation (ABC) to offer "a more truthful interpretation of history" than the ARBC would offer citizens.[28] DeForest, who had ties to SCLC and had participated in its 1968 campaign against poverty at Resurrection City, argued that the planned Bicentennial was irrelevant to the majority of African Americans. To make the event meaningful to black citizens, DeForest's group pressured the Department of the Interior to identify African American historical sites as national landmarks. With funds provided under a contract with the National Park Service, the ABC successfully increased the number of black historic sites on the National Register of Historic Places from three to sixty during the 1970s.[29]

DeForest also recognized the significance of the Bicentennial's local race problem. At the time, the DCBC's membership was composed primarily of prominent white business leaders; in fact, only six of its twenty-six members were black. Appalled, DeForest criticized the group for its lack of diversity, accused it of accomplishing little besides emphasizing the federal and festive elements of Bicentennial activities, and took members to task for producing a plan that only served to line their own pockets. The DCBC took umbrage at DeForest's accusations. It blamed the ARBC, rather than its own members, for narrowly tailoring its programming. The group claimed that it had tried to implement urban renewal programs, but complained that it was hamstrung by federal influences. Negotiations with officially designated national planners was like "negotiating with George III and his Court," local commission members reported. Their comments indicated that national officials had stymied their efforts to improve black neighborhoods. But they could not refute DeForest's charges that their membership body was not diverse.[30]

In 1970, as the ARBC deliberated over Washington's role in the national festivities, the DCBC headed toward collapse. According to DeForest, the District's Bicentennial planning could be characterized by low visibility, a lack of enthusiasm, and insufficient funds. In fact, he reported that some members of the city's Bicentennial Commission did not even know that they had been selected to serve on it. Mark Evans, a radio and television executive, Board of

Trade director, and DCBC member, stepped in to preside over the ruins of the commission during the critical months before the ARBC selected its host city. But the group eventually disbanded due to members' general lack of direction and enthusiasm.[31]

White House officials demanded more from the city's leaders. In September 1971, at the White House's behest, Mayor Walter Washington held a conference with some of the District's major stakeholders to redefine the city's role in the Bicentennial and revitalize the defunct DCBC. Mirroring the national shift to recruit private enterprise to the Bicentennial, the mayor invited the city's major financial, real estate, and downtown business groups to attend. A diverse group of black citizens and black-run organizations joined the predominantly white Board of Trade, Downtown Progress, and planning and design representatives to discuss the city's Bicentennial programming. This group included city council member Sterling Tucker; Marion Barry, head of Pride, Inc., and chairman of the Pilot District Project's Citizens' Board; the United Planning Organization, the city's Community Action Agency; higher education representatives; and church leadership. As Deputy Mayor Graham Watt boasted to White House Advisor Bud Krogh, the participants were "most certainly a force to be reckoned with," and he expressed the hope that they would "enhance the President's program for the Nation's Capital," a directive that had become increasingly vague.[32]

Held at the Linden Hill Hotel in suburban Maryland, the conference revealed that even among the city's major stakeholders, the divisions over urban renewal were great. The business leaders in attendance expressed interest in developing private sector activities and initiatives that would have a lasting impact on the city. In fact, among their top proprieties was a convention center and sports arena. Black participants, on the other hand, mentioned public housing; the reconstruction of the riot corridors; the development of Fort Lincoln, a new federally funded urban community on the city's northeastern edge; and an overall improved system of urban renewal as pressing issues. Notably, 50 percent of those interviewed during the conference felt that improved race relations should be one of the Bicentennial's main concerns, while 35 percent suggested a comprehensive drug treatment program in jails and prisons. It was clear to those in attendance that if any of the proposed projects materialized, they would be divisive.[33]

Given the mimetic reforms that the Johnson administration had ushered in during the late 1960s, skeptics of the Linden Hill conference did not believe that the city's black leaders would radicalize the Bicentennial. For them, the mayor's renewed interest in resuscitating the DCBC—at the White House's urging, no less—attracted the wrong type of attention. They feared that the conference only served to repopulate the DCBC with the same calculating Washingtonians who had tried to profit from the riots. "With the Bicentennial coming, some greedy niggers and whites who tried once in 1968 to take over planning for all the burned out corridors are playing their games again," the 14th Street Community Planning Team, a group of community representatives and professional planners, said unhappily. For them, Linden Hill was proof that the interracial coalition of local politicians and business groups that coalesced around the pretext of Bicentennial planning would once again overlook the city's larger black population for their own monetary gain.[34]

The Afro-American Bicentennial Corporation expanded on this idea. DeForest's group suggested that the Linden Hill conference mirrored the District's own colonial relationship with the federal government. "Most would favor an approach that will be free of all taint of colonialism imposed by a small, secretly selected elite in obtaining a more representative Bicentennial Commission for the District of Columbia," it reported. The DCBC claimed not to alienate the local community through its plans and activities. But to DeForest's group, the Maryland summit suggested otherwise. It maintained that not even a reconstituted DCBC would look out for the interests of all Washingtonians.[35]

Despite opponents' skepticism of the Linden Hill conference, they did see one promising outcome of the summit. James Gibson, president of the Metropolitan Washington Planning and Housing Association (MWPHA), accepted the DCBC's chairmanship. Born in Atlanta in 1934, Gibson grew up three blocks from Martin Luther King. After he completed college at Duquesne University, he served an army stint in Germany. Then Gibson threw himself into the civil rights movement. At age twenty-five, he became executive secretary of the NAACP's Atlanta chapter. In Washington, Gibson presided over the MWPHA, a group that represented the city's lower-income residents and challenged the city's planning policies. Under Gibson's watch, the MWPHA shed its white leadership and transformed into a black advocacy group. In 1971, the veteran civil rights activist and community organizer accepted the DCBC chairmanship because he believed "there is a set of values that a black American brings to the Bicentennial."[36] Gibson spoke on behalf of many of the city's black residents. "Their patience is dead," he said, "and not likely to be any less dead in 1976." By taking up the mantle of the predominantly white prodevelopment group, Gibson hoped to inject into the commission a new urgency for social programming and urban renewal efforts that would impact the residents in areas damaged by the 1968 riots.[37]

Gibson's belief that the national celebration could foster productive dialogue between the city's black and white residents guided his leadership of the organization. In December 1971, Gibson, with the help of Board of Trade director Mark Evans, used the lessons of the Afro-American Bicentennial Corporation and the Linden Hill conference to diversify the D.C. Bicentennial Commission by widely recruiting new membership. Evans boasted that the new commission comprised a variety of residents "from black militants to white bank presidents and from artists to real estate developers."[38] Gibson believed that the reorganization would help bring about social change and major urban improvements. But the new leader faced two major challenges. First, he had to divert the committee's focus away from the development of the city's downtown core. Second, he had to solicit financial contributions from the ARBC, which kept a watchful eye over Bicentennial planning. Gibson quickly discovered that it would be difficult to accomplish both tasks.[39]

To Gibson's credit, he did succeed in expanding the local Bicentennial Commission's programmatic scope. Under his watch, the DCBC began to address social and economic development, community recreation and cultural facilities, improved health care, adequate housing, and education. But the ARBC consistently rebuffed its efforts. It routinely withheld information, planning assistance, and attention to its programming. To Gibson's chagrin, the White House was no help in the matter. Instead of improving communications and coordination between the local and national organizations, it also rejected local input. "We shall pursue District planning with an eye toward accommodating whatever the national organizations and panels develop in the future," White House Aide Andre Buckles said dismissively in 1972. Buckles comments indicated that much like the D.C. Crime Bill, when it came to urban affairs, the White House had no problem marginalizing local government officials and imposing a federal agenda upon the city.[40]

During the Bicentennial planning period, some groups shifted their focus away from the immediate fights against Nixon's overly punitive anticrime crusade and urban renewal plans to the underlying injustice that haunted these fights: the lack of home rule. Rather than lobby for municipal elections, the D.C. League of Women Voters took up the cause of congressional representation, a less racially fraught proposition. Months of planning and hard work by local members prompted the national League of Women Voters to adopt congressional voting representation for District residents as a focal point of its fiftieth-anniversary campaign, dubbed "Year of the Voter." In 1970, the League pressed its thirteen hundred chapters to collect 1.5 million signatures in support of voting representation for District residents. The petition drive began on

Marcher at the 1970 League of Women Voters parade shows her disappointment with the District's colonial status in Congress by displaying tea bags on her umbrella. (Star Collection, D.C. Public Library © *Washington Post*)

Tax Day, April 15, and carried the slogan "D.C.—Last Colony." In recognition of the need to broaden home rule's appeal beyond its white middle-class constituency to appeal to young black women, the D.C. chapter added the slogan "Congressional Representation—Right On." By the end of its campaign, the League had come close to its ambitious goal, collecting 1.2 million signatures. In executing its campaign, the lobbying group brought national attention to the issue of disenfranchisement at the same time as Nixon's crime bill unfavorably drew the city into the spotlight.[41]

The League's petition built congressional momentum to establish a nonvoting delegate in the House of Representatives. Against the recommendation of the House District Committee chairman John McMillan, both houses of Congress passed the D.C. Delegate Act. This pleased Nixon adviser Pat Moynihan, who had pushed for a set of home rule proposals as chair of the White House Urban Affairs Council. Despite a heavy-handed federal approach to issues of justice and policing in D.C., Nixon had long voiced support for self-government. The fact that the white middle-class League of Women Voters had executed a far less controversial campaign than Marion Barry's Free D.C. campaign four years earlier made the moderate proposal more palatable. Thus, on September 22, 1970, without a public statement or ceremony, he signed the bill into law and provided for a special election in 1971.[42]

Momentum for statehood built during the campaign for congressional representation. Some of the city's more militant activists were frustrated by the pace and tenor of home rule efforts. Specifically, they viewed the nonvoting delegate position as another mimetic reform handed down by the federal government. Determined to make D.C. the fifty-first state, a group of black activists, including Black United Front leader Reverend Douglas Moore and black journalist Chuck Stone, formed the D.C. Statehood Committee in 1969. The following year, white *D.C. Gazette* editor Sam Smith penned a persuasive article outlining the case for statehood. Together with Julius Hobson, they established a third party, the D.C. Statehood Party, and ran Hobson against Walter Fauntroy for the District's nonvoting delegate seat. Hobson did not want to participate in a political system that left congressional oversight intact. Nevertheless, he ran for the position in the hopes that he could advocate for statehood from the House floor.[43]

A coalition of black nationalists, antifreeway activists, and New Leftists backed Hobson and demanded immediate statehood. During the campaign, Hobson reasoned that statehood was the most efficient solution to the city's educational, housing, and transportation crises. For starters, it only needed a congressional majority to approve it rather than require a constitutional amendment. There were a few glaring problems with Hobson's platform. First, one could find little support inside Congress for the issue. Second, statehood did not address the pressing question of the federal payment, which Congress provided the city in exchange for the nontaxable land it occupied. Yet Hobson hoped that by adopting it as his platform, he could help make the issue more mainstream.[44]

On the other side, Fauntroy garnered support from black church leaders, national liberal activists, and a large majority of the city's white liberal voters. The more politically moderate coalition favored a gradualist approach to self-government. Concerned about the federal payment and the longer-term fight for self-determination, Fauntroy made a home rule bill and full voting representation in Congress the center of his campaign. After campaigning with Coretta Scott King, he easily defeated Hobson, who had mounted a third-party challenge from the left, and white Republican city council member John Nevius to claim the congressional seat in March 1971.[45]

In late 1970 and early 1971, as the congressional election was underway, a group of well-connected local activists mapped out a strategy to turn the fight for home rule into a national campaign. Building off of its successful campaign for congressional representation, the D.C. League of Women Voters, along with the local chapter of Americans for Democratic Action, met with Fauntroy on the eve of his electoral victory to organize a coalition of national organizations that would work toward home rule and voting representation for District residents. In July, their efforts coalesced into the Coalition for Self-Determination. In a show of bipartisan support for home rule, Fauntroy accepted the cochairmanship alongside African American senator Edward Brooke.[46]

Never before had the fight for democracy in the nation's capital been adopted by such a broad coalition. The Coalition for Self-Determination succeeded in attracting a diverse group of national partners, including Common Cause, SCLC, the NAACP, and the United Auto Workers. The local coalition included the D.C. chapters of these national organizations as well as the Washington Urban League, the Committee for Aid and Development of Latin Americans in the Nation's Capital, and the Jewish Community Council. Together, the group combined well-organized constituent pressure, local volunteer efforts, and an effective behind-the-scenes lobbying campaign to fight for home rule. But for all its effective techniques, the coalition lacked local involvement from more militant black activists like Hobson or groups like the D.C. Statehood Party. In fact, the Coalition counted few Washingtonians as members. It was not a grassroots organization, and it struggled with how much to involve potentially explosive Washingtonians. But there was another reason residents did not get involved: they simply were not concerned with the intricacies of the various strategies hatched to win self-determination. Meanwhile the Coalition knew that the issue of statehood had little popular support, whereas the more gradualist efforts it championed were more palatable to citizens across the country in the tumultuous racial and political climate of the 1970s.[47]

As the newest member of the House of Representatives, Fauntroy fought doggedly for home rule. In 1972, the delegate mapped out the contours of the District's governance for members of the Democratic National Committee: men from South Carolina, Texas, Mississippi, Georgia, and Kentucky decided whether the District could impose a tax on tobacco or have a publicly owned bus system, how much local tax residents had to pay, and how the city could spend those tax revenues. "Because the District is a colony, we must make our appeals to the national institutions which, under our unjust system, hold the power over our lives," Fauntroy said. But he warned that "the people of the

District are unwilling to be patient much longer."[48] After successfully lobbying the Democratic National Committee for the inclusion of a "strong and specific" home rule plank, Fauntroy found himself the target of local leaders' opprobrium, this time for persuading presidential candidate George McGovern to excise the right to statehood from his 1972 party platform. Statehood advocates claimed Fauntroy had sabotaged their efforts to preserve his congressional powers. Fauntroy had spent his civil rights and political careers making deals on behalf of black Washingtonians. To him, this was no different. Unbothered by the criticism, he forged ahead with a bigger campaign.[49]

In the early 1970s, Fauntroy called on a network of activists he had cultivated during his work with SCLC to lead a new southern voting registration drive. He focused primarily on congressional districts in which an increase in black votes could provide a margin of victory. The delegate even traveled down to Representative John McMillan's Sixth Congressional District to campaign for the challenger, John Jenrette, in the 1972 Democratic primary. By directing funds and attention to an intense primary race in South Carolina, Fauntroy helped mobilize previously disenfranchised African Americans to upset the long-standing House District Committee chairman, thereby removing the District's biggest obstacle to home rule. After McMillan's twenty-four-year reign, black congressman Charles Diggs Jr. (D-Mich.) assumed the chairmanship of the House District Committee and vowed to restore democracy to the District.[50]

In a year of nationwide despair over economic conditions, the ongoing Vietnam War, and rising political scandals, the Nixon administration recognized that a symbolic gesture toward democracy could bolster its public image. As the White House looked ahead to November's election, some staff members emphasized home rule legislation as the culmination of its 1968 campaign pledge to focus on Washington's local problems and as an important addition to the rhetoric surrounding the upcoming Bicentennial celebration. Others highlighted home rule's ability to demonstrate the president's commitment to racial equality and enhance his image among African Americans nationally, as the issue continued to be among the goals of the NAACP, the Congressional Black Caucus, and other civil rights groups. Through extensive research, the Nixon administration discovered that it provoked no adverse political reaction from white citizens across the country. "Few stand to lose their jobs, to have their property values decreases, or to have their children bused to school because D.C. gets home rule," aides explained. Thus, it began to seriously explore the idea of granting home rule in advance of the 1976 Bicentennial.[51]

During the summer of 1973, the Afro-American Bicentennial Corporation seized on the issue of home rule. During its July 4 celebration, black actor James Earl Jones gave a rousing rendition of Frederick Douglass's 1852 Fourth of July speech. He spoke to an audience of politically disenfranchised District residents at Cedar Hill, Douglass's Anacostia home. Douglass's speech, which Jones eloquently recited, had called American liberty and patriotism into question by pointing to the gross injustice to which the government subjected African Americans. Its inclusion in the day's festivities provided political poignancy to the ABC-led event.[52]

The program, cosponsored with the National Park Service, also featured D.C. Delegate Walter Fauntroy. In an inspiring speech, Fauntroy told audience members, "The District of Columbia will never be worthy of the title, 'The Nation's Capital,' so long as its citizens are taxed without representation and denied the constitutionally guaranteed right to local self-government." By including Fauntroy's politicized speech at the event, staged just outside the city's tourist landscape, the ABC asked citizens to consider exactly who spoke for D.C. residents.[53]

In an attempt to demonstrate to city residents that it did care about all Washingtonians, the DCBC sponsored a two-day citywide celebration in October 1973. In selecting its downtown location, event planners attempted to mend the city's fractured social geography. As the *Washington Post* noted, all residents, black and white, "could pretend that they lived in a city like any other." At the festivities, held on Fifteenth and H Streets, participants danced to live music and sampled ethnic cuisine from a variety of restaurants. The *Post* excitedly described the transformation the celebration had on the ordinarily impersonal facade of Washington's built environment. According to the paper, "The usual austerity of the environment, the impersonality of colonnades and manicured grounds were softened, at least temporarily, by a factor usually forgotten in discussions of Washington: people."[54] According to DCBC chairman James Gibson, the event, a warm-up to the official Bicentennial celebration, succeeded in showing that "we can mix across a range of races and cultures."[55] But it could only provide a brief escape. Reclaiming the seat of power, if only for two days, could not conceal the fact that the federal government still asserted political control over the District. Nor could it shake skeptics' sense that prodevelopment stakeholders still guided the DCBC's mission.

Tensions continued to mount toward the end of 1973. In November, the White House backed away from its $18 million commitment to local economic development and social programs for the celebration. According to the White House, new proposals for local programming would now require congressional authorization, a task it knew would be exceedingly difficult to achieve.

The Nixon administration's new mandate impeded local Bicentennial efforts. Instead of appealing to Congress, White House officials encouraged the D.C. government and the DCBC to work directly with private organizations, including the Board of Trade and the Washington Area Convention and Visitors Bureau, to efficiently increase tourist services and revenues for the upcoming celebration. In doing so, they undermined the appointed black government and redirected funds away from the very programming that the reconstituted DCBC had fought to promote.[56]

The loss of federal funds threatened job training programs, neighborhood arts programs, and small business assistance programs. The White House, city council vice chairman Sterling Tucker complained, cared too much about anticipated tourists, about whom he did not "give much of a damn."[57] Furious, DCBC chairman James Gibson criticized the White House for derailing local efforts. He objected to its recommendation to turn to private developers to channel the upcoming surge of tourist dollars into permanent local gain and accused officials of breaking their promise to invest in the majority-black city. The fact that the federal government stripped the city of urban renewal funds as it invested in overly punitive crime programming was not lost on the District's black leaders.[58]

The Washingtonian's James Seymore detected a fundamental irony in the responses of local black leaders like Gibson and Tucker. "The Bicentennial clearly reveals Washington's basic schizophrenia," he said. "On the one hand," he explained, "we expect home rule for the District. On the other we expect the federal government to come in and do the Bicentennial for us." "The initiative," Seymore concluded, "has to come from the community." Yet what the journalist failed to recognize was that Gibson and Tucker's outrage stemmed from the federal government's callous disregard of Washington's black residents who lived in neighborhoods outside the monumental core—areas where residents remained disenfranchised and bore the consequences of harsh federal laws like the D.C. Crime Bill. With the federal government controlling the purse strings for the celebration, they knew that community efforts were futile.[59]

During the planning period, the White House continued to whittle its $18 million pledge down to under $3 million. It left the D.C. Bicentennial Commission scrambling for money, even though its local programs promised to commemorate the Bicentennial as much as the tourist attractions that received millions in federal Bicentennial aid. The DCBC claimed to make the most of its limited funds. Yet the D.C. Chamber of Commerce, the black-run counterpart to the white Board of Trade, remained skeptical of its work. Established in 1938, the D.C. Chamber of Commerce's membership included independent black businesspeople, professionals, and minority trade and professional groups in the D.C. area. It focused on the concerns of small business owners, with a particular emphasis on affecting economic change and development in the inner city. It criticized the local Bicentennial Commission for raising expectations that it would "revolutionize" the D.C. economy and then commissioning projects that did not account for the needs of the whole community. Its criticism pointed once again to the divisiveness of urban planning under limited home rule. Because Johnson's reorganization plan had politically fractured black Washington, and because white stakeholders and black leaders vied for power in the absence of elected representation, urban renewal, much like anticrime measures, remained a contentious issue in the public sphere.[60]

Representative Diggs forced the House District Committee to reckon with another contentious issue when he, along with Walter Fauntroy, pressed forward with home rule legislation. The congressman knew he had to walk a cautious line. He felt a sense of duty toward Washington residents to craft home rule legislation that provided them real representation and afforded the local government meaningful powers, but he was aware that he presided over a committee steeped in Jim Crow traditions and filled with home rule opponents who carried enough veto power to keep any bill stalled in the House.

As Sterling Tucker testified to the committee, home rule legislation needed to include a locally elected mayor and city council; local legislative authority over the city's affairs; full budgetary authority, including the right to determine the city's priorities and raise and allocate revenues; and an automatic federal payment to the city. Diggs knew that House members would never agree to all of these demands. So he offered several concessions to the House's southern Democrats, including full control of the city's budget, approval over judicial appointments, presidential authority to take over control of the local police force in an emergency, and a prohibition on the city council from changing the city's criminal code. His gamble paid off. Diggs won the support of Representative William Natcher, the powerful chairman of the D.C. Appropriations Subcommittee who had held up funds for the city's subway system until the House overrode his opposition four years earlier. Now he persuaded his Democratic colleagues to support Diggs, rendering the House District Committee's Republican clique powerless to further stall the bill. Yet Diggs's concessions locked into conference a bill with far more limited provisions than he had originally intended.[61]

Generally speaking, the fight for home rule was split between activists and the majority of D.C. residents, black and white, on one side and the city's powerful business community on the other. The reception to Diggs's political compromise was more complicated. On the one hand, D.C. statehood activists decried the move. Reverend David Eaton, pastor of the All Souls Unitarian Church, went so far as to accuse Diggs of "selling his soul" in his deal with Natcher.[62] On the other hand, the Federation of Citizens Associations supported Diggs's concession to retain congressional line-item control over the District budget. But that was the only praise it doled out. As Federation president Dr. Ellis Haworth told members of the Senate-House conference in October 1973, none of its recommendations were incorporated into the pending legislation. "Congress should understand that there is a substantial group of District citizens, many of whom are represented by this Federation, who do not favor the change from the present system of appointment by the president," Haworth stated, adding, "We see little likelihood that an elected local government will be more efficient, more responsive, or better able to balance federal and local interests, nor do we expect our taxes to be lower or our schools better."[63] Conservative officials agreed. As late as December 22, 1973, two days before Nixon signed the home rule legislation into law, White House Deputy Ken Cole vowed to work with the Republican leadership "to get as conservative and limited a bill as possible."[64]

For the most part, the Nixon administration succeeded. Because Republicans were convinced that Diggs would accept almost any bill that the White House deemed acceptable, they had crafted an extremely limited version of home rule with broad presidential and congressional controls. Under the Home Rule charter, Congress could enact legislation for the District on any subject and veto any act of the city council; the president had veto power over municipal legislation; and the city government's budget was still a part of the federal budget process. In addition, the president would appoint local judges, and the U.S. Attorney for the District of Columbia, another presidential appointee, would serve as the city prosecutor—meaning that the city would not elect its own district attorney.[65]

A few amendments were rejected. Senator William Scott (R-Va.) had fought to transfer jurisdiction for the Lorton Correctional Complex in Virginia from the District government to the Department of Justice, while Senator Norris Cotton (R-N.H.) had introduced an amendment to allow the president to appoint the city's chief of police. Yet still, on account of pressure from legislators from Virginia and Maryland, the city's closely supervised tax powers explicitly precluded the enactment of a commuter tax. Meanwhile, the administration used its influence with House District members to ensure a measure providing the president with emergency powers over local police.[66]

One notable exception to the trend of limited self-government was the bill's provisions for Advisory Neighborhood Commissions (ANCs), added at the request of Congressman Don Fraser (D-Minn.). Provided that residents approved the referendum, the city's new charter would allow for the election of roughly 360 unpaid representatives to thirty-six neighborhood councils, each divided into single neighborhood districts for every two thousand residents. The idea, which was supported by community activists, was to give neighborhoods a larger say in local affairs by allowing elected ANC commissioners to present their positions and recommendations on policy issues to various District government agencies, the executive branch, and the city council. In a bill that worked to limit avenues for autonomy, the ANCs offered potentially substantive spaces for participatory democracy.[67]

As activists and legislators debated home rule legislation, national Bicentennial organizers had their own politically and racially fraught issues with which to contend. In 1972, the People's Bicentennial Commission, established by antiwar activist Jeremy Rifkin one year earlier to provide "revolutionary alternatives for the Bicentennial years," launched a public attack on the ARBC. As one of the most vocal critics of the Bicentennial's commercialization, the group educated citizens on the radical potential of political democracy and embedded in its message a critique of capitalism and urban development that resonated with D.C. activists.[68] To draw further attention to the hypocrisy of the Bicentennial, it released several of the ARBC's internal memos to the press. The memos portrayed the organization as a top-down commission with little interest in the upcoming celebration. Following their release, the *Washington Post* charged the ARBC with "politics, commercialism and jingoism."[69] Journalists also accused Nixon of stacking the ARBC with Republican members to further a conservative agenda. This news spawned a congressional investigation into its activities. Despite a lack of concrete evidence against the ARBC, the organization lost its political capital and public credibility; it had become enmeshed within a greater legitimation crisis presiding over the Nixon administration.[70]

At the end of 1973, as Nixon handed District residents greater control over local affairs, he reorganized the American Revolution Bicentennial Commission into the American Revolution Bicentennial Administration (ARBA). He then appointed John Warner, former secretary of the navy, to run the organization. These changes provided the ARBA with greater autonomy while distancing it from the federal government. The ARBA's new mission differed only slightly from the ARBC's old mission. But, at Warner's request, the group's officers explored ways to include people of all ages, race, and gender in the Bicentennial's programming. Thus, in 1973 and 1974, in the years after the DCBC reorganized under chairman James Gibson to better incorporate black residents' needs, the ARBA held its own series of conferences to deal with the issues that Native Americans, women, and ethnic and racial groups had with its plans for the Bicentennial.[71]

In June 1974, James Gibson and Monsignor Geno Baroni, director of the National Center for Urban Ethnic Affairs, cosponsored a meeting for ethnic and racial groups in the capital. The meeting attracted more than seventy-five participants representing a cross-section of national and community organizations. Concerned with the problems that plagued most cities, they came together to lobby for urban renewal programs and craft Bicentennial projects to stimulate local economic development. Under the ARBA's watchful eye, participants formed the Bicentennial Ethnic Racial Council to offer feedback to the main body. In this instance, the ARBA took a proactive approach to accommodate dissent. As its report indicated, the conference signaled a landmark moment, the first in which a federal agency collaborated with such a diverse group of community representatives.[72]

Then, in 1975, just one year before the Bicentennial, the ARBA created a twenty-five-member Advisory Council to increase public representation in the planning process. The new council included distinguished black writer Maya Angelou and Malcolm X's widow, Betty Shabazz. But the ARBA's approach to inclusivity resulted in a depoliticized showcase of cultural pluralism. More importantly, in its inclusion of racial and ethnic groups in the celebration, it managed to sidestep the era's racial politics—something that Washingtonians could not avoid, especially in the new era of home rule.[73]

THE REDEVELOPMENT OF PENNSYLVANIA AVENUE

In the period after the 1968 riots and Poor People's Campaign, local white stakeholders focused on urban development in an attempt to control the flow of federal funds into the city's downtown core. The debates around the redevelopment of Pennsylvania Avenue during the Bicentennial planning period illustrate how these white stakeholders used the celebration as a vehicle to execute their vision over the opposition of residents who lived outside the central business district. They did not enact these plans alone. Much as they had done with federal anticrime legislation, select black municipal appointees lent their support to nationally oriented urban development efforts. Their largely prodevelopment positions reveal the compromises they made as they negotiated their roles as intermediaries between the federal government and D.C. residents in the lead-up to home rule.

In the late eighteenth century, French engineer Pierre L'Enfant conceived of Pennsylvania Avenue as a grand thoroughfare that would connect the Executive Mansion and the Capitol. By World War II, Pennsylvania Avenue had become the nation's greatest ceremonial and processional route. Home to a vast array of federal structures, including the Federal Trade Commission, the National Archives, the Department of Justice, and the U.S. Post Office, it had earned D.C. the nickname "city of marble." Yet it was run-down, with parking lots and deteriorating buildings lining the northern side of the avenue. To Pat Moynihan's great consternation, private business hesitated to build along the avenue. "This is the most valuable real estate in the world," the White House advisor exclaimed. "This is not any downtown," he added. "It's the center of the capital of the United States for God's sake."[74]

As the counselor to the president for urban affairs, and the previous executive secretary of the White House Urban Affairs Council, Moynihan used his position to prioritize the Pennsylvania Avenue project. Moynihan had come to the White House fresh from Harvard University, where he had served as a professor in the Graduate School of Education and as the director of the Joint Center for Urban Studies. Often considered a liberal within Nixon's inner circle, he helped craft national urban policy but had never been in a position to implement a project of this magnitude. Instead, while chairing the Urban Affairs Council, he had forged ahead on issues related to government building location, patterns of youth unrest, food stamp programs, and the exodus of Native Americans from reservations to cities. Moynihan had another reason to champion the Pennsylvania Avenue redesign: after John Kennedy's assassination in 1963, Jackie Kennedy had requested that the project continue apace. Moynihan was determined to honor the slain president by finally creating the great thoroughfare Kennedy had envisioned.[75]

While Moynihan initiated the redevelopment of Pennsylvania Avenue, officials, planners, and business owners disagreed over the shape of development. The Board of Trade, which often had the ear of the White House when it came to local affairs, met with Moynihan to discuss the project. The BOT told Moynihan that neither existing municipal agencies nor federal agencies could resuscitate the avenue. A new entity was needed, it believed, to balance federal and local concerns with the desire to recruit private investment.[76] Moynihan agreed. In June 1970, one month before Nixon signed the D.C. Crime Bill into law, the White House aide worked with the president on a strategy to utilize federal funds to stimulate private commercial development between the Capitol and the White House. Moynihan knew the president would view it as a minor issue. But for him, it was the most important urban legislation on

Patrick Moynihan and President Richard Nixon tour the redevelopment area of Pennsylvania Avenue. (CORBIS/Corbis via Getty Images)

which the president had yet deliberated. It would, he argued, create "the first truly modern central city in the world." Moynihan firmly believed that the redevelopment project ought to serve as the focal point of the Bicentennial. As an added benefit, he thought it would help Nixon leave his stamp on the city. "I count this as no small matter," he said.[77]

Following conversations with the BOT, Moynihan mapped out the contours and technical details of a new, quasi-public corporation that would handle the redevelopment efforts. The corporation would be empowered to draft detailed plans for developing Pennsylvania Avenue and would have the power of eminent domain, allowing it to aggregate and clear land for viable commercial investment. As outlined, the project would eventually recoup its costs, though Moynihan explained that the corporation would first have to borrow funds—up to $125 million—from the Treasury Department to finance it. Guided by the White House's directive, and during the early stages of Bicentennial planning, Congress moved into action. In September 1970, it proposed the Federal City Bicentennial Development Corporation (FCBDC) Act to establish a new development corporation to revive the stretch of Pennsylvania Avenue between the Capitol and the White House.[78]

Whereas the *Washington Post* did not back the government's invasive law-and-order measures, it heartily supported upgrading Pennsylvania Avenue, a view that aligned with its historical support for redevelopment. The paper reasoned that the FCBDC's plan would provide a good opportunity to accomplish several tasks at once: increase the city's tax base with commercial development, keep downtown businesses alive, and provide amenities for tourists. In fact, it argued that more than other city projects, this one represented the best combination of local and national interests. "The grand axis between the Capitol and the White House" was a lifeline, said the paper, for "our dingy downtown." "It would be self-defeating and nothing short of idiotic for this city to refuse a federal effort to re-emphasize the national significance of this city and thereby to strengthen the lifeline," the *Post* argued.[79] But not everyone wanted to tie the city's fate to its national standing. Incorporating the Pennsylvania Avenue redevelopment project within the Bicentennial's scope gave some home rule proponents pause. They interpreted it as a sign that the federal government would once again bypass the needs of black Washingtonians, refuse to relinquish real power, and fail to redistribute significant resources to them.

The *Washington Star*, which, along with the *Washington Post*, helped set the city's urban agenda, pushed back against Congress's FCBDC proposal. It scrutinized the proposed development corporation and called into question its tenuous connection to the Bicentennial celebration. Instead of serving as a capstone project for the nation's two hundredth birthday, the *Star* viewed the FCBDC as a wedge issue between blacks and whites. Moreover, it described the projected redevelopment as "a middle-class bastion between the government and the ghetto."[80]

The Metropolitan Washington Planning and Housing Association agreed. In the fall of 1970, just two months after the federal government passed its D.C. Crime Bill, and one year before its president, James Gibson, became chair of the D.C. Bicentennial Commission, the group launched a grassroots campaign against Congress's plan.[81] Speaking for the group, Gibson chastised "the heavy, authoritarian hand of the federal government" for trying to impose on the District a plan that ignored residents' needs and threatened the stability of a city already torn by racial and class strife.[82] The group accused Congress of limiting planning to a small section of Pennsylvania Avenue rather than relating it to the city's larger social and cultural geography. To the MWPHA, the FCBDC's limited focus on Pennsylvania Avenue suggested that the government was once again leveraging its city for ceremonial purposes rather than human needs. In order to make the Bicentennial more democratic, it reasoned, the celebration had to improve the quality of life of all Washington residents. Why, the group wondered, was the government unwilling to make large-scale changes to the city's urban landscape? The answer was clear: much like its callous disregard of black lives in favor of punitive law-and-order measures, the government readily positioned black Washingtonians outside the scope of worthy urban planning projects.[83]

The FCBDC was in the crosshairs of debates over the redevelopment of Pennsylvania Avenue and larger arguments over who should govern the city. To black activists who had been pushed to the margins of political power, one thing was clear: the FCBDC's mission would not improve the lives of the city's lower-income residents, many of whom lived in Pennsylvania Avenue's Anacostia neighborhood, far from the White House. As one local architect noted candidly, "Everyone knew the plans were intended to enhance a short, but symbolically charged, parade route—not to make a symbolic tie between diverse parts of the city by fixing up the whole avenue."[84] In fact, by unilaterally constituting the corporation's board of directors, Congress ignored the wishes of local government officials, who had asked for greater representation. The bill's lack of provisions for citizen participation particularly frustrated local activists, reinforcing their suspicions that the new Pennsylvania Avenue would become another federal enclave rather than a welcoming site for residents.[85]

The Washington Planning Workshop expanded on these sentiments. The community development center, run by a young black Washington architect named Taylor Culver, was one of eighty-two outfits across the country that aimed to "build for the community." Harlem architects created the first shop in 1964 to offer architectural services and training to residents. Under Nixon, the Office of Economic Opportunity denied the centers a $70,000 grant, so they worked with bare-bones staff and relied on volunteer expertise to make building for the poor more economically feasible. Culver founded D.C.'s chapter in 1971 and had, in the span of one year, designed a drug clinic, offered expertise to poor residents who claimed to have been defrauded by the Federal Housing Administration, and presented plans for playgrounds in blighted areas to the D.C. City Council. He strongly opposed the proposed development corporation. He pointed out the particular hypocrisy of the government creating the FCBDC, intended to guild Pennsylvania Avenue, at a time when it claimed to be looking for ways to "save" the nation's cities. The bill did not attempt to "rescue" the riot-torn sectors of the city. Instead, Culver argued, it threatened to eliminate a large portion of the District's tax base, along with needed revenue from small businesses along Pennsylvania Avenue, in exchange for "a paved vista best suited for massive military parades" and "blocks of sterile buildings completely barren of human scale." For Culver, the bill added insult to a long list of citywide injuries, including the decades-long urban renewal project in Southwest, the exodus of white residents to the suburbs, and, most recently, the

1968 riots. Thus, he urged Congress to "bring the people back, not just between 8 A.M. and 6 P.M., but at all hours of the day and evening."[86]

The Pennsylvania Avenue project even sparked tensions within Downtown Progress. Created by the highly influential Federal City Council, Downtown Progress primarily represented large businesses and produced extensive plans to redevelop D.C.'s former downtown retail core. While members allied around the cause of urban development, the displacements outlined in the FCBDC's plan created divisions within the organization. The *Washington Post* attended one of its ten confrontational sessions, observing that "voices of frustration and anger filled the conference room of Downtown Progress. . . . Together they formed a cacophony of disparate and often conflicting interests." James Gibson, now chairman of the D.C. Bicentennial Commission, presided over the meeting. Previously opposed to the redevelopment project, Gibson shifted positions. He even acted as a referee between businesspeople as they debated the bill's merits.[87]

At risk of dislocation, the group's small business owners opposed the FCBDC. During congressional hearings in the spring of 1972, Harry Hahn, a local businessman whose store would be one of the first impacted by the redevelopment project, testified against it. Hahn was the owner of the Hub Furniture Company, located one block from Pennsylvania Avenue on 7th and D Streets NW. If development proponents got their way, Hahn's store would be one of its first casualties. Even so, Hahn recognized the importance of the avenue to Washington's local economy. He told the subcommittee that he believed local residents had an obligation to the tourists who visited and contributed to the city's economy and welcomed the redevelopment of Pennsylvania Avenue. Yet for Hahn, the project had to comprise just one piece of a more comprehensive redevelopment plan needed—one that would include the burned-out corridors of the 7th Street, 14th Street, H Street, and Anacostia neighborhoods.[88]

Overall, Hahn spoke forcefully on the subject of race. His testimony focused on the potential exodus of downtown businesses to the suburbs, the need for low-income African Americans to have a place to shop and work, and the exclusion of owners and tenants from the decision-making process. Hahn's family had opened Hub Furniture Company in 1902. His store, as well as other businesses located on the 7th Street corridor, catered to less affluent, inner-city residents. "You just cannot ignore this tremendous segment of the Washington population," he warned the subcommittee. In addition to catering to a lower-income black clientele, 50 percent of Hub Furniture Company's employees were black, some in managerial positions and most residents of the inner city. Crafting a tactical argument based on the racial stereotypes that southern members of Congress trafficked in, Hahn warned that Hub's closure would force his employees to join the ranks of the unemployed and potentially place them on the "already overburdened welfare rolls."[89]

Mortimer Lebowitz, president of Morton's department stores, also testified against the project. Like the nearby Hub Furniture, Morton's building was included in the proposed redevelopment area. And, like Hahn, Lebowitz acknowledged the challenges that Congress's proposed legislation posed to his black customers and employees. With rentals from the corporation priced "six or eight times our current costs," Lebowitz reasoned that merchants would be forced to relocate, thereby depriving the poor of a place to shop.[90]

The strands of opposition to the FCBDC were not as well coordinated as the prodevelopment sector's support for it. During the congressional hearings, Downtown Progress testified in favor of it. So did Robert Gray, a city-planning director. He believed that the FCBDC could help the city overcome its major obstacles to downtown revitalization, including the District's tarnished image as the crime capital—one that, ironically, Nixon had cemented.[91] In the lead-up to both home rule and the Bicentennial, Mayor Walter Washington also made a strong case for urban development. He hailed the project, emphasizing the ways that it would improve residents' quality of life. Moreover, the legislation would, he believed, make Pennsylvania Avenue a vibrant center of downtown activity, including "new private investment, new jobs, new and improved housing, additional services for our people, new social and cultural activities, and last but certainly not least, more revenue for the city." In touting the project's local benefits, he sided with the federal government as well as the city's white stakeholders, who had previously been some of his biggest critics.[92]

In October 1972, Congress passed the Pennsylvania Avenue legislation with few concessions to local activists. According to the FCBDC's promotional materials, "Congress determined that the national interest required that the area . . . be developed and used in a manner suitable to its ceremonial, physical, and historic relationship" to the federal government and to the surrounding "governmental buildings, monuments, memorials and parks." The legislation did call for the creation of a seven-member advisory group to the commission composed of area merchants and property owners. Yet this only served to enhance white stakeholders' power. Meanwhile, the final version of the bill provided the corporation with eminent domain and omitted a provision allowing for a veto by the D.C. government and the National Planning Commission. This omission effectively guaranteed that any plan submitted to Congress would consider the needs of tourists and the federal government above those of the city's residents. By denying local officials a veto and granting more seats to white stakeholders, the federal government continued to undermine black leadership under Johnson's limited home rule plan.[93]

Congress also came to the realization that such a massive undertaking could not be completed by 1976. Thus, it changed the broadly named FCBDC to the more narrowly tailored Pennsylvania Avenue Development Corporation (PADC). However, as Bill Hart, national Bicentennial Commission chairman, told President Nixon, "The Bicentennial remains a convenient vehicle to urge speedy legislative action in hopes that at least a partially rejuvenated Pennsylvania Avenue will greet people in 1976." Congress agreed with Hart, using the celebration to justify federal intervention in urban affairs even as it absolved itself of any expectation of meaningful urban renewal outside Washington's monumental core.[94]

In 1973, the PADC began substantive planning activities. A fifteen-member staff held more than one hundred meetings with representatives of District and federal government agencies, community groups, and business and professional associations before preparing a formal plan for congressional approval. In 1974, the corporation came up with a plan that the *Washington Star* believed had a better chance of succeeding than anything that had preceded it. The PADC looked to balance economic utility with the goal of housing residents, preserving small businesses, and protecting retail specialty areas. It proposed 4.2 million square feet of new office space, 800,000 square feet of new retail space, 400 to 700 additional hotel rooms, and a new 1,500-unit residential community. According to the *Star*, the PADC's plan promised "sensitivity to the real needs of human beings." The paper conceded, however, that developers continued to give a muddled account of where low-income residents fell on their spectrum of priorities.[95]

The Board of Trade spoke excitedly about the PADC's new plan to revitalize the avenue by introducing mixed commercial and residential spaces with new landscaping, lighting, paving, and public open spaces. Unlike the government's traditional demolition model of urban renewal, the PADC approached Washington's downtown more gingerly. The Board of Trade was particularly impressed with its extensive historic preservation program, its proposal for the restoration of the Willard Hotel and other landmark buildings, and the avenue's projected amenities for residents and visitors alike—including places to eat and shop and cultural activities for tourists.[96]

In June 1974, less than six months before Washington's first municipal elections, the appointed city council made its suggestions to the PADC—suggestions that only served to enhance the city's monumental profile. It advocated changing Pennsylvania Avenue's image through a variety of cosmetic improvements, including landscaping, the restoration of historic buildings, and tours of the area. The city council did try to remain sensitive to racial matters. For example, it suggested that the PADC prepare an employment program with special provisions for equity investment and business development opportunities for minority group members. It also demanded that the PADC provide low- and moderate-income residencies in its housing proposal for the area. But the council largely shrugged off its financial responsibility for the project. "Public expenditures," it clarified, "are to be provided by the federal government as a special National effort to revitalize this historic Avenue." Tightening the city's purse strings, it clarified that District funds would not be made available. Because the Pennsylvania Avenue project developed during but expanded out of the exigencies of the Bicentennial celebration, the question of who could and should govern the city undergirded debates over urban development.[97]

In 1974, *Washington Star* reporter Benjamin Forgey offered readers a discouraging view of the PADC's progress. "Stand on the corner of 8th and E streets and look south," Forgey instructed. "Deteriorating buildings, empty stores, dirty streets, speculators' parking lots, dismal retail strips, a ludicrous waste of a great urban space, and the gibberish of construction . . . helps to give these blocks and the rest of downtown the ambience of a war zone after a devastating attack from the air."[98] During subsequent years, disagreements continued to delay the PADC's plan. A substantial portion of that controversy dealt with the question of historic preservation. Nevertheless, Congress approved it in May 1975. But with so much of the area in disrepair and funding still uncertain, the city's prodevelopment sector looked to another project to energize Washington's local economy in the lead-up to the Bicentennial.[99]

THE EISENHOWER CONVENTION CENTER

In the late 1960s and early 1970s, convention centers sprang up in major cities like Baltimore, Houston, Indianapolis, St. Louis, and Atlanta. But in D.C., development proponents had trouble converting tourist dollars into badly needed infrastructure for the city. Mark Evans, former chairman of the city's Bicentennial Commission, fumed. The Board of Trade had long advocated for the construction and maintenance of auditoriums, cultural venues, and stadiums. The civic center was no exception. As the Board of Trade director argued, the city would continue to commit economic suicide without a major convention center. Evans had first proposed the idea of a convention center-sports arena complex when the city was competing with Philadelphia and Boston for

Bicentennial hosting duties. After the ARBC chose Philadelphia in 1970, he lobbied House District Committee member Joel Broyhill to introduce legislation authorizing the construction of a similar project.[100]

The BOT invested significant time and energy into developing an attractive proposal. In 1971, it partnered with the National Capital Planning Commission, which had final approval over federal land use and building construction, to develop a plan. Using information from a recent government feasibility study, they prepared a booklet of design possibilities to present to the federal government. To further sell the project, the Washington Area Convention and Visitors Bureau, a group started by the BOT in 1931, produced a brochure advertising the civic center, complete with blueprints detailing meeting rooms, exhibit hall specifications, and building dimensions.[101]

In response, the Public Buildings and Grounds Subcommittee of the House Public Works Committee unanimously approved a measure to build a $108 million convention center–sports arena complex as a memorial to former president Dwight D. Eisenhower. In advancing the legislation, Congressman Kenneth J. Gray (D-Ill.), who cosponsored the bill with Broyhill, sought to rely on a never-before-used provision of the 1959 Public Buildings Act that required approval of only the larger Senate and House Public Works Committees and not the entire body of Congress, provided the president found it "in the public interest." In preparing to test the provision, Gray hoped that the committees could sidestep public controversy. His decision revealed once again how the lack of home rule allowed the federal government to continue to insert itself into local issues.[102]

As debate over the convention center heated up in the spring and summer of 1972, the BOT published an open letter to President Nixon and to members of Congress as a full-page ad that ran in both the *Washington Star* and the *Washington Post*. Other like-minded groups, including the Hotel Association of Washington, D.C., Inc., Downtown Progress, the Federal City Council, and the Washington Board of Realtors, Inc.—as well as the black middle-class D.C. Federation of Civic Associations—joined the BOT in stating the case for the construction of the Civic Center.[103] Two days later, President Nixon responded with his own letter to Congressman Gray, chairman of the House Public Works Committee. Nixon supported the idea of a civic center or sports arena in downtown Washington to draw citizens from across the country to the capital. As Gray's committee reviewed the legislation, he expressed his full support for the bill. "This takes on special significance as we approach the 1976 Bicentennial in which the Washington metropolitan region will play a major role," the president added, acknowledging the capital's significance to the celebration. [104]

Thinking beyond the Bicentennial's needs, Nixon trusted that the venue would have a trickle-down effect, filtering tourist dollars to the neighborhood level. However, he believed that the long-term developmental, managerial, and financial responsibility for such a project resided with the District of Columbia rather than the federal government. For that reason, he called for measures that would force the District's municipal government to construct and finance the project on its own. The Washington Area Convention and Visitors Bureau, which was primarily financed by tourist-oriented businesses in the city, was pleased. Likewise, the Board of Trade eagerly accepted the president's endorsement. It reprinted Nixon's letter to Gray in its August newsletter to draw further attention to the anticipated project.[105]

Congressional proponents hoped that the Dwight D. Eisenhower Memorial Bicentennial Civic Center would accomplish three goals: to provide a convention facility to contribute to the commemoration of the nation's Bicentennial year, a facility to encourage commercial and economic activity within Washington, and a fitting memorial to former President Eisenhower. The central features of the proposal included a thirty-year purchase contract with private investors, a federal subsidy of up to $14 million to the D.C. government, and necessary funds for relocation efforts. Considering the city's fraught history with federal relocation efforts, the latter provision immediately caught residents' eyes.[106]

Congressional members conferred with an assortment of federal and local organizations before recommending a site in Northwest D.C., bounded by 8th, H, and 10th Streets and New York Avenue. Just south of Mount Vernon Square, the site resided in the heart of what Downtown Progress called "Washington's Downtown Urban Renewal Area," home to sixty-one households, eighty-two businesses and institutions, and a forthcoming Metro stop. Recalling the heated debates around the Southwest Redevelopment Project, the Nixon White House requested a more collaborative process. It asked that "the legitimate concerns of merchants, working people, and residents in those neighborhoods receive fair consideration in the planning and location process." However, it left the details up to Congress, once again punting the needs of local Washingtonians to another branch of government.[107]

Much like the warm welcome they gave the government-led Pennsylvania Avenue redevelopment plan, the city's booster organizations hailed the proposed civic center project. They believed that the location meshed well with the city's other urban renewal plans. Moreover, they anticipated that it would create a demand for approximately 3,000 new jobs, 3,400 hotel rooms, 2,500 restaurant seats, and 90,000 square feet of commercial space. The local city council agreed, as did a mix of public and private organizations, including the Redevelopment Land Agency, National Capital Planning Commission, and D.C. Bicentennial Commission.[108]

Community activists demanded a chance to respond. The eight-block area targeted for construction pit Washington's powerful business community against a growing coalition of residents, small business owners, and churchgoers. They had their opportunity on February 17, 1972. On that day, Representative Gray held one of four public hearings on the project at the Greater New Hope Baptist Church, the project's proposed site. The irony of a congressional representative from Illinois holding hearings about local development in D.C. was not lost on the three hundred residents who packed into the church that evening. The hearing started at 5 P.M. and lasted well past midnight. That night, the project's opponents identified the displacement of residents and businesses, the decrease in the amount of property subject to real estate taxation, and its impact on Chinatown as their major concerns. "I'd like the Chinese community to stay together," George Moy, owner of a neighborhood Chinese restaurant, said. "The way it looks now, we're going to be in Southwest, Northwest, all over the city," he warned, alluding to the previous relocation of black residents for the Southwest Redevelopment Project. King David, a lawyer and area churchgoer, vowed to take the matter to court. "I will hold this up until hell freezes over," he claimed.[109]

Churchgoers also struggled with the prospect of relocation. Reverend Charles Hamilton, pastor of the church that hosted the hearing that night, told the subcommittee that his fifteen-hundred-member congregation had paid $150,000 for the building eighteen years earlier and had paid the mortgage off in eleven years. "We love this place," he said. "This is where we come on Sunday mornings to have our spiritual strength renewed." Reverend S. Everett Guiles and members of the twelve hundred families who worshipped at Turner Memorial African Methodist Episcopal Church also pushed back against the legislation. The project would mean the loss of the building that they had purchased twenty years earlier and paid off seven years ago.[110]

That evening, the project's opponents were outmatched by a unified front of white business and trade groups. Representatives from the Board of Trade, the Hotel Association of Washington, and the Restaurant and Beverage Association of Washington joined Downtown Progress to express their support. They testified that a convention center would revitalize a deteriorating downtown area and boost the city's tourist and hotel economy. Downtown Progress used the meeting as an opportunity to counter opponents' specific charges. The group's response hinged on optimistic readings of relocation assistance, construction values, and the government's willingness to cooperate with Chinese organizations. They did, however, make one key concession. After Reverend Hamilton's testimony, and on account of pressure from the Metropolitan Washington Planning and Housing Association, the organization recommended reducing the size of the site and moving it farther west to minimize any adverse effects to the Chinese community, the businesses on Furniture Row, or the two churches.[111]

Downtown Progress's highly professional technical staff used the Bicentennial as a vehicle to lobby for changing the identity of downtown Washington. By the early 1970s, members knew black residents were gaining greater political influence. So they crafted a more inclusive message—one that differed dramatically from their messaging following the 1968 riots. "The downtown cannot afford to be exclusively a black downtown, a local downtown, a national downtown or a tourist-trap downtown," the organization said. "The participation of the black community at all levels will be central to this," it conceded. For Downtown Progress, the convention center would serve as a benchmark of racial progress for the city. It would be "a vital center which has risen from a period of intense social conflict and physical reconstruction, under the administration of a black mayor and with a citizenry which is 70 percent black," it said in recognition of the city's changing racial demographics. But Downtown Progress refused to acknowledge the divisiveness of urban planning, the negative consequences of downtown development, or the continued need for resources in the city's riot-torn neighborhoods.[112]

Much to activists' disappointment, the District's black leaders aligned with the city's business community in prioritizing outside visitors over local residents. Just as he had with the Pennsylvania Avenue project, Mayor Walter Washington readily endorsed the convention center proposal. "The Eisenhower Civic Center will address an unmet need in our city by providing space and facilities for major national and international scholarly, scientific, cultural and business organizations to meet in the Capital City," the mayor said. Mayor Washington joined the city's business community in urging swift approval of legislation to assist in the development of the center, which he believed would "keep the city moving."[113]

Likewise, Walter Fauntroy, the local SCLC leader, former city council member, and current congressional delegate, voiced his support for the civic center. Since 1966, the civil rights leader had run the Model Inner City Community

Organization, which allowed black community leaders to redirect federal officials' urban renewal agenda and reclaim the tools of urban planning and development for their own purposes. In refusing to relinquish control of its neighborhood to private developers or government planners, MICCO demonstrated the power of citizen participation in a city that lacked participatory democracy. However, on account of his position in Congress, Fauntroy's opponents, including members of the Redevelopment Land Agency, forced him to resign from MICCO. Without Fauntroy's leadership, MICCO was vulnerable to further attacks by the land clearance agency, which ultimately dismantled the community participation component of its program. By removing Fauntroy and defanging MICCO, the federal government sent a clear message to the city. It might have permitted the District electoral representation, but it would work to limit the influence of the city's black politicians. But by the early 1970s, Fauntroy himself had taken up the mantle of urban development. Writing in the Board of Trade's August 1972 newsletter, he said, "A civic center . . . is one of the most urgently needed projects to further the revitalization of downtown Washington." This was a far cry from his advocacy on behalf of the city's poor residents.[114]

The D.C. Chamber of Commerce, which had opposed the redevelopment of Pennsylvania Avenue, also endorsed the civic center project. Unlike Washington and Fauntroy, the black-run group did address the racial disparities that cast a shadow over all discussions about downtown development. According to the group's president, W. Ronald Evans, the fact that the capital was 72 percent black while blacks owned under 10 percent of the city's businesses was a great tragedy. Yet the commerce group believed that the construction of the convention center would benefit the black community. It reasoned that construction, subcontracting, concessional, and service-related contracts would provide jobs for underemployed and unemployed African Americans, just as it had with the Washington Metro project. The Chamber of Commerce's position pointed to a larger trend: the mimetic reforms implemented by the Johnson administration to marginalize radical black activists led to increased support for urban development by the city's black leaders.[115]

Reverend Hamilton's decision to reverse his position on the convention center's location bolsters this point. To the surprise of his congregation, the reverend announced the church's willingness to relocate. Hamilton's decision was inspired by assurances that Congress would reduce the proposed site from twenty-five to fifteen acres and, instead of a civic center and sports arena complex, only build one facility, thereby leaving room for the preservation of the church. Hamilton's endorsement came as a relief to those who had frowned upon black activists' passionate protests in Southwest D.C. years earlier. Moreover, it indicated to black municipal government officials and to white business and trade groups that a new coalition of urban development proponents could reengineer Washington as home rule neared.[116]

In the fall of 1972, they learned they would have their chance. In October, Congress authorized the D.C. government to build a municipal convention center. In doing so, it threw specific questions about the center's funding, development, construction, operations, and maintenance into the public domain. The Board of Trade issued a statement of gratitude on behalf of the prodevelopment coalition. "In perhaps no other District of Columbia project has there been evidenced such unanimity of support," the organization's president, John Stadtler, told President Nixon. But Stadtler was wrong.[117]

The Eisenhower Center was still at the center of community disputes. That same month, the Black United Front came out in opposition of the project. Speaking on behalf of BUF, Reverend Douglas Moore launched a vitriolic attack against the project. Moore suggested that the civic center did not represent "good economics or good politics." According to Moore, the project was part of what he considered a "no growth" industry. More importantly, he criticized Mayor Walter Washington and Councilman Sterling Tucker, the city's most prominent black government officials, for supporting it. Moore, a radical activist from North Carolina, was unafraid to challenge them. He had fought a groundbreaking campaign to end segregation in Durham during the 1950s. There, he had worked closely with Martin Luther King until his perceived radicalism threatened other civil rights leaders who persuaded King to disaffiliate him from SCLC in 1960. Moore was not alone in his disappointment. On the heels of Nixon's anticrime bill, black activists on the margins of local political power were deeply frustrated with the city's black leaders for their lack of advocacy on behalf of black residents.[118]

Upset, opponents continued to organize against the construction of the civic center. In September 1973, the D.C. Statehood Party, together with representatives of several small downtown businesses, sued the city, Downtown Progress, and the Redevelopment Land Agency. They pursued legal action to bar federal and local officials from making further progress on the building of the convention center. The plaintiffs called the legislation unconstitutional and argued that the defendants had violated their duties, not to mention the environmental and relocation stipulations of the legislation. The lawsuit served to further align Downtown Progress with local government officials. The two groups worked closely to strategize, brief, and argue the case. On September 17, 1973, the District Federal Court entered an order supporting the defendants, thereby thwarting community activists.[119]

Although the plaintiffs had lost the case, they remained vocal in their opposition to the project. They had a friend in Tedson Meyers, a white Democrat on the D.C. City Council. Nixon appointed the attorney in 1972 to achieve party and racial balance on the council. His work spearheading local crime fighting efforts in his diverse neighborhood of Adams Morgan especially appealed to the president. But once on the council, Meyers led the municipal opposition against downtown development. He helped stop legislation to build the freeway system and challenged the economic feasibility and necessity of the civic center project. With requests for federal funding denied, and private funding pending, he questioned the city's logic in using taxpayers' money to pay for the project. Meyers wondered where the convention center should rank in the city's priorities. "Does the answer to development . . . lie in major construction projects which boost real estate taxes? Or does it lie in projects which stimulate the redevelopment of a resident population able to support a more stable income tax base?" he asked. For Meyers, the Eisenhower Center did not represent an effective solution to Washington's urban crisis. Black activists agreed, positioning Meyers, rather than the council's black members, as an ally in the fight against downtown development.[120]

D.C. Gazette editor Sam Smith agreed with Meyers. In November 1973, the local activist humorously advertised the sale of the convention center on the cover of the newspaper: "For Sale: 300,000 square feet of warehouse space in changing neighborhood right in the heart of downtown Washington. Take possession free and clear of existing tenants for no money down and only $5 million a year for thirty years. . . . Only $65 million. Taxpayers will finance. This bargain will not last long. Call W. E. Washington." By publishing the ad, Smith highlighted several of the problems opponents had with the project. He also pointed to the unique coalition that had formed against the construction of the center, including black parishioners, furniture storeowners, and Chinese residents. According to Smith, they were joined by "residents who don't like the idea of the city being remade in the image of Mark Evans," a jab at the broadcaster and former D.C. Bicentennial Commission chairman, who seemed to have a hand in every major development project. The longtime home rule advocate believed that decisions about the city's fate should not be left to federal officials, unelected municipal representatives, and the city's powerful white business and real estate groups.[121]

Edmond Kanwit, a local government economist in the Urban and Transportation Department, also expressed skepticism about the project. Testifying before the local city council just one month before Congress passed the D.C. Home Rule Act, Kanwit placed self-determination at the center of his critique. He suggested that sharp changes in both local and national outlook demanded a reconsideration of the Eisenhower Center. Kanwit cited a lengthy list of local particularities and national forces that called the construction of the center into question. Strong deterrents to building the center included the city's imminent home rule; national economic policy concerned with combating inflation; pessimistic studies on the center's ability to meet its operating and capital costs; the accelerated exodus of middle-class residents and businesses to the suburbs; and the failure of public and private interests to rebuild after the riots. He concluded that the economic and political climate at the end of 1973 "demands a more socially aware calculus than heretofore," especially as local problems festered.[122]

In his testimony, Kanwit also illustrated the harmful way that national imperatives and patriotic sentiment undergirded the Eisenhower Center project in specific and local urban development in general. "There is a brutal irony in a campaign to ram this project down the throats of a disenfranchised population in commemoration of the bicentennial of the revolutionary uprising against Colonial taxation without representation," he said, waxing political. Kanwit was not a prominent leader or high-level bureaucrat. But that in itself was telling. By explicitly referencing the city's political disenfranchisement, he illustrated the heavy hand that national politics played in local governance under limited home rule.[123]

National imperatives had already guided the decision to turn the building into an impressive memorial to President Eisenhower. *Washington Star* reporter Martin Nolan suggested that the project's proponents wanted to name the convention center after the former president "to grease things in Congress." Nolan had a different recommendation. He proposed naming the building the Julius A. Hobson Convention Center, a title that would honor the black activist who had captivated the city's political imagination for decades.[124] Congress ignored his suggestion. However, the issue of erecting a memorial on private land continued to cause problems for the project's viability. Chinese-led organizations petitioned Congress to relocate the Eisenhower Center to government-owned land in accordance with the established precedents for all other presidential memorials. Meanwhile, city council member Tedson Meyers suggested that Congress donate the land and funds as compensation for the civic center's dual purpose.[125]

Congress tried to persuade Washingtonians to pay for the project through appeals to their greater national duty. It made a fatal mistake, however, in trying to do so in the months before the city's first elections under the D.C. Home Rule Act. This infuriated black congressman Charles Diggs, John McMillan's replacement as chairman of the House District Committee. In March 1974, Diggs tried to halt a referendum on the project, telling House District Committee members that it was inconsistent with the Home Rule Act to bypass the mayor and city council prior to local elections. Doing so, he feared, would signal that they did not trust local black officials and would serve as a reminder of their tendency to undercut their authority. While Congress's legislative history already illustrated this, Diggs did not think it was prudent for them to do so again so close to the advent of local municipal elections.[126]

One local black council member thought otherwise. Nixon appointee Marguerite Selden, an Urban League member and retired assistant superintendent of D.C. public schools, told Representative Diggs she planned to vote in favor of the proposed plan. Nixon appointed Selden, a black Democrat, in March 1973 to replace Stanley Anderson, the only remaining member of the original city council. Her appointment left the political and racial makeup of the council the same: six Republicans and three Democrats, and six black members and three white members. But with the addition of Selden, no members resided east of the Anacostia River in neighborhoods that, on account of white flight during the 1950s and 1960s, had become predominantly black. In a letter to the House District chairman, Selden noted that she, too, was concerned about the project's financial consequences. "But," she added, "I believe the citizens of the Nation's Capital may sometimes need to place their posture as residents of the Capital of our country above community risks."[127]

When it came time for the city council to vote on whether or not to permit a voter referendum on the proposed convention center, Selden was not present. Neither was John Nevius, the white Republican chairman of the D.C. City Council. The remaining members voted 5–2 not to put it on the ballot. As one frustrated Washingtonian said, "It is a sad reminder that the vestiges of voter disenfranchisement still lives on in these post Home Rule days. It is ironic that those who now lead us at City Hall—and who hope to obtain our vote for representation under the new Home Rule Charter—would be the ones to relegate us to those 'pre–Home Rule' days when Congress was the 'tail that wagged the dog.'"[128]

The council's decision not to solicit community input was further evidence of the growing interracial alliance of politicians and business groups that used the Bicentennial to justify reshaping the city's urban landscape. But the coalition's goal to develop Washington's downtown continued to exclude any plans to improve the station of the city's poor black residents. Although the national Bicentennial celebration was quickly becoming peripheral to the project, these black and white stakeholders continued to leverage the city's national symbolism for their own local priorities, pushing the most disadvantaged Washingtonians further to the margins.

BICENTENNIAL BLUES

On July 4, 1976, the moment that the American Revolution Bicentennial Administration had spent years planning for had finally arrived. Originally cast in the liberal mold of President Lyndon Johnson's Great Society, the government's handover of the national ceremony to corporate America indicated the larger political and social changes underway as the country's postwar political order crumbled. "After a decade of racial tensions, assassinations, scandal, rising inflation, embattled campuses and eroding public trust, what was there left to celebrate?" the ARBA asked. "There was plenty," it defiantly declared.[129]

The Bicentennial weekend kicked off that Friday evening with a solemn ceremony at the National Archives, located on Pennsylvania Avenue. Though construction crews had not yet broken ground, Congress had approved the Pennsylvania Avenue Development Corporation's plan a year earlier. Later that weekend, over a million people gathered on the Mall for the National Pageant of Freedom and Fireworks Display, hosted by "Happy Birthday USA," a nonprofit citizen's group. Tourists traveling from out of town could stop in the National Visitor Center, located at the city's train station, to watch the nine-and-a-half-minute "Welcome to Washington" slide show. Walking along the Mall, they could participate in the Smithsonian's twelve-week Festival of American Folk Life, sponsored in part by American Airlines and General Foods Corporation, and visit its newly opened National Air and Space Museum. From there, they could glance over at the FBI's new headquarters at the J. Edgar Hoover Building. If tourists sought even more adventure, the ARBA's *Visitors Guide to the Nation's Capital* listed side trips to Maryland, Virginia, West Virginia, and even Pennsylvania. But in the District, visitors found little to do outside the National Mall. The purposeful lack of programming beyond the Mall hid the city's economic and racial divisions and ignored the city's low-income black residents. According to James Gibson, "There will be a splendid array of Bicentennial activities for the affluent in this town, but who can afford the Kennedy Center?"[130]

Under the Nixon administration, the government's willingness to use federal assistance to address social problems drastically diminished. This, combined with the political turmoil of the era, forced a reconfiguration of the Bicentennial that profoundly changed Washington. Under the pretense of Bicentennial planning, the federal government, white business and trade groups, and local black officials prioritized development projects over social and economic renewal programs and more readily partnered with private developers. As this coalition's power strengthened, urban renewal projects that offered more radical opportunities for citizen participation fell by the wayside.

Planners flagged two projects in particular for urban renewal under the Bicentennial's early programmatic scheme that never achieved their potential to address the District's racial and economic disparities. The first was the development of Fort Lincoln, a former military post located in Northeast D.C. In November 1966, President Johnson signed legislation creating Model Cities, a program intended to bring federal coordination and planning expertise to over one hundred cities. As part of its Great Society and War on Poverty programming, Model Cities was an ambitious federal aid program with a simple goal: to help get the poor out of central city slums. Johnson had the idea that housing for the urban poor could be built on surplus federal land, a plan that did not require relocation and one that had at its disposal a few critical resources: available land, federal funds, and the ability to bypass Congress. Local housing advocates were particularly excited about the opportunity to designate excess federal land for public housing. But Johnson foisted the project, which he announced in August 1967, upon the new local government, thereby dictating the parameters of the city's urban renewal efforts.[131]

The Department of Housing and Urban Development took Johnson's idea to house the urban poor and morphed it into a program to build model communities, "new towns in town," that would reflect quality design and social balance. It targeted Fort Lincoln, which held 335 wooded acres on the eastern edge of the District about to be vacated by the Department of Justice. Under Johnson's guidance, planners emphasized social service delivery and citizen participation—the newest ideas in community planning. Planners envisioned housing for fifteen thousand of the city's poor residents, with four thousand dwellings for families of varied incomes, a federal employment center, and a possible satellite campus for the District's Federal City College. After the dispossessions occasioned by the Southwest Project, some feared that Fort Lincoln would become another "showcase program for the middle class"—especially after black homeowners objected to the presence of public housing in their neighborhood. However, as the Bicentennial came into view, the project's national proponents promised a commitment to racial and economic integration and to community participation.[132]

Nixon did not deliver on Johnson's promise to remake Fort Lincoln. The change of administrations hampered the urgency, creativity, and scope of the project. What was once Johnson's pet project—dubbed "Fort Lyndon" by the press—lost its sponsors when Nixon came into office. After that, the area was relegated to government-subsided commercial development. In 1971, the same year that black residents identified the development of Fort Lincoln as a pressing issue at the Linden Hill Bicentennial conference, the Redevelopment Land Agency assumed jurisdiction over it and selected the Westinghouse Corporation as its sole developer. "Fort Lincoln New Town will be a balanced community in which persons of all social, economic and racial backgrounds can live together in a quality urban environment," national Bicentennial Commission chairman Bill Hart optimistically told President Nixon in 1972. But Nixon paid little attention to the project's development. Meanwhile, as the federal government minimized the importance of urban renewal programming to the Bicentennial, it rolled out a new plan for higher-income occupancy at the site. In doing so, it once again marginalized local officials' input and ignored the needs of the city's poor black residents.[133]

Under Lyndon Johnson's direction, the government had also promised to tackle the redevelopment of the Bolling Air Force Base. Located along the Anacostia River, the base was a nine-hundred-acre site controlled by the Department of Defense. Due to conflicting air traffic at the nearby Washington National Airport, its runways had been closed since 1962. In 1965, Congress targeted 432 acres of the site for urban renewal. Frustrated that no action had been taken since then, the D.C. Coalition of Conscience, a self-described "catalyst and protest group" led by Reverends Walter Fauntroy and Channing Phillips and comprising various religious and civil rights organizations, hatched a plan to descend on the base, "by land and by sea," in August 1966. The group's goal was to draw attention to its demand to use the land for the city's inadequately housed residents. The "civil rights invasion," as the *Post* described it, caught the attention of the base's commander, who coordinated with the MPD and FBI to investigate the matter.[134]

Frustrated that its plans were leaked to the press, the group arrived at the base two days ahead of schedule. One hundred fifty airmen, air force police, and base firemen greeted the two hundred protestors, including Fauntroy, Phillips, members of CORE and the NAACP, as well as public housing residents, and black schoolchildren. The encounter was cordial but once again pointed to the challenge of catalyzing meaningful urban renewal without home rule. The air force and Department of Defense had no issue with Washington residents. In fact, the Pentagon repeatedly said that it had no further use for the majority of the land at the base. The opposition rested with Congress and, specifically, with Congressman L. Mendel Rivers, chairman of the House Armed Services Committee. Following the coalition's demonstration, Rivers insisted that the entire base was needed for military expansion. He objected to the property's use for the construction of low-income housing on the grounds that it should not be used for the "social concoctions of some idiots around Washington." The congressman backed his words with action. In his leadership role on the House Armed Services Committee, he extended the military's exclusive use of the land for another five years, thereby blocking plans for eight thousand new housing units on the base. Johnson, who had expressed his general support for the urban renewal plan, did not intervene.[135]

In the aftermath of the 1968 riots, the city's municipal officials renewed their commitment to the base's progressive redevelopment. So did the ARBC. It continued to welcome the Bolling Air Force Base as a national model for urban development as late as 1973. But much like what it did with Fort Lincoln, Congress severed the Southwest D.C. project's connections to the Bicentennial. Instead, the Department of Defense announced its plan to develop the entire nine-hundred-acre site as a "Little Pentagon," providing for over one thousand military housing units. Upset, D.C. City Council members fired back. "We do not accept the proposition that this very large tract of land should remain forever under the exclusive jurisdiction of the military," city council chairman John Nevius told Congress. "In my opinion," vice chairman Sterling Tucker added, "it would be a serious mistake to devote this entire tract to activities which make no financial or social contribution to the local economy." Their opinions did not matter. In the absence of strong congressional representation, the D.C. government lacked the political power to prevent the Defense Department from executing its plan.[136]

The unfulfilled potential of urban renewal plans was just one sign that the Bicentennial had promised too much. In 1975, James Gibson described his feelings toward the upcoming celebration as "angry, frustrated, disillusioned, outraged, hurt, [and] mad." He resigned as DCBC chairman after three and a half years of service just one year before the main event. On resigning, Gibson acknowledged that the goal of using the event to help the city's poor neighborhoods by sponsoring construction projects and festivals there "has been realized only to a very limited extent." "Obviously it is a failure not to have brought off the rebuilding of the riot corridors and the development of Ft. Lincoln or a downtown civic center," he said, adding, "We have not lived up to the expectations of the 'Great Society.'"[137] Gibson criticized the mayor and white business leaders for their unwillingness to provide the necessary financial support to rebuild the city's neighborhoods devastated during the 1968 riots. In an interview he gave just one month before the Bicentennial, Gibson pulled out a 1972 issue of the DCBC's newsletter with the headline "A New D.C. in 4 Years!" "It was simply no longer credible," Gibson admitted. "My departure symbolized that."[138]

Black citizens across the country wrestled with similar feelings. One month before the Bicentennial, *Ebony* published an editorial, entitled "The Bicentennial Blues," to dramatize the juxtaposition between the Bicentennial's language and the racial violence that continued to occur throughout the country. The photographs appended to the editorial depicted white men brutally attacking an African American citizen with an American flag during an antibusing rally outside Boston's City Hall two months earlier.[139] Then, on July 31, 1976, Vernon Jordan, executive director of the National Urban League, commented on the celebration's unfulfilled promises in the *Baltimore Afro-American*: "Today it is black people who have largely opted out of the nonsensical empty celebrations of the Bicentennial and instead have directed America's attention to its unfinished business of constructing the third century of national life built on the noble promises of 1776," Jordan said.[140] ARBA administrator John Warner dismissed Jordan's comments and the *Ebony* piece. "Naturally I am sorry that some people chose not to take part because of past wrongs. But I am proud and pleased to report that a great many Blacks . . . did participate in substance and spirit. As a result," Warner explained, "we all have gained a better understanding and appreciation for each other."[141]

Certainly the Afro-American Bicentennial Corporation and the Bicentennial Ethnic Racial Council won fights for recognition and inclusion in the festivities. Thanks to their work, even the American Freedom Train, the largest national project for the upcoming Bicentennial celebration, became a lesson in racial tolerance. In one of its twenty-six cars, viewers could find a shrine to the civil rights movement, including Dr. King's black robe, one of his Bibles, and a life-size replica of his pulpit from his Atlanta-based Ebenezer Baptist Church. In the interactive experience, viewers could also look at one of the four movie projectors simultaneously flashing scenes from the various peace marches he led around the country.[142]

Backed by five major U.S. corporations, the Freedom Train traveled to forty-eight states in 1975 and 1976. Over the course of its journey, 5.5 million citizens visited it, as the country's small cities and towns proudly hosted the train. But when the Freedom Train headed toward the Washington area in September 1976, the D.C. Bicentennial Commission refused to welcome it into the District. Instead, the federal government hosted the train to little fanfare at

The Freedom Train passes through Rockville, Maryland, on its way to the Pentagon. It did not stop in Washington, D.C. (Star Collection, D.C. Public Library © *Washington Post*)

the Pentagon. After a five-day stay in Arlington, Virginia, the train headed to Miami, where it ushered in the New Year.[143]

As the Freedom Train made its way across the country, its assorted civil rights relics appeared outdated. African Americans were demanding more from the federal government, assuming local political power, and changing the shape of urban governance in the seventies. Through its patriotic tone, pageantry, and celebration of the American spirit, the Bicentennial sought to mask these new realities by erasing race from its national narrative. But this proved to be an impossible task in the majority-black District, which held its first municipal elections in the lead-up to the historic celebration.

In the early 1970s, white development proponents worked to counter the exodus of businesses and the flow of capital from cities across the country. However, in Washington, white boosters' relationship to the federal government set them apart from other business and trade groups. Their connections to the White House and their lifeline to the members of Congress who supervised the city's budget made them uniquely powerful stakeholders. During the early Bicentennial planning period, they worried that home rule would threaten their control over city politics. But as local elections neared, black political leaders expressed a keen interest in the urban development of the city's downtown. Together with groups like the Board of Trade and Downtown Progress, they privileged business interests over residents and parking garages and pedestrian malls over residential reconstruction.

Although they were successful in helping initiate the Pennsylvania Avenue and Eisenhower Convention Center projects, their plans failed to meet the Bicentennial's deadlines. But at some point during the planning period, that stopped mattering. In 1977, even as new battles over historic preservation bogged down plans for the avenue, and the Eisenhower Center faded into oblivion inside of Congress, Downtown Progress claimed that it had accomplished enough to close shop. After eighteen years of major involvement in downtown revitalization, the influential organization believed that the city's majority-black municipal government would finish enacting its vision.[144]

The use of the nation's two hundredth birthday to usher in the redevelopment of downtown D.C. offers a stark reminder that business and political elites often use civic pride to steamroll dissent. Moreover, it demonstrates clearly the limits of the 1974 home rule legislation. As the celebration faded from local memory, the coalition of local politicians and business groups that coalesced under the pretext of Bicentennial planning paved the way for the next several decades of downtown-focused development. But the activists who had dedicated their lives to the fight for home rule had a different vision for the new era of municipal politics.

CONCLUSION

CIVIL RIGHTS, LAW AND ORDER, AND URBAN DEVELOPMENT IN THE POST-HOME RULE ERA

We know elected politics is not the be-all
and end-all. It is only one thing.
—New School for Afro-American Thought
cofounder Gaston Neal, April 1988

Home rule wasn't freedom, it was more like a snake
that took 20 years to squeeze life from its victim.
—*Washington Post* reporters David Vise and
Howard Schneider, December 1995

A HISTORIC MOMENT

On a warm Thursday in May 1974, Clifford Alexander, a forty-year-old black attorney and former head of the Equal Employment Opportunity Commission, marched into D.C.'s District Building to kick off his mayoral campaign. Standing in front of the City Council Chambers, Alexander took aim at Mayor Walter Washington. In the six and a half years since President Johnson had appointed Washington to office, the city bore witness to major riots, rising crime rates, housing decay, and controversial urban renewal and development efforts. Alexander criticized Washington for allowing the District's rents to rise dramatically, for the slow pace of rebuilding efforts in the city's riot corridors, and for his failure to select African Americans and women for high-level appointments. Ninety people, young and middle-aged, black and white, nodded and applauded enthusiastically in the air-conditioned room.[1]

The mayor responded two days later at his own campaign kickoff. "Somebody says, 'Where have you been?'" the fifty-nine-year-old statesman told the jubilant, sweat-soaked audience in the Masonic Temple at Tenth and U Streets NW. "My answer to that is open your eyes. You'll see this city is on its way to getting together like no other city in the country." Alexander and Washington spent the next four months embroiled in a heated yet civil campaign for the local Democratic Party's nomination. As residents in the overwhelmingly Democratic city knew, the primary winner would continue on to face an uncompetitive Republican challenger in November's mayoral race. Mayor Washington ultimately defeated Alexander in a close primary race and, as predicted, cruised to victory, finally able to govern with a mandate from the local electorate.[2]

Home rule opened varying degrees of political power to black militants. In 1969, the Black United Front had asked members to resign rather than sit on a fraudulent city council. But following the establishment of the D.C. Congressional Delegate in 1970, and on the eve of council elections, it had a different outlook. According to Reverend Channing Phillips, "The development of electoral politics in the District since 1968 rules out the possibility and the necessity of forming a new front."[3] And, in fact, activists comprised nine of the thirteen members on the first elected city council. Julius Hobson, running on the Statehood Party's ticket, won an at-large seat, as did Reverend Jerry Moore, a Republican and Baptist minister. Hobson and Moore won their seats in large part because the 1973 Home Rule Act stipulated that only two candidates from any one party could be elected as at-large council members. The two spots taken by the Democratic Party went to Free D.C. leader and school board president Marion Barry and the Black United Front's Douglas Moore, who ran a campaign that downplayed his image as a dashiki-clad, aggressive black nationalist to emphasize lesser-known aspects of his character, like his experience as a teacher, minister, and organizer. Community organizer and fellow BUF leader Willie Hardy won the seat to represent Ward 7, a position she held until 1980. Supported by the city's white business interests and middle-class black residents, the Urban League's Sterling Tucker won the council's chairmanship.[4]

With the advent of home rule, local politics quickly became even more participatory. In 1974, residents approved the referendum to the city's new charter providing for the election of thirty-six unpaid Advisory Neighborhood Commissions. Following the first election of commissioners in 1976, the ANCs began considering a wide range of issues on the neighborhood level, including traffic patterns, street improvements, liquor licenses, police protection, and trash collection. By institutionalizing the ANCs, the city hoped to ensure high levels of citizen input on issues directly affected by government action, much as the War on Poverty had tried to ensure with its "maximum feasible participation" mandate.[5]

While home rule provided many local black activists with new powers, it remained to be seen how the new governing structure would affect the city's low-income residents. In the early 1970s, 56 percent of Washington's black families fell below the poverty line, as compared to 13.7 percent of white families. Of those, 46 percent earned less than $8,000 a year. The average annual income of D.C. families on public assistance was only $1,409, 53.7 percent below the national poverty level. In 1972, total underemployment in the city was estimated at $100,000—equivalent to nearly 30 percent of the workforce. Approximately forty thousand families in D.C. were in need of better housing, and roughly five thousand families were on the waitlist for public housing.[6]

Mayor Washington, along with the first elected city council, tackled rent control, the rebuilding of riot-torn areas, and the expansion of the job market to lower unemployment rates. But municipal officials only made so much headway on these issues during their first four years in office. For his part, Mayor Washington had trouble harnessing the new city bureaucracy to tackle long-term local needs. He did, however, demonstrate a keen sensitivity to the concerns of the city's business community and worked hard to promote extensive downtown urban development. The council also catered to the District's powerful white stakeholders by decreasing benefits under the city's workers compensation law—a long-standing concern of the business community. Moreover, after initially trying to enact stricter rent-control laws, the council soon worked to loosen controls to benefit landlords.[7]

If the 1974 mayoral election served to restore to the District an elected municipal government, the 1978 election functioned as a referendum on the city's civil rights movement. Following years of turning inward under the Nixon administration's paternalistic supervision, the mayor's political circle had shrunk, consisting primarily of other black elites. His administration faced increasing criticism from neighborhood activists for failing to address the problems that plagued the city and for its inability to create a more powerful framework to empower D.C. residents. This opened the door to a challenge from both city council chairman Sterling Tucker and at-large city council member Marion Barry in the Democratic primary.[8]

Since the politically moderate Washington and Tucker had already secured the vote of the black middle class, the former SNCC leader knew that he had to broaden his electoral base if he wanted to win the election. Thus, Barry took

U.S. Supreme Court justice Thurgood Marshall, the first African American to serve on the high court, swears in Marion Barry. (Star Collection, D.C. Public Library © *Washington Post*)

his message to the poorest sections of the city. He reached out to the constituents that he had worked with through Pride, Inc., in the late 1960s and early 1970s. His platform moved beyond the earlier civil rights movement's emphasis on integration to include more expansive community-based services and social welfare goals. Aware that Washington's business community could be a major source of campaign revenue, and adept at soliciting funds from white contributors since his days fund-raising for SNCC, Barry also carefully cultivated the support of downtown business interests, winning the *Washington Post*'s endorsement in the process.[9]

In 1978, Barry narrowly defeated Washington and Tucker in the three-way primary race for the Democratic Party mayoral nomination. While Barry carried only 27 percent of the black vote overall, as compared to 38 percent for Washington and 32.7 percent for Tucker, he won the white vote by a wide margin, receiving 52 percent of their support to lay claim to the office. Having earned their votes on the campaign trail, the activist and staunch home rule supporter would have to balance the interests of poor, black voters with those of his white, Northwest D.C. constituents.[10]

Barry was mayor of D.C. from 1979 to 1991, and then again from 1995 to 1999, with a six-month stint in jail and a term on the city council in between. He followed a wave of black mayors in large urban cities, including Kenneth Gibson of Newark, Coleman Young of Detroit, Tom Bradley of Los Angeles, Maynard Jackson of Atlanta, and Walter Washington himself. Their results had been mixed. White flight, the disappearance of urban manufacturing jobs, persistent poverty, and rising crime rates cast a shadow over their reigns and provided fodder for their opponents. Barry was determined to make D.C. a showcase for black political power and prove critics of black leadership wrong. He established an ambitious social welfare program for the District and recruited talent from across the country to enact it. But rather than building consensus, Barry became a polarizing figure. His courtship of white voters solicited criticism from those concerned that he would sacrifice the principle of self-government. Their concerns were not wholly unfounded. Thanks to the fiscal constraints imposed on the city by the federal government, including a low federal payment and the inability to tax commuters, pressure to emphasize development policies grew. As Barry knew, the key to rebuilding the city increasingly lay with private developers. Like other big-city black mayors in the 1970s, Barry zealously courted the corporate sector on becoming mayor. Yet it remained to be seen what this would mean for black self-determination.[11]

In some ways, Barry's tenure reveals the limits of black protest politics. Activists had harnessed the energy of the modern movement, breaking down Jim Crow laws and inching their way toward democracy, first with mayor and city council appointments, then with school board elections and the institution of a nonvoting delegate. Unsatisfied, Walter Fauntroy, the city's first congressional delegate, pushed harder. He capitalized on the creative strength of the civil rights movement to overthrow House District Committee chairman John McMillan. Together with a broad interracial coalition of activists, he helped pave the way for the city's first mayoral and city council elections in one hundred years. But the civil rights movement could only carry the District's desire for democracy so far in a city circumscribed by a congressionally dictated home rule bill. As Barry translated activism into institutionalized politics, he reckoned with a $100 million deficit, oversaw a bloated city government, and was forced to work under the oversight of a Congress with the authority to veto any decision made by the District's city council. Even so, Barry spent his first term—arguably his most successful—balancing the city's budget, conducting the first audit of the city government in one hundred years, and reducing the city's debt. He also oversaw the redevelopment of the city's downtown and created thousands of public sector jobs for D.C. residents.[12]

Barry was reelected in 1982 with 80 percent of the vote and another endorsement, albeit a less enthusiastic one, from the *Washington Post*. However, the 1980s proved to be difficult for Barry and local municipal politics. Barry's administration misused city funds, continued to bloat the workforce with patronage jobs, and presided over municipal social services that were in shambles. Republican-inspired investigations of his administration also undermined black political power in the federal city. While the investigations were not entirely unfounded, U.S. attorneys overzealously pursued Barry and his associates. Between 1978 and 1989, they obtained convictions or guilty pleas in a number of cases against members of his administration, including two convictions against high-ranking officials during his second term. Ivanhoe Donaldson, Barry's onetime campaign manager and former deputy mayor for economic development, pleaded guilty in 1985 to federal theft and cover-up charges after it was revealed that he stole over $190,000 in D.C. government money. Then, in 1990, the FBI famously arrested Barry and indicted him on thirteen counts for drug offenses. Barry was eventually convicted on two misdemeanor counts and served six months in a federal penitentiary before resuming his political career.[13]

Barry's conviction played into the hands of Republican partisans interested in undermining Democrats nationally. More broadly speaking, the continued pursuit of black officials for criminal wrongdoing worked to aggressively diminish Congress's respect for the D.C. government. It also provided ammunition for members of Congress who wanted to intervene more in the city's affairs. But they would still have to contend with Barry, who resurrected his political career in 1992. He ran for and won the council seat representing Ward 8, his new home east of the Anacostia River. His campaign centered on rallying the Ward's poorer voters with promises to bring power, hope, and resources to the neglected section of the city. The grassroots politics and campaign tactics that Barry had honed in the 1960s came back in play once again, in large part because the systemic issues self-determination intended to address had not been resolved by the passage of home rule.[14]

LINGERING ISSUES

Washington experienced a delayed but fruitful rebirth following the 1968 riots, especially when compared to other cities like Detroit, Cleveland, and Newark, where riots had also occurred. Even so, when it came to urban development, the trajectories of the civic center and Pennsylvania Avenue projects revealed how onerous it was to add to the District's infrastructure under continued federal oversight, especially when Congress refused to relinquish complete political control over the city's downtown development. In 1977, the Bicentennial was a distant memory, but the Eisenhower Center lingered in public debate. The civic center, which had been authorized in 1972, continued to fall to the mercy of congressional committees. "You could easily conclude," the *Washington Post* argued, "that the not-so-good old days of colonial rule were still with us." Kentucky representative William Natcher, no friend to D.C. residents, understood the Senate Subcommittee's rejection of funds as a "direct repudiation as far as home rule is concerned." This frustrated local development enthusiasts, who understood that a convention center would attract new business, create new jobs, and generate new revenue. "On one hand," WTOP-TV 9 said in frustration, "Congress complains that the District does not do enough to help itself," but "on the other hand, Congress moves to deny the city one of the most promising tools for self-help." Yet the Eisenhower project found little traction inside Congress.[15]

The home rule era did eliminate some of the bureaucratic barriers necessary to execute the convention center project. In 1978, the D.C. City Council imposed a special hotel tax to fund downtown convention space. In April 1980, the city finally broke ground on the project. In December 1983, it opened for business at 10th and H Streets and New York Avenue, becoming the fourth-largest convention facility in the nation, with over eight hundred thousand square feet of exhibition space. But when it came to urban development, members of Congress continued to hamstring local municipal officials. For example, a Maryland Democrat attached a rider that prohibited hanging a scoreboard from the ceiling or from building the kind of fixed permanent seating found in large arenas in the facility. Congress's 1983 fiscal appropriations bill went so far as to prohibit the center "from booking sports events, concerts, circuses, rodeos and other such evens that traditionally have been held in existing facilities." Suburban interests prevented the D.C. government from maximizing profits on the convention center in part because they saw it as competition with Maryland's Capital Centre, a concert and sports venue located southeast of D.C. that seated nineteen thousand and hosted Washington's hockey and basketball teams. Their interference revealed once again the limits of the 1973 Home Rule Act in granting the District self-determination.[16]

The opening of the Metro subway stations and convention center in downtown D.C., as well as the construction and renovation of hotels, stores, theaters, restaurants, and office buildings in the 1980s, improved negative perceptions of the city's downtown. So did the "striking transformation" of Pennsylvania Avenue, whose redevelopment was pursued by the Pennsylvania Avenue Development Corporation, the quasi-public agency that bought declining properties on and near the avenue and resold them to developers for new construction and renovation.[17] During the 1970s and early 1980s, the Pennsylvania Avenue project had been enmeshed in debates over historic preservation. Organizations like Don't Tear It Down, which formed in 1971 and grew to twelve hundred members over the decade, began with the mission to save the Old Post Office. After the PADC issued its proposal in 1974, further opposition arose over its demolition plans. In 1977, the PADC responded with a historic preservation plan of its own. Major funding, construction work, and land acquisition followed. But as one of the leaders of Don't Tear It Down explained to Congress, the PADC was still exempt from local and federal laws, and therefore not subject to even the District's own Historic Landmark and Historic District Protection Act, which had passed in 1978, thanks in large part to its lobbying efforts. In 1982, the PADC accommodated historic preservation groups with a new master plan and then persuaded private corporations to invest more than $1.5 billion in executing it. By the end of the decade, every block on the north side of the avenue had undergone a major revival. As the *Post* wrote excitedly on the twenty-year anniversary of the riots, "There is so much construction downtown that scaffolding, cranes, wrecking machinery and workers in hard hats can be seen on virtually every major block in the area."[18]

The city's riot-torn areas followed a different trajectory. Traveling down the 14th Street NW, 7th Street NW, and H Street NE corridors, one still found boarded-up buildings, broken glass, garbage littering the streets, drug dealers, and homeless citizens. Empty lots continued to sit next to older stores that had survived the riots. A sprinkling of rehabilitated and new apartment buildings had been built, while longtime residents continued to wait for repairs. Mayor Barry sympathized with residents as landlords sought to vacate properties to make way for new development. But the racially charged gentrification issue proved difficult for the man who had won the mayoral seat by courting, in part, white gentrifiers and developers. Barry knew that the District needed the tax revenue that redevelopment promised. Thus, low-income residents' needs lost out as a coalition of black officials, bankers who had previously been accused of redlining or refusing loans for projects in riot-torn areas, young white developers, and community groups previously hostile to business interests came together to profit off of the rebuilding of the historically black commercial districts.[19]

When it came to the issue of crime, black municipal officials faced a more complicated crucible of issues. According to legal scholar James Forman Jr., they wrestled with increasing violence, drug use, and drug addiction to heroin and, later, crack. Crack cocaine had a particularly devastating affect on the District. In 1969, 45 percent of male jail detainees tested positive for heroin, up from 3 percent in the early 1960s. But by 1987, 60 percent of Washington arrestees tested positive for crack cocaine. The rise in drug addiction and the drug trade led to increases in youth gang activity, boarded-up housing in low-income neighborhoods, robberies, and murder.[20]

No one in the black community knew the best way to combat rising drug use and murder rates. As Forman argues, during the late 1970s and 1980s, city officials considered several different policy proposals, including the decriminalization of marijuana, drug treatment, and increased sentences. Ultimately D.C.'s mayor and city council members embraced the law-and-order rhetoric they inherited from the Nixon administration, passed tougher laws under a supportive Congress, and adopted more aggressive policing practices well into the 1990s. Recognizing that the crime issue was an issue on which he could campaign, Barry himself claimed the mantle of drug warrior until he fell victim to his own addiction. D.C. also appointed its first black police chief, Burtell Jefferson, a staunch advocate for mandatory minimum sentencing, to lead the nation's first black-majority police department in 1978. During this time period, the city's budget for police and corrections rose to $1.1 billion, a 61.5 percent increase, but the city's courts and jails remained overcrowded, thanks in large part to the number of black citizens whom officials locked up. During the 1980s, D.C. became known as the "murder capital of the world," the logical conclusion to Nixon's "crime capital" and failed War on Crime.[21]

Forman has three explanations for the rise in black-led punitive crime policy. First, he contends that black officials did not see mass incarceration coming. Instead, their small decisions, made over time, contributed to the rise of mass incarceration. Second, he argues, middle-class and elite blacks were shielded from some of the most punitive policing practices and held poorer blacks, including those that tended toward criminal activity, in lower regard. Third, he asserts, "African-Americans have *always* viewed the protection of black lives as a civil rights issue, whether the threat comes from police officers or street criminals."[22] But this was not a foregone conclusion, especially not in Washington during the late 1960s and early 1970s. Instead, the federal government's surveillance over the city in the era leading up to home rule shaped the parameters for the punitive turn in black Washington.

One major issue neglected by Forman is that Congress systematically curtailed the city's jurisdiction over criminal justice. After Nixon largely abandoned the District following the passage of his 1970 crime bill, local officials were initially granted more authority over the crime problem. Yet the president continued to have emergency powers over the local police, and the Senate still confirmed judges appointed by the mayor to the D.C. Court of Appeals and the D.C. Superior Court. Even under home rule, the city council could not make changes to the criminal code. As political scientist Michael Fauntroy argues, Congress used its authority to, in part, govern morality in the District. In 1981, for example, Congress overturned the city council's major reform of the criminal laws defining and punishing sexual offenses. And from 1987 to 1989, Congress required the District to establish and fund a free telephone hotline so that Maryland residents living near Lorton Reformatory could learn about any disturbances at the prison.[23]

Suburban legislators continued to try to influence District policy in the area of criminal justice. In 1989, Representative Stanford E. Parris (R-Va.) sponsored legislation to establish a National Capital Public Safety Administrator, to be housed in the White House. The bill also called for the transfer of key services, including police, fire, emergency medical services, and the detention of persons accused or convicted of crimes in the District to the president. Moreover, it required the construction of a prison inside the District in order to close Lorton Reformatory, located in Parris's district. This failed attempt followed earlier successes, like Parris's ability to get Congress to block a D.C. government plan to select new police officers by lottery—an effort on Mayor Barry's part to increase the number of minority policemen in the District.[24]

Parris had exerted a particularly strong influence on D.C. affairs during the 1980s. According to the *Washington Post*, he was "emerging as a 1980s version of former representative Joel Broyhill, the Arlington conservative who tied the city in parliamentary knots for decades"—a comparison Parris said he would not dispute.[25] Although Parris maintained that he was not anti–home rule, he continued to intervene in D.C. proposals, going as far as to successfully delay an attempt to increase the federal payment to the city by invoking a seldom-used quorum call in the District Committee. Parris's oversight, like Broyhill's and McMillan's before his, reflected a conflation of suburban-interests and racism to undermine self-determination. Over the decade, suburban interests continued to influence and intervene in local issues like taxation, the lottery, economic development, higher education, and criminal justice, way beyond their call to protect the federal interest.[26]

Washington's welfare rights activism also left a multifaceted legacy. During the 1960s, welfare recipients channeled their energy into boycotts, sit-ins, lawsuits, and lobbying efforts. Through War on Poverty programming, many developed skills—and even careers—as organizers and succeeded in shifting attention toward their communities' needs. In a city where political participation was severely restricted, low-income black women found in the welfare rights movement space to enact their own visions of a just society. During the 1970s, some continued to translate their skills into paid employment in social service agencies, while others established advocacy centers, job programs, and childcare facilities. One such woman, Loretta Ross, took up the issue of reproductive rights and antiviolence activism. Ross, a Howard University graduate and sexual assault survivor who experienced sterilization abuse from a defective intrauterine device at the age of twenty-three, became the director of the D.C. Rape Crisis Center, the only center at the time run primarily by and for women of color. Ross was representative of the hundreds of black women who used their experiences to press for changes in public assistance programs, fight against sex-based oppression and sexual violence, and expand notions of rights and participatory democracy.[27]

After Nixon took office, welfare funds continued to fall short of federal cost of living standards as federal officials set budgets inadequate to meet the needs of the city's poor. As Congress undertook broad welfare reform measures, as the Supreme Court issued rulings that limited welfare rights, and as understaffed and underfunded local agencies eliminated welfare programs, many of welfare rights activists' earlier victories were reversed. The changes made by the federal government during the early 1970s wound up bringing welfare activists and city administrators together, as the two groups collaborated to oppose fiscal and programmatic cuts at the federal level. But their partnership also moved the fight to reform welfare policy off the streets and into government buildings, necessitated the mobilization of fewer women, and forced activists to compromise and moderate their demands. As they dedicated their lives to welfare reform, they became peripheral to the home rule movement, generally leaving the more mainstream black leaders to assume political positions once it was implemented.[28]

MAKING SENSE OF HOME RULE

The era from 1973 to 1995 represented a distinct governing phase in D.C. politics. The passage of home rule was a triumph of coalition politics. But activists continued to push for more democratic representation. In 1975, District activists, along with a coalition of bipartisan congressional allies led by Delegate

Walter Fauntroy and Self-Determination for D.C., a national advocacy group founded in 1971, tried to strengthen home rule through the passage of a D.C. Voting Rights Amendment to the Constitution. The amendment would allow D.C. to receive two senators and proportional representation in the House, as granted to the fifty states. Activists implemented a national lobbying campaign to bring constituent pressure to bear on reluctant members of Congress. In 1978, they succeeded in helping the amendment pass by the two-thirds majority needed in the House and Senate. However, it fell short of the thirty-eight states needed to ratify it and expired in September 1985.[29]

As the voting rights amendment failed, statehood activists employed a different strategy to expand the parameters of home rule. Although Julius Hobson had passed away in 1977 after a battle with leukemia, those critical of home rule took up the mantle of statehood during the mid-1980s. They argued that statehood was needed to address the weaknesses of the Home Rule Act, to counter the injustice of disenfranchisement, and to remedy the issue of taxation without representation. Thirteen statehood bills were introduced between the 98th and 107th Congresses, but only two—one in 1987 and one in 1993—made it out of the House District Committee. The 1993 bill, the only one in which Congress took a floor vote, was defeated 277–153. On its defeat, Senator Edward Kennedy (D-Mass.) said, "The denial of the District of Columbia representation in Congress condemns the citizens of the District to second class status and makes a mockery of the principles of representative Democracy on which the nation was founded."[30]

The powers retained by Congress, particularly those related to revenue generation, created an untenable financial structure for the District. The deficiencies embedded in the 1973 Home Rule bill severely undercut the ability of the city to protect itself against poor fiscal times. It had left the city with an enormous pension liability and the responsibility to provide services usually administered by state governments. At the same time, Congress refused to provide an adequate federal payment to compensate the city for the nontaxable land it occupied while also restricting the city's ability to tax nonresident income. Thus, the District had to provide state-level services, including provisions for courts, Medicaid, welfare, prisons, and higher education, on a municipal budget. To fund these services, the District government levied state-type taxes, like personal and business income taxes, not typically levied by cities. The deficiencies in these programs were exacerbated during the 1980s, when the nature of the problems that traditionally confronted the D.C. government expanded. For example, it encountered a rise in the level of violent crime, gun use, and drug abuse and an increase in the number of people on public aid. With increasing poverty and the closing of many federally run mental health facilities, homelessness became an increasingly visible problem. The District's HIV/AIDS rate surpassed many West African nations to become the highest in the United States, and the city's public school system continued to struggle with high dropout rates and inadequate facilities.[31]

White flight to the suburbs, followed by black flight to formerly white suburbs, further contributed to the city's financial troubles. As wealthier residents continued to move away, they took their tax dollars with them. Between 1970 and 1980, the D.C. population dropped from 756,700 to 638,333 and to 606,900 by the 1990 census. Middle-class migration to the suburbs resulted in a large proportion of low- and high-income households. Congress exacerbated the problem of suburban migration by resisting residency requirements for municipal employment. From 1991 to 1994, the city witnessed a 10 percent reduction in the total number of income taxpayers and a 20 percent decline in the number of working D.C. residents. Almost 64 percent of D.C.'s tax filers earned less than $30,000 in 1995. The city's black population—celebrated in 1957 as the majority—began to decrease in the 1980s, partially on account of drug violence, but also due to high city taxes, low-quality public schools, and increased racial tensions. With fewer people able to shoulder the cost of the resources needed by the city's poorest residents, a devastating fiscal crisis erupted.[32]

D.C.'s fiscal crisis represented a host of federal and local issues, including questionable internal oversight of city funds, government inefficiency, budget deficits, increasing crime and violence, declining population, and deteriorating public schools. As Fauntroy argues, "The financial crisis was the inevitable outgrowth of a fatally flawed state-county-local government design with dwindling resources to cope by itself with the overwhelming urban challenges."[33]

D.C. elected officials' responses to the fiscal crisis—including poor management, corruption, and deception—contributed to the erosion of the limited home rule that had been granted and led to increased congressional scrutiny of the District during the 1980s and 1990s. In the early 1990s, outside investigations found corruption in the city's police department, housing agency, foster care system, and prisons. Moreover, the 1992 Republican Party platform called for "closer and responsible Congressional scrutiny of the city, federal oversight of its law enforcement and courts, and tighter fiscal restraints over its expenditures," pointing to the partisan politics at play in D.C. governance—especially after Washington residents elected Sharon Pratt Dixon as mayor and Eleanor Holmes Norton as the Democratic nonvoting delegate to the House of Representatives, a position she continues to hold to this day, in 1990.[34]

In 1995, Congress revealed the true limits of the 1973 Home Rule Act when it passed the D.C. Financial Responsibility and Management Assistance Act to respond to D.C.'s fiscal crisis. The act created an unelected five-member D.C. Control Board, to which Congress gave authority over virtually every function of District governance. It listed as its rationale for the control board the financial emergency in Washington; the D.C. government's "failure to provide its citizens with effective, efficient services in areas such as education, health care, crime prevention, trash collection, drug abuse treatment and prevention, human services delivery, and the supervision and training of government personnel"; and the long-term financial impact of resident and businesses migration out of the District.[35] Some also viewed it as punishment for the District's reelection of Barry as mayor for a fourth time in 1994. In fact, Congressman Newt Gingrich (R-Ga.), the soon-to-be Speaker of the House, called Barry's nomination "a tragic moment for this country" and predicted that the former mayor would have "an impossible time trying to deal with Congress."[36]

In 1997, Congress once again exerted its influence, creating the National Capital Revitalization and Self-Government Improvement Act to further expand the managerial and oversight responsibilities of the Control Board, which operated until September 2001. The legislation reduced Mayor Barry and the D.C. City Council's authority over District affairs by shifting financial responsibility for a number of local functions to the federal government. As a result, the federal government assumed financial and administrative responsibilities for the District's largest fiscal burdens—its unfunded pension liability for vested teachers, police, firefighters, and judges, which by 1997 had grown to $4.9 billion. But it also assumed more control over D.C. governance. Congress, for example, agreed to increase the federal share of the city's Medicaid costs from 50 to 70 percent in exchange for increased oversight of the program.[37]

Similarly, the federal government took complete control of the city's beleaguered criminal courts and prisons, including control of sentencing guidelines. During the 1980s, overcrowding at Lorton Reformatory resulted in the rapid deterioration of its facilities and prisoner-led uprisings over the poor living conditions in the 98 percent black male prison population during the late 1980s and early 1990s. By 1995, Lorton incarcerated roughly 7,300 inmates, 44 percent more people than originally intended. Facilities were so inadequate that from 1995 to 1996, National Park Police had to airlift inmates to get medical attention nearly fifty times. In 1997, Congress took over the D.C. criminal justice system and closed Lorton, transferring its prisoners to jails far away from their families. The federalization and subsequent closing of Lorton represented the culmination of decades of lobbying on the part of suburban interests, beginning with federal legislators' fight to include it in the House version of the 1970 D.C. Crime Bill and their failed amendment to the 1973 Home Rule Act.[38]

By the end of the 1990s, Congress had direct management responsibility for the city's public schools, the police department, financial management, fire and emergency medical services, public works, administrative services, corrections, human services, consumer and regulatory affairs, employment services, housing and community development, personnel, and procurement. Moreover, reporting shifted from the mayor and city council to the control board and chief management officer, a position created by the 1997 act. Congress also decided to end the federal payment, the annual transfer of federal funds that compensated the city for lost property tax revenue incurred because of the federal government's presence. The economic downturn was not exclusive to the nation's capital. New York City, Cleveland, and Philadelphia all endured fiscal crises, all of which were worse than what D.C. faced. But while not as dire, Congress responded more dramatically to the capital's, giving the D.C. Control Board more power and authority than any of the other panels established to combat the financial crisis.[39]

Congress imposed on D.C. a governing regime that set out to repair the city's fiscal crisis while halting the policy advance of black interests—even as it appointed Anthony Williams, a black bureaucrat and future D.C. mayor, as its first chief financial officer. As political scientist Daryl B. Harris argues, "Democracy in the District took a battering in the 1990s not because of who was mayor but because of the colonialist tendencies of Congress."[40] *Democracy's Capital* shows how Congress shaped the limits of black political power in the federal city in the 1960s and 1970s, leading to the unsustainable governing system with which District residents still live. The federal government's desire to dictate the shape and substance of the city's programs and policies transcends officials' desire to give democratic rights to District residents.

The Johnson and Nixon administrations directly and indirectly limited the democratic possibilities of the nation's capital. Through intense battles over the War on Poverty and War on Crime, Washingtonians fought for greater political control and participatory democracy. In the mid-1960s, radical activists channeled new energy into the movement for self-government, harnessing the power of low-income black residents in ways that the civil rights movement had not yet done. But because the War on Poverty privileged issue-based activism and prioritized low-income and often female-driven mobilization, it diverted financial resources and the attention of militant activists away from movements around the larger issue of home rule. Moreover, Johnson's reorganization plan fractured black Washington politically, undermined grassroots activism, and prompted black municipal appointees to forge partnerships with local white business interests and conservative white lawmakers to implement a prodevelopment agenda and maintain traditional governing structures at the expense of the city's black residents—actions that laid the foundation for D.C. governance for the next fifty years. Meanwhile, the War on Crime, part of the burgeoning anticrime apparatus built to punish black bodies and marginalize radical activists, curbed their efforts to achieve true self-determination.

In the aftermath of the 1968 riots, activists and organizations that sought to represent Washington's voiceless citizens turned from the issue of home rule to activism around community control, riot rebuilding, police reform, and urban renewal. Groups that represented the interests of Washington's middle class, on the other hand, shifted their focus to changing the underlying injustice that haunted the city: the lack of home rule. The gradualist efforts that more moderate black, predominantly male leaders advocated for helped usher in compromise legislation that formed the basis for two decades of governance. By the 1990s, the growing national support for conservative policies and opposition to black political power resonated with an increasingly powerful plurality. Although Congress could no longer exclude black Washingtonians from the democratic process, it could still police local policy and enforce racial inequalities.

Congress never did relinquish its ultimate authority over District affairs, and full democracy in the nation's capital remains out of reach. The city has always had to compete for funds in the context of race, suburban interests, and national political concerns. The erosion of home rule was a combination of partisan politics, city-suburban politics, and congressional intervention. Scholars and activists generally agree that until there is a supportive president willing to work for the passage of full representation for the District, a Congress willing to support it, and a national network of sympathetic organizations willing to rally around it, then D.C. residents will never have the rights to self-determination enjoyed by all other U.S. citizens.

But perhaps that is still not enough. When black leaders fought for home rule in the 1970s, they returned to traditional tactics, like national consensus building and lobbying for congressional support. In the process, they lost the backing of black militants who had turned to other pressing grassroots issues.

Only when more radical dreams of democracy are fashioned to incorporate the voices of those consistently marginalized, and elected politics are no longer seen as an alternative to activism and protest but as an arm of a larger revolution, will our country "make D.C. mean Democracy's Capital," as civil rights and Black Power organizations fought for in the mid-twentieth century.[41]

ACKNOWLEDGMENTS

It is a great pleasure to thank all of those who have directly and indirectly supported this project. As a young scholar at Wesleyan University, I had the privilege to participate in a dynamic Center for African American Studies and work closely with Anne DuCille, Ashraf Rushdy, and Gayle Pemberton. Renee Romano took me on as a thesis student and was a great mentor. Yale University was an incredible place to do my doctoral work, and that is a testament to the wonderful people who filled its halls. I benefited from conversations and classes with Elizabeth Alexander, George Chauncey, Kathleen Cleaver, Matt Jacobson, Jennifer Klein, Joanne Meyerowitz, and Steve Pitti. I was also fortunate to learn from a number of scholars from different years and fields who are doing brilliant work, including Francesca Ammon, Betsy Beasley, Kathleen Belew, Andrew Friedman, Joe Fronczak, Jay Garcia, Josh Glick, Sarah Haley, Betty Luther Hillman, Scott Saul, Brandon Terry, Jason Ward, and Sandy Zipp. Katherine Mooney, and Jeff Gonda have remained gracious friends.

Glenda Gilmore, Jean-Christophe Agnew, and Jonathan Holloway brought a diverse set of questions and specialties to this project, all of which are evident in its pages. The idea for this project originated in Jonathan's office, and his generosity and commitment to this project were invaluable. I was not surprised by, though I was certainly grateful for, Glenda and Jean-Christophe's insightful feedback and compatible advice. Perhaps it was a coincidence that they both retired as I was finishing up my book, but the two trips to New Haven that I made in the span of two weeks in May 2018 reenergized me as I finished revising the book. Jean-Christophe pushed me to take intellectual risks that I otherwise would not have. He helped me move beyond the sheer accumulation of information to craft a narrative, timeline, and map that would function as the architecture and signature of my own interpretation. And Glenda encouraged me to think big, be bold, and ask good questions. She has taught us all what it means to write history like black lives matter. She is a model scholar and is responsible for both the title of my book and for turning me into a historian. Having attended both of their retirement celebrations, I know I am not the only one who owes my career to these scholars. I am honored to add my name to the lists.

Thanks to everyone at the University of North Carolina Press, including Cate Hodorowicz, Christi Stanforth, and Dylan White, who aided in the publication of this book. It is inadequate to say that the readers' reports I received were helpful. My anonymous reviewers at the University of North Carolina Press and elsewhere provided me with critical and constructive feedback that changed the manuscript for the better. They went above and beyond the call of duty, and for that I am grateful. Heather Thompson and Rhonda Williams are fantastic series editors, and I am thrilled to be among the wonderful scholars publishing in the Justice, Power, and Politics series. I am particularly grateful to my editor, Brandon Proia, who shared my enthusiasm for this project from the very beginning. His willingness to debrief on a moment's notice, ability to break down seemingly monumental tasks into achievable assignments, and good humor made him a pleasure to work with.

At the archives, I received good guidance from Greg Cumming at the Richard Nixon Presidential Library; Joellen ElBashir at Howard University's Moorland-Spingarn Research Center; Allen Fisher at the Lyndon Baines Johnson Presidential Library; Sarah Leavitt at the National Building Museum; Anne McDonough at the Historical Society of Washington, D.C.; Athena Smith and the helpful staff at George Washington University's Special Collections Research Center; and Derek Gray at the Martin Luther King Jr. Memorial Library. My first research trip to the MLK Library corresponded to Derek's first week on the job, and years later he assisted me with last-minute photo requests and permissions.

A John Morton Blum Fellowship from Yale University and an Albert J. Beveridge Grant from the American Historical Association underwrote the book's main archival research. A fellowship from the Mrs. Giles Whiting Foundation supported its writing. A one-year position at the United States Military Academy provided me time to think about revisions. Working for Colonel Ty Seidule, and with Greg Daddis, Major Andy Forney, Major Rory McGovern, and Major Danny Sjursen, was an honor. Meanwhile, chairs, commenters, and copanelists at countless conferences, including Chris Agee, Joe Crespino, Mike Durfee, Alex Elkins, Max Felker-Kantor, Lily Geismer, Elizabeth Hinton, Kwame Holmes, Julilly Kohler-Hausmann, Tim Lombardo, Heather Thompson, and Leah Wright Rigueur, helped sharpen my thinking about the book.

At the University of Florida (UF), a Humanities Enhancement Award supported the book's completion. UF's College of Liberal Arts and Sciences and

Center for the Humanities and the Public Sphere (Rothman Endowment) generously awarded a publication subvention grant. Several other groups and centers at UF helped further this project, including the Bob Graham Center for Public Service; the Center for the Study of Race and Race Relations; and the members of the Mellon Intersections Working Group on Mass Incarceration, comprising Stephanie Birch, Elizabeth Dale, Katheryn Russell-Brown, Jodi Schorb, and Heather Vrana. My colleagues in the History Department gave me a warm welcome and continued support. I am particularly grateful to Jeff Adler, Jack Davis, Matt Gallman, Bill Link, Steve Noll, and Paul Ortiz for their advice and guidance. Most important, I owe great thanks to the women in my department, who helped shepherd me through my early years at UF—especially Michelle Campos, Nina Caputo, Elizabeth Dale, Lily Guerra, and Jessica Harland-Jacobs. Louise Newman edited the introduction in short order to get the manuscript ready to submit. Sheryl Kroen invited me to work with her at a critical juncture. She has become a dear friend and an inspiring mentor. I am also lucky to have excellent colleagues in the African American Studies Program. I have learned so much from my friend and confidant Manoucheka Celeste. Though no longer at UF, Ibram Kendi continues to provide gracious mentorship and a shining example of courageous scholarship.

The university is teeming with talented people I am honored to work with, including Jennifer Jones, Rachel Nelson, Lourdes Santamaría-Wheeler, Lisa Scott, Carlos Suarez, and Trysh Travis. Valerie and George Atohi, Brooke and Ivan Davis, Meredith DeFranco, Jess and Robb Holmes, Lisa Johnson, and Laura and Chris Porter made and continue to make life down here more enjoyable. John Asalone, Sarah Firshein, Emily Hager, Annette LoVoi, Eleanor Morrison, Catharine Richert, and Jake Wolman make life, in general, better. Meanwhile, my in-laws, Peter and Mary Beth Durant, housed me in Washington for short and long research trips, provided transportation to and from the many archives I visited, and dropped everything to assist me with one of the very last book-related tasks. I've known them for almost twenty years and am lucky to call them family.

In the fall of 2017, I was run over by a car while out on an early morning run. I could not have made a full recovery without the immediate assistance of Dr. Ethan Dean; the help of the nurses at Shands Hospital; the kindness of John Phillips, DPT; the surgical care of Dr. Jennifer Hagen and Dr. Michael Moser; the support of my patient and funny physical therapists, Josh Barabas and Zach Sutton; and the encouragement of my miracle worker, Mary Horn. As other working parents know, arranging child care, school pickups, and after-school activities is a careful balancing act, even under the best of circumstances. Our sons have grown into independent, thoughtful kids thanks to the care of a team of child-care providers from Brooklyn to Gainesville, including Sandra Rodney, Jordan Davis Corley, and the staff and teachers at St. John's Kids, Helen Owen Carey, Open Arms, GASP, Flowers Montessori, and Littlewood Elementary School.

While pregnant with my second son, I met three wonderful women, Mollie Bort, Amanda Donovan, and Kyle Tilley, whose daily chatter continues to bring me joy. In Gainesville, I literally ran into Eva George. I could not have found a kinder, funnier, and more supportive running partner. Although she moved away as I was finishing my book, she is always in my heart.

Above all, I am thankful for my family's support. With unconditional love, Larry Pearlman put me through my ninja training. Marian Fischer Pearlman made sure I stayed afloat while offering her own good council both to me and to a new generation of Philadelphia women. Together they gave me the courage to speak out against racial injustice and the drive to finish this book. Greg, Julia, and Gracie Pearlman kept me motivated throughout. Leaving this tremendous familial unit for the South was not easy, but their visits, group texts, and FaceTime calls keep me connected to them. I will never be able to thank them sufficiently for their help after my accident, and I am grateful to have them by my side. I am also lucky to live near my grandparents, Barbara and Louis Fischer, whose company I treasure. And though Lee Samuels lives on the other coast, I know how proud she is.

The first person I saw when I woke up in the hospital was my husband, Fletcher Durant. When I tested the "in sickness and in health" promise of our marriage, he showed me more love, patience, and kindness than I thought one could humanely summon. Unfortunately for him, I picked a book topic that he was also interested in. Our endless conversations on walks in the park, during long car rides, and in more emails than I can count breathed life into this project when it needed it most. He is my most trusted counsel, my biggest cheerleader, and the one who read every single page more than once. I could not have done this without him. My only regret is that I can only thank him here once.

Our sons, Felix Everett and Milo Freeland, have known this project their whole lives. I carried Felix on stage with me at my graduate school commencement ceremony, but he has carried me through this project. His imagination, curiosity, and sense of justice—formed during countless Black Lives Matter protests in the streets of New York City and dinnertime conversations about race relations—has relieved me of my guilt when I have to work instead of listen to him weave his own creative tales. I arrived at UF five months pregnant with Milo, who has grown into a sweet and strong-willed boy with whom I share a special bond—in part because he insists on nothing less than my full attention. They are smart, kind, funny, and brave, and I am excited to watch them grow. I could have done this without them, but it would have been far less joyful. A year that began in the hospital and culminated with my manuscript submission did not deserve to be as good as it was. It is because of these three that it was possible.

NOTES

ABBREVIATIONS

ARBA
American Revolution Bicentennial Administration

BAA
Baltimore Afro-American

BOTR-GWU
Greater Washington Board of Trade Records, Special Collections Research Center, Gelman Library, The George Washington University, Washington, D.C.

BUF
Black United Front

CCR-GWU
District of Columbia City Council Records, Special Collections Research Center, Gelman Library, The George Washington University, Washington, D.C.

Committee of 100-GWU
Committee of 100 on the Federal City Records (Part I), Special Collections Research Center, Gelman Library, The George Washington University, Washington, D.C.

DPR-MLKL
Downtown Progress Records, D.C. Community Archives, Martin Luther King Jr. Memorial Library, Washington, D.C.

EX FG
Federal Government

EX HU
Human Rights

FCAR-MLKL
District of Columbia Federation of Citizens Associations Records, D.C. Community Archives, Martin Luther King Jr. Memorial Library, Washington, D.C.

JHP-MLKL
Julius W. Hobson Papers, D.C. Community Archives, Martin Luther King Jr. Memorial Library, Washington, D.C.

LBJL
Lyndon Baines Johnson Presidential Library, Austin, Texas

NYT
New York Times

Proposal to the ARBC
A Proposal to the American Revolution Bicentennial Commission from the District of Columbia Bicentennial Commission, Maryland Bicentennial Commission,

and Virginia Independence Bicentennial Commission, Washington, D.C., September 1969

RBOH-MSRC-HU
: Ralph Bunche Oral History Collection, Moorland-Spingarn Research Center, Howard University, Washington, D.C.

RNPL
: Richard Nixon Presidential Library, Yorba Linda, California

SMOF
: Staff Member and Office Files

SNCCP
: Student Nonviolent Coordinating Committee Papers, 1959–1972, microfilm, Sterling Memorial Library, Yale University, New Haven, Connecticut

WFP-GWU
: Walter E. Fauntroy Papers, Special Collections Research Center, Gelman Library, The George Washington University, Washington, D.C.

WHCF
: White House Central Files

WHSF
: White House Subject Files

WP
: *Washington Post*

WS
: *Washington Star*

INTRODUCTION

1. According to political scientist Michael K. Fauntroy, "Home rule refers to a governmental status in which authority and responsibility for management of a unit of government falls to that unit of government, subject to the parameters set by a superior unit of government. Domestically, home rule is seen in the context of relationships between cities and states or between counties and states." Fauntroy, "Home Rule for the District of Columbia," 23–24. The Constitution states: "To exercise exclusive Legislation in all Cases whatsoever, over such District (not exceeding ten Miles square) as may, by Cession of particular States, and the acceptance of Congress, become the Seat of the Government of the United States." U.S. Constitution, art. 1, sec. 8.

2. Reverend Channing Phillips, interview by Katherine M. Shannon, July 13, 1967, Washington, D.C., RBOH-MSRC-HU.

3. Dr. George Wiley, interview by James Mosby, date not recorded, Washington, D.C., RBOH-MSRC-HU.

4. For broad surveys on the 1960s, see Gitlin, *The Sixties*; Blum, *Years of Discord*; Anderson, *The Movement and the Sixties*; Lytle, *America's Uncivil Wars*. On the broad contours of the seventies, see Bailey and Farber, *America in the Seventies*; Schulman and Zeilizer, *Rightward Bound*.

5. On SNCC, see Carson, *In Struggle*; Payne, *I've Got the Light of Freedom*. On Black Power, see Ogbar, *Black Power*; Joseph, *The Black Power Movement*; Williams, *Concrete Demands*. For a variety of studies on the Black Panthers, see Murch, *Living for*

the City; Cleaver and Katsiaficas, *Liberation, Imagination, and the Black Panther Party*; Alondra Nelson, *Body and Soul*; Bloom and Martin, *Black against Empire*.

6. For two excellent historical studies connecting the carceral state and the welfare state, see Hinton, *From the War on Poverty to the War on Crime*, and Kohler-Hausmann, *Getting Tough*. On scholarship outside of history that examines interactions between the welfare and the carceral systems, see Garland, *The Culture of Control*; Wacquant, *Punishing the Poor*; Beckett and Western, "Governing Social Marginality"; Soss, Fording, and Schram, *Disciplining the Poor*; Gustafson, *Cheating Welfare*.

7. On the Great Society, see Zelizer, *The Fierce Urgency of Now*; Milkis and Mileur, *The Great Society and the High Tide of Liberalism*; Unger, *The Best of Intentions*. On the War on Poverty, see Michael B. Katz, *The Undeserving Poor*. On the ways poor communities struggled to reshape the War on Poverty on the ground, see Orleck and Hazirjian, *The War on Poverty*; Orleck, *Storming Caesar's Palace*; Williams, *The Politics of Public Housing*; Germany, *New Orleans after the Promises*; Levenstein, *A Movement without Marches*; Goldstein, *Poverty in Common*. On "maximum feasible participation," see Orleck, "Introduction: The War on Poverty from the Grass Roots Up," 2.

8. Over the last twenty years, some historians have focused on Washington's many subcultures while others have taken a variety of geographical approaches to the study of D.C. history. See, for example, David K. Johnson, *The Lavender Scare*; Valk's excellent *Radical Sisters*; Repak, *Waiting on Washington*; Cary, *Urban Odyssey*; Abbott, *Political Terrain*. Pioneering studies like Gillette's *Between Justice and Beauty* and, more recently, Ruble's *Washington's U Street* focus on the racial implications of urban planning and the city's popular black U Street neighborhood respectively. See also Jaffe and Sherwood, *Dream City*, and Siegel, *The Future Once Happened Here*. Jaffe and Sherwood focus on the ways that black political power in general, and Marion Barry's rule in specific, led to the city's demise after the passage of home rule measures in 1973. They do not offer an examination of the importance of Black Power strategies and organizations to the fight for civil rights in the District. Siegel uses Washington, D.C., as a case study, along with New York and Los Angeles, to analyze the negative effects of liberal social policies. Meanwhile, scholars who examine Washington, D.C.'s political status rarely engage substantively with its racial history. Jamin Raskin, Mark Richards, and Charles Harris have done important work on the issue of voting rights, Congressional governance, and the tension between federal and local interests. Raskin, "Is This America?"; Richards, "The Debates over the Retrocession of the District of Columbia, 1801–2004"; Charles Wesley Harris, *Congress and the Governance of the Nation's Capital*. The following take up the issue of race and move beyond simply documenting the passage of home rule legislation to explain many of its causes: Zigas, *Left with Few Rights*; Diner, "The Black Majority"; Walters and Travis, *Democratic Destiny and the District of Columbia*.

9. A notable exception is Asch and Musgrove's *Chocolate City*, an excellent history of race and democracy in D.C. In 2017, former public defender and law professor James Forman Jr. took a much-needed critical approach to local black leaders' decisions to bolster the prison industrial complex while trying to protect black constituents. But this superb study does not examine the impact of the federal government on local politics. Forman, *Locking Up Our Own*.

10. For scholarship on community-level protests, see Morris, *The Origins of the Civil*

Rights Movement; Dittmer, *Local People*; Fairclough, *Race and Democracy*; Payne, *I've Got the Light of Freedom*. On the relationship between civil rights and Black Power, see Tyson, *Radio Free Dixie*; Williams, *Black Politics / White Power*; Hill, *The Deacons for Defense*; Countryman, *Up South*; Woodard, *Nation within a Nation*; Jeffries, *Bloody Lowndes*. Studies that follow the movement into the 1970s and examine the movements it inspired include Grady-Willis, *Challenging U.S. Apartheid*; Orleck, *Storming Caesar's Palace*; Oropeza, *¡Raza Si! ¡Guerra No!*

11. For the best study on how the administrations of John F. Kennedy through Ronald Reagan transformed the welfare state into a punitive carceral state, see Hinton, *From the War on Poverty to the War on Crime*. In particular, Hinton shows how, over the course of the Johnson presidency, social welfare programs that expanded educational and job training opportunities to urban residents came to be supplanted by police department "recreational" programs that only enhanced law enforcement surveillance. See also Kohler-Hausmann, "Guns and Butter"; Germany, *New Orleans after the Promises*; Maddison, "'In Chains 400 Years . . . and *Still* in Chains in DC!,'" particularly 187–90.

12. The carceral state is a term that refers to the institutions, laws, customs, and politics that have created what political scientists Vesla Weaver and Amy Lerman call "a punishment-oriented system of governance" in modern America. Weaver and Lerman, "Political Consequences of the Carceral State," 2. This was in large part thanks to historian Heather Ann Thompson's warning, in 2010, that scholars have overlooked late twentieth-century mass incarceration and have "not yet begun to sort out its impact on the social, economic, and political evolution of the postwar period." Thompson, "Why Mass Incarceration Matters." For compelling studies on other major transformations, including the history of urban segregation, municipal politics, and suburban expansion in the postwar era, see, for example, Kruse, *White Flight*; Lassiter, *The Silent Majority*; Self, *American Babylon*; and Sugrue, *The Origins of the Urban Crisis*.

13. See Gottschalk, *The Prison and the Gallows*; Thompson, "Why Mass Incarceration Matters"; Beckett and Herbert, *Banished*; Marion, *A History of Federal Crime Control Initiatives, 1960–1993*; Walker, *Popular Justice*; Gest, *Crime and Politics*.

14. On the powerful role of racism in federal crime policy, particularly the ideology of racial liberalism and its naturalization of links between criminality and blackness, see Hinton, *From the War on Poverty to the War on Crime*; Murakawa, *The First Civil Right*; Weaver, "Frontlash"; Beckett, *Making Crime Pay*.

15. Murakawa, *The First Civil Right*; Hinton, *From the War on Poverty to the War on Crime*.

16. For two different arguments linking crime policy to a backlash to civil rights, see Edsall and Edsall, *Chain Reaction*, and Alexander, *The New Jim Crow*. For scholarship on popular pressure arising from consternation about crime, see Fortner, *Black Silent Majority*; Enns, *Incarceration Nation*; Flamm, *Law and Order*. For a longer view that does not attribute the development of the carceral state solely to the conservative backlash to demographic changes and civil rights gains, see Muhammad, *The Condemnation of Blackness*.

17. See, for example, Fortner, *Black Silent Majority*; Miller, "The Invisible Black Victim." Fortner's *Black Silent Majority* received heavy criticism from other "war on crime" scholars. Khalil Muhammad, for example, notes that Fortner does not locate

the "visible hand of racism" in police brutality, redlining, segregation, and job discrimination. Additionally, Muhammad laments that *Black Silent Majority* promotes the harmful myth that "nothing stands in the way of racial equality except black people's own choices and behavior." Muhammad, "'Black Silent Majority,' by Michael Javen Fortner." Similarly, Donna Murch notes, "Absent from *Black Silent Majority* is an examination of what happens when a marginalized community facing mass capital abandonment, job loss, and an urgent public health crisis is presented only one policy option: more policing and punishment." By attempting to locate black agency, Fortner fails to appreciate how U.S. political dynamics circumscribed policy options for African Americans. Murch, "Who's to Blame for Mass Incarceration?" For more nuanced studies of how black communities confronted crime and policing in the 1960s and beyond, see Felker-Kantor, *Policing Los Angeles*; Murch, "Crack in Los Angeles"; Stauch, "Wildcat of the Streets"; Pihos, "Police, Race, and Politics in Chicago."

18. Forman, *Locking Up Our Own*, 10.

19. This book serves as one response to Heather Thompson's call for work that shows how the carceral expansion affected other urban transformations. See Thompson, "Why Mass Incarceration Matters"; Hinton, *From the War on Poverty to the War on Crime*; Kohler-Hausmann, *Getting Tough*. On political responses to the rising drug epidemic, see Murch, "Crack in Los Angeles"; Durfee, "Crack Era Reform."

20. Michael B. Katz, *Why Don't American Cities Burn?*, 87–88.

21. Michael B. Katz, *Why Don't American Cities Burn?*, 86.

22. Charles Cassell, interview by Robert E. Wright, December 31, 1968, Washington, D.C., RBOH-MSRC-HU.

23. On the impact of the partnerships formed between white business interests and the federal government on urban planning and development, see Harvey, *The Urban Experience*, chapter 9; Don Mitchell, "Postmodern Geographical Praxis?"; Cindi Katz, "Hiding the Target"; Hackworth, *The Neoliberal City*; Vitale, *City of Disorder*. On black-led partnerships with white stakeholders, see, for example, Stone, *Regime Politics*; Thompson, *Whose Detroit*.

24. See, for example, Fergus, *Liberalism, Black Power, and the Making of American Politics, 1965–1980*; Joseph, *Waiting 'til the Midnight Hour*; Joseph, *The Black Power Movement*; Woodard, *Nation within a Nation*; Tyson, *Radio Free Dixie*; Ogbar, *Black Power*; Countryman, *Up South*; Self, *American Babylon*; Grady-Willis, *Challenging U.S. Apartheid*.

25. Joseph, "The Black Power Movement, Democracy, and America in the King Years," 1003. In cities like Philadelphia and Newark, Black Power fundamentally altered the composition of black leadership. But in Washington, the federal government circumscribed Black Power's radical possibilities.

26. Sundiata Keita Cha-Jua and Clarence Lang best articulated the call for scholarship that situates Black Power politics in the postwar city and urban political economy. Cha-Jua and Lang, "The 'Long Movement' as Vampire." On urban coalition building in Atlanta during the postwar era, including black elected officials' desire for the political and economic benefits from redevelopment and the power of white stakeholders to help marshal resources, see Stone, *Regime Politics*.

27. Diner, *Democracy, Federalism and the Governance of the Nation's Capital, 1790–1974*, 4–22; Zigas, *Left with Few Rights*, 13–14.

28. Abbott, "Perspectives on Urban Economic Planning," 9–10. The 1871 territorial government consisted of a governor, an eleven-member council, and a Board of Public Works, all appointed by the president. In 1873, President Ulysses Grant appointed the board's most influential member, Alexander Shepherd, to the new governorship. The powerful political boss authorized large-scale projects to modernize Washington but overspent three times the approved budget and bankrupted the city. Charles Wesley Harris, *Congress and the Governance of the Nation's Capital*, 3–5. According to historian Constance Green, many white residents did not mind their disenfranchisement at the hand of the federal government as it kept black power in check. Green, *Washington: Capital City, 1879–1950*, 5. For more on the rise and retrenchment of local Reconstruction policies in Washington, see Masur's excellent study, *An Example for All the Land*.

29. Manning, "Multicultural Washington, D.C.," 331–32; Green, *The Secret City*, 18–19; Abbott, "Perspectives on Urban Economic Planning," 15; Moore, *Leading the Race*, chapter 8. For an overview of black life in Washington during the nineteenth century, see Green, *The Secret City*, 13–155; Lewis, *District of Columbia*, 3–80. For more on Howard's centrality to black intellectual life, see Holloway, *Confronting the Veil*. On the centerpiece of the city's black secondary educational system, M Street High School, see Robinson, "The M Street High School, 1891–1916"; Stewart, *First Class*.

30. Yellin, *Racism in the Nation's Service*, 1–8; Manning, "Multicultural Washington, D.C.," 333; Gilmore, *Defying Dixie*, 17–18; Sullivan, *Days of Hope*, 46–47, 53. Spearheaded by Secretary of the Interior Harold L. Ickes, the Interior Department hired African Americans to fill white-collar positions, integrated housing projects and national parks, and established an in-house advisory position to monitor race relations in all federal agencies during the 1930s. Biles, *The South and the New Deal*, 119.

31. Manning, "Multicultural Washington, D.C.," 334.

32. Manning, "Multicultural Washington, D.C.," 335. For general trends on black migration and ensuing housing shortages in urban America, see Mohl, "Race and Housing in the Postwar City." In 1949, the Supreme Court ruled racial covenants unenforceable in court. See Gonda, *Unjust Deeds*.

33. Ammon, "Commemoration amid Criticism," 176–78, 182. On housing conditions for low-income black residents, see Borchert, *Alley Life in Washington*. On the idea of Washington as a national laboratory for urban policy, see Gillette, "A National Workshop for Urban Policy." On the consequences of policies to combat urban decay, see, for example, Teaford, "Urban Renewal and Its Aftermath"; Silver, *Twentieth-Century Richmond*; Bednarek, *Changing Image of the City*; Hirsch, *Making the Second Ghetto*; Mohl, "Making the Second Ghetto in Metropolitan Miami, 1940–1960." On white flight more broadly, see Kenneth T. Jackson, *Crabgrass Frontier*; Lassiter, *The Silent Majority*; Kruse, *White Flight*; Nicolaides, *My Blue Heaven*.

34. The Southwest D.C. quadrant was a majority-black area just south of Independence Avenue and the National Mall, east of South Capitol Street, and north of P Street. Gutheim and Lee, *Worthy of the Nation*, 235; Ammon, "Commemoration amid Criticism," 182, 196; Gillette, *Between Justice and Beauty*, 164. After the organization began demolishing buildings in the spring of 1954, lawsuits from business owners challenging the agency's powers to condemn land overwhelmed the District courts. In

October, the Supreme Court sided with the RLA. In *Berman v. Parker*, it unanimously affirmed the RLA's right to condemn land occupied by "miserable and disreputable housing," in the spirit of public interest. The same year as the Supreme Court ruled racial segregation in public schools unconstitutional in the landmark *Brown v. Board of Education* decision, it granted the RLA authority to forcibly remove black residents from their homes and relocate them to other neighborhoods. Gutheim and Lee, *Worthy of the Nation*, 318; Gillette, "A National Workshop for Urban Policy," 14. According to the Supreme Court's decision, written by Justice William O. Douglas, "In the present case, Congress and its authorized agencies attack the problem of the blighted parts of the community on an area rather than on a structure-by-structure basis. . . . The experts concluded that if the community were to be healthy, if it were not to revert again to a blighted or slum area, as though possessed by a congenital disease, the area must be planned as a whole." *Berman v. Parker*. As Steven Diner argues, "Southwest urban renewal accelerated the emergence of new, all-black neighborhoods in other parts of the city . . . particularly east of the Anacostia River." Diner, "The Black Majority," 253.

35. Quoted in Diner, "The Black Majority," 255; Zachary Schrag, *The Great Society Subway*, 23; Smith, *Captive Capital*, 216. On other slum removal efforts, see Hirsch, *Making the Second Ghetto*; Mohl, "Making the Second Ghetto in Metropolitan Miami, 1940–1960"; Sugrue, *The Origins of the Urban Crisis*; Schuyler, *A City Transformed*; Bauman, *Public Housing, Race and Renewal*; Teaford, *The Rough Road to Renaissance*; Schwartz, *The New York Approach*.

36. Lewis, *District of Columbia*, 121–23; Gilbert, *Ten Blocks from the White House*, 3–4; Gillette, "A National Workshop for Urban Policy," 18.

37. Charles Wesley Harris, *Congress and the Governance of the Nation's Capital*, 6. On southern conservatives' campaigns to preserve the white social order more broadly, see Ward, *Defending White Democracy*. According to one Washington journalist, the Senate committee in particular was viewed as a "proving ground for junior members or a dumping ground for embarrassing ones." Jaffe and Sherwood, *Dream City*, 27.

38. Ward, *Defending White Democracy*, 71–72. See also Fleegler, "Theodore G. Bilbo and the Decline of Public Racism, 1938–1947."

39. Bilbo's tenure as House District Committee chair ended not because District residents protested forcefully enough but because his outspoken support of segregation back home garnered the attention of the NAACP. In 1947, NAACP Executive Director Walter White submitted an exhaustive report to the Senate Campaign Investigation Committee documenting Bilbo's voter intimidation practices in Mississippi. On reviewing this evidence, the Committee decided to bar Bilbo from taking his seat in the Senate and, consequently, on the District Committee. However, Bilbo died before the Senate could formally censure him. Lewis, *District of Columbia*, 180; Lawson, *Running for Freedom*, 23–25; Berman, *The Politics of Civil Rights in the Truman Administration*, 54.

40. "The Board of Trade," *Washington Afro-American*, March 13, 1965; Abbott, "Perspectives on Urban Economic Planning," 10. On the influence of business interests on the city, see, for example, Cummings, *Business Elites and Urban Development*; Weiss, *The Rise of the Community Builders*; Cohen, *A Consumers' Republic*; Bloom, *Merchant of Illusion*; Stevens, *Developing Expertise*; Rubin, *Insuring the City*. On the historical

relationships between business interests and built space more broadly, see, for example, Isenberg, *Downtown America*; Hornstein, *A Nation of Realtors*; Sandoval-Strausz, *Hotel*; Richard Harris, *Building a Market*.

41. Derthick, *City Politics in Washington, D.C.*, 89–93.

42. Derthick, *City Politics in Washington, D.C.*, 89–93; Smith, *Captive Capital*, 23, 26. On the importance of business-based growth consensus and growth coalitions in shaping public decisions in American cities, see, for example, Molotch and Logan, *Urban Fortunes*; Gottidiener, *The Social Production of Urban Space*; Elkin, "Twentieth Century Urban Regimes"; Fleischmann and Feagin, "The Politics of Growth-Oriented Urban Alliances"; Mollenkopf, *The Contested City*.

43. Asch and Musgrove, *Chocolate City*, 193; Elsie Carper, "Federation to Bar New Mixed Unit," *WP*, November 14, 1964; Mike DeBonis, "In 'One City,' Two D.C. Civic Federations," *WP*, March 3, 2013. The 1964 controversy erupted over the membership of one of its groups, the Lamond-Riggs Citizens Association, which had named a black woman as a delegate to the larger body. The Federation expelled the group in May but reinstated it two months later. Although the main body agreed to retain member associations that had already integrated, it voted to ban any new integrated groups. In January 1966, the Lamond Riggs Citizens Association withdrew from the Federation due to the long-standing controversy over its whites-only policy. Carper, "Federation to Bar New Mixed Unit"; "Group Quits Federation of Citizens," *WP*, January 5, 1966. On the role of neighborhood improvement associations before the 1960s, see Sugrue, "Crabgrass-Roots Politics." Statistics on the number of neighborhood associations represented by the Federation vary. Scholars have estimated that it represented nearly seventy neighborhood groups during the late 1940s. In the 1960s, the Federation said it represented thirty-four groups, while city planner Martha Derthick estimated that it represented fifty-two. See Vose, *Caucasians Only*, 197; Ward, *Defending White Democracy*, 74; Statement, George W. Brady to D.C. Council, March 15, 1969, FCAR-MLKL, box 2, folder 1968–1969 Office Files Book 2; Derthick, *City Politics in Washington, D.C.*, 109.

44. This term, now standard in the urban studies lexicon, was developed by sociologist Harvey Molotch in his seminal paper "The City as a Growth Machine" and expanded on in his book *Urban Fortunes* (with John R. Logan). In these works, Molotch revises established understandings of urban theory by arguing that social actions rather than interpersonal market or geographic necessities shape cities. Especially important in shaping cities was, he argued, the real estate interests of those whose properties gain value when growth takes place. These actors make up what Molotch termed "the local growth machine."

45. Abbott, "Perspectives on Urban Economic Planning," 11; Ruble, *Washington's U Street*, 61; "The Board of Trade." According to the League of Women Voters of the District of Columbia, "The most powerful organized opposition to self-government comes from the Metropolitan Washington Board of Trade. While it worked hard to get the Presidential vote for Washington and has continued to press for voting representation on Congress, the Board of Trade argues against local government." Report, "D.C.—Last Colony," prepared by the League of Women Voters of the District of Columbia, March 1970, JHP-MLKL, series 6, box 1, folder Home Rule (1 of 8) 1962–80.

46. Diner, *Democracy, Federalism and the Governance of the Nation's Capital, 1790–1974*, 37, 41–45; Zigas, *Left with Few Rights*, 24, 35.

47. For studies of D.C.'s pre-1960s civil rights protests and demonstrations, see Asch and Musgrove, *Chocolate City*; Green, *The Secret City*; Jones, "Before Montgomery and Greensboro"; Gilmore, *Defying Dixie*, 385–92; Quigley, *Just Another Southern Town*; Pacifico, "'Don't Buy Where You Can't Work.'"

48. Scholar J. Samuel Walker has aggregated the best data from the riots. See *Most of 14th Street Is Gone*, 98.

49. A note on terminology: I have chosen to use the terms "riot," "rebellion," "disorder," "disturbance," and "uprising" interchangeably so as not to privilege one interpretation over another. The term "riot" has negative connotations and, though it was used in contemporary sources, including press coverage and government investigations, does not fully account for what happened in Washington, D.C. Specifically, the term does not capture the grievances of rioters living in poor neighborhoods who had long sought to better the material conditions in which they lived. Nor does it convey the root causes of the violence and destruction that transpired in April 1968. For further discussions on this terminology, see Seligman, "'But Burn—No'"; Thompson, "Urban Uprisings"; Elkins, "Stand Our Ground."

50. Fauntroy, "Home Rule for the District of Columbia," 23–24.

CHAPTER 1

1. See Higginbotham, foreword to *Freedom North*. On the symbolism of black protest at the Lincoln Memorial, see Sandage, "A Marble House Divided." For more on protest on the National Mall, see Barber, *Marching on Washington*. On ways that King's "I Have a Dream" speech has been contorted to serve different political purposes, see Hall's 2004 presidential address to the Organization of American Historians, later published as "The Long Civil Rights Movement and the Political Uses of the Past." Nikhil Pal Singh was also at pains to disrupt the "master narrative" advanced by the nation-state to deradicalize and denationalize the movement. See Singh, *Black Is a Country*, especially pages 1–14.

2. Asch and Musgrove, *Chocolate City*, 338; Sellers, *The River of No Return*, 62; Reverend Channing Phillips, interview by Katherine M. Shannon; Susanna McBee, "4000 Troops Set for Use on Aug. 28: No Trouble Expected," *WP*, August 22, 1968. According to August Meier and Elliot M. Rudwick, cooperation at the March on Washington came at the cost of considerable compromise and was precarious at best. Meier and Rudwick, *CORE*, 224. Studies that minimize local contributions to the March on Washington—and to the civil rights movement more generally—include Garrow, *Bearing the Cross*; Branch, *Pillar of Fire*; Weisbrot, *Freedom Bound*.

3. "The Board of Trade," *Washington Afro-American*, March 13, 1965.

4. Abbott, "Perspectives on Urban Economic Planning," 10–11; Report, "D.C.—Last Colony," League of Women Voters of the District of Columbia, March 1970, JHP-MLKL, series 6, box 1, folder Home Rule (1 of 8) 1962–80; Draft Position on Proposed Legislation, July 30, 1968, FCAR-MLKL, box 2, folder 1968–1969 Office Files Book 1; Smith, *Captive Capital*, 23. On the racial motivations of white community and business

groups in other locales, see, for example, Sugrue, *The Origins of the Urban Crisis*; Crespino, *In Search of Another Country*; Lassiter, *The Silent Majority*; Kruse, *White Flight*.

5. Hobson spent one quarter at Columbia before leaving for Howard. The activist explained that he was disenchanted with the university's large classes and felt he needed more academic training. At Howard, Hobson found a better intellectual fit. He studied with visiting Marxist professors like Paul Sweezy (from the University of New Hampshire), Otto Nathan (an economist and executor of Albert Einstein's will), Corliss Lamont (from Columbia University). He did not graduate. Susan Jacoby, "Julius Hobson: The Man behind the Mouth," *The Washingtonian*, April 1969; "Julius Hobson: A Goad for Change," *WP*, July 2, 1972; Matthews, "The Politics of Julius W. Hobson, Sr., and the District of Columbia Public School System," 72; Cynthia Gorney, "Julius Hobson Sr. Dies: Activist Stirred Up City for 25 Years," *WP*, March 24, 1977.

6. Julius W. Hobson, interview by Katherine Shannon, July 3, 1967, Washington, D.C., RBOH-MSRC-HU; Gorney, "Julius Hobson Sr. Dies."

7. Among other positions, Hobson served as PTA president of Slowe Elementary and Woodbridge Elementary School, vice president of the citywide Federation of Civic Associations, president of the Woodridge Civic Association, and a member of Americans for Democratic Action. Matthews, "The Politics of Julius W. Hobson, Sr., and the District of Columbia Public School System," 73.

8. Hobson liked to say that his political career began on the day he walked his son past the all-white neighborhood school to the bus stop so that he could attend a segregated, overcrowded school across town. Gorney, "Julius Hobson Sr. Dies."

9. John Lindsay, "Justice Will Probe Police Department: NAACP Charges of Brutality to Be Aired," *WP*, July 26, 1957. Hobson's 1957 investigation into the Metropolitan Police Department's promotion practices came to the attention of the House District Committee chairman John McMillan (D-S.C.). McMillan encouraged the D.C. Commissioners to dismiss the investigation. The D.C. Commissioners eventually cleared Police Chief Robert Murray of charges of brutality and racial discrimination. Elsie Carper, "Chief Murray Is Exonerated of Police Bias: Charges by NAACP Not Substantiated," *WP*, November 8, 1957.

10. An interracial group of college students, including future black civil rights leaders James Farmer and Bayard Rustin, created CORE in 1942 in Chicago, Illinois. At the time, Farmer was the Race Relations Secretary for the Fellowship of Reconciliation (FOR), a Christian pacifist organization founded in 1915. Farmer had originally developed and presented his idea for CORE to FOR in 1942. Although members decided not to sponsor his group, they gave Farmer permission to start it that year. Because CORE leaders believed Washington was an important location for conducting nonviolent direct action projects, they had established a presence there long before 1961. From 1947 to 1954, CORE held annual interracial summer workshops in Washington. In 1949, Washington, D.C., area CORE members formed a local chapter called the Washington Interracial Workshop. But without the support of the national summer workshops, which ended in 1954, the local chapter disbanded in early 1955. It had lain dormant for over five years when Julius Hobson assumed leadership. Farmer, *Lay Bare the Heart*, 84–105, 110–16; Arsenault, *Freedom Riders*, 30; Kosek, *Acts of Conscience*, 86–190; Meier and Rudwick, *CORE*, 1–39, 45, 50–54; Bell, *CORE and the Strategy of Nonviolence*, 8–9. For more on the Freedom Rides, see Arsenault, *Freedom Riders*.

11. Farmer, *Lay Bare the Heart*, 153.

12. Bell, *CORE and the Strategy of Nonviolence*, 19.

13. Farmer, *Lay Bare the Heart*, 111.

14. The fact that CORE did not have a southern base hurt the organization in the early 1960s. According to SNCC member Cleveland Sellers, many of the black students who joined SNCC would have formed southern CORE chapters had CORE had the infrastructure to absorb new members in the South. Sellers, *The River of No Return*, 37. By 1962, with the exception of Boston and Columbus, every chapter in a major city—including New Haven, Brooklyn, New York, Newark, Philadelphia, Baltimore, and Washington—had a black chairman. Meier and Rudwick, *CORE*, 198.

15. "Julius Hobson," *city Side*, WTOP, aired March 8, 1964, transcript, JHP-MLKL, series 1, box 1, folder CORE Correspondence.

16. Charles Conconi, "Goodbye Mr. Hobson: The Last Interview," *The Washingtonian*, May 1977.

17. Julius W. Hobson, interview by Katherine Shannon; Gorney, "Julius Hobson Sr. Dies"; "CORE Ready to Test Fair Housing Order," *WP, February 2, 1964*; "CORE Starts 2 Additional 'Dwell-Ins,'" *WP*, August 17, 1963; "Trenton Park Settles Apartment Grievance," *WP*, July 2, 1964. The campaign against D.C.'s public utilities companies led to a permanent court injunction to prevent Hobson from encouraging people to paste stickers over the holes in punch-card utility bills. Smith, *Captive Capital*, 258.

18. Lewis, *District of Columbia*, 182.

19. Booker, "Washington's Civil Rights Maverick."

20. Smith, *Captive Capital*, 256.

21. Julius W. Hobson, interview by Katherine Shannon.

22. Julius W. Hobson, interview by Katherine Shannon; Wendell P. Bradley, "State Dept. Will Step Up Fight against Rte. 40 Discrimination," *WP*, October 29, 1961; "Rte. 40 Freedom Riders to Test Delaware Also," *WP*, November 7, 1961; Holder, "Racism toward Black African Diplomats during the Kennedy Administration"; "New CORE Post for J. W. Hobson," *BAA*, July 21, 1962. As southeastern regional director, Hobson supervised chapters in Florida, Alabama, South Carolina, Virginia, North Carolina, Georgia, and West Virginia. Memo, undated, JHP-MLKL, series 1, box 1, folder CORE Correspondence.

23. "11 Negro Leaders Hit School Boycott Plan," *WP*, March 11, 1964.

24. Quoted in "Julius Hobson," *city Side*, WTOP, aired March 8, 1964, transcript.

25. "11 Negro Leaders Hit School Boycott Plan"; "D.C. School Boycott Called Off"; "School Head Meets with CORE Chief," *WP*, March 24, 1964. On Brooklyn CORE's controversial school boycotts, see Jacoby, *In Someone Else's House*, chapter 1.

26. Valk, *Radical Sisters*, 22–23.

27. The list of accusations against Hobson included charges that he violated CORE rules and procedures in action projects; violated CORE's by-laws in regard to internal disagreements and news media; misused his role as a regional representative; violated CORE's constitution; and permitted irregularities in the membership list. Minutes, Steering Committee Meeting, May 22, 1964, JHP-MLKL, series 1, box 1, folder CORE Correspondence.

28. "CORE Factions March at Hospital, Other Sites," *Washington Daily News*, June 22, 1964.

29. Letter, Julius Hobson to James Farmer, June 22, 1964, JHP-MLKL, series 1, box 1, folder CORE Correspondence.

30. CORE had also suspended a leader in the Dayton, Ohio, chapter earlier that year and the entire Brooklyn CORE chapter in April. Meier and Rudwick, *CORE*, 286; William J. Raspberry and Robert E. Baker, "Hobson Expelled by National CORE," *WP*, June 21, 1964.

31. Minutes, 1962, JHP-MLKL, series 1, box 1, folder CORE Convention Minutes; Meier and Rudwick, *CORE*, 314.

32. Farmer, *Lay Bare the Heart*, 258–60. On Brooklyn CORE's 1964 stall-in, see Purnell, "Drive Awhile for Freedom." For more on Brooklyn CORE, see Purnell, *Fighting Jim Crow in the County of Kings*.

33. "Editorial," WTOP, aired July 6 and 7, 1966, transcript, JHP-MLKL, series 2, box 3, folder Association of Community Teams Correspondence; Edward McHale, "McKissick, New Chief of CORE, Tells His Views," *Chicago Defender*, January 15, 1966. For CORE, the Black Power slogan meant two things: an emphasis on the cohesion and race pride of the black community and the building up of political power through independent black voting blocs. Bell, *CORE and the Strategy of Nonviolence*, 16–17. On the role of whites in CORE, see Meier and Rudwick, *CORE*, chapter 10. On the increasing militancy in the civil rights movement, see, for example, Jeffries, *Bloody Lowndes*; Hill, *The Deacons for Defense*.

34. "Editorial," *Washington Afro-American*, June 27, 1964.

35. Julius W. Hobson, interview by Katherine Shannon.

36. Charles Conconi, "Goodbye Mr. Hobson: The Last Interview."

37. Valk, *Radical Sisters*, 22–24.

38. Julius W. Hobson, interview by Katherine Shannon; Bart Barnes, "ACT Chapter Planned Here by Hobson," *WP*, July 7, 1964; Pamphlet, JHP-MLKL, series 2, box 3, folder ACT Correspondence. Gloria Richardson Dandridge is best known for her work in Cambridge, Maryland. For more on the black activist, see Levy, "Gloria Richardson and the Civil Rights Movement in Cambridge, Maryland."

39. John Matthews, "Julius W. Hobson: The Gadfly for District's Negro Militants," *Sunday Star*, April 16, 1967.

40. Matthews, "The Politics of Julius W. Hobson, Sr., and the District of Columbia Public School System," 82.

41. Smith, *Captive Capital*, 257.

42. Matthews, "Julius W. Hobson: The Gadfly for District's Negro Militants."

43. William Chapman, "Black Power Group Goal High Politics," *WP*, July 9, 1965.

44. Susan Filson, "Civil Rights Case Here Is Held Vital," *WP*, July 23, 1966; Smith, *Captive Capital*, 185; *Hobson v. Hansen*. For more on Judge J. Skelly Wright and his work in New Orleans, see Fairclough, *Race and Democracy*, 199–200, 234–38, 242–47, 255–56, 262–63. For more on *Hobson v. Hansen*, see Matthews, "The Politics of Julius W. Hobson, Sr., and the District of Columbia Public School System."

45. The Deacons knew that CORE practiced nonviolence and agreed to respect its philosophy during its demonstrations. But they told James Farmer that when CORE was not demonstrating, the Deacons would determine their response "in consultation with their consciences and their God." The Deacons went on to protect Farmer during

his visits to Bogalusa, Louisiana. Farmer, *Lay Bare the Heart*, 285–91; Hill, *The Deacons for Defense*, 2–3, 224.

46. William Raspberry, "Bogalusa Unit Plans Move to D.C.," *WP*, March 30, 1966.

47. Raspberry, "Bogalusa Unit Plans Move to D.C."

48. Michael Janofsky, "The Comeback Man in the News: From Disgrace to 'Amazing Grace,'" *NYT*, September 14, 1994; Arthur S. Brisbane, "Marion Barry Just Wants to Be Loved," *WP*, April 26, 1987. For more on Barry, see Agronsky, *Marion Barry*. For descriptions of the sit-in movement, see Weisbrot, *Freedom Bound*, 19–44; Morris, *The Origins of the Civil Rights Movement*; Chafe, *Civilities and Civil Rights*.

49. Ransby, *Ella Baker and the Black Freedom Movement*, 239–40; Civil Rights Movement Veterans, "1960."

50. Milton Coleman, "Marion Barry: The Activist Denies He's Changed," *WP*, January 2, 1979.

51. Monroe W. Karmin, "Calm in the Capital," *Wall Street Journal*, June 23, 1967.

52. See in particular Jones, "Before Montgomery and Greensboro"; Gilmore, *Defying Dixie*, 385–92; Quigley, *Just Another Southern Town*; Pacifico, "'Don't Buy Where You Can't Work.'"

53. Karmin, "Calm in the Capital."

54. Quoted in Smith, *Captive Capital*, 164.

55. Donaghy, "Walter Fauntroy"; Karmin, "Calm in the Capital."

56. Hayes Johnson also argues that Muslim groups like the Nation of Islam were able to make inroads with poor black residents because they felt like the black middle class had turned their back on them. Hayes Johnson, *Dusk at the Mountain*, 166, 199.

57. "Further Local Boycotts Are Considered by SNCC," *WP*, January 26, 1966. Howard Gillette Jr. says the boycott involved one hundred thousand people. Gillette, *Between Justice and Beauty*, 191.

58. Quoted in Jaffe and Sherwood, *Dream City*, 45.

59. Asch and Musgrove, *Chocolate City*, 343–44; Agronsky, *Marion Barry*, 123; Marion Barry, Letter of Support, reel 58, SNCCP; "Store Boycott Planned by New Rights Group Supporting Home Rule," *WP*, February 22, 1966; Dan Morgan, "Barry Finds Home Rule a Frustrating Battle," *WP*, July 25, 1966; Robert Asher, "Boycott over Home Rule Deplored," *WP*, February 24, 1966.

60. William Raspberry, "Barry Is New Catalyst for Change Here," *WP*, March 9, 1966.

61. Sachse, "D.C. Home Rule Movement, 1966–1973," 33. For scholarship that examines the local struggle in the wake of new federal laws like the Civil Rights Act and Voting Rights Act in Alabama, see Ashmore, *Carry It On*.

62. William Raspberry, "Tactics Meant Failure for Free D.C. Movement," *WP*, March 22, 1966; William Clopton, "150 Shops Show 'Free D.C.' Stickers," *WP*, March 5, 1966; Willard Clopton and Leroy F. Aarons, "Home Rulers Start Boycott at 100 Stores: H Street NE Area Is First," *WP*, March 6, 1966.

63. Clopton and Aarons, "Home Rulers Start Boycott at 100 Stores"; Willard Clopton and John Carmody, "Free D.C.'ers End Drive in Northeast: Merchants Report Slight Impact," *WP*, March 13, 1966; Sachse, "D.C. Home Rule Movement, 1966–1973," 27–38.

64. Raspberry, "Barry Is New Catalyst for Change Here."

65. William Clopton, "The Genesis and the Exoduses of Free D.C. Movement: Already Left Mark," *WP*, April 24, 1966.

66. Willard Clopton, "NAACP Drops Support of Free D.C. Campaign: Splits with SNCC," *WP*, March 12, 1966; Valk, *Radical Sisters*, 25–26.

67. Sue Cronk, "Free D.C. Movement Termed Immoral, Un-American by Trade Board Head," *WP*, April 5, 1966.

68. William Raspberry, "Foe of Home Rule Fears Graft, Crime," *WP*, April 11, 1966.

69. Marion Barry, Letter of Support, reel 58, SNCCP; Asher, "Boycott over Home Rule Deplored"; "Home Rule Defeated," *WP*, October 11, 1966; Gillette, *Between Justice and Beauty*, 192.

70. Jean R. Hailey, "Barry Quits SNCC Post to Aid Poor," *WP*, January 19, 1967.

71. Wiley Austin Branton, interview by James Mosby, Part 2, October 20, 1969, Washington, D.C., RBOH-MSRC-HU.

72. Flanagan, "Lyndon Johnson, Community Action, and Management of the Administrative State." For more on the War on Poverty and CAP, see Forget, "A Tale of Two Communities."

73. Wiley Austin Branton, interview by James Mosby, Part 2; Flanagan, "Lyndon Johnson, Community Action, and Management of the Administrative State."

74. Branton's most famous case began in 1956, when he agreed to represent Little Rock high school students and their families who wished to integrate the all-white Central High School in Little Rock. That case, *Aaron v. Cooper*, soon involved the national NAACP and attorney Thurgood Marshall, among others. It ultimately went to the Supreme Court, where it became the second major statement, after *Brown v. Board of Education*, on school integration. Heller Anderson, "Wiley Branton, Early Desegregation Lawyer, Dies," *NYT*, December 17, 1988; Kilpatrick, "Wiley Austin Branton and the Voting Rights Struggle"; Asch and Musgrove, *Chocolate City*, 347.

75. "Broyhill Says Radicals Run UPO, Pride," *WP*, November 8, 1967; Wiley Austin Branton, interview by James Mosby, part 2; Asch and Musgrove, *Chocolate City*, 348.

76. Wiley Austin Branton, interview by James Mosby, part 2.

77. Wiley Austin Branton, interview by James Mosby, part 2.

78. Valk, "'Mother Power,'" 34–36; Asch and Musgrove, *Chocolate City*, 348.

79. Asch and Musgrove, *Chocolate City*, 348–49; Valk, *Radical Sisters*, 26–29.

80. Asch and Musgrove, *Chocolate City*; Valk, *Radical Sisters*; Wolfe, "'Maximum Feasible Participation,'" 92–93.

81. Leon, "Marion Barry, Jr.," 69–71; Asch and Musgrove, *Chocolate City*, 350; Valk, *Radical Sisters*, 13–14.

82. Valk, *Radical Sisters*, 33–34.

83. McMillan served as chairman from 1948 until 1972. Charles Wesley Harris, *Congress and the Governance of the Nation's Capital*, 5–6. In 1965, the House of Representatives took a home rule bill out of McMillan's committee, voting 213–183 to bring the bill to the floor. Although the bill failed, the action indicated that other representatives had grown tired of McMillan's totalitarian rule over Washington. Harris and Thornton, *Perspectives of Political Power in the District of Columbia*, 85.

84. Bart Barnes, "Joel T. Broyhill, 86: Vigorous 11-Term N.Va. Congressman," *WP*, September 27, 2006.

85. Jaffe and Sherwood, *Dream City*, 44–45; Johnson quoted in Califano, *The Triumph and Tragedy of Lyndon Johnson*, 229; Asch and Musgrove, *Chocolate City*, 344.

86. Califano, *The Triumph and Tragedy of Lyndon Johnson*, 228; Walker, *Most of 14th Street Is Gone*, 26.

87. Johnson, "Special Message to the Congress: The Nation's Capital, February 27, 1967."

88. Walker, *Most of 14th Street Is Gone*, 22; Flamm, *Law and Order*, 125.

89. "Johnson Orders New D.C. Rule," *WP*, June 2, 1967.

90. Johnson, "Special Message to the Congress: The Nation's Capital, February 27, 1967."

91. Califano, *The Triumph and Tragedy of Lyndon Johnson*, 230.

92. House Debate, Congressional Record (August 9, 1967), 21960.

93. House Debate, Congressional Record (August 9, 1967), 21960.

94. "House Accepts New D.C. Rule," *WP*, August 10, 1967; Elsie Carper, "Johnson Orders New D.C. Rule," *WP*, June 2, 1967; Asch and Musgrove, *Chocolate City*, 351.

95. Califano, *The Triumph and Tragedy of Lyndon Johnson*, 230–31.

96. Jaffe and Sherwood, *Dream City*, 53–54.

97. Jaffe and Sherwood, *Dream City*, 54; Jay Matthews, "City's 1st Mayoral Race, as Innocent as Young Love," *WP*, October 11, 1999.

98. When President Johnson approached Washington about the mayor-commissioner position, he initially declined; if he was to govern the District, he wanted to have control of the Metropolitan Police Department. After much deliberation, Johnson relented and granted him such authority, much to the consternation of *WP* owner Katharine Graham, who had recommended that the president retain control over the local police. Diner, "The Black Majority," 258.

99. Stuart Auerbach, "'Convention' Set to Advise LBJ," *WP*, August 17, 1967; Hollie West, "Black Power Group Sets Advisory Vote," *WP*, August 16, 1967.

100. "Hobson Wins City Straw Vote," *WP*, August 22, 1967; Robert Asher, "Barry Assails LBJ Prospects for Council," *WP*, September 16, 1967. Notably Walter Washington, not yet appointed to the mayoral position, received thirteen votes.

101. Asher, "Barry Assails LBJ Prospects for Council."

102. Robert Kaiser, "City's New Council Takes Oath: Model Rule, War on Crime Urged by LBJ at Ceremony," *WP*, November 4, 1967; Remarks, Lyndon Johnson at Swearing In of Walter Washington and Thomas Fletcher, September 28, 1967, "D.C. Commissioners 2 of 2," box 12, White House Office Files of Joseph A. Califano, LBJL.

103. Katz, *Why Don't American Cities Burn?*, 87–88.

104. Reverend Channing Phillips, interview by Katherine M. Shannon.

105. Jaffe and Sherwood, *Dream City*, 57.

106. Leon Dash, "White Racists, 'Uncle Toms' Make Up City Council, Black Power Unit Says," *WP*, October 4, 1967.

107. Sellers, *The River of No Return*, 60.

108. Ransby, *Ella Baker and the Black Freedom Movement*, 239–40; Civil Rights Movement Veterans, "1960"; Sellers, *The River of No Return*, 57, 60; Dion T. Diamond, interview by Kay Shannon, November 11, 1967, Washington, D.C., RBOH-MSRC-HU. NAG worked with Washington CORE to help desegregate Route 40 in 1961 and

assisted SCLC with March on Washington logistics in 1963. See "Police Seize 8 in Disorders on Rte. 40," *WP*, December 17, 1961; Sellers, *The River of No Return*, 62. For an excellent biography of Carmichael, see Joseph, *Stokely*.

109. Michael T. Kaufman, "Stokely Carmichael, Rights Leader Who Coined 'Black Power,' Dies at 57," *NYT*, November 16, 1998; Paula Spahn, "The Undying Revolutionary," *WP*, April 8, 1998; Carmichael and Thelwell, *Ready for Revolution*, 171–215. For more on the birth and life of SNCC, see Carson, *In Struggle*; Jeffries, "SNCC, Black Power and Independent Political Party Organizing in Alabama, 1964–1966."

110. Ture and Hamilton, *Black Power*, 44.

111. Gilbert, *Ten Blocks from the White House*, 60; Kaufman, "Stokely Carmichael, Rights Leader Who Coined 'Black Power,' Dies at 57."

112. Charles Cassell, interview by Robert E. Wright. See also Reginald Booker, interview by Robert E. Wright, July 24, 1970, Washington, D.C., RBOH-MSRC-HU. Carmichael left occasionally for SNCC's Atlanta headquarters as well as trips to Havana and Hanoi. According to Winston Grady-Willis, "The geographical base of the executive committee had shifted slightly northward. A 'Washington, D.C., clique' led by Carmichael and Ivanhoe Donaldson had supplanted the previous Nashville and Atlanta leadership circles." Grady-Willis, *Challenging U.S. Apartheid*, 97. Black activists had established a similar coalition, the Negro Community Council, in 1962, though it disbanded within a year. Robert C. Maynard, "D.C. Negro Leaders Work to Maintain Uneasy Coalition," *WP*, January 12, 1968.

113. Reverend Channing Phillips, interview by Katherine M. Shannon.

114. Charles Cassell, interview by Robert E. Wright.

115. William Raspberry, "Samaritan Seizes Every Chance to Wage Own Poverty Program," *WP*, October 17, 1965.

116. Carolyn Lewis, "Black Power Leader Endorses the 'Camp-In,'" *WP*, March 10, 1968; Scottie Lanahan, "Willie Has the Word," *WP*, September 23, 1966; Rosemarie Tyler, "Willie Hardy Looks for Warm Bodies, Free Minds to Vote," *BAA*, December 8, 1962; Eve Edstrom, "Anacostia Citizens Carry Public Welfare Load," *WP*, November 15, 1962; Raspberry, "Samaritan Seizes Every Chance to Wage Own Poverty Program."

117. Charles Cassell, interview by Robert E. Wright. In the same interview, Cassell listed Washington's ACT, led by Julius Hobson, among the militant organizations he admired.

118. "Pastor Who Permitted Stokely Speech Keeps Post."

119. Reverend Channing Phillips, interview by Katherine M. Shannon; Robert C. Maynard, "D.C. Negro Leaders Work to Maintain Uneasy Coalition," *WP, January 12, 1968.*

120. Robert C. Maynard, "Urban League Wary of Black United Front," *WP*, January 18, 1968; Maynard, "D.C. Negro Leaders Work to Maintain Uneasy Coalition."

121. Maynard, "Urban League Wary of Black United Front."

122. Reginald Booker, interview by Robert E. Wright.

123. Reginald Booker, interview by Robert E. Wright.

124. Robert C. Maynard, "Negroes to Drive for Unity," *WP*, January 11, 1968.

125. "Editorial," WTOP, aired January 12 and 13, 1968, transcript, JHP-MLKL, series 6, box 35, folder ACT-Black United Front.

126. Position on Proposed Legislation, July 30, 1968, FCAR-MLKL, box 2, folder 1968–1969 Office Files Book 1.

127. Charles Cassell, interview by Robert E. Wright; Asch and Musgrove, *Chocolate City*, 370.

CHAPTER 2

1. Memo, Stephen Pollak to Lyndon Johnson, April 26, 1967, EX FG, box 267, WHCF, LBJL. The federal government may have been afraid of SNCC but, according to journalist Clay Risen, it did not have good reason to be. "As SNCC radicalized, it shrank in size and influence. By 1967, it was practically bankrupt. . . . In 1964 SNCC had three hundred permanent staffers; by fall 1967, it had about twenty-five, including part-timers. Many of them were under indictment for draft refusal. Most weren't getting paid. Their anti-white radicalism had cost them dearly." Risen, *A Nation on Fire*, 87. For more on SNCC's new phase, see Jeffries, "SNCC, Black Power and Independent Political Party Organizing in Alabama, 1964–1966," 171–93; Payne, *I've Got the Light of Freedom*, chapter 13; Grady-Willis, *Challenging U.S. Apartheid*. On this new stage in other locales, see Hill, *The Deacons for Defense*; Countryman, *Up South*; Woodard, *Nation within a Nation*; Orleck, *Storming Caesar's Palace*. On Black Power as a distinct concept and decisive break from the civil rights movement, see Cha-Jua and Lang, "The 'Long Movement' as Vampire."

2. Monroe W. Karmin, "Calm in the Capital," *Wall Street Journal*, June 23, 1967. For more on the riots in Newark and Detroit, see Krasovic, *The Newark Frontier*; Mumford, *Newark*, chapters 5 and 6; Fine, *Violence in the Model City*.

3. Memo, Harry McPherson to Lyndon Johnson, August 8, 1967, EX FG, box 267, WHCF, LBJL.

4. Katz, *Why Don't American Cities Burn?*, 91; Gordon and Moriss, "Presidential Commissions and the Law Enforcement Administration"; Weaver, "More Than Words"; Simon, *Governing through Crime*.

5. Hechinger and Taylor, "Black and Blue," 10.

6. Proposal, Black United Front, September 25, 1968, WFP-GWU, box 18, folder 7; Hechinger and Taylor, "Black and Blue," 8; "John B. Layton, 60's Chief of Capital Police," *NYT*, October 8, 1989.

7. Hechinger, "Black and Blue," 8, 10, 13. Gilbert, *Ten Blocks from the White House*, 7. John Hechinger was a fifth-generation white Washingtonian, Yale graduate, and head of the D.C.-based Hechinger Company, a hardware store chain founded by his father in 1911. Johnson had appointed him to head the city council in November 1967.

8. Karmin, "Calm in the Capital"; Walker, *Most of 14th Street Is Gone*, 22.

9. Memo, Stephen Pollak to Lyndon Johnson, April 24, 1967, "FG 216 District of Columbia (3-16-67–5-31-67)," box 267, WHCF, LBJL.

10. Walker, *Most of 14th Street Is Gone*, 28.

11. Gillon, *Separate and Unequal*; Walker, *Most of 14th Street Is Gone*, 29–30.

12. Walker, *Most of 14th Street Is Gone*, 31–32; "One Hot Night," *WP*, August 2, 1967; "City Names Grievance Task Force," *WP*, August 2, 1967; Diner, "The Black Majority," 258.

13. Irv Chapman and Bob Clark, "Attorney General Ramsey Clark," *Issues and Answers*, American Broadcasting Company, aired May 12, 1968, transcript, "Washington D.C.—Issues and Answers 5-12-68," box 35, Personal Papers of Ramsey Clark, LBJL. Even White House officials called Clark "Ramsey the Marshmallow" for his moderate positions on law and order. O'Reilly, *Racial Matters*, 266. For more on Clark's positions on law and order, see "Justice Department: The Ramsey Clark Issue."

14. Remarks, Ramsey Clark at Planning Session for Conferences of Local Officials on Prevention and Control of Civil Disorder, November 17, 1967, "Civil Disorder Training Conferences 67–68 (2 of 2)," box 62, Papers of Ramsey Clark, LBJL; Clayton Fritchey, "Urban Violence Dips for First Time in 5 Years," *WS*, September 9, 1968; Walker, *Most of 14th Street Is Gone*, 40.

15. Flamm, *Law and Order*, 129–30.

16. Flamm, *Law and Order*, 129–30; Walker, *Most of 14th Street Is Gone*, 31–32; President's Commission on Crime in the District of Columbia, *Report on the Metropolitan Police Department*, 2, 66–67, 72, 74, 83.

17. Flamm, *Law and Order*, 129–30; Walker, 31–32; President's Commission on Crime in the District of Columbia, *Report on the Metropolitan Police Department*, 2, 66–67, 72, 74, 83.

18. Robert G. Kaiser and Hollie I. West, "Mayor, Council Panel to Meet on Police Brutality Charges: Brutality Charge to Be Aired," *WP*, November 21, 1968; Robert G. Kaiser, "Council Agrees to Leave Police Probe to Mayor: Police Probe to Be Left to Mayor Meeting Closed to Public," *WP*, November 22, 1967; Asch and Musgrove, *Chocolate City*, 353.

19. Walker, *Most of 14th Street Is Gone*, 37.

20. Murphy and Commissioner, *A View from the Top of American Law Enforcement*, 103.

21. Walker, *Most of 14th Street Is Gone*, 39.

22. Hechinger and Taylor, "Black and Blue," 12; James Lardner, "Murphy's Law Commissioner: A View from the Top of American Law Enforcement," *WP*, February 12, 1978; Martin Weil, "Patrick V. Murphy, Who Advocated Police Restraint during 1968 D.C. Riots, Dies at 91," *WP*, December 17, 2011.

23. U.S. House Committee on the District of Columbia, Anti-Riots Hearing before Subcommittee No. 4; Weaver, "Frontlash," 250, 254. See also Orr, "Congress, Race, and Anticrime Policy," 234–35.

24. Statement, Fred M. Vinson Jr., before Subcommittee for House District Committee on H.R. 12328, October 4, 1967, "D.C. Planning for Riots 1967–1968," box 72, Papers of Ramsey Clark, LBJL; Flamm, *Law and Order*, 130–32; Johnson, Memorandum of Disapproval of the District of Columbia Crime Bill, November 13, 1966; Johnson, "Statement upon Signing the District of Columbia Crime Bill, December 27, 1967."

25. Price, "King to King," 106–7.

26. Price, "King to King," 106–7. See also Walker, *Most of 14th Street Is Gone*, 277; Drea, *McNamara, Clifford, and the Burdens of Vietnam, 1965–1969*, 90.

27. U.S. Riot Commission, *Report of the National Advisory Commission on Civil Disorders*, 1; Thomas Talburt, "Riot Remedy Is Costly," *Washington Daily News*, March 1,

1968. For more on the Kerner Commission and its legacy, see Gillon, *Separate and Unequal*; Flamm, *Law and Order*, 104–10; Harris and Curtis, *Locked in the Poorhouse*; Abu-Lughod, *Race, Space and Riots in Chicago, New York, and Los Angeles*, chapter 8.

28. Gillon, *Separate and Unequal*, 237.

29. Address, Lyndon Johnson, March 13, 1968, Speeches, box 118, WHCF, LBJL.

30. Chronological sequence of events commencing with Dr. Martin Luther King's assassination, "D.C. Planning for Riots 1967–1968," box 72, Papers of Ramsey Clark, LBJL.

31. Risen, *A Nation on Fire*, 56; Gilbert, *Ten Blocks from the White House*, 17–18.

32. United Press International, April 5, 1968, "Carmichael Investigation 1968," box 61, Papers of Ramsey Clark, LBJL; Newsletter, April–May 1968, reel 52, SNCCP. According to SNCC's Washington branch, over twenty SNCC members remained in the office when the police teargassed it. A national guardsman allegedly said, "Your leader started this so suffer." United Press International, April 5, 1968, "Carmichael Investigation 1968."

33. Schaffer, "The 1968 Washington Riots in History and Memory," 5; Gilbert, *Ten Blocks from the White House*, 20–22.

34. "The Second Sacking of Washington."

35. Gilbert, *Ten Blocks from the White House*, 56–57.

36. Gilbert, *Ten Blocks from the White House*, 28, 71–72, 86–87.

37. Gilbert, *Ten Blocks from the White House*, 28, 71–72, 86–87.

38. Flamm, *Law and Order*, 146; Interim Report of the Committee for the Administration of Justice under Emergency Conditions, EX HU 2, box 20, WHCF, LBJL; Gilbert, *Ten Blocks from the White House*, 74–75, 92.

39. Flamm, *Law and Order*, 146; Interim Report of the Committee for the Administration of Justice under Emergency Conditions; Gilbert, *Ten Blocks from the White House*, 74–75, 92.

40. Michael Adams, "D.C. Officials Show Grief, Ire," *WS*, April 6, 1968.

41. Adams, "D.C. Officials Show Grief, Ire."

42. Carolyn Lewis, "Women Leaders Mourn Loss of Dr. King," *WP*, April 6, 1968.

43. Adams, "D.C. Officials Show Grief, Ire."

44. Adams, "D.C. Officials Show Grief, Ire"; United Press International, April 8, 1968, "Carmichael Investigation 1968," box 61, Papers of Ramsey Clark, LBJL.

45. Interim Report of the Committee for the Administration of Justice Under Emergency Conditions, EX HU 2, box 20, WHCF, LBJL; Gilbert, *Ten Blocks from the White House*, 74.

46. Schaffer, "The 1968 Washington Riots in History and Memory," 17–18; Interim Report of the Committee for the Administration of Justice Under Emergency Conditions, EX HU 2, box 20, WHCF, LBJL.

47. There were 15,530 troops deployed in Washington, 13,682 from the regular army and 1,848 from the National Guard. Report, City Council Public Hearings, BOTR-GWU, box 285, folder 28; Gilbert, *Ten Blocks from the White House*, appendix 1, 224–25; Walker, *Most of 14th Street Is Gone*, 98, 103.

48. Estimated Impact on Washington's Economy Resulting from the Civil Disorders during the Period April 4–15, 1968, June 10, 1968, BOTR-GWU, box 285, folder 28;

Interim Report of the Committee for the Administration of Justice under Emergency Conditions, EX HU 2, box 20, WHCF, LBJL.

49. According to Michael Flamm, the president "demanded and consumed details that were beneath the notice of a chief executive." Flamm, *Law and Order*, 132.

50. Interim Report of the Committee for the Administration of Justice under Emergency Conditions, EX HU 2, box 20, WHCF, LBJL; chronological sequence of events commencing with Dr. Martin Luther King's assassination, "D.C. Planning for Riots 1967–1968," box 72, Papers of Ramsey Clark, LBJL; Memo, Joseph Califano to Lyndon Johnson, April 6, 1968, EX HU 2, box 20, WHCF, LBJL.

51. Charles Duncan, interview by Robert E. Wright, December 11, 1968, Washington, D.C., RBOH-MSRC-HU.

52. Statement, John W. Hechinger, May 10, 1968, BOTR-GWU, box 285, folder 28.

53. Statement, John W. Hechinger, May 10, 1968.

54. Memo, BUF to all members, April 23, 1968, JHP-MLKL, series 6, box 35, folder ACT-Black United Front.

55. Report, City Council Public Hearings, BOTR-GWU, box 285, folder 28.

56. "School Vote Bill Adopted," *WP*, April 3, 1968; Ellen Hoffman, "School Election Bill Signed," *WP*, April 23, 1968; Report, City Council Public Hearings, BOTR-GWU, box 285, folder 28.

57. Report, City Council Public Hearings, BOTR-GWU, box 285, folder 28.

58. Report, City Council Public Hearings.

59. Statement, John W. Hechinger, May 10, 1968, BOTR-GWU, box 285, folder 28.

60. Report, City Council Public Hearings, BOTR-GWU, box 285, folder 28.

61. Report, City Council Public Hearings.

62. Report, City Council Public Hearings.

63. Report, "A Police Department in Trouble: Racial Discrimination and Misconduct in the Police Department of Washington, D.C.," National Capital Area Civil Liberties Union, August 1, 1968, EX FG, box 271, WHCF, LBJL.

64. Gilbert, *Ten Blocks from the White House*, 32–33.

65. Letter, Joseph H. Deckman to Mr. O. L. Weir, April 8, 1968, BOTR-GWU, box 284a, folder 34.

66. David Lawrence, "Tragedy of Riots Deep-Rooted," *U.S. News and World Report*, n.d., BOTR-GWU, box 286, folder 2.

67. Gilbert, *Ten Blocks from the White House*, 42–43.

68. Report, City Council Public Hearings.

69. Report, City Council Public Hearings.

70. Walker, *Most of 14th Street Is Gone*, 106–8.

71. Walker, *Most of 14th Street Is Gone*, 106–8.

72. Letter, William Calomiris to Employers of Metropolitan Washington, April 10, 1968, BOTR-GWU, box 285, folder 9.

73. Quoted in Janak, "The New American Discrimination—Eminent Domain"; Gillette, *Between Justice and Beauty*, 146, 270.

74. Letter, Joseph H. Deckman to Mr. O. L. Weir, April 8, 1968, BOTR-GWU, box 284a, folder 34; Gilbert, *Ten Blocks from the White House*, 42.

75. Letter, Joseph H. Deckman to Mr. O. L. Weir, April 8, 1968.

76. Letter, Bill Langhenry to Ramsey Clark, May 13, 1968, BOTR-GWU, box 284a, folder 34.

77. Letter, John Jarboe to Lyndon Johnson, May 9, 1968, BOTR-GWU, box 284a, folder 34.

78. Memo, Mike Manatos to Lyndon Johnson, April 11, 1968, EX HU 2, box 20, WHCF, LBJL.

79. Flamm, *Law and Order*, 162–63, 173–78, 180–81.

80. Speech, Ramsey Clark, April 17, 1968, "Washington D.C.-American Society of Newspaper Editors 4-17-68," box 35, Papers of Ramsey Clark, LBJL.

81. Telegram, Joel L. Evins to Ramsey Clark, April 9, 1968, "Carmichael Investigation 1968," box 61, Papers of Ramsey Clark, LBJL.

82. Lawrence Spivak and Carl Stern, "Attorney General Ramsey Clark," *Meet the Press*, National Broadcasting Company, aired April 7, 1968, transcript, box 35, Papers of Ramsey Clark, LBJL.

83. Thomas A. Lane, *Public Affairs*, May 25, 1968, BOTR-GWU, box 287, folder 17. For more on Public Safety Director Patrick Murphy's campaign for racial justice within the MPD, see Hechinger, "Black and Blue."

84. President's Commission on Crime in the District of Columbia, *Report on the Metropolitan Police Department*, 84.

85. Richard Wilson, "Police Buildup a Non-extremist Riot Approach," *WS*, April 19, 1968.

86. Robert Kaiser, "Last GIs Pull Out of City," *WP*, April 17, 1968.

87. Wilson, "Police Buildup a Non-extremist Riot Approach." For more on the riots in Chicago following King's assassination, see Abu-Lughod, *Race, Space and Riots in Chicago, New York, and Los Angeles*, chapter 3; Risen, *A Nation on Fire*, chapter 10.

88. Quoted in Letter, John Jarboe to Lyndon Johnson, May 9, 1968, BOTR-GWU, box 284, folder 34.

89. Walter E. Fauntroy, interview by Edward Thompson III, February 23, 1973, and March 5, 1973, Washington, D.C., RBOH-MSRC-HU.

90. Michael Harris, interview by Robert E. Martin, June 25, 1968, Washington, D.C., RBOH-MSRC-HU.

91. Lawrence Spivak and Carl Stern, "Attorney General Ramsey Clark," *Meet the Press*, National Broadcasting Company, aired April 7, 1968, transcript, box 35, Papers of Ramsey Clark, LBJL.

92. "The Mindless Mob Spurns Dr. King's Creed," *WP*, April 7, 1968.

93. Crosby Noyes, "District Deserves High Marks in Riot Control," *WS*, n.d., BOTR-GWU, box 286, folder 2.

94. "Editorial," WMAL, aired the week of April 14, 1968, transcript, BOTR-GWU, box 284a, 34.

95. Risen, *A Nation on Fire*, 116; "While Washington Burned," *Washington Daily News*, April 8, 1968; "The Mindless Mob Spurns Dr. King's Creed," *WP*, April 7, 1968.

96. "While Washington Burned."

97. The City's Response," *Washington Evening Star*, April 9, 1968.

98. "Guard Found Duty Rough, Residents Friendly," *WS*, April 21, 1968.

99. Gilbert, *Ten Blocks from the White House*, 112.

100. "Editorial," WMAL, aired the week of April 14, 1968, transcript, BOTR-GWU, box 284a, 34; Donald Johnson, "Singer Brown Cooled Crowd," *Boston Globe*, April 7, 1968; Jackson, "Petey Greene Talks Down the Riots, 1968."

101. "The Mindless Mob Spurns Dr. King's Creed."

102. Clarence Mitchell Jr., interview by Robert Martin, December 6, 1968, Washington, D.C., RBOH-MSRC-HU.

103. Lawrence, "Tragedy of Riots Deep-Rooted," *U.S. News and World Report*, n.d., BOTR-GWU, box 286, folder 2; Walker, *Most of 14th Street Is Gone*, 102; Gilbert, *Ten Blocks from the White House*, 150, 154. Police arrested twenty-seven federal employees and fifteen municipal government workers for riot-connected offenses. According to Ben Gilbert, "After hearings in April, Congress passed a law directing that, thereafter, anyone convicted of a felony connected with a riot or civil disturbance would be barred from employment by the federal government and the city government for five years. U.S. Civil Service regulations in existence at the time of the April riots also called for the removal of any government employees convicted of a riot-connected felony." Gilbert, *Ten Blocks from the White House*, 152–53.

104. Memo, John Macy to Lyndon Johnson, EX HU 2, box 20, WHCF, LBJL.

105. Risen, *A Nation on Fire*, 91; Phil Casey, "Carmichael Warns of 'Retaliation,'" *WP*, April 6, 1968. Police arrested H. Rap Brown in Cambridge Maryland in June 1967 for inciting to riot. Brown had been chairman of SNCC for less than one month when arrested. For more on Brown, see his autobiography, Al-Amin, *Die, Nigger, Die!*

106. Carmichael Press Conference, "Carmichael Investigation 1968," box 61, Papers of Ramsey Clark, LBJL.

107. Carmichael Press Conference, "Carmichael Investigation 1968"; Gilbert, *Ten Blocks from the White House*, 65.

108. Gilbert, *Ten Blocks from the White House*, 221.

109. Carmichael Press Conference, "Carmichael Investigation 1968"; "Restraint by Police Calms Angry Crowd," *WP*, April 4, 1968; Gilbert, *Ten Blocks from the White House*, 65.

110. Gilbert, *Ten Blocks from the White House*, 62–64. Howard students had founded the Nonviolent Action Group (NAG), a campus organization determined to "nag the conscience of Washington." Sellers, *The River of No Return*, 60.

111. Memo, Larry Temple to Lyndon Johnson, April 5, 1968, EX HU 2, box 20, WHCF, LBJL; chronological sequence of events commencing with Dr. Martin Luther King's assassination, "D.C. Planning for Riots 1967–1968," box 72, Papers of Ramsey Clark, LBJL.

112. Gilbert, *Ten Blocks from the White House*, 65.

113. United Press International, April 8, 1968, "Carmichael Investigation 1968," box 61, Papers of Ramsey Clark, LBJL.

114. Memo, Nathaniel Kossack, April 15, 1968, "Carmichael Investigation 1968," box 61, Papers of Ramsey Clark, LBJL.

115. *Associated Press*, April 22, 1968, "Carmichael Investigation 1968," box 61, Papers of Ramsey Clark, LBJL. For more on the Fair Housing Act, see Zasloff, "The Secret History of the Fair Housing Act."

116. Gilbert, *Ten Blocks from the White House*, 93.

117. Telegram, Joe L. Evins to Ramsey Clark, April 9, 1968, "Carmichael Investigation 1968," box 61, Papers of Ramsey Clark, LBJL.

118. O'Reilly, *Racial Matters*, 266; Minutes, Washington, D.C. Riot and Future Planning, April 15, 1968, EX HU 2, box 20, WHCF, LBJL.

119. Lawrence Spivak and Carl Stern, "Attorney General Ramsey Clark," *Meet the Press*, National Broadcasting Company, aired April 7, 1968, transcript, box 35, Papers of Ramsey Clark, LBJL.

120. Carson, *In Struggle*, 277, 292; Carmichael with Thelwell, *Ready for Revolution*, 676; Robert Maynard, "SNCC without Carmichael Is Faltering," *WP*, September 20, 1968; Leon Dash, "Bigger BUF Role Seen for Carmichael," *WP*, August 24, 1968; "Stokely in Senegal," *WP*, September 8, 1968. According to Clayborne Carson, "Johnson administration officials apparently had decided that any attempt to prosecute Carmichael might not succeed and, in any case, would have the unacceptable effect of making Carmichael a martyr." Carson, *In Struggle*, 277.

121. Interim Report of the Committee for the Administration of Justice under Emergency Conditions, EX HU 2, box 20, WHCF, LBJL. According to CAJ's report, the mayor relied on a statutory provision "giving the District of Columbia power to enact reasonable and usual police regulations. His action, necessary as it was, is open to challenge on the basic ground that curfews in this country are so rare and so plainly intended for unusual circumstances, that they cannot be viewed "as usual police regulations." See also Walker, *Most of 14th Street Is Gone*, 112.

122. Robert G. Kaiser, "Mayor Gains Wide Support in 1st 7 Months," *WP*, June 2, 1968.

123. Gillette, *Between Justice and Beauty*, 173; Asch and Musgrove, *Chocolate City*, 349.

124. Minutes, August 7, 1968, WFP-GWU, box 16, folder 14; Gillette, *Between Justice and Beauty*, 209; Smith, *Captive Capital*, 288.

125. Memo, Ramsey Clark to J. Edgar Hoover, May 29, 1968, "D.C. Matters 1967–1968," box 85, Papers of Ramsey Clark, LBJL.

CHAPTER 3

1. For more on the political tradition of marching on Washington, see Barber, *Marching on Washington*.

2. On civil rights declension narratives, see Hall, "The Long Civil Rights Movement and the Political Uses of the Past." Historians generally view SCLC's Poor People's Campaign as a failure. See Garrow, *Bearing the Cross*; Fairclough, *To Redeem the Soul of America*; McKnight, *The Last Crusade*. The exception is Mantler's excellent *Power to the Poor*. However, even this study privileges cities like Chicago, Denver, Los Angeles, and Albuquerque over Washington's local community.

3. Henry Hampton, *Eyes on the Prize II Interview with Marian Wright Edelman*. See also Thomas F. Jackson, *From Civil Rights to Human Rights*, 333; Mantler, *Power to the Poor*, 94.

4. King, "Statement delivered at press conference announcing the Poor People's Campaign." On the Bonus March, see Barber, *Marching on Washington*, chapter 3.

5. Sandage, "A Marble House Divided," 156; Sellers, *The River of No Return*, 62; Pauley, "John Lewis 'Speech at the March on Washington,'" 24; Yglesias, "It May Be a Long, Hot Spring in the Capital."

6. David Halvorsen, "Cancel Rights Marches," *Chicago Tribune*, August 27, 1966.

7. Jesse Lewis, "King Begins Tour Here on Call for Home Rule: 500 Crowd Rally Sponsor King Tour," *WP*, August 5, 1965; John Carmody, "Dr. King Pushes Shaw-Area Renewal: Shaw-Area Renewal Pushed by Dr. King," *WP*, March 13, 1967; Garrow, *Bearing the Cross*, 436; Asch and Musgrove, *Chocolate City*, 349–50.

8. King, "A Time to Break Silence." See Thomas F. Jackson, *From Civil Rights to Human Rights*; Honey, *To the Promised Land*.

9. McGraw, "An Interview with Andrew J. Young," 328; Report, Meeting of the Interreligious Committee, March 7, 1968, "Poor People's Campaign #1," box 6, Papers of Warren Christopher, LBJL; Yglesias, "It May Be a Long, Hot Spring in the Capital."

10. Fairclough, *To Redeem the Soul of America*, 165–66. For more on Young's life, see Young, *An Easy Burden*.

11. Report, Meeting of the Commission on Racial Justice, March 5, 1968, "Poor People's Campaign #1," box 6, Papers of Warren Christopher, LBJL.

12. McGraw, "An Interview with Andrew J. Young," 327–28; McKnight, *The Last Crusade*, 21.

13. Report, Meeting of the Interreligious Committee, March 7, 1968, "Poor People's Campaign #1," box 6, Papers of Warren Christopher, LBJL.

14. Report, Meeting of the Interreligious Committee, March 7, 1968, "Poor People's Campaign #1."

15. Report, Meeting of the Interreligious Committee, March 7, 1968, "Poor People's Campaign #1."

16. Memo, Kevin Maroney to Ramsey Clark, March 20, 1968, "Poor People's Campaign #1," box 6, Papers of Warren Christopher, LBJL.

17. Report, Meeting of the Commission on Racial Justice, March 5, 1967, "Poor People's Campaign #1," box 6, Papers of Warren Christopher, LBJL. Tensions had been building between SCLC and SNCC for years. See Fairclough, *To Redeem the Soul of America*, 315–17, 365; Jeffries, "SNCC, Black Power and Independent Political Party Organizing in Alabama, 1964–1966."

18. Memo, Kevin Maroney to Ramsey Clark, March 20, 1968, "Poor People's Campaign #1," box 6, Papers of Warren Christopher, LBJL.

19. Memo, Kevin Maroney to Ramsey Clark, May 3, 1968, "Poor People's Campaign #1." box 6, Papers of Warren Christopher, LBJL.

20. Memo, Fred M. Vinson Jr. to Warren Christopher, December 5, 1967, "Poor People's Campaign #1," box 6, Papers of Warren Christopher, LBJL; McKnight, *The Last Crusade*, 22.

21. Report, Meeting of the Interreligious Committee, March 5, 1968, "Poor People's Campaign #1," box 6, Papers of Warren Christopher, LBJL.

22. Memo, Fred Vinson Jr. to Ramsey Clark, March 6, 1968, "Poor People's Campaign #1," box 6, Papers of Warren Christopher, LBJL.

23. Memo, Matthew Nimetz to Warren Christopher, April 18, 1968, "Poor People's Campaign #1," box 6, Papers of Warren Christopher, LBJL.

24. Memo, Joseph Califano to Lyndon Johnson, April 17, 1968, EX HU 2, box 20, WHCF, LBJL. See also Dallek, *Flawed Giant*, 520–29.

25. Lawrence Spivak and Carl Stern, "Attorney General Ramsey Clark," *Meet the Press*, National Broadcasting Company, aired April 7, 1968, transcript, box 35, Papers of Ramsey Clark, LBJL; McKnight, *The Last Crusade*, 110.

26. Minutes, Washington D.C. Riot and Future Planning, May 7, 1968, "HU 2 FG 216 11-23-63–5-15--68," box 20, WHCF, LBJL.

27. Irv Chapman and Bob Clark, "Attorney General Ramsey Clark," *Issues and Answers*, American Broadcasting Company, aired May 12, 1968, transcript, "Washington D.C.—Issues and Answers 5-12-68," box 35, Personal Papers of Ramsey Clark, LBJL.

28. Irv Chapman and Bob Clark, "Attorney General Ramsey Clark," *Issues and Answers*.

29. Irv Chapman and Bob Clark, "Attorney General Ramsey Clark," *Issues and Answers*.

30. Information Center Memorandum No. 1, May 16, 1968, "Poor People's Campaign #2," box 7, Papers of Warren Christopher, LBJL.

31. Letter, J. Edgar Hoover to J. Walter Yeagley, May 9, 1968, "Poor People's Campaign #1," box 6, Papers of Warren Christopher, LBJL.

32. McKnight, *The Last Crusade*, 107; Minutes, Washington D.C. Riot and Future Planning, May 7, 1968, "HU 2 FG 216 11-23-63–5-15-68," box 20, WHCF, LBJL.

33. Memo, Matthew Nimetz to Joseph Califano, April 25, 1968, FG 216 District of Columbia (4-1-68–5-17-68)," box 268, WHCF, LBJL.

34. Memo, Warren Christopher to Joseph Califano, April 27, 1968, "FG 216 District of Columbia (4-1-68–5-17-68)," box 268, WHCF, LBJL.

35. Minutes, Washington D.C. Riot and Future Planning, May 7, 1968, "HU 2 FG 216 11-23-63–5-15-68," box 20, WHCF, LBJL; Walker, *Most of 14th Street Is Gone*, 113.

36. "A Threat of Anarchy in Nation's Capital."

37. Quoted in Mantler, "Black, Brown and Poor," 143.

38. McKnight has contextualized the Memphis march as part of the PPC's first phase. McKnight, *The Last Crusade*, 53–63; Young, *An Easy Burden*, 458.

39. Quoted in Mantler, "Black, Brown and Poor," 155.

40. McKnight, *The Last Crusade*, 87.

41. "A Threat of Anarchy in Nation's Capital."

42. Irna Moore, "Machen Predicts Poor March Will Trigger Round of Violence," *WP*, April 22, 1968.

43. Memo, Joseph Califano to Lyndon Johnson, May 9, 1968, "FG 216 District of Columbia (4-1-68–5-17-68)," box 268, WHCF, LBJL.

44. Letter, Frederick M. Bohen to Burton Langhenry, April 24, 1968, BOTR-GWU, box 284A, folder 34.

45. Minutes, April 25, 1968, FCAR-MLKL, box 2, folder 1967–1968 Office Files.

46. Letter, John Jarboe to Lyndon Johnson, May 9, 1968, BOTR-GWU, box 284A, folder 34.

47. "Trade Board Asks MPs to Augment D.C. Police," *Washington Daily News*, May 30, 1968.

48. Minutes, Washington D.C. Riot and Future Planning, May 7, 1968, "HU 2 FG 216 11-23-63–5-15-68," box 20, WHCF, LBJL.

49. Minutes, Washington D.C. Riot and Future Planning, May 7, 1968.

50. Memo, Nash Castro to Fred Vinson Jr., April 2, 1968, "Poor People's Campaign #1," box 6, Papers of Warren Christopher, LBJL; McKnight, *The Last Crusade*, 109.

51. William Raspberry, "Fauntroy Ponders Dual Role in Dr. King's Spring Drive," *WP*, February 14, 1968.

52. Memo, Joseph Califano to Lyndon Johnson, May 9, 1968, "FG 216 District of Columbia (4-1-68–5-17-68)."

53. Memo, Nash Castro to Fred Vinson Jr., April 2, 1968, "Poor People's Campaign #1," box 6, Papers of Warren Christopher, LBJL; McKnight, *The Last Crusade*, 109; Memo, Ramsey Clark to Larry Levenson, June 3, 1968, "Poor People's March May 1968—6-19-68," box 74, Clark Papers, LBJL.

54. 90 Cong. Rec. (May 13, 1968) (statement of Rep McMillan), BOTR-GWU, box 284A, folder 34.

55. Quoted in Gilbert, *Ten Blocks from the White House*, 199.

56. Gilbert, *Ten Blocks from the White House*, 118, 197, 199; Mantler, "Black, Brown and Poor," 153; Paul W. Valentine, "Marshals Picked from Gangs," *WP*, May 17, 1968.

57. Memo, John R. McDonough to Ramsey Clark, May 21, 1968, "Poor People's Campaign #2," box 7, Papers of Warren Christopher, LBJL; Memo, Nathaniel E. Kossack to Duty Officers, May 20, 1968, "Poor People's March May 1968—6-19-68," box 74, Personal Papers of Ramsey Clark, LBJL.

58. James Edward Peterson, interview by Kay Shannon, July 3, 1968, Washington, D.C., RBOH-MSRC-HU; Mantler, "Black, Brown and Poor," 149.

59. Robert Rippley, interview by Katherine M. Shannon, July 13, 1967, Washington, D.C., RBOH-MSRC-HU.

60. Katz, *Why Don't American Cities Burn?*, 91.

61. Willard Clopton Jr., "President Rules Out March Ban," *WP*, March 31, 1968.

62. Judith Martin, "They Could Write 'How to March on Washington,'" *WP*, March 4, 1968.

63. "Resurrection City Grows by Leaps in Washington," *BAA*, May 18, 1968.

64. William H. Moyer, interview by Kay Shannon, July 7, 1968, Washington, D.C., RBOH-MSRC-HU; San Francisco Quakers, "Memorial Statement."

65. Memo, Roger W. Wilkins to Ramsey Clark, March 13, 1968, "Poor People's Campaign #1," box 6, Papers of Warren Christopher, LBJL.

66. Press Conference, Stokely Carmichael, April 7, 1968, transcript, "Carmichael Investigation 1968," box 61, Clark Papers, LBJL. See Fairclough, *To Redeem the Soul of America*, 315–17, 365.

67. Mantler, "Black, Brown and Poor," 152.

68. Mantler, "Black, Brown and Poor," 307. In fairness to the *Courier*'s coverage, Carmichael did storm out of the meeting over the issue of nonviolence. *Pittsburgh Courier*, February 17, 1968.

69. James Edward Peterson, interview by Kay Shannon.

70. Daily Summary, May 27, 1968, "Poor People's Campaign #2," box 7, Papers of Warren Christopher, LBJL.

71. Newsletter, May–June 1968, reel 58, SNCCP.

72. Tony Henry, interview by Kay Shannon, July 15, 1968, Washington, D.C., RBOH-MSRC-HU.

73. Willard Clopton Jr. and William R. MacKaye, "Clerics Stage a Silent Vigil for Peace," *WP*, February 7, 1968; Paul W. Valentine, "Coalition Accuses SCLC of Triggering Disturbances," *WP*, June 29, 1968; Minutes, May 22, 1968, WFP-GWU, box 16, folder 14.

74. Myra MacPherson, "Rich Negroes Aid the Poor People," *NYT*, May 17, 1968; Jean White, "King Appeals to Negro Middle Class," *WP*, February 9, 1968.

75. Clyde Aveilhe, interview by Robert E. Martin, June 18, 1968, Washington, D.C., RBOH-MSRC-HU.

76. Michael Harris, interview by Robert E. Martin; "Colleges Deny Facilities to Poor March Classes," *WP*, May 22, 1968. American, Georgetown, George Washington, and Catholic Universities issued the statement through the Consortium of Universities.

77. Ewart Brown, interview by Robert E. Martin, September 14, 1968, Washington, D.C., RBOH-MSRC-HU.

78. Michael Harris, interview by Robert E. Martin.

79. Clyde Aveilhe, interview by Robert E. Martin.

80. Stephen S. Rosenfeld, "Poor People's U. in Convocation," *WP*, June 11, 1968.

81. Honey, *Going Down Jericho Road*, 183–84.

82. Bernadette Carey, "Middle Class Now Has Its Own Campaign," *WP*, May 9, 1968.

83. Carey, "Middle Class Now Has Its Own Campaign."

84. Carolyn Lewis, "Resurrection City Women Confront D.C. Counterparts," *WP*, May 26, 1968.

85. Thomas F. Jackson, *From Civil Rights to Human Rights*, 357; Mantler, *Power to the Poor*, 105, 134–35; Valk, "'Mother Power,'" 34; Elsie Carper, "Mother's Day Parade Opens Drive by Poor," *WP*, May 13, 1968.

86. Memo, Roger W. Wilkins to Ramsey Clark, March 13, 1968, "Poor People's Campaign #1."

87. Carol Honsa, "Nine Protesters Fired by UPO," *WP*, April 20, 1968; Bernadette Carey, "7 Dismissed Workers Lash Back at UPO," *WP*, April 23, 1968.

88. Carl Bernstein, "Resurrection City Wears Out D.C. Officials' Welcome," *WP*, June 23, 1968; Mantler, "Black, Brown and Poor," 205.

89. Bernstein, "Resurrection City Wears Out D.C. Officials' Welcome"; Katie Mettler, "The Day Anti–Vietnam War Protesters Tried to Levitate the Pentagon," *WP*, October 19, 2017.

90. Mantler, "Black, Brown and Poor," 189, 204–6; McKnight, *The Last Crusade*, 113, 116; Wright, "Civil Rights 'Unfinished Business,'" 428.

91. Paul W. Valentine, "Marchers Plan Capitol Protest," *WP*, June 24, 1968.

92. Memo, Nash Castro to Warren Christopher, May 29, 1968, "Poor People's Campaign #2," box 7, Papers of Warren Christopher, LBJL.

93. Mantler, "Black, Brown and Poor," 207; Wright, "Civil Rights 'Unfinished Business,'" 477. For an excellent analysis of the media's role, see Mantler, "Black, Brown and Poor," chapter 5.

94. Mantler, "Black, Brown and Poor," 328, 330.

95. Telegram, Joe Pool to Ramsey Clark, June 4, 1968, "Poor People's Campaign #2," box 7, Papers of Warren Christopher, LBJL.

96. Ben Franklin, "Rustin Quits March; Calls Aims Unclear," *NYT*, June 8, 1968; Mantler, "Black, Brown and Poor," 328, 330.

97. "Sterling Tucker: Veteran Crusader for Negro Cause," *WP*, June 8, 1968; "Sterling Tucker to Head D.C. League," *BAA*, September 22, 1956; "Job Discriminated Cited in District," *BAA*, November 30, 1957; "Capital Heartbeat: Tucker for Welfare Job," *BAA*, March 9, 1963; "NYC Poverty Post Offered Urban League Secretary," *BAA*, May 21, 1966; Willard Clopton Jr., "Rustin Quits March; Tucker New Choice," *WP*, June 8, 1968; Irna Moore, "Tucker Will Direct 'Day of Support," *WP*, June 10, 1968.

98. "Black Power Backers Take Pot Shots at Established Groups," *BAA*, August 12, 1967.

99. "Sterling Tucker: Veteran Crusader for Negro Cause."

100. *Associated Press*, June 19, 1968, folder 10–4 Civil Rights—Poor People's Campaign, box 16, Campaign 1968 Research Files, RNPL.

101. Thomas F. Jackson, *From Civil Rights to Human Rights*, 358; Mantler, *Power to the Poor*, 173.

102. *Associated Press*, "50,000 Hear Leader of Poor Vow to Keep Resurrection City in Capital," *Toledo Blade*, June 20, 1968; "Police Tear Gas Curbs Marchers," *WP*, June 21, 1968.

103. "Police Tear Gas Curbs Marchers."

104. Michael Harris, interview by Robert E. Martin; "Police Tear Gas Curbs Marchers"; Valentine, "Marchers Plan Capitol Protest."

105. Quoted in Gilbert, *Ten Blocks from the White House*, 201–2.

106. Memo, Stanley Krysa to Duty Officer File, June 21, 1968, "Poor People's Campaign #2," box 7, Papers of Warren Christopher, LBJL; Conference Summary, Duty Officer File, June 20, 1968, "Poor People's Campaign #2," box 7, Papers of Warren Christopher, LBJL; Gilbert, *Ten Blocks from the White House*, 201; "Officials Agree Not to Extend Resurrection City's Permit," *WP*, June 22, 1968; "Abernathy Demands 2 Agencies Probe Tear-Gassing," *WP*, June 24, 1968.

107. Bernstein, "Resurrection City Wears Out D.C. Officials' Welcome."

108. Charles Duncan, interview by Robert E. Wright.

109. Resolution, Kalorama Citizens Association, October 10, 1968, FCAR-MLKL, box 2, folder 1968–1969 Office Files Book 1.

110. David A. Jewell and Paul W. Valentine, "The Troubles of Resurrection City," *WP*, June 21, 1968; Mantler, *Black and Brown*, 340. Ralph Abernathy denied that Jackson had ever been the chief of security. "Abernathy Denies 'Violence' Charge," *WP*, June 21, 1968.

111. Conference Summary, Duty Officer File, June 20, 1968, "Poor People's Campaign #2," box 7, Papers of Warren Christopher, LBJL; Paul W. Valentine, "343 Poor Marchers Arrested," *WP*, June 25, 1968.

112. Robert C. Maynard, "A Symbol—How It Changed," *WP*, June 22, 1968.
113. McKnight, *The Last Crusade*, 107.
114. Ben Franklin, "Troops Ordered into Washington to Curb Outbreak," *NYT*, June 25, 1968.
115. Wilkins, *A Man's Life*, 221.
116. Valentine, "343 Poor Marchers Arrested"; Gilbert, *Ten Blocks from the White House*, 202.
117. Charles Duncan, interview by Robert E. Wright; Second Supplemental Report, Operation of the District of Columbia Criminal Justice System Following the Mass Arrests on June 24–25, 1968, "Poor People's Campaign #2," box 7, Papers of Warren Christopher, LBJL; Minutes, Washington D.C. Riot and Future Planning, May 7, 1968, "HU 2 FG 216 11-23-63–5-15-68," box 20, WHCF, LBJL; "City Calls Curfew in Disorders after Police Clear Out Campsite," *WP*, June 25, 1968.
118. Mantler, "Black, Brown and Poor," 208 and, more broadly, chapter 5.
119. Gilbert, *Ten Blocks from the White House*, 206.
120. Jesse Jackson, "Resurrection City," 67.
121. Kay Shannon, interview by Claudio Rawles, August 12, 1968, Washington, D.C., RBOH-MSRC-HU.
122. Valk, "'Mother Power,'" 38, 40–41.
123. Mantler, *Power to the Poor*, 183–84, 211.
124. Tony Henry, interview by Kay Shannon.
125. BUF, "The June 24th Trick Bag," JHP-MLKL, DC Public Library, series 6, box 35, folder ACT-Black United Front.
126. BUF, "The June 24th Trick Bag."
127. Maynard, "A Symbol—How It Changed."
128. William Raspberry, "March Lacked 1963's Mood," *WP*, June 21, 1968.
129. Maynard, "A Symbol—How It Changed."
130. Neary, "A New Resolve."
131. "A Threat of Anarchy in Nation's Capital."
132. Statement, Richard Nixon, September 27, 1968, folder Crime in Washington, D.C., box 98, Pre-Presidential Papers, RNPL.

CHAPTER 4

1. Carl Sims, "NE Youths Demand Suspension of Policeman Who Slew Suspect," *WP*, May 6, 1967.
2. Robert C. Kaiser, "Youths Push Probe of Brooker Death," *WP*, May 10, 1967; "Officer Fatally Hurt on Way to Shooting," *WP*, May 3, 1967; "Brooker Death Probe Hit by 5 Witnesses," *WP*, June 2, 1967; Thomas W. Lippman, "Here's History of Police-Citizen Deaths in Washington since January," *WP*, October 13, 1968; Leonard Downie Jr., "Policeman's Slaying of Youth Ruled 'Justifiable Homicide,'" *WP*, May 4, 1967.
3. "Byrd, Broyhill Denounce Brooker Death Probe," *WP*, May 12, 1967.
4. Proposal for Neighborhood Control of the Police in the Black Community, Black United Front, September 25, 1968, WFP-GWU, box 18, folder 7.
5. Memo, Pat Buchanan to Martin Anderson, n.d., folder Crime—General, box 21,

Campaign 1968 Research Files, RNPL. On the racial coding of crime, see, for example, Mendelberg, *The Race Card*; Barlow, "Race and the Problem of Crime in *Time* and *Newsweek* Cover Stories, 1946–1995."

6. Statement, Richard Nixon, June 22, 1968, box 95, Pre-Presidential Papers, RNPL. Historian Michael W. Flamm argues, "For conservatives, black crime would become the means by which to mount a flank attack on the civil rights movement when it was too popular to assault directly." Flamm, *Law and Order*, 15. See also Barkan, *Protesters on Trial*; Button, *Black Violence*; Cronin, Cronin, and Milakovich, *U.S. v. Crime in the Streets*.

7. The Disaster Center, "United States Crime Rates 1960–2012"; Federal Bureau of Investigation, "Uniform Crime Reporting Statistics"; Weaver, "Frontlash," 260.

8. Material for the President's Discussion with Walter Washington and Tom Fletcher, October 3, 1967, "D.C. Commissioners 2 of 2," box 12, White House Office Files of Joseph A. Califano, LBJL.

9. Press Release, November 13, 1967, folder Crime—Republicans (Republican Task Force on Crime), box 23, Campaign 1968 Research Files, RNPL.

10. Dallek, *Flawed Giant*, 528–29.

11. Flamm, *Law and Order*, 132–34, 140; Weaver, "Frontlash," 253–59; Orr, "Congress, Race, and Anticrime Policy," 235–36.

12. Kohler-Hausmann, *Getting Tough*, 32–33; Flamm, *Law and Order*, 132–34, 140; Weaver, "Frontlash," 253–59; Orr, "Congress, Race, and Anticrime Policy," 235–36. On the Safe Streets Act and Law Enforcement Assistance Administration, see Hinton, *From the War on Poverty to the War on Crime*; Thompson, "Why Mass Incarceration Matters," 729–31; Parenti, *Lockdown America*, 6–23; and Simon, *Governing through Crime*, 89–102. According to Weaver, "It was understood that if the money went to cities, agencies controlled by liberal Democrats and blacks in city government would administer it. Alternatively, if the money was channeled through at the state level, governors would have discretion over how the money was used and the majority of governors were ideologically conservative." Weaver, "Frontlash," 255.

13. Address, Lyndon Johnson, March 13, 1968, "SP 2-3-1968-FG 216 D.C. Message 3-13-68," box 118, LBJL.

14. Statement, Lyndon Johnson, July 3, 1968, "FG 216 District of Columbia (5-18-68)," box 268, WHCF, LBJL.

15. Quoted in Flamm, *Law and Order*, 130.

16. Statement, Richard Nixon, June 22, 1968, box 9, Pre-Presidential Papers, RNPL.

17. Statement, Richard Nixon, September 27, 1968, folder Crime in Washington, D.C., box 98, Pre-Presidential Papers, RNPL.

18. Statement, Richard Nixon, October 21, 1968, folder Statement on Crime, box 101, Pre-Presidential Papers, RNPL.

19. Statement, Richard Nixon, October 22, 1968, folder Dayton Rally Statement Re Crime, box 101, Pre-Presidential Papers, RNPL.

20. Quoted in Irv Chapman and Bob Clark, "Attorney General Ramsey Clark," *Issues and Answers*, American Broadcasting Company, aired May 12, 1968, transcript, "Washington D.C.—Issues and Answers 5-12-68," box 35, Personal Papers of Ramsey Clark, LBJL; Baum, *Smoke and Mirrors*, 5.

21. Marquis Childs, "Ramsey Clark: The Quiet Target," *WP*, September 9, 1968.

22. Newsletter, *Greater Washington Board of Trade News* 15, no. 6 (June 1968), BOTR-GWU, box 185, folder 12.

23. Position on Proposed Legislation, July 30, 1968, FCAR-MLKL, box 2, folder 1968–1969 Office Files Book 1.

24. "Fauntroy Calls Front 'Wrong,'" *WP*, July 9, 1968; "Serving the City," *WP*, July 11, 1968.

25. Leon Dash, "Slaying of Police Defended: Black United Front Calls It 'Justifiable,'" *WP*, July 6, 1968; "Police Brutality Real Concern of Black Front," *WP*, July 14, 1968.

26. "Is BUF Vindicated?," *Washington Afro-American*, July 20, 1968.

27. Resolution, Kalorama Citizens Association, October 10, 1968, FCAR-MLKL, box 2, folder 1968–1969 Office Files Book 1.

28. Report, "A Police Department in Trouble: Racial Discrimination and Misconduct in the Police Department of Washington, D.C.," National Capital Area Civil Liberties Union, August 1, 1968, EX FG, box 271, WHCF, LBJL.

29. "New Cry: Pay Police to Live Here," *Washington Afro-American*, March 22, 1969; Proposal, Black United Front, September 25, 1968, WFP-GWU, box 18, folder 7.

30. Proposal, Black United Front, September 25, 1968, WFP-GWU, box 18, folder 7; Robert Levey, "Councilman Supports Front's Police Goals: Front Gets Support of Councilman," *WP*, July 22, 1968.

31. William Raspberry, "Layton Wasn't Hep to New Problems," *WP*, July 9, 1969.

32. Letter, Joseph A. Mosesso and Morris H. Clark to Randle Highlands Citizens Association, January 21, 1969, FCAR-MLKL, box 2, folder 1968–1969 Office Files Book 2.

33. Statement, Federation of Citizens Associations to D.C. Council's Public Safety Committee, August 16, 1968, FCAR-MLKL, box 2, folder 1968–1969 Office Files Book 1.

34. Statement, Federation of Citizens Associations to D.C. Council's Public Safety Committee, August 16, 1968.

35. "Black Front Seeks Broyhill's Arrest," *WP*, December 2, 1968.

36. William Raspberry, "Nixon's D.C. Policy: What Will He Do?," *WP*, November 8, 1968; Statement, Richard Nixon, January 31, 1969, FCAR-MLKL, box 2, folder 1968–1969 Office Files Book 2.

37. Robert Hinton, "Black Front Says Tucker Was Ousted," *WP*, February 18, 1969.

38. Statement, Richard Nixon, January 31, 1969.

39. Memo, John Ehrlichman to Robert Mayo, February 23, 1970, folder Howard Messner, box 23, WHSF, SMOF: Egil Krogh, RNPL; Memo, John Ehrlichman to Richard Nixon, November 10, 1969, folder Memos, box 51, WHSF, SMOF: John D. Ehrlichman, RNPL.

40. Epstein, *Agency of Fear*, 64–65; Baum, *Smoke and Mirrors*, 16.

41. Address, John Mitchell, February 19, 1971, folder National Advisory Commission on Criminal Justice Standards and Goals, box 28, WHSF, SMOF: Egil Krogh, RNPL; Marion, *A History of Federal Crime Control Initiatives, 1960–1993*, 87; Memo, John Ehrlichman to Robert Mayo, February 23, 1970; Memo, John Ehrlichman to Richard Nixon, November 10, 1969.

42. Letter, Joseph A. Mosesso and Morris H. Clark to Randle Highlands Citizens

Association, January 21, 1969, FCAR-MLKL, box 2, folder 1968–1969 Office Files Book 2.

43. Letter, Joseph A. Mosesso and Morris H. Clark to Randle Highlands Citizens Association, January 21, 1969.

44. Letter, Osby L. Weir to Richard Nixon, February 5, 1969, folder District of Columbia, box 71, WHSF, SMOF: Egil Krogh, RNPL; Letter, George Brady to Richard Nixon, January 7, 1969, FCAR-MLKL, box 2, folder 1968–1969 Office Files Book 2.

45. Letter, David Rein to Gilbert Hahn, March 20, 1969, CCR-GWU, box 51; Mary Wiegers, "Dialogue between Black and White," *WP*, February 11, 1969; Statement, Federation of Citizens Associations, January 9, 1969, FCAR-MLKL, box 2, folder 1968–1969 Office Files Book 2.

46. "Nixon's Plan for D.C.," *Washington Daily News*, February 1, 1969.

47. Letter, Richard Nixon to Richard Hollander, February 5, 1969, folder District of Columbia, box 1, WHCF, Subject Files, EX FG 106, RNPL.

48. Memo, Richard Nixon to John Mitchell, February 4, 1969, folder District of Columbia, box 71, WHSF, SMOF: Egil Krogh, RNPL.

49. Tydings, foreword to "District of Columbia Court Reorganization, 1970," 478.

50. Memo, Bud Krogh to John Ehrlichman, September 15, 1969, folder Chron File, Memos, September, 1969, box 1, WHSF, SMOF: Egil Krogh, RNPL; Marion, *A History of Federal Crime Control Initiatives, 1960–1993*, 88.

51. Ted Lewis, *New York Daily News*, "Capital Stuff," September 12, 1969.

52. Memo, Bud Krogh to Don Santarelli, September 16, 1969, folder Chron File, Memos, September, 1969, box 1, WHSF, SMOF: Egil Krogh, RNPL.

53. Memo, Bud Krogh to Don Santarelli, September 16, 1969.

54. Smith, *Captive Capital*, 153.

55. Robert Asher, "Council Posts Set by Nixon," *WP*, January 31, 1969; Irma Moore, "Choice of Hahn for Council Criticized," *WP*, February 14, 1969; Hinton, "Black Front Says Tucker Was Ousted." In July, BUF had dismissed all white attendees during a discussion of community policing. Tucker protested the move by walking out and had not attended a meeting since.

56. Briefing Paper for Meeting with Gil Hahn, November 20, 1969, folder Gilbert Hahn, box 72, WHSF, SMOF: Egil Krogh, RNPL.

57. Memo, John Ehrlichman to Richard Nixon, November 10, 1969, folder Memos, box 51, WHSF, SMOF: John D. Ehrlichman, RNPL; Robert F. Levey, "Deputy Mayor Named," *WP*, November 13, 1969; Memo, Bud Krogh to Dwight Chapin, November 4, 1969, folder Chron File, Memos, November, 1969, box 1, WHSF, SMOF: Egil Krogh, RNPL.

58. Memo, Bud Krogh to Don Santarelli, September 16, 1969; Memo, Bud Krogh to Dick Blumenthal, October 1, 1969, folder Chron File, Memos, October, 1969, box 1, WHSF, SMOF: Egil Krogh, RNPL.

59. Memo, Bud Krogh to John Ehrlichman, September 15, 1969; Memo, John Ehrlichman to Herb Klein, September 15, 1969, folder Chron File, Memos, September, 1969, box 1, WHSF, SMOF: Egil Krogh, RNPL.

60. Memo, Richard Blumenthal to Hugh Sloan, October 10, 1969, folder D.C. Visit—President (1969–1970), box 26, WHCF, SMOF: Andre Buckles, RNPL.

61. Memo, Daniel Moynihan to John Ehrlichman, October 24, 1969, folder Citizens' Group (1969), box 6, WHCF, SMOF: Andre Buckles, RNPL.

62. Memo, Daniel Moynihan to John Ehrlichman, October 24, 1969.

63. Memo, Daniel Moynihan to John Ehrlichman, October 24, 1969.

64. "Fauntroy Pushed as Council Head," *WP*, January 23, 1969.

65. Memo, Daniel Patrick Moynihan to John Ehrlichman, November 10, 1969, folder Correspondence—Memos to Staff, Ehrlichman, box 7, WHCF, SMOF: Daniel Patrick Moynihan, RNPL.

66. Message, Walter Washington to the annual meeting of the Washington Home Rule Committee, November 26, 1968, BOTR-GWU, box 368, folder 13; Press Release, Richard Nixon, October 22, 1968, folder Statement on Washington, D.C., box 101, Pre-Presidential Papers, RNPL.

67. Memo, John Ehrlichman to Richard Nixon, November 10, 1969, folder Memos, box 51, WHSF, SMOF: John D. Ehrlichman, RNPL.

68. Memo, Richard Blumenthal to Bud Krogh, November 5, 1969, folder D.C. Government (1969–70), box 11, WHCF, SMOF: Andre Buckles, RNPL.

69. Memo, Bud Krogh to John Ehrlichman, November 10, 1969, folder Mayor Washington, box 72, WHSF, SMOF: Egil Krogh, RNPL; Memo, for Richard Nixon, November 10, 1969, folder Mayor Washington, box 72, WHSF, SMOF: Egil Krogh, RNPL.

70. Talking Points for Richard Nixon, November 10, 1969, folder Mayor Washington, box 72, WHSF, SMOF: Egil Krogh, RNPL.

71. Memo, John Ehrlichman to Richard Nixon, November 10, 1969, folder Memos, box 51, WHSF, SMOF: John D. Ehrlichman, RNPL.

72. Memo, Stephen Hess to Bud Krogh, November 6, 1969, folder Articles (Crime), box 2, WHCF, SMOF: Andre Buckles, RNPL.

73. Summary of Remarks of Sterling Tucker Delivered at the Men's Day Service 19th Street Baptist Church, October 26, 1969, CCR-GWU, box 50; *Record*, November 5, 1969, folder Articles (Crime), box 2, WHCF, SMOF: Andre Buckles, RNPL.

74. Summary of Remarks of Sterling Tucker Delivered at the Men's Day Service 19th Street Baptist Church, October 26, 1969; *Record*, November 5, 1969.

75. Memo, Bud Krogh to Dave Miller, January 26, 1970, folder Chron File, Memos, January 1970, box 2, WHSF, SMOF: Egil Krogh, RNPL.

76. Simpson F. Lawson, "Washington and the White House: What Have They Done for Us Lately?," n.d., folder D.C. Government (1969–70), box 11, WHCF, SMOF: Andre Buckles, RNPL.

77. Memo, Bud Krogh to Ginger Savell, January 14, 1970, folder Chron File, Memos, January, 1970, box 2, WHSF, SMOF: Egil Krogh, RNPL.

78. Letter, Daniel Patrick Moynihan to John Ehrlichman, January 28, 1970, folder Correspondence—Memos to Staff, Ehrlichman, box 7, WHCF, SMOF: Daniel Patrick Moynihan, RNPL.

79. Letter, Daniel Patrick Moynihan to John Ehrlichman, January 26, 1970, folder Correspondence—Memos to Staff, Ehrlichman, box 7, WHCF, SMOF: Daniel Patrick Moynihan, RNPL.

80. Memo, Ken Cole to Bud Krogh, January 21, 1970, folder Crime Message (1970), box 23, WHSF, SMOF Egil Krogh, RNPL; Memo, January 23, 1970, folder President's

Meeting with Mayor, Friday January 23, 1970, box 28, WHSF, SMOF: Egil Krogh, RNPL.

81. Notes on Street Crime and D.C. Government, Bud Krogh to D.C. Crime File, January 19, 1970, folder Meeting with President 12-22-69—Abernathy, McMillan, Nielsen, box 28, WHSF, SMOF: Egil Krogh, RNPL.

82. Memo, Bud Krogh to Bill Timmons, January 21, 1970, folder Chron File, Memos, January, 1970, box 2, WHSF, SMOF: Egil Krogh, RNPL.

83. Memo, January 23, 1970, folder President's Meeting with Mayor, Friday January 23, 1970, box 28, WHSF, SMOF: Egil Krogh, RNPL; Memo, January 23, 1970, folder President's Meeting with Mayor, Friday, January 23, 1970, box 28, WHSF, SMOF: Egil Krogh, RNPL; Press Conference, Walter Washington, January 23, 1970, folder President's Meeting with Mayor, Friday January 23, 1970, box 28, WHSF, SMOF: Egil Krogh, RNPL.

84. William Trombley, "Mayor Walter Washington," *Los Angeles Times*, March 13, 1969.

85. Reginald Booker, interview by Robert E. Wright.

86. Smith, *Captive Capital*, 156.

87. Memo, John R. Brown III to John Ehrlichman, January 29, 1970, folder Mayor Washington, box 72, WHSF, SMOF: Egil Krogh, RNPL

88. Memo, Bud Krogh to Richard Nixon, May 22, 1970, folder President's Meeting with Mayor, Friday May 22, 1970, box 28, WHSF, SMOF: Egil Krogh, RNPL; Weaver, "Frontlash," 261.

89. Memo, Bud Krogh to Richard Nixon, May 22, 1970; Weaver, "Frontlash," 261.

90. Memo, Donald Santareilli to Egil Krogh, May 27, 1970, folder Mayor Washington, box 72, WHSF, SMOF: Egil Krogh, RNPL.

91. Memo, Bud Krogh to John Ehrlichman, June 8, 1970, folder Mayor Washington, box 72, WHSF, SMOF: Egil Krogh, RNPL.

92. Memo, White House staff to Richard Nixon, October 8, 1969, folder District of Columbia (7-1-69 to 12-31-69), box 1. WHCF, Subject Files, EX FG 106, RNPL; Memo, Bud Krogh to John Ehrlichman, October 9, 1969, folder Correspondence—Memos to Staff, Ehrlichman, box 7, WHCF, SMOF: Daniel Patrick Moynihan, RNPL.

93. "Congress Clears Controversial D.C. Crime Control Bill."

94. "Congress Clears Controversial D.C. Crime Control Bill."

95. The four were Brock Adams (D-Wash.), Charles C. Diggs Jr. (D-Mich.), Donald M. Fraser (D-Minn.) and Andrew Jacobs Jr. (D-Ind.) They also objected to what they believed were overly punitive juvenile provisions, including that a child age sixteen accused of certain violent crimes would be tried as an adult, that a child age fifteen accused of a felony could be transferred to an adult court, and that the standard of proof for finding a juvenile guilty was a "preponderance of the evidence." "Congress Clears Controversial D.C. Crime Control Bill."

96. "Congress Clears Controversial D.C. Crime Control Bill."

97. Marion, *A History of Federal Crime Control Initiatives, 1960–1993*, 88; Packer, "A Special Supplement: Nixon's Crime Program and What It Means."

98. Letter, George Brady to Joseph Tydings and John McMillan, April 3, 1970, folder D.C. Crime (1969–73), box 9, WHCF, SMOF: Andre Buckles, RNPL.

99. "Congress Clears Controversial D.C. Crime Control Bill."

100. "Congress Clears Controversial D.C. Crime Control Bill"; Statement, City Council, March 20, 1970, CCR-GWU, box 9.

101. Statement, City Council, March 20, 1970, CCR-GWU, box 9; Statement, Gilbert Hahn, March 21, 1970, CCR-GWU, box 9.

102. William Raspberry, "Why Federalize Lorton?," *WP*, March 2, 1970.

103. Memo, n.d., folder Current D.C. Issues, box 9, WHCF, SMOF: Andre Buckles, RNPL.

104. Letter, Edward Kennedy and Sam Ervin, May 15, 1970, folder D.C. Legislative Package (1969–1970), box 24, WHSF, SMOF: Egil Krogh, RNPL; "Congress Clears Controversial D.C. Crime Control Bill."

105. "Congress Clears Controversial D.C. Crime Control Bill"; Statement, Senator Eagleton, July 13, 1970, folder D.C. Crime Bill (1970), box 23, WHSF, SMOF: Egil Krogh, RNPL.

106. Memo, Samuel C. Jackson to Richard Nixon, May 26, 1970, folder No-Knock (1970), box 24, WHSF, SMOF: Egil Krogh, RNPL; Richard Pearson, "Samuel C. Jackson Dies," *WP*, September 29, 1982.

107. Howe, "David Eaton."

108. Memo, Samuel C. Jackson to Richard Nixon, May 26, 1970, folder No-Knock (1970), box 24, WHSF, SMOF: Egil Krogh, RNPL.

109. William Raspberry, "Crime Drawing Blacks, Police Closer Together," *WP*, January 25, 1970.

110. Memo, Samuel C. Jackson to Richard Nixon, May 26, 1970, folder No-Knock (1970), box 24, WHSF, SMOF: Egil Krogh, RNPL.

111. Memo, Bud Krogh to John Ehrlichman, May 27, 1970, folder Chron File, Memos, May 1970, box 3, WHSF, SMOF: Egil Krogh, RNPL.

112. Remarks, Gerald Ford, July 15, 1970, folder D.C. Crime Bill (1970), box 23, WHSF, SMOF: Egil Krogh, RNPL; "Congress Clears Controversial D.C. Crime Control Bill."

113. Nixon, "Remarks on Signing the District of Columbia Court Reform and Criminal Procedure Act of 1970"; Banks, *Judicial Politics in the D.C. Circuit Court*, 28. A state-level court system was established for D.C. But by eliminating appellate review by the allegedly lenient U.S. Court of Appeals, Congress ended its ability to act as a local state Supreme Court in criminal matters. Moreover, it effectively transformed the powerful D.C. District Court into an ordinary federal court of appeals. For more on the D.C. Crime bill's effect on the D.C. Circuit Court's judicial role, agenda, and scope of its judicial policy making, see Banks, *Judicial Politics in the D.C. Circuit Court*, 26–32; Rohmann and Morris, *Calmly to Poise the Scales of Justice*, 233–35. While the federal courts of the D.C. Circuit Court lost an important part of their jurisdiction, their influence over other areas grew. According to Rohmann and Morris, "The District Court and the Court of Appeals would become the major forum for the adjudication of cases precipitated by the burst of legislation, passed during the Johnson and Nixon administrations, that greatly enlarged the role of the federal government." Rohmann and Morris, *Calmly to Poise the Scales of Justice*, 235.

114. Notes, Edwin Harper, July 15, 1972, folder Ed Harper Input, box 65, WHCF, SMOF: Leonard Garment, RNPL; Alfred E. Lewis, "5 Held in Plot to Bug Democrats'

Office Here," *WP*, June 18, 1972; Notes, Edwin Harper, July 15, 1972, folder Ed Harper Input, box 65, WHCF, SMOF: Leonard Garment, RNPL.

115. Memo, John Ehrlichman to White House Staff, April 7, 1972, folder D.C. Crime Meeting w Schecter (TIMES), box 23, WHSF, SMOF: Egil Krogh, RNPL; Speech, Gilbert Hahn Jr., July 8, 1971, CCR-GWU, box 9; The Disaster Center, "United States Crime Rates 1960–2012." Vesla Weaver writes, "However, an analysis by the Brookings Institution found that the decrease was due to a change in the value of stolen goods, decreasing the number of crimes classified as burglary or larceny." Weaver, "Frontlash," 261.

116. Notes, Edwin Harper, July 15, 1972, folder Ed Harper Input, box 65, WHCF, SMOF: Leonard Garment, RNPL.

117. Message, Walter Washington to the annual meeting of the Washington Home Rule Committee, November 26, 1968, BOTR-GWU, box 368, folder 13.

118. Bard and Shellow, *Issues in Law Enforcement*, 187; Asch and Musgrove, *Chocolate City*, 368.

119. Fortner, *Black Silent Majority*, 154.

120. Bernadette Carey, "Black Front Plans War against Crime," *WP*, December 31, 1968.

121. "Crime's Primary Victims," *WP*, January 6, 1969.

122. Bard and Shellow, *Issues in Law Enforcement*, 187.

123. Bard and Shellow, *Issues in Law Enforcement*, 184, 188; William Raspberry, "D.C. Model Precinct in Trouble," *WP*, July 22, 1968; William Raspberry, "Pilot Precinct Merits a Test," *WP*, November 13, 1968; Kweit and Kweit, *People and Politics in Urban America*, 388.

124. Speech, Sterling Tucker, February 5, 1970, folder D.C. Street Crime, box 25, WHSF, SMOF: Egil Krogh, RNPL.

125. William Raspberry, "Creator-Director Chief Obstacle to Implementing Police Project," *WP*, October 31, 1969; Bard and Shellow, *Issues in Law Enforcement*, 189, 191.

126. Raspberry, "Creator-Director Chief Obstacle to Implementing Pilot Project"; Bard and Shellow, *Issues in Law Enforcement*, 189, 191.

127. Proposal, The Third District Pilot Police Project, folder Model Precinct Project (1970–71), box 16, WHCF, SMOF: Andre Buckles, RNPL; William Raspberry, "Pilot District Objections Narrowing," *WP*, October 29, 1969; Asch and Musgrove, *Chocolate City*, 369.

128. William Raspberry, "Police-Community Program Damaged by 2-Year Wrangle," *WP*, January 23, 1970; Asch and Musgrove, *Chocolate City*, 368.

129. Donald E. Graham, "Pilot District Again Periled," *WP*, March 28, 1971; Richard E. Prince, "City to Finance Police Project Temporarily," *WP*, July 2, 1971; Paul W. Valentine, "Pilot District Project, Nearly Out of Money, Seeks Extension," *WP*, August 6, 1972; Richard E. Prince, "Five Years Change Marion Barry: Sphere of Influence Widens," *WP*, November 7, 1971.

130. Smith, *Captive Capital*, 288.

131. Paul W. Valentine, "OEO Extends D.C.'s Police Pilot Project," *WP*, February 14, 1970; Richard E. Prince, "Angry Pilot Police Project Board Rejects OEO Restriction on Grant," *WP*, May 1, 1970; Bart Barnes, "OEO Study Criticizes D.C. Pilot Police Plan,"

WP, August 2, 1971; "D.C. Pilot Police-Community Project Dies for Want of Money," *WP*, November 9, 1973.

132. "Cutting the Crime Rate."

133. Simpson F. Lawson, "Washington and the White House: What Have They Done for Us Lately?," n.d., folder D.C. Government (1969–70), box 11, WHCF, SMOF: Andre Buckles, RNPL.

134. Speech, Gilbert Hahn Jr., July 8, 1971, CCR-GWU, box 9. Opposition to Hahn's reappointment stemmed from both local and national Republicans, including House Minority Leader Gerald Ford, who had complained to the White House that Hahn had acted irresponsibly as city council leader. Stephen Green, "Mitchell Obtains New Hahn Term," *WP*, January 29, 1972. According to the *Post*, the city council chairman had angered congressmen as well as the business community by pushing consumer regulations and controversial parking fees, among other legislative proposals. "Gilbert Hahn Jr.; Nixon Pick to Lead D.C. Council," *WP*, October 8, 2008. Hahn's actions sharply contrasted the mayor's. Walter Washington had taken measures to avoid angering congressional legislators and members of the Nixon administration and had worked hard to gain Republican businesspeople's support. Hahn refused to do so. As a result, he clashed with both Washington and the Nixon White House in his attempts to expand the council's authority. But his effort to forge a council independent from the whims of the federal politicians who controlled the city's budget had its price. Smith, *Captive Capital*, 151; Richard E. Prince, "Nixon's Rapprochement with Mayor Led to Hahn's Ouster," *WP*, April 17, 1972.

135. Fortner, *Black Silent Majority*, 154; Kirk Scharfenberg, "Inner City Residents Prefer 'Tough' Police," *WP*, March 15, 1972; editorial quoted in Fortner, *Black Silent Majority*, 161.

CHAPTER 5

1. Memo, John Dean to John Ehrlichman, January 21, 1971, folder Re Crime Fight, box 25, WHSF, SMOF: John W. Dean III, RNPL.

2. Carroll Kilpatrick, "President Looks Ahead to Our 200th Birthday," *WP*, July 9, 1966; ARBA, *Bicentennial of the United States*, 1:55. The ARBC's thirty-four original members included seventeen public representatives and seventeen government officials—including four senators, four representatives, and nine ex- officio members from various parts of the federal government. The public members included citizens associated with leading universities, former presidents of the American Bar Association, and a variety of businessmen and cultural figures. ARBA, *Bicentennial of the United States*, 1:241.

3. ARBA, *Bicentennial of the United States*, 1:244; Zaretsky, *No Direction Home*, 144.

4. ARBA, *Bicentennial of the United States*, 1:242.

5. Wolf Von Eckardt, "Mission 76: A Spanking New Capital," *WP*, April 14, 1968. On early Bicentennial planning in Philadelphia, see Feffer, "Show Down in Center City"; Knowles, "Staying Too Long at the Fair."

6. Von Eckardt, "Mission 76: A Spanking New Capital"; "Mission 76," *WP*, April 14, 1968. Carl Abbott argues that in Washington, metropolitan newspapers "assumed

responsibility for proposing, analyzing, and promoting views of feasible economic futures." The *Post*, in particular, he asserts, had institutional memory and staying power and thus could "contribute significantly to working new ideas into coherent wholes." Abbott, "Perspectives on Urban Economic Planning," 19–20. On the idea of Washington as a model city, see Gillette, *Between Justice and Beauty*.

7. Robert A. Peck, "Federal Fortresses," *WP*, February 19, 1977. According to one local architect, the FBI building was a "great concrete hulk midway along the historic link between White House and Congress. The siting of this brooding monolith symbolizes that the FBI might be monitoring the connection between branches of government, too." Wiebenson, "Symbol Power," 20.

8. "The Mission '76 Idea," *WP*, February 22, 1970.

9. William Ecenbarger, "Boston, Philadelphia Vie for Bicentennial," *WP*, April 3, 1969; Wolf Von Eckardt, "Some Look Forward," *WP*, March 29, 1970.

10. Wolf Von Eckardt, "'Mission '76: An Idea v. Fireworks," *WP*, April 20, 1969.

11. In 1960, the BOT commissioned and presented a proposal to the three-man President's Commission charged with determining if and where the United States should have a World's Fair in 1964. The board even contracted renowned architect and urban planner Victor Gruen to prepare a study on the proposed site. Huxtable, "Out of a Fair, a City"; Derthick, *City Politics in Washington, D.C.*, 89–93; Clarke, "Washington Board of Trade."

12. ". . . And Six Years from Today," *WP*, July 4, 1970; "The Mission '76 Idea."

13. Proposal to the ARBC, folder ABC (American Revolution Bicentennial Commission) (2 of 4), box 10, WHCF, SMOF: Bradley H. Patterson Jr., RNPL; Addendum to Proposal of National Capital Historic Region Bicentennial Committee prepared by Downtown Progress, April 1970, DPR-MLKL, box 40, folder Downtown Design and Development Program 1967–71; Priscilla R. Crane, "Letter to the Editor," *WP*, April 9, 1970; Von Eckardt, "Some Look Forward."

14. Letter, Francine Storch and Jonathan Green to Jane Shay, March 18, 1970, folder American Revolution Bicentennial (5 of 5), box 3, WHCF, SMOF: Andre Buckles, RNPL.

15. Report, Proposal to the ARBC, folder ABC (American Revolution Bicentennial Commission) (2 of 4), box 10, WHCF, SMOF: Bradley H. Patterson Jr., RNPL; Addendum to Proposal of National Capital Historic Region Bicentennial Committee prepared by Downtown Progress, April 1970, DPR-MLKL, box 40, folder Downtown Design and Development Program 1967–71; Crane, "Letter to the Editor"; Von Eckardt, "Some Look Forward."

16. Memo, Charlie McWhorter to Leonard Garment, June 15, 1970, folder ABC (American Revolution Bicentennial Commission) (2 of 4), box 10, WHCF, SMOF: Bradley H. Patterson Jr., RNPL; Letter, Bill Safire to John Ehrlichman, March 4, 1970, folder PR 8-1 American Bicentennial Celebration (1969–70), WHCF, Subject Files, Public Relations 8-1, RNPL.

17. ARBA, *Bicentennial of the United States*, 1:225, 246, 244; William L. Claiborne, "D.C. Loses Bid for Bicentennial," *WP*, July 2, 1970. The ARBC officially scrapped the international exposition in May 1972. See Knowles, "Staying Too Long at the Fair," 104–8.

18. William L. Claiborne, "Nixon Reserves View on Bicentennial Plans," *WP*, July 4, 1970.

19. Memo, Charlie McWhorter to Leonard Garment, June 15, 1970, folder ABC (American Revolution Bicentennial Commission) (2 of 4), box 10, WHCF, SMOF: Bradley H. Patterson Jr., RNPL.

20. Letter, Arthur D. Kallen to Mr. H. McKittrick, June 19, 1970, folder American Revolution Bicentennial Commission, box 2, WHCF, SMOF: Andre Buckles, RNPL.

21. Walker, *Most of 14th Street Is Gone*, 124–26.

22. Asch and Musgrove, *Chocolate City*, 360–62; Gillette, "A National Workshop for Urban Policy," 22–26; Zachary Schrag, *The Great Society Subway*, chapter 5.

23. Asch and Musgrove, *Chocolate City*, 360–63; Gillette, "A National Workshop for Urban Policy," 22–26; Zachary Schrag, *The Great Society Subway*, chapter 5.

24. Asch and Musgrove, *Chocolate City*, 364–66; Zachary Schrag, *The Great Society Subway*, 123, chapter 5.

25. Walker, *Most of 14th Street Is Gone*, 128–29; Zachary Schrag, *The Great Society Subway*, 163–64. For an excellent study on the Washington Metro, see Zachary Schrag, *The Great Society Subway*. The "Mid City" line eventually was named the Green Line and did not open until 2001.

26. Statement, Joseph B. Danzansky, before the Subcommittee on Business, Commerce and Fiscal Affairs of the House Committee on the District of Columbia, November 10, 1971, DPR-MLKL, box 40, folder Downtown Development Corporation 1970–74; J. Y. Smith, "Joseph B. Danzansky Dies at Age 65," *WP*, November 9, 1979; Asch and Musgrove, *Chocolate City*, 358.

27. Press statement, Sterling Tucker, September 16, 1971, CCR-GWU, box 22.

28. ARBA, *Bicentennial of the United States*, 1:194.

29. Jane Rippeteau, "Huge Bicentennial Influx is Expected," *WP*, August 2, 1974; Eugene L. Meyer, "Neglected Black Historic Sites Recorded for Bicentennial," *WP*, April 14, 1973; Angela Terrell, "Black Landmarks," *WP*, August 3, 1974; "Around Town," *WP*, August 11, 1975. For more on ABC's preservation efforts, see Pauline Gaskins Mitchell, "The History of Mt. Zion United Methodist Church and Mt. Zion Cemetery."

30. James Seymore, "Let Them Eat Birthday Cake," *The Washingtonian*, July 1971.

31. Report, Proposal to the ARBC, folder ABC (American Revolution Bicentennial Commission) (2 of 4), box 10, WHCF, SMOF: Bradley H. Patterson Jr., RNPL; "The Spirit of '76," *WP*, May 15, 1971.

32. Memo, Graham Watt to Bud Krogh, September 27, 1971, folder Bicentennial 1971, box 2, WHCF, SMOF: Andre Buckles, RNPL; Report, Proposal to the ARBC, folder ABC (American Revolution Bicentennial Commission) (2 of 4), box 10, WHCF, SMOF: Bradley H. Patterson Jr., RNPL.

33. Memo, September 18, 1971, folder Bicentennial—D.C. (2 of 2), box 12, WHCF, SMOF: Bradley H. Patterson Jr., RNPL; Memo, Graham Watt to Bud Krogh, September 27, 1971.

34. Statement, 14th Street Community Planning Team, n.d., CCR-GWU, box 22.

35. Afro-American Bicentennial Corporation, "Beyond the Fireworks of 76: A Quest for a Continuing Revolution," Washington, D.C., November 1971, folder Bicentennial—D.C. (2 of 2), box 12, WHCF, SMOF: Bradley H. Patterson Jr., RNPL.

36. Margot Hornblower, "James Gibson: Resignation but Not a Sense of Failure," *WP*, July 3, 1975.

37. Wolf Von Eckardt, "Bicentennial: Before, After," *WP*, October 9, 1971.

38. Von Eckardt, "Bicentennial: Before, After."

39. Hornblower, "James Gibson: Resignation but Not a Sense of Failure."

40. Report, Washington Bicentennial, folder Washington Bicentennial (1972), box 26, WHCF, SMOF: Andre Buckles, RNPL.

41. Zigas, *Left with Few Rights*, 40; Sachse, "D.C. Home Rule Movement, 1966–1973," 80.

42. Zigas, *Left with Few Rights*, 40–41; Diner, "The Black Majority," 259.

43. Musgrove, "'Statehood Is Far More Difficult,'" 5–7. Stone was the associate director of the American Committee on Africa, and the White House correspondent and editor of the *Washington Afro-American* until he was named editor-in-chief of the *Chicago Defender* in 1963. From 1965 to 1967, Stone served as special assistant to Congressman Adam Clayton Powell Jr., writing speeches and directing activities for the House Education and Labor Committee.

44. Musgrove, "'Statehood Is Far More Difficult,'" 5; Asch and Musgrove, *Chocolate City*, 378–79. In 1972, Hobson was diagnosed with multiple myeloma, cancer of the bone marrow. The disease left him wheelchair bound and in constant pain until his death in 1977.

45. Musgrove, "'Statehood Is Far More Difficult,'" 5; Asch and Musgrove, *Chocolate City*, 378–79; Zigas, *Left with Few Rights*, 40–41; Diner, "The Black Majority," 259.

46. Statement, Walter Fauntroy, July 29, 1971, folder D.C. Home Rule 1971 (1 of 2), box 13, WHCF, SMOF: Andre Buckles, RNPL.

47. Zigas, *Left with Few Rights*, 42; Sachse, "D.C. Home Rule Movement, 1966–1973," 93–94.

48. News Release, Testimony of Congressman Walter Fauntroy before the Platform Committee of the Democratic National Committee, June 23, 1972, WFP-GWU, box 15, folder 1.

49. Lewis, *District of Columbia*, 1186–87.

50. Gillette, *Between Justice and Beauty*, 190. The 1964 Voting Rights Act helped Fauntroy's campaign. In John McMillan's district, registration efforts following its implementation resulted in an increase of black voters registered to vote, from 3 percent in 1964 to 28 percent in 1972. Fauntroy, "Home Rule for the District of Columbia," 25.

51. Memo, White House staff to John Ehrlichman, n.d., folder Home Rule (1971–73), box 13, WHCF, SMOF: Andre Buckles, RNPL; Issues and Considerations, n.d., folder Home Rule (1971–73), box 13, WHCF, SMOF: Andre Buckles, RNPL.

52. Eugene L. Meyer, "To Him, Your (July 4) Celebration Is a Sham," *WP*, July 5, 1973.

53. Meyer, "To Him, Your (July 4) Celebration Is a Sham."

54. Joel Dreyfuss, "In Celebration of the Capital City," *WP*, October 27, 1973. On the foreboding nature of the built environment, see Zukin, *Landscapes of Power*; Davis, *City of Quartz*.

55. Hornblower, "James Gibson: Resignation but Not a Sense of Failure."

56. Federal Bicentennial Program for the District of Columbia, n.d., folder Bicentennial 1973, box 3, WHCF, SMOF: Andre Buckles, RNPL.

57. "$18 Million Bicentennial Aid Assured," *WP*, November 11, 1973.

58. Kirk Scharfenberg, "Panel: '76 Fete Derailed: White House Said to Renege on Fund Plan," *WP*, October 2, 1973.

59. James Seymore, "The Fizzling of the Bicentennial," *The Washingtonian*, July 1973.

60. Stephen J. Lynton, "Bicentennial Projects Shows Split in City," *WP*, July 3, 1976; "District of Columbia Chamber of Commerce, *First Word* 1, no. 2 (March 1973), BOTR-GWU, box 146, folder 1.

61. Memo, Ken Cole to Richard Nixon, December 22, 1973, folder D.C. Home Rule 1973 (2 of 2), box 14, WHCF, SMOF: Andre Buckles, RNPL; Charles Wesley Harris, *Congress and the Governance of the Nation's Capital*, 9; "Congress Clears Controversial D.C. Crime Control Bill."

62. Editorial, "The Twists in the Road to Home Rule," *WP*, October 10, 1973; Zigas, *Left with Few Rights*, 46.

63. Memo, Dr. Ellis Haworth to members of the Senate-House Conference, October 25, 1973, folder District of Columbia Self-Government and Government Reorganization Act, box 23, WHCF, SMOF: Andre Buckles, RNPL.

64. Memo, Ken Cole to Richard Nixon, December 22, 1973, folder D.C. Home Rule 1973 (2 of 2), box 14, WHCF, SMOF: Andre Buckles, RNPL; Zigas, *Left with Few Rights*, 46.

65. Memo, Dana Mead to Ken Cole, July 9, 1973, folder District of Columbia (1-6-73 to 7-27-74) (1 of 2), box 2, WHCF, Subject Files, EX FG 106, RNPL; Lewis, *District of Columbia*, 186; Diner, "The Black Majority," 260.

66. "Congress Clears Controversial D.C. Crime Control Bill"; Senate Debate, Congressional Record (July 10, 1973), 22935–22977; Memo, Dana Mead to Ken Cole, July 9, 1973, folder District of Columbia (1-6-73 to 7-27-74) (1 of 2), box 2, WHCF, Subject Files, EX FG 106, RNPL; Lewis, *District of Columbia*, 186; Diner, "The Black Majority," 260.

67. See Council of the District of Columbia, "Office of the Advisory Neighborhood Commissions"; Asch and Musgrove, *Chocolate City*, 380.

68. Daly, "The Peoples Bicentennial Commission."

69. ARBA, *Bicentennial of the United States*, 1:246.

70. Bodnar, *Remaking America*, 231; Capozzola, "'It Makes You Want to Believe in the Country,'" 32, 36–37; Zaretsky, *No Direction Home*, 148. For more on the People's Bicentennial Commission, see Bodnar, *Remaking America*, 234–37.

71. ARBA, *Bicentennial of the United States*, 1:248; ARBA, *National Bicentennial Ethnic and Racial Council Conference Report, January 20–22, 1975*, 2.

72. ARBA, *Bicentennial of the United States*, 1:197; ARBA, *National Bicentennial Ethnic and Racial Council Conference Report, January 20–22, 1975*, 2; Bodnar, *Remaking America*, 237; Capozzola, "It Makes You Want to Believe in the Country,'" 34; "Blacks Form Caucus at Bicentennial Meeting," *BAA*, February 1, 1975.

73. "Bicentennial Unit to Be Increased," *BAA*, September 23, 1972; Bodnar, *Remaking America*, 232; Zaretsky, *No Direction Home*, 151.

74. Eugene L. Meyer, "Hill Stirs on Pennsylvania Ave. Plan," *WP*, August 20, 1970. On the religious symbolism of Pennsylvania Avenue, see Meyer, *Myths in Stone*, 15–20, 70–73. On the national significance of the avenue, see Barber, *Marching on Washington*, 5–6, 8; Lewis, *District of Columbia*, 33.

75. Congress designated the area as a National Historic Site in 1965 and considered

the project one of the city's "sacred cows." Katzman, *Daniel Patrick Moynihan*, 82; Hess, *The Professor and the President*, 48–59.

76. Fact Sheet on the Pennsylvania Avenue Plan, n.d., BOTR-GWU, box 310, folder 2.

77. Memo, Daniel Patrick Moynihan to Richard Nixon, June 8, 1970, folder Federal City Bicentennial Development Corp (Bill and Message) (1 of 4), box 24, WHCF, SMOF: Daniel Patrick Moynihan, RNPL.

78. Memo, Daniel Patrick Moynihan to Richard Nixon, June 8, 1970. On the history of the "quasi-governmental sector," see Radford, "From Municipal Socialism to Public Authorities."

79. "Whose Heavy Hand?," *WP*, September 30, 1970.

80. Christopher Weight, "Businessmen Fret," *WS*, November 15, 1970. On the *Washington Star*'s role in setting discourse in the city, see Abbott, "Perspectives on Urban Economic Planning," 20.

81. Ellen Hoffman, "D.C. Group to Fight Avenue Bill," *WP*, September 30, 1970. In only a few short years, the MWPHA had gone through dramatic changes. According to local activist Sam Smith, it had been "the preserve of white noblesse obligers" but had quickly transformed into a black advocacy group. Smith, *Captive Capital*, 255.

82. "Whose Heavy Hand?"

83. Statement, John Anthony, before the House Committee on Interior and Insular Affairs on the Federal City Bicentennial Development Corporation, September 18, 1970, folder Pa. Ave Commission Correspondence (5 of 5), box 32, WHCF, SMOF: Daniel Patrick Moynihan, RNPL.

84. Wiebenson, "Symbol Power," 19.

85. The mayor, the chairman of the city council, and four D.C. residents were among the fifteen directors of the corporation, several short of a majority. "A New Design for the Grand Design," *WP*, August 21, 1972.

86. Sarah Booth Conroy, "Culver: A Man with a Plan," *WP*, January 9, 1972; Statement, Washington Planning Workshop on Pennsylvania Avenue Development Corporation, August 22, 1972, BOTR-GWU, box 308, folder 18.

87. Eugene L. Meyer, "Downtown Progress: Renewal Frustration, Conflict," *WP*, August 29, 1972.

88. Statement, Harry H. Hahn, before the Subcommittee on National Parks and Recreation, April 13, 1972, BOTR-GWU, box 308, folder 18.

89. Statement, Harry H. Hahn, before the Subcommittee on National Parks and Recreation, April 13, 1972. The linkages between race and welfare are well established in the literature. See, for example, Kohler-Hausmann, *Getting Tough*; Gilens, *Why Americans Hate Welfare*; Quadagno, *The Color of Welfare*.

90. Abbott Combes, "Grand Plan for Avenue Is Attacked," *WP*, April 15, 1972.

91. Statement, Robert N. Gray, before the House Subcommittee on National Parks and Recreation on Interior and Insular Affairs on HR 10751, CCR-GWU, box 22; Memo, Richard Weinstein to Knox Banner, May 11, 1972, DPR-MLKL, box 25, folder unknown.

92. Statement, Mayor Walter Washington, before the Subcommittee on Parks and Recreation on Interior and Insular Affairs, n.d., CCR-GWU, box 24.

93. The Pennsylvania Avenue Plan 1974, PADC, October 1974, 1.

94. Letter, Bill Hart to Richard Nixon, October 19, 1972, folder Washington Bicentennial (1972), box 26, WHCF, SMOF: Andre Buckles, RNPL. Congress authorized the corporation to borrow up to $50 million from the U.S. Treasury or from private interests. Kirk Scharfenberg, "Nixon Gets Pa. Avenue Renewal Bill," *WP*, October 19, 1972.

95. Benjamin Forgey, "A Pennsylvania Avenue for the People, Not Just Parades," *WS*, April 16, 1974. The plan also provided for 130 units per acre, as compared to 200 units per acre for an average high-rise apartment and roughly 30 to 40 units an acre on a typical street of row houses in Washington. Fact Sheet on the Pennsylvania Avenue Plan, n.d., BOTR-GWU, box 310, folder 2.

96. Fact Sheet on the Pennsylvania Avenue Plan, n.d., BOTR-GWU, box 310, folder 2. According to urban historian Zachary Schrag, "Rather than massive demolition, they envisioned public improvements throughout downtown, coupled with 'spot action' to remove pockets of blight." Zachary Schrag, *The Great Society Subway*, 203.

97. Memo, Edward B. Webb Jr. to Council Members, June 21, 1974, CCR-GWU, box 24.

98. Benjamin Forgey, "At Long Last the Phoenix May Be Stirring," *WS*, April 15, 1974.

99. Berry, "Statement of Max Berry, Chairman PADC, before House Subcommittee on Government Operations and Metropolitan Affairs." On the history of and fight to preserve the Old Post Office building, see Kassan, "The Old Post Office Building in Washington, D.C."

100. "Is the Convention Center Necessary?," *Washington Afro-American*, October 1, 1977; Bart Barnes, "Sports Arena Fight: Progress vs. People: D.C. Area Residents, Businessmen at Odds on Sports Arena Plan," *WP*, February 13, 1972. On the building and business of convention centers, see Petersen, *Convention Centers, Stadiums and Arenas*; Fenich, *The Dollars and Sense of Convention Centers*; Robert R. Nelson, "Convention Centers as Catalysts for Local Economic Development"; Ford, *America's New Downtowns*, chapter 4; Van Uffelen, *Convention Centers*.

101. National Capital Planning Commission, "The Dwight D. Eisenhower Memorial Bicentennial Civic Center (never built)"; Washington Area Convention and Visitors Bureau, "Brochure for the Eisenhower Memorial Bicentennial Civic Center."

102. Stephen Green, "Sports, Civic Center Backed: D.C. Sports Arena, Convention Center Approved," *WP*, February 2, 1972.

103. Greater Washington Board of Trade, "Open Letter to President and Congress Urging Passage of Eisenhower Civic Center Bill."

104. Letter, Richard Nixon to Kenneth Gray, August 17, 1972, reprinted in *Metropolitan Washington Board of Trade News* 27, no. 8 (August 1972), BOTR-GWU, box 184, folder 33.

105. Letter, Richard Nixon to Kenneth Gray, August 17, 1972.

106. Informational Summary Proposed Convention/Sports Arena Complex Mount Vernon Square, n.d., DPR-MLKL, box 62, folder SA—CC (1 of 2); Memo, Christine Blackwell to Robert Gray, January 19, 1973, DPR-MLKL, box 63, folder SA—CC (1 of 2). The actual facility would be 550,000 square feet and would include a large exhibit space, meeting rooms, and associated facilities for convention delegates. Questions and Answers Regarding D.C. Convention Center Legislation, n.d., DPR-MLKL, box 62,

folder SA—CC (1 of 2); Dwight D. Eisenhower Memorial Bicentennial Civic Center, July 13, 1971, CCR-GWU, box 1; Summary of Proposal, July 1973, CCR-GWU, box 1.

107. Address, Richard Nixon, February 4, 1972, BOTR-GWU, box 142a, folder 25; Informational Summary Proposed Convention/Sports Arena Complex Mount Vernon Square, n.d., DPR-MLKL, box 62, folder SA—CC (1 of 2); Memo, Christine Blackwell to Robert Gray, January 19, 1973, DPR-MLKL, box 63, folder SA—CC (1 of 2).

108. Summary of Proposal, July 1973, CCR-GWU, box 1; Report, Dwight D. Eisenhower Memorial Bicentennial Civic Center, September 1973, folder Eisenhower Center (1971–74), box 9, WHCF, SMOF: Andre Buckles, RNPL; Washington, D.C., Convention Center/Sports Arena Fact Sheet, n.d., DPR-MLKL, box 64, folder CC-SA (1 of 2).

109. Bart Barnes, "Cut in Arena Site Fails to Satisfy Local Critics," *WP*, February 18, 1972; Bart Barnes, "New Hearings Are Set on Arena Proposal," *WP*, February 9, 1972; "Some Facts on the Eisenhower Convention Center," *D.C. Gazette*, November 14, 1973; Petition to U.S. Congress, Mayor-Commissioner Walter Washington, and D.C. City Council Chairman John A. Nevius Re: The Eisenhower Civic Center Memorial and the Chinese Community, CCR-GWU, box 1.

110. Barnes, "Cut in Arena Site Fails to Satisfy Local Critics."

111. Barnes, "Cut in Arena Site Fails to Satisfy Local Critics"; Memo, Robert Gray to Knox Banner, December 16, 1971, DPR-MLKL, box 24, folder Exec Comm 1971 A; Memo, Richard Weinstein to Knox Banner, DPR-MLKL, box 25, folder unknown.

112. Streets for the People Program, Downtown Progress, December 12, 1972, CCR-GWU, box 22.

113. Walter Washington, "We Must Keep Moving," *Metropolitan Washington Board of Trade News* 27, no. 8 (August 1972), BOTR-GWU, box 184, folder 33.

114. Walter Fauntroy, "Back the Center with Bipartisan Support," *Metropolitan Washington Board of Trade News* 27, no. 8 (August 1972), BOTR-GWU, box 184, folder 33; Gillette, *Between Justice and Beauty*, 209; Smith, *Captive Capital*, 288.

115. W. Ronald Evans, "A Piece of the Action," *Metropolitan Washington Board of Trade News* 27, no. 8 (August 1972), BOTR-GWU, box 184, folder 33.

116. "Eisenhower Center Vote Nears," *Metropolitan Washington Board of Trade News* 27, no. 8 (August 1972), BOTR-GWU, box 184, folder 33. Bart Barnes, "Sports Arena Fight: Progress vs. People: D.C. Area Residents, Businessmen at Odds on Sports Arena Plan," *WP*, February 13, 1972. Other factors contributed to the elimination of the arena from the plan. During the summer of 1972, Abe Pollin, D.C. businessman and owner of the Baltimore Bullets NBA franchise, was awarded a new NHL franchise. He wanted to consolidate his teams into one Washington arena and agreed to let his teams play in the Eisenhower Civic Center, provided it could be ready for the 1974–75 season. As the Eisenhower project stalled, Pollin shifted gears. Much to the frustration of the Board of Trade, he began work on a privately financed arena in Largo, Maryland. Clarke, "Washington Board of Trade."

117. Letter, John W. Stadtler to Richard Nixon, n.d., folder Eisenhower Center (1971–74), box 9, WHCF, SMOF: Andre Buckles, RNPL; A bill to amend the Public Buildings Act of 1959, Revised Draft, July 31, 1972 DPR-MLKL, box 64, folder CC-SA (1 of 2).

118. Reverend Douglas Moore, "Reply to WRC-TV editorial on the Eisenhower

Bicentennial Civic Center," editorial, WRC-TV, aired February 22, 1974, transcript, CCR-GWU, box 1; Branch, *Parting the Waters*, 260–99.

119. "D.C. Groups Sue to Halt NW Center," *WP*, September 6, 1972; Memo, Christine Blackwell to Robert Gray, October 23, 1973, DPR-MLKL, box 25, folder Exec Comm (Illegible).

120. Tedson J. Meyers, "The Eisenhower Center: Its Risk . . . ," *WP*, March 9, 1974; "Halting Freeways and Blazing Trails."

121. Sam Smith, "Through Mt. Vernon Square with Bonds and Boondoggle," *D.C. Gazette*, November 1973; Sam Smith, "The Greater Washington Astrodud," *D.C. Gazette*, March 8, 1972.

122. Statement, Edmond L. Kanwit, before the Committee on Environment and Business Development of the District of Columbia City Council, November 27, 1973, CCR-GWU, box 1.

123. Statement, Edmond L. Kanwit, before the Committee on Environment and Business Development of the District of Columbia City Council, November 27, 1973, CCR-GWU, box 1.

124. Martin F. Nolan, "Unconventional Proposal," *WS*, April 10, 1977. Nolan was a few decades early in his suggestion. In 2006, the city council approved legislation to name the newest convention center, built in 2003, after the city's first home rule mayor, Walter Washington.

125. Petition to U.S. Congress, Mayor-Commissioner Walter Washington, and D.C. City Council Chairman John A. Nevius Re: The Eisenhower Civic Center Memorial and the Chinese Community, CCR-GWU, box 1; Memo, Tedson Meyers to D.C. City Council members, December 15, 1973, CCR-GWU, box 1. For more on Washington's Chinese community, see Chow, "From Pennsylvania Avenue to H Street, NW."

126. Stephen Green, "Rep. Diggs Fights Vote on NW Center," *WP*, March 9, 1974.

127. Kirk Scharfenberg, "2 Women to Get Council Seats," *WP*, March 6, 1973; letter, Marguerite C. Selden to Charles C. Diggs Jr., December 15, 1973, CCR-GWU, box 1. In fact, only two out of the thirteen council members even stayed for the entire day of public hearings on the civic center. After the mayor's representatives and the BOT testified, the rest of the members left without listening to opponents testify against the bill.

128. David Jamison, "No Referendum," Letter to the Editor, *WP*, February 24, 1974; LaBarbara Bowman, "Referendum for Center Voted Down: Referendum for Center Denied," *WP*, February 12, 1974.

129. ARBA, *Bicentennial of the United States*, 1:7.

130. Hornblower, "James Gibson: Resignation but Not a Sense of Failure"; ARBA, *Bicentennial of the United States*, 1:16, 100, 253; Stephen J. Lynton and Patricia Camp, "Ford Leads Solemn July 4 Tribute," *WP*, July 3, 1976; Paul Hodge and Martin Weil, "20,000 Attend Visitor Center Debut," *WP*, July 5, 1976; Lynton, "Bicentennial Projects Shows Split in City"; ARBA, *Visitor's Guide to the Nation's Capital*. See also Wright, "White City to White Elephant."

131. Derthick, "Defeat at Fort Lincoln"; Flanagan, "Lyndon Johnson, Community Action, and Management of the Administrative State," 601.

132. Smith, *Captive Capital*, 280; Burby, Weiss, and Zehner, "A National Evaluation of Community Services and the Quality of Life in American New Towns"; Letter, Bill Hart to Richard Nixon, October 19, 1972, folder Washington Bicentennial (1972), box 26, WHCF, SMOF: Andre Buckles, RNPL; Gillette, *Between Justice and Beauty*, 179. For a comprehensive examination of Fort Lincoln, see Derthick, "Defeat at Fort Lincoln."

133. Letter, Bill Hart to Richard Nixon, October 19, 1972, folder Washington Bicentennial (1972), box 26, WHCF, SMOF: Andre Buckles, RNPL; Derthick, "Defeat at Fort Lincoln," 28; Smith, *Captive Capital*, 220; Gillette, *Between Justice and Beauty*, 184–85.

134. Maddison, "'In Chains 400 Years . . . and *Still* in Chains in DC!,'" 173; Willard Clopton Jr., "Rights 'Invasion' Plan Puts Bolling on Alert," *WP*, July 31, 1966.

135. Harrison Young and Peter Winterble, "Coalition Invades Bolling, Promptly Gets Tour," *WP*, August 3, 1966; "A Tent at Bolling," *WP*, August 4, 1966; Jack Eisen, "Proposal to Keep Bolling, Anacostia under Military Control Draws Fire," *WP*, August 12, 1966; Lewis, *District of Columbia*, 127; Memo, Dana Mead to Richard Nixon, May 31, 1973, folder Anacostia (1972–73), box 2, WHCF, SMOF: Andre Buckles, RNPL; Gillette, *Between Justice and Beauty*, 179.

136. Statement, John Nevius to the Federal Projects Committee, National Capital Planning Commission, n.d., CCR-GWU, box 22; Letter, Sterling Tucker to Ben Reifel, March 1, 1973, CCR-GWU, box 22; Lewis, *District of Columbia*, 128; Smith, *Captive Capital*, 77.

137. Hornblower, "James Gibson: Resignation but Not a Sense of Failure."

138. Lynton, "Bicentennial Projects Shows Split in City"; Adam Bernstein, "A. Knighton Stanley, a Civil Rights Leader and D.C. Pastor, Dies at 76," *WP*, September 25, 2013.

139. Zaretsky, *No Direction Home*, 154; "The Bicentennial Blues."

140. Vernon E. Jordan, "To Be Equal," *BAA*, July 31, 1976.

141. ARBA, *Bicentennial of the United States*, 1:197.

142. "Freedom Train Spans 200 Years of History," *BAA*, November 8, 1975.

143. "Freedom Train Runs Out of Steam," *WP*, March 29, 1975; Margot Hornblower, "Capital Area May Shunt the Freedom Train," *WP*, January 30, 1976; "Freedom Train Will Arrive in Area on Friday," *WP*, September 23, 1976; Lynn Darling, "Freedom Train: Short, Dazzling Trip," *WP*, September 26, 1976. The train, reminiscent of the 1947–49 project of the same name, carried historical documents as well as an assortment of cultural items, including a *Vogue* magazine cover, a model of the Dallas–Fort Worth airport, and a "wetback disguise," used by Mexicans to cross the border undetected. It visited 137 cities in forty-eight states by the end of 1976. The sponsoring corporations, including Pepsico, General Motors, and Kraftco, put up the seed money for the project; the remainder, approximately $13 million out of the $18 million budgeted, was raised from foundations, sales of merchandise on the train, and from the $1 to $1.50 admission tickets. Margot Hornblower, "Ford Talks about Train for Freedom," *WP*, December 20, 1974; ARBA, *The Bicentennial of the United States of America*, 1:119, 253. For more on the earlier Freedom Train, see Kammen, *Mystic Chords of Memory*, 573–76; Little, "The Freedom Train"; "Freedom Train Spans 200 Years of History," *BAA*, November 8, 1975.

144. Notes for Bob Linowes for breakfast meeting with major contributors, December 28, 1977, BOTR-GWU, box 310, folder 2.

CONCLUSION

1. LaBarbara Bowman, "Alexander Opens Race for Mayor," *WP*, May 10, 1974.

2. Jay Mathews, "City's 1st Mayoral Race, as Innocent as Young Love," *WP*, October 11, 1999; Judy Luce Mann, "Washington Announces for Mayor," *WP*, May 12, 1974.

3. Alice Bonner, "Absence Saps D.C. Influence," *WP*, November 23, 1972.

4. Megan Rosenfeld, "Barry, Moore Lead Parties in At-Large City Council Races," *WP*, September 11, 1974.

5. ANCs presented their positions and recommendations to District government agencies, the executive branch, and the city council. See Council of the District of Columbia, "Office of the Advisory Neighborhood Commissions."

6. Valk, "'Mother Power,'" 39; Smith, *Captive Capital*, 120; Diner, "The Black Majority," 261; Lewis, *District of Columbia*, 192.

7. Smith, *Captive Capital*, 120; Diner, "The Black Majority," 261; Lewis, *District of Columbia*, 192.

8. Gillette, *Between Justice and Beauty*, 191.

9. Gillette, *Between Justice and Beauty*, 191.

10. Vernon Loeb, "Barry Brings Halt to Turbulent D.C. Saga," *WP*, May 22, 1998.

11. Gillette, *Between Justice and Beauty*, 190; Ruble, *Washington's U Street*, 230; Asch and Musgrove, *Chocolate City*, 394.

12. Leon, "Marion Barry, Jr.," 77; Gillette, *Between Justice and Beauty*, 197.

13. Leon, "Marion Barry, Jr.," 78–79.

14. Leon, "Marion Barry, Jr.," 80.

15. "Convention Center Impasse," *WP*, October 19, 1977; Zachary Schrag, *The Great Society Subway*, 123; "Hope Remains for Convention Center Funds," WTOP-TV 9, September 12–13, 1977, DPR-MLKL, box 66, folder SA-CC. Support for the project came from the city's elected political bodies, the Advisory Neighborhood Commission covering the site area, the Chinese community that would have been dislocated, MWPHA, VOICE, and business organizations such as the BOT, Chamber of Commerce, Downtown Progress, and Washington Hotel Association. Organized labor, such as the Hotel and Restaurant Employees Union Local 25, the Greater Washington Central Labor Council, and the Washington Building and Construction Trades Council also lent their support to the project. Major Points about the Washington Civic Center, August 19, 1977, DPR-MLKL, box 65, folder: Sports Arena Convention and Civic Center.

16. Fauntroy, *Home Rule or House Rule?*, 119.

17. Kenneth Bredemeier and Mary Jordan, "Downtown Shaking Off Riot Images," *WP*, April 8, 1988.

18. Bednar, *L'Enfant's Legacy*, 24; Gutheim and Lee, *Worthy of the Nation*, 358; Gordon, "Statement of Karen Gordon on Behalf of Don't Tear It Down."

19. John Mintz, "Investors Reclaiming Riot Corridors," *WP*, April 7, 1988.

20. Muhammad, "Power and Punishment: Two New Books about Race and Crime."

21. By 1991, an estimated 42 percent of black men ages eighteen to thirty-five were in jail, on probation, or being sought on a warrant. Fauntroy, *Home Rule or House Rule?*, 134; Muhammad, "Power and Punishment." For a different perspective on Burtell Jefferson, see Williams and Kellough, "Leadership with an Enduring Impact."

22. Muhammad, "Power and Punishment."

23. Fauntroy, "Home Rule for the District of Columbia," 35; Fauntroy, *Home Rule or House Rule?*, 12, 78.

24. Walters, "Introduction: An Administered System of Government," 9; Fauntroy, *Home Rule or House Rule?*, 110–11, 124; Philip Schrag, "The Future of District of Columbia Home Rule," 314.

25. Donald P. Baker and Michael Isikoff, "Rep. Parris Emerges as District's 1980s Version of Broyhill," *WP*, September 28, 1981.

26. Fauntroy, *Home Rule or House Rule?*, 124–25.

27. Valk, "'Mother Power,'" 36, 50–51; "Voices of Feminism Oral History Project: Narrators." For more on black radical feminists' fights during the 1970s, see Valk, *Radical Sisters*.

28. Valk, "'Mother Power,'" 36, 49–52; Valk, *Radical Sisters*, 8.

29. It passed the House 289–127 and Senate 67–32. Sixteen states ratified it. Fauntroy, "Home Rule for the District of Columbia," 37; Asch and Musgrove, *Chocolate City*, 380–81.

30. Quoted in Fauntroy, *Home Rule or House Rule?*, 3.

31. Zigas, *Left with Few Rights*, 69.

32. Fauntroy, *Home Rule or House Rule?*, 15–17, 105, 107, 110–11, 138; Zigas, *Left with Few Rights*, 69.

33. Fauntroy, *Home Rule or House Rule?*, 16.

34. In 1990, Walter Fauntroy stepped down from the congressional seat he had held since 1971 in order to run for mayor. Musgrove, "'Statehood Is Far More Difficult,'" 10; "The Vision Shared: The Republican Platform, Uniting Our Family, Our Country, Our World."

35. Fauntroy, "Home Rule for the District of Columbia," 37–38; U.S. Statutes at Large, "District of Columbia Financial Responsibility and Management Assistance Act of 1995."

36. Quoted in Zigas, *Left with Few Rights*, 70; Yolanda Woodlee, "Uncertainties Arise on Morning after GOP Triumph, Barry Can Expect Cool Reception on Capitol Hill," *WP*, November 10, 1994.

37. Fauntroy, *Home Rule or House Rule?*, 172, 188, 199; Fauntroy, "Home Rule for the District of Columbia," 37–38.

38. Tang, "The Old Lorton, Virginia Prison Is Being Turned into Homes."

39. Fauntroy, *Home Rule or House Rule?*, 183; Fauntroy, "Home Rule for the District of Columbia," 38–39; Zigas, *Left with Few Rights*, 72. By September 2001 the city had succeeded in passing four balanced budgets, gaining a stable bond rating, and had repaid its U.S. Treasury loans. With those targets met, the city fulfilled the criteria set forth in the 1995 legislation to move out from under the supervision of the Control Board. On September 30, 2001, the Control Board officially suspended its operations

and transferred home rule authority back to the mayor and city council. Zigas, *Left with Few Rights*, 78.

40. Daryl B. Harris, "The High Tide of Pragmatic Black Politic," 116.

41. District branch letterhead, Part 26—Selected Branch Files, 1940–1955, reel 7, series A, *Papers of the National Association for the Advancement of Colored People*, microfilm, Sterling Memorial Library, Yale University.

BIBLIOGRAPHY

ARCHIVAL COLLECTIONS

Austin, Texas
Lyndon Baines Johnson Presidential Library
New Haven, Connecticut
Yale University, Sterling Memorial Library
Papers of the National Association for the Advancement of Colored People
Student Nonviolent Coordinating Committee Papers, 1959–1972
Washington, D.C.
The George Washington University, Special Collections Research Center, Gelman Library
Greater Washington Board of Trade Records
District of Columbia City Council Records
Committee of 100 on the Federal City Records (Part I)
Walter E. Fauntroy Papers
Howard University, Moorland-Spingarn Research Center
Ralph Bunche Oral History Collection
Martin Luther King Jr. Memorial Library
D.C. Community Archives
District of Columbia Federation of Citizens Associations Records
Julius W. Hobson Papers
Downtown Progress Records
Yorba Linda, California
Richard Nixon Presidential Library

GOVERNMENT DOCUMENTS

House Debate, Congressional Record (August 9, 1967), 21960.

The Pennsylvania Avenue Plan 1974, Pennsylvania Avenue Development Corporation, October 1974.

President's Commission on Crime in the District of Columbia. *Report on the Metropolitan Police Department*. Vol. 1. Washington, D.C.: U.S. Government Printing Office, 1966.

Senate Debate, Congressional Record (July 10, 1973), 22935–77.

U.S. House Committee on the District of Columbia, Anti-Riots Hearing before Subcommittee No. 4, 90th Cong., 1st sess., 1967.

U.S. Riot Commission. *Report of the National Advisory Commission on Civil Disorders*. Washington, D.C.: U.S. Government Printing Office, 1968.

U.S. Statutes at Large. "District of Columbia Financial Responsibility and Management Assistance Act of 1995." April 17, 1995, 109 Stat. 97.

LEGAL CASES

Aaron v. Cooper, 358 U.S. 1, 78 S.Ct. 1399 (1958)
Berman v. Parker, 348 U.S. 26 (1954)
Brown v. Board of Education, 347 U.S. 483 (1954)
Hobson v. Hansen, 269 F. Supp. 401 (D.C. 1967)

NEWSPAPERS

Associated Press
Baltimore Afro-American
Boston Globe
Chicago Defender
Chicago Tribune
D.C. Gazette
Los Angeles Times
New York Daily News
New York Times
Pittsburgh Courier
The Sunday Star
Toledo Blade
Wall Street Journal
Washington Afro-American
Washington Daily News
The Washingtonian
Washington Post
Washington Star

BOOKS, ARTICLES, DISSERTATIONS, AND THESES

Abbott, Carl. "Perspectives on Urban Economic Planning: The Case of Washington, D.C., since 1880." *Public Historian* 11, no. 2 (Spring 1989): 5–21.

———. *Political Terrain: Washington, D.C., from Tidewater Town to Global Metropolis*. Chapel Hill: University of North Carolina Press, 1999.

Abu-Lughod, Janet L. *Race, Space and Riots in Chicago, New York, and Los Angeles*. New York: Oxford University Press, 2007.

Agronsky, Jonathan. *Marion Barry: The Politics of Race*. Latham, N.Y.: British American Publishers, 1991.

Al-Amin, Jamil (H. Rap Brown). *Die, Nigger, Die!* New York: Dial, 1969.

Alexander, Michelle. *The New Jim Crow: Mass Incarceration in the Age of Colorblindness*. New York: New Press, 2012.

Ammon, Francesca Russello. "Commemoration amid Criticism: The Mixed Legacy of Urban Renewal in Southwest Washington, D.C." *Journal of Planning History* 8, no. 3 (August 2009): 175–220.

Anderson, Terry H. *The Movement and the Sixties*. New York: Oxford University Press, 1995.

ARBA (American Revolution Bicentennial Administration). *The Bicentennial of the United States of America: A Final Report to the People.* Washington: American Revolution Bicentennial Administration, 1977.

———. *National Bicentennial Ethnic and Racial Council Conference Report, January 20–22, 1975.* Washington, D.C.: ARBA, 1975.

———. *Visitor's Guide to the Nation's Capital.* Washington, D.C.: ARBA, 1976.

Arsenault, Raymond. *Freedom Riders: 1961 and the Struggle for Racial Justice.* New York: Oxford University Press, 2006.

Asch, Christopher, and Derek Musgrove. *Chocolate City: A History of Race and Democracy in the Nation's Capital.* Chapel Hill: University of North Carolina Press, 2017.

Ashmore, Susan Youngblood. *Carry It On: The War on Poverty and the Civil Rights Movement in Alabama, 1964–1972.* Athens: University of Georgia Press, 2008.

Bailey, Beth, and David Farber, eds. *America in the Seventies.* Lawrence: University Press of Kansas, 2004.

Banks, Christopher P. *Judicial Politics in the D.C. Circuit Court.* Baltimore: Johns Hopkins University Press, 1999.

Barber, Lucy G. *Marching on Washington: The Forging of an American Political Tradition.* Berkeley: University of California Press, 2002.

Bard, Morton, and Robert Shellow. *Issues in Law Enforcement: Essays and Case Studies.* Reston, Va.: Reston Publishing Company, 1976.

Barkan, Steven E. *Protesters on Trial: Criminal Justice in the Southern Civil Rights and Vietnam Anti-war Movements.* New Brunswick, N.J.: Rutgers University Press, 1985.

Barlow, Melissa Hickman. "Race and the Problem of Crime in *Time* and *Newsweek* Cover Stories, 1946–1995." *Social Justice* 25, no. 2 (Summer 1998): 149–83.

Baum, Dan. *Smoke and Mirrors: The War on Drugs and the Politics of Failure.* Boston: Little, Brown, 1996.

Bauman, John F. *Public Housing, Race and Renewal: Urban Planning in Philadelphia, 1920–1974.* Philadelphia: Temple University Press, 1987.

Beckett, Katherine. *Making Crime Pay: Law and Order in Contemporary American Politics.* New York: Oxford University Press, 1997.

Beckett, Katherine, and Steve Herbert. *Banished: The New Social Control in Urban America.* New York: Oxford University Press, 2009.

Beckett, Katherine, and Bruce Western. "Governing Social Marginality: Welfare, Incarceration and the Transformation of State Policy." In *Mass Imprisonment: Social Causes and Consequences*, edited by David Garland, 35–50. London: Sage, 2001.

Bednar, Michael. *L'Enfant's Legacy: Public Open Spaces in Washington, D.C.* Baltimore: Johns Hopkins University Press, 2006.

Bednarek, Janet R. Daly. *Changing Image of the City: Planning for Downtown Omaha, 1945–1973.* Lincoln: University of Nebraska Press, 1992.

Bell, Inge Powell. *CORE and the Strategy of Nonviolence.* New York: Random House, 1968.

Berman, William C. *The Politics of Civil Rights in the Truman Administration.* Columbus: Ohio State University Press, 1970.

"The Bicentennial Blues." *Ebony*, June 1976, 152–53.

Biles, Roger. *The South and the New Deal*. Lexington: University Press of Kentucky, 1994.

Bloom, Joshua, and Waldo E. Martin Jr. *Black against Empire: The History and Politics of the Black Panther Party*. Oakland: University of California Press, 2013.

Bloom, Nicholas Dagen. *Merchant of Illusion: James Rouse, America's Salesman of the Businessman's Utopia*. Columbus: Ohio State University Press, 2004.

Blum, John Morton. *Years of Discord: American Politics and Society, 1961–1974*. New York: W. W. Norton, 1991.

Bodnar, John E. *Remaking America: Public Memory, Commemoration, and Patriotism in the Twentieth Century*. Princeton, N.J.: Princeton University Press, 1992.

Booker, Simeon. "Washington's Civil Rights Maverick." *Ebony*, May 1965, 140–45.

Borchert, James. *Alley Life in Washington: Family, Community, Religion, and Folklife in the City, 1850–1970*. Urbana: University of Illinois Press, 1980.

Branch, Taylor. *Parting the Waters: America in the King Years 1954–1963*. New York: Simon & Schuster, 1988.

———. *Pillar of Fire: America in the King Years, 1963–1965*. New York: Simon & Schuster, 1998.

Burby, Raymond J., III, Shirley F. Weiss, and Robert B. Zehner. "A National Evaluation of Community Services and the Quality of Life in American New Towns." *Public Administration Review* 35, no. 3 (May–June 1975): 229–39.

Button, James W. *Black Violence: Political Impact of the 1960s Riots*. Princeton, N.J.: Princeton University Press, 1978.

Califano, Joseph A. *The Triumph and Tragedy of Lyndon Johnson: The White House Years*. 1991; reprint, New York: Simon & Schuster, 2015.

Capozzola, Christopher. "'It Makes You Want to Believe in the Country': Celebrating the Bicentennial in an Age of Limits." In *America in the Seventies*, edited by Beth Bailey and David Farber, 29–49. Lawrence: University Press of Kansas, 2004.

Carmichael, Stokely, and Ekwueme Michael Thelwell. *Ready for Revolution: The Life and Struggles of Stokely Carmichael (Kwame Ture)*. New York: Scribner, 2003.

Carson, Clayborne. *In Struggle: SNCC and the Black Awakening of the 1960s*. Cambridge, Mass.: Harvard University Press, 1981.

Cary, Francine Curro, ed. *Urban Odyssey: A Multicultural History of Washington, DC*. Washington, D.C.: Smithsonian Institution Press, 1996.

Chafe, William. *Civilities and Civil Rights: Greensboro, North Carolina, and the Black Struggle for Freedom*. New York: Oxford University Press, 1980.

Cha-Jua, Sundiata Keita, and Clarence Lang. "'The 'Long Movement' as Vampire: Temporal and Spatial Fallacies in Recent Black Freedom Studies." *Journal of African American History* 92, no. 2 (Spring 2007): 265–88.

Chow, Esther Ngan-ling. "From Pennsylvania Avenue to H Street, NW: The Transformation of Washington's Chinatown." In *Urban Odyssey*, edited by Francine Curro Cary, 190–207. Washington, D.C.: Smithsonian Institution Press, 1996.

Cleaver, Kathleen, and George Katsiaficas, eds. *Liberation, Imagination, and the Black Panther Party: A New Look at the Panthers and Their Legacy*. New York: Routledge, 2001.

Cohen, Lizabeth. *A Consumers' Republic: The Politics of Mass Consumption in Postwar America*. New York: Knopf, 2003.
"Congress Clears Controversial D.C. Crime Control Bill." *CQ Almanac* 1970, 26th ed. Washington, D.C.: Congressional Quarterly, 1971: 05-208–05-219.
Countryman, Matthew. *Up South: Civil Rights and Black Power in Philadelphia*. Philadelphia: University of Pennsylvania Press, 2006.
Crespino, Joseph. *In Search of Another Country: Mississippi and the Conservative Counterrevolution*. Princeton, N.J.: Princeton University Press, 2007.
Cronin, Thomas E., Tania Z. Cronin, and Michael F. Milakovich. *U.S. v. Crime in the Streets*. Bloomington: University of Indiana Press, 1981.
Cummings, Scott, ed. *Business Elites and Urban Development: Case Studies and Critical Perspectives*. Albany: State University of New York Press, 1988.
"Cutting the Crime Rate: How Nation's Capital Does It." *U.S. News and World Report*, April 10, 1972.
Dallek, Robert. *Flawed Giant: Lyndon Johnson and His Times, 1961–1973*. New York: Oxford University Press, 1998.
Dávila, Arlene M. *Barrio Dreams: Puerto Ricans, Latinos, and the Neoliberal City*. Berkeley: University of California Press, 2004.
Davis, Mike. *City of Quartz: Excavating the Future in Los Angeles*. London: Verso, 1990.
"D.C. School Boycott Called Off." *Jet*, April 16, 1964.
Derthick, Martha. *City Politics in Washington, D.C.* Boston: Joint Center for Urban Studies of the Massachusetts Institute of Technology and Harvard University, 1962.
———. "Defeat at Fort Lincoln." *Public Interest* 20 (Summer 1970): 3–39.
Diner, Steven J. "The Black Majority: Race and Politics in the Nation's Capital." In *Snowbelt Cities: Metropolitan Politics in the Northeast and Midwest since World War II*, edited by Richard M. Bernard, 247–66. Bloomington: Indiana University Press, 1990.
———. *Democracy, Federalism and the Governance of the Nation's Capital, 1790–1974*. Washington: Center for Applied Research and Urban Policy, University of the District of Columbia, 1987.
Dittmer, John. *Local People: The Struggle for Civil Rights in Mississippi*. Urbana: University of Illinois Press, 1994.
Donaghy, Daniel. "Walter Fauntroy." In *Encyclopedia of African American History, 1896 to the Present: From the Age of Segregation to the Twenty-First Century*, edited by Paul Finkelman, 196. New York: Oxford University Press, 2009.
Drea, Edward. *McNamara, Clifford, and the Burdens of Vietnam, 1965–1969*. Vol. 6 of Secretaries of Defense Historical Series. Washington, D.C.: Historical Office, Office of the Secretary of Defense, 2011.
Durfee, Michael. "Crack Era Reform: A Brief History of Crack Cocaine and the Rise of Mass Incarceration." Ph.D. diss., State University of New York, Buffalo, 2015.
Edsall, Thomas Byrne, and Mary Edsall. *Chain Reaction: The Impact of Race, Rights, and Taxes on American Politics*. New York: Norton, 1991.

Elkin, Stephen L. "Twentieth Century Urban Regimes." *Journal of Urban Affairs* 7 (Spring 1985): 11–28.

Elkins, Alex. "Stand Our Ground: The Street Justice of Urban American Riots, 1900–1968." *Journal of Urban History* 42 (March 2016): 419–37.

Enns, Peter K. *Incarceration Nation: How the United States Became the Most Punitive Democracy in the World*. New York: Cambridge University Press, 2016.

Epstein, Edward Jay. *Agency of Fear: Opiates and Political Power in America*. New York: Putnam, 1977.

Fairclough, Adam. *Race and Democracy: The Civil Rights Struggle in Louisiana, 1915–1972*. Athens: University of Georgia Press, 1995.

———. *To Redeem the Soul of America: The Southern Christian Leadership Conference and Martin Luther King, Jr.* Athens: University of Georgia Press, 1987.

Farmer, James. *Lay Bare the Heart: An Autobiography of the Civil Rights Movement*. New York: Arbor House, 1985.

Fauntroy, Michael K. "Home Rule for the District of Columbia." In *Democratic Destiny and the District of Columbia: Federal Politics and Public Policy*, edited by Ronald W. Walters and Toni-Michelle C. Travis, 21–44. Lanham, Md.: Lexington Books, 2010.

———. *Home Rule or House Rule? Congress and the Erosion of Local Governance in the District of Columbia*. Lanham, Md.: University Press of America, 2003.

Feffer, Andrew. "Show Down in Center City: Staging Redevelopment and Citizenship in Bicentennial Philadelphia, 1974–1977." *Journal of Urban History* 30, no. 6 (September 2004): 791–825.

Felker-Kantor, Max. *Policing Los Angeles: Race, Resistance, and the Rise of the LAPD*. Chapel Hill: University of North Carolina Press, 2018.

Fenich, George Girard. *The Dollars and Sense of Convention Centers*. New Brunswick, N.J.: Rutgers University Press, 1992.

Fergus, Devin. *Liberalism, Black Power, and the Making of American Politics, 1965–1980*. Athens: University of Georgia Press, 2009.

Fine, Sidney. *Violence in the Model City: The Cavanagh Administration, Race Relations, and the Detroit Riot of 1967*. Ann Arbor: University of Michigan Press, 1989.

Flamm, Michael W. *Law and Order: Street Crime, Civil Unrest, and the Crisis of Liberalism in the 1960s*. New York: Columbia University Press, 2005.

Flanagan, Richard M. "Lyndon Johnson, Community Action, and Management of the Administrative State." *Presidential Studies Quarterly* 31, no. 4 (2001): 585–608.

Fleegler, Robert L. "Theodore G. Bilbo and the Decline of Public Racism, 1938–1947." *Journal of Mississippi History* 68 (Spring 2006): 1–27.

Fleischmann, Arnold, and Joe R. Feagin. "The Politics of Growth-Oriented Urban Alliances." *Urban Affairs Quarterly* 23 (December 1987): 207–32.

Ford, Larry R. *America's New Downtowns: Revitalization or Reinvention?* Baltimore: Johns Hopkins University Press, 2003.

Forget, Evelyn L. "A Tale of Two Communities: Fighting Poverty in the Great Society (1964–68)." *History of Political Economy* 43, no. 1 (2011): 199–223.

Forman, James, Jr. *Locking Up Our Own: Crime and Punishment in Black America*. New York: Farrar, Straus and Giroux, 2017.

Fortner, Michael Javen. *Black Silent Majority: The Rockefeller Drug Laws and the Politics of Punishment*. Cambridge, Mass.: Harvard University Press, 2015.
Garland, David. *The Culture of Control: Crime and Social Order in Contemporary Society*. Chicago: University of Chicago Press, 2001.
Garrow, David J. *Bearing the Cross: Martin Luther King, Jr., and the Southern Christian Leadership Conference*. New York: William Morrow, 1986.
Germany, Kent. *New Orleans after the Promises: Poverty, Citizenship, and the Search for the Great Society*. Athens: University of Georgia Press, 2007.
Gest, Ted. *Crime and Politics: Big Government's Erratic Campaign for Law and Order*. New York: Oxford University Press, 2001.
Gilbert, Ben W. *Ten Blocks from the White House: Anatomy of the Washington Riots of 1968*. New York: Frederick A. Praeger, 1968.
Gilens, Martin. *Why Americans Hate Welfare: Race, Media, and the Politics of Antipoverty Policy*. Chicago: University of Chicago Press, 1999.
Gillette, Howard. *Between Justice and Beauty: Race, Planning, and the Failure of Urban Policy in Washington, D.C.* Baltimore: Johns Hopkins University Press, 1995.
Gillette, Howard, Jr. "A National Workshop for Urban Policy: The Metropolitanization of Washington, 1946–1968." *Public History* 7 (Winter 1985): 7–27.
Gillon, Steven M. *Separate and Unequal: The Kerner Commission and the Unraveling of American Liberalism*. New York: Basic Books, 2018.
Gilmore, Glenda Elizabeth. *Defying Dixie: The Radical Roots of Civil Rights, 1919–1950*. New York: W. W. Norton & Co., 2008.
Gitlin, Todd. *The Sixties: Years of Hope, Days of Rage*. New York: Bantam Books, 1987.
Goldstein, Alyosha. *Poverty in Common: The Politics of Community Action during the American Century*. Durham, N.C.: Duke University Press, 2012.
Gonda, Jeffrey D. *Unjust Deeds: The Restrictive Covenant Cases and the Making of the Civil Rights Movement*. Chapel Hill: University of North Carolina Press, 2015.
Gordon, Alain R., and Norval Moriss. "Presidential Commissions and the Law Enforcement Administration." In *American Violence and Public Policy: An Update of the National Commission on the Causes and Prevention of Violence*, edited by Lynn A. Curtis, 117–32. New Haven, Conn.: Yale University Press, 1985.
Gottidiener, Mark. *The Social Production of Urban Space*. Austin: University of Texas Press, 1985.
Gottschalk, Marie. *The Prison and the Gallows: The Politics of Mass Incarceration in America*. Cambridge, Mass.: Cambridge University Press, 2006.
Grady-Willis, Winston. *Challenging U.S. Apartheid: Atlanta and Black Struggles for Human Rights, 1960–1977*. Durham, N.C.: Duke University Press, 2006.
Green, Constance. *The Secret City: A History of Race Relations in the Nation's Capital*. Princeton, N.J.: Princeton University Press, 1967.
———. *Washington: Capital City, 1879–1950*. Princeton, N.J.: Princeton University Press, 1963.
Gustafson, Kaaryn S. *Cheating Welfare: Public Assistance and the Criminalization of Poverty*. New York: New York University Press, 2011.

Gutheim, Frederick Albert, and Antoinette J. Lee. *Worthy of the Nation: The History of Planning for the National Capital*. Washington, D.C.: Smithsonian Institution Press, 1977.

Hackworth, Jason. *The Neoliberal City: Governance, Ideology, and Development in American Urbanism*. Ithaca, N.Y.: Cornell University Press, 2007.

Hall, Jacquelyn Dowd. "The Long Civil Rights Movement and the Political Uses of the Past." *Journal of American History* 91, no. 4 (March 2005): 1233–63.

Harris, Charles Wesley. *Congress and the Governance of the Nation's Capital: The Conflict of Federal and Local Interests*. Washington, D.C.: Georgetown University Press, 1995.

Harris, Charles Wesley, and Alvin Thornton. *Perspectives of Political Power in the District of Columbia: The Views and Opinions of 100 Members of the Local Political Elite*. Washington, D.C.: National Institute of Public Management, 1981.

Harris, Daryl B. "The High Tide of Pragmatic Black Politic: Mayor Anthony Williams and the Suppression of Black Interests." In *Democratic Destiny and the District of Columbia*, edited by Ronald W. Walters and Toni-Michelle Travis, 103–20. Lanham, Md.: Lexington Books, 2010.

Harris, Fred R., and Lynn A. Curtis. *Locked in the Poorhouse: Cities, Race, and Poverty in the United States*. Lanham, Md.: Rowman & Littlefield, 1998.

Harris, Richard. *Building a Market: The Rise of the Home Improvement Industry, 1914–1960*. Chicago: University of Chicago Press, 2012.

Harvey, David. *The Urban Experience*. Baltimore: Johns Hopkins University Press, 1985.

Hechinger, John W., and Gavin Taylor. "Black and Blue: The D.C. City Council vs. Police Brutality." *Washington History* 11, no. 2 (1999): 4–23.

Hess, Stephen. *The Professor and the President: Daniel Patrick Moynihan in the Nixon White House*. Washington, D.C.: Brookings Institution Press, 2015.

Higginbotham, Evelyn Brooks. Foreword to *Freedom North: Black Freedom Struggles outside the South, 1940–1980*, edited by Jeanne Theoharis and Komozi Woodard, xiii–xiv. New York: Palgrave Macmillan, 2003.

Hill, Lance E. *The Deacons for Defense: Armed Resistance and the Civil Rights Movement*. Chapel Hill: University of North Carolina Press, 2004.

Hinton, Elizabeth. *From the War on Poverty to the War on Crime: The Making of Mass Incarceration in America*. Cambridge, Mass.: Harvard University Press, 2016.

Hirsch, Arnold R. *Making the Second Ghetto: Race and Housing in Chicago, 1940–1960*. Chicago: University of Chicago Press, 1983.

Holder, Calvin B. "Racism toward Black African Diplomats during the Kennedy Administration." *Journal of Black Studies* 14, no. 1 (September 1983): 31–48.

Holloway, Jonathan Scott. *Confronting the Veil: Abram Harris Jr., E. Franklin Frazier, and Ralph Bunche, 1919–1941*. Chapel Hill: University of North Carolina Press, 2002.

Honey, Michael K. *Going Down Jericho Road: The Memphis Strike, Martin Luther King's Last Campaign*. New York: W. W. Norton, 2007.

———. *To the Promised Land: Martin Luther King and the Fight for Economic Justice*. New York: W. W. Norton, 2018.

Hornstein, Jeffrey M. *A Nation of Realtors: A Cultural History of the Twentieth-Century American Middle Class*. Durham, N.C.: Duke University Press, 2005.
Isenberg, Alison. *Downtown America: A History of the Place and the People Who Made It*. Chicago: University of Chicago Press, 2004.
Jackson, Jesse. "Resurrection City: The Dream . . . the Accomplishments." *Ebony*, October 1968, 65–74.
Jackson, Kenneth T. *Crabgrass Frontier: The Suburbanization of the United States*. New York: Oxford University Press, 1985.
Jackson, Thomas F. *From Civil Rights to Human Rights: Martin Luther King, Jr., and the Struggle for Economic Justice*. Philadelphia: University of Pennsylvania Press, 2007.
Jacoby, Tamar. *In Someone Else's House: America's Unfinished Struggle for Integration*. New York: Free Press, 1998.
Jaffe, Harry, and Tom Sherwood. *Dream City: Race, Power, and the Decline of Washington, D.C.* New York: Simon & Schuster, 1994.
Jeffries, Hasan Kwame. *Bloody Lowndes: Civil Rights and Black Power in Alabama's Black Belt*. New York: New York University Press, 2009.
———. "SNCC, Black Power and Independent Political Party Organizing in Alabama, 1964-1966." *Journal of African American History* 91, no. 2 (Spring 2006): 171-193.
Johnson, David K. *The Lavender Scare: The Cold War Persecution of Gays and Lesbians in the Federal Government*. Chicago: University of Chicago Press, 2004.
Johnson, Hayes. *Dusk at the Mountain: The Negro, the Nation, and the Capital*. New York: Doubleday & Co., 1962.
Jones, Beverly W. "Before Montgomery and Greensboro: The Desegregation Movement in the District of Columbia, 1950–1953." *Phylon* 43, no. 2 (1982): 144–54.
Joseph, Peniel E. "The Black Power Movement, Democracy, and America in the King Years." *American Historical Review* 114, no. 4 (October 2009): 1001–16.
———. *Stokely: A Life*. New York: Basic Books, 2014.
———. *Waiting 'til the Midnight Hour: A Narrative History of Black Power in America*. New York: Henry Holt and Company, 2006.
———, ed. *The Black Power Movement: Rethinking the Civil Rights–Black Power Era*. New York: Routledge, 2006.
"Justice Department: The Ramsey Clark Issue." *Time*, October 18, 1968.
Kammen, Michael G. *Mystic Chords of Memory: The Transformation of Tradition in American Culture*. New York: Knopf, 1991.
Kassan, Gail Karesh. "The Old Post Office Building in Washington, D.C.: Its Past, Present and Future." *Records of the Columbia Historical Society* (1971–72): 570–95.
Katz, Cindi. "Hiding the Target: Social Reproduction in the Privatized Urban Environment." In *Postmodern Geography: Theory and Praxis*, edited by Claudio Minca, 93–111. Oxford: Blackwell, 2001.
Katz, Michael B. *The Undeserving Poor: America's Enduring Confrontation with Poverty*. New York: Oxford University Press, 2013.
———. *Why Don't American Cities Burn?* Philadelphia: University of Pennsylvania Press, 2012.

Katzman, Robert A. *Daniel Patrick Moynihan: The Intellectual in Public Life*. Washington, D.C.: Woodrow Wilson Center Press, 2004.

Kilpatrick, Judith. "Wiley Austin Branton and the Voting Rights Struggle." *University of Arkansas at Little Rock Law Review* 26, no. 4 (Summer 2004): 641–701.

King, Martin Luther, Jr. "A Time to Break Silence." In *A Testament of Hope: The Essential Writings and Speeches of Martin Luther King, Jr.*, edited by James M. Washington, 231–44. San Francisco: HarperCollins, 1986.

Knowles, Scott Gabriel. "Staying Too Long at the Fair: Philadelphia Planning and the Debacle of 1976." In *Imagining Philadelphia: Edmund Bacon and the Future of the City*, edited by Scott Gabriel Knowles, 78–111. Philadelphia: University of Pennsylvania Press, 2009.

Kohler-Hausmann, Julilly. *Getting Tough: Welfare and Imprisonment in 1970s America*. Princeton, N.J.: Princeton University Press, 2017.

———. "Guns and Butter: The Welfare State, the Carceral State, and the Politics of Exclusion in the Postwar United States." *Journal of American History* 102, no. 1 (June 2015): 87–99.

Kosek, Joseph Kip. *Acts of Conscience: Christian Nonviolence and Modern American Democracy*. New York: Columbia University Press, 2009.

Krasovic, Mark. *The Newark Frontier: Community Action in the Great Society*. Chicago: University of Chicago Press, 2016.

Kruse, Kevin. *White Flight: Atlanta and the Making of Modern Conservatism*. Princeton, N.J.: Princeton University Press, 2007.

Kweit, Robert W., and Mary Grisez Kweit. *People and Politics in Urban America*. 2nd ed. New York: Taylor & Francis, 1999.

Lassiter, Matthew D. *The Silent Majority: Suburban Politics in the Sunbelt South*. Princeton, N.J.: Princeton University Press, 2007.

Lawson, Steven F. *Running for Freedom: Civil Rights and Black Politics in America since 1941*. Philadelphia: Temple University Press, 1991.

Leon, Wilmer J., III. "Marion Barry, Jr.: A Politician for the Times." In *Democratic Destiny and the District of Columbia*, edited by Ronald W. Walters and Toni-Michelle Travis, 61–86. Lanham, Md.: Lexington Books, 2010.

Levenstein, Lisa. *A Movement without Marches: African American Women and the Politics of Poverty in Postwar Philadelphia*. Chapel Hill: University of North Carolina Press, 2009.

Levy, Peter B. "Gloria Richardson and the Civil Rights Movement in Cambridge, Maryland." In *Groundwork: Local Black Freedom Movement in America*, edited by Jeanne Theoharis and Komozi Woodard, 97–115. New York: New York University Press, 2005.

Lewis, David Levering. *District of Columbia: A Bicentennial History*. New York: Norton, 1976.

Little, Stuart J. "The Freedom Train: Citizenship and Postwar American Culture, 1946–1949." *American Studies* 34 (1993): 35–67.

Lytle, Mark H. *America's Uncivil Wars: The Sixties from Elvis to the Fall of Richard Nixon*. New York: Oxford University Press, 2006.

Maddison, Catherine. "'In Chains 400 Years . . . and *Still* in Chains in DC!': The

1966 Free DC Movement and the Challenges of Organizing in the City." *Journal of American Studies* 41, no. 1 (2007): 169–92.
Manning, Robert D. "Multicultural Washington, D.C.: The Changing Social and Economic Landscape of a Post-Industrial Metropolis." *Ethnic and Racial Studies* 21, no. 2 (March 1998): 328–55.
Mantler, Gordon K. "Black, Brown and Poor: Martin Luther King Jr., the Poor People's Campaign and Its Legacies." Ph.D. diss., Duke University, 2008.
———. *Power to the Poor: Black-Brown Coalition and the Fight for Economic Justice, 1960–1974*. Chapel Hill: University of North Carolina Press, 2013.
Marion, Nancy. *A History of Federal Crime Control Initiatives, 1960–1993*. Westport, Conn.: Praeger, 1994.
Masur, Kate. *An Example for All the Land: Emancipation and the Struggle over Equality in Washington, D.C.* Chapel Hill: University of North Carolina Press, 2010.
Matthews, Martina Pinkney. "The Politics of Julius W. Hobson, Sr., and the District of Columbia Public School System." Ph.D. diss., Ohio State University, 1981.
McGraw, James R. "An Interview with Andrew J. Young." *Christianity and Crisis* 27 (January 1968): 324–30.
McKnight, Gerald D. *The Last Crusade: Martin Luther King, Jr., the FBI, and the Poor People's Campaign*. Boulder: Westview, 1998.
Meier, August, and Elliott M. Rudwick. *CORE: A Study in the Civil Rights Movement, 1942–1968*. New York: Oxford University Press, 1973.
Mendelberg, Tali. *The Race Card: Campaign Strategy, Implicit Messages, and the Norm of Equality*. Princeton, N.J.: Princeton University Press, 2001.
Meyer, Jeffrey F. *Myths in Stone: Religious Dimensions of Washington, D.C.* Berkeley: University of California Press, 2001.
Milkis, Sidney M., and Jerome M. Mileur, eds. *The Great Society and the High Tide of Liberalism*. Amherst: University of Massachusetts Press, 2005.
Miller, Lisa L. "The Invisible Black Victim: How American Federalism Perpetuates Racial Inequality in Criminal Justice." *Law and Society Review* 44, no. 4 (December 2010): 805–37.
Mitchell, Don. "Postmodern Geographical Praxis? The Postmodern Impulse and the War against Homeless People in the 'Post-justice' City." In *Postmodern Geography: Theory and Praxis*, edited by Claudio Minca, 57–92. Oxford: Blackwell, 2001.
Mitchell, Pauline Gaskins. "The History of Mt. Zion United Methodist Church and Mt. Zion Cemetery." *Records of the Columbia Historical Society* 51 (1984): 103–18.
Mohl, Raymond A. "Making the Second Ghetto in Metropolitan Miami, 1940–1960." *Journal of Urban History* 21, no. 3 (March 1995): 395–427.
———. "Race and Housing in the Postwar City: An Explosive History." *Journal of the Illinois State Historical Society* 94, no. 1 (Spring 2001): 8–30.
Mollenkopf, John. *The Contested City*. Princeton, N.J.: Princeton University Press, 1983.
Molotch, Harvey. "The City as a Growth Machine: Toward a Political Economy of Place." *American Journal of Sociology* 82, no. 2 (September 1976): 309–32.

Molotch, Harvey, and John R. Logan. *Urban Fortunes: The Political Economy of Place.* Berkeley: University of California Press, 1987.

Moore, Jacqueline M. *Leading the Race: The Transformation of the Black Elite in the Nation's Capital, 1880–1920.* Charlottesville: University Press of Virginia, 1999.

Morris, Aldon D. *The Origins of the Civil Rights Movement: Black Communities Organizing for Change.* New York: Free Press, 1986.

Muhammad, Khalil Gibran. *The Condemnation of Blackness: Race, Crime, and the Making of Modern Urban America.* Cambridge, Mass.: Harvard University Press, 2010.

Mumford, Kevin. *Newark: A History of Race, Rights, and Riots in America.* New York: New York University Press, 2007.

Murakawa, Naomi. *The First Civil Right: How Liberals Built Prison America.* New York: Oxford University Press, 2014.

Murch, Donna. "Crack in Los Angeles: Crisis, Militarization, and Black Response to the Late Twentieth-Century War on Drugs." *Journal of American History* 102, no. 1 (June 2015): 162–73.

———. *Living for the City: Migration, Education and the Rise of the Black Panther Party in Oakland, California.* Chapel Hill: University of North Carolina Press, 2010.

Murphy, Patrick V., and Thomas Plate Commissioner. *A View from the Top of American Law Enforcement.* New York: Simon & Schuster, 1977.

Musgrove, George Derek. "'Statehood Is Far More Difficult': The Struggle for D.C. Self-Determination, 1980–2017." *Washington History* 29, no. 2 (Fall 2017): 3–17.

Neary, John. "A New Resolve: Never to Be Invisible Again." *Life*, June 28, 1968, 28–29.

Nelson, Alondra. *Body and Soul: The Black Panther Party and the Fight against Medical Discrimination.* Minneapolis: University of Minnesota Press, 2011.

Nelson, Robert R. "Convention Centers as Catalysts for Local Economic Development." Ph.D. diss., University of Delaware, 2000.

Nicolaides, Becky M. *My Blue Heaven: Life and Politics in the Working-Class Suburbs of Los Angeles, 1920–1965.* Chicago: University of Chicago Press, 2002.

Ogbar, Jeffrey O. G. *Black Power: Radical Politics and African American Identity.* Baltimore: Johns Hopkins University Press, 2004.

O'Reilly, Kenneth. *Racial Matters: The FBI's Secret File on Black America, 1960–1972.* New York: Free Press, 1989.

Orleck, Annelise. "Introduction: The War on Poverty from the Grass Roots Up." In *The War on Poverty: A New Grassroots History*, edited by Annelise Orleck and Lisa Gayle Hazirjian, 1–28. Athens: University of Georgia Press, 2011.

———. *Storming Caesar's Palace: How Black Mothers Fought Their Own War on Poverty.* Boston: Beacon, 2005.

Orleck, Annelise, and Lisa Gayle Hazirjian, eds. *The War on Poverty: A New Grassroots History, 1964–1980.* Athens: University of Georgia Press, 2011.

Oropeza, Lorena. *¡Raza Si! ¡Guerra No! Chicano Protest and Patriotism during the Viet Nam War Era.* Berkeley: University of California Press, 2005.

Orr, Marion. "Congress, Race, and Anticrime Policy." In *Black and Multiracial*

Politics in America, edited by Yvette M. Assensoh and Lawrence J. Hanks, 225–56. New York: New York University Press, 2000.

Pacifico, Michele F. "'Don't Buy Where You Can't Work': The New Negro Alliance of Washington." *Washington History* 6, no. 1 (Spring/Summer 1994): 66–88.

Packer, Herbert L. "A Special Supplement: Nixon's Crime Program and What It Means." *New York Review of Books*, October 22, 1970.

Parenti, Christian. *Lockdown America: Police and Prisons in the Age of Crisis*. New York: Verso, 2000.

"Pastor Who Permitted Stokely Speech Keeps Post." *Jet*, November 2, 1967.

Pauley, Garth E. "John Lewis 'Speech at the March on Washington' (28 August 1963)." *Voices of Democracy* 5 (2010): 18–36.

Payne, Charles. *I've Got the Light of Freedom: The Organizing Tradition and the Mississippi Freedom Struggle*. 1995; reprint, Berkeley: University of California Press, 2007.

Petersen, David C. *Convention Centers, Stadiums and Arenas*. Washington, D.C.: Urban Land Institute, 1989.

Pihos, Peter. "Police, Race, and Politics in Chicago." Ph.D. diss., University of Pennsylvania, 2015.

Price, Barrye La Troye. "King to King: A Study of Civil Unrest and Federal Intervention from 1968 to 1992." Ph.D. diss., Texas A&M University, 1997.

Purnell, Brian. "Drive Awhile for Freedom: Brooklyn CORE's 1964 Stall-In and Public Discourses on Protest Violence." In *Groundwork: Local Black Freedom Movements in America*, edited by Jeanne Theoharis and Komozi Woodard, 45–75. New York: New York University Press, 2005.

———. *Fighting Jim Crow in the County of Kings: The Congress of Racial Equality in Brooklyn*. Lexington: University Press of Kentucky, 2013.

Quadagno, Jill S. *The Color of Welfare: How Racism Undermined the War on Poverty*. New York: Oxford University Press, 1994.

Quigley, Joan. *Just Another Southern Town: Mary Church Terrell and the Struggle for Racial Justice in the Nation's Capital*. New York: Oxford University Press, 2015.

Radford, Gail. "From Municipal Socialism to Public Authorities: Institutional Factors in the Shaping of American Public Enterprise." *Journal of American History* 90, no. 3 (December 2003): 863–90.

Ransby, Barbara. *Ella Baker and the Black Freedom Movement: A Radical Democratic Vision*. Chapel Hill: University of North Carolina Press, 2003.

Raskin, Jamin. "Is This America? The District of Columbia and the Right to Vote." *Harvard Civil Rights–Civil Liberties Law Review* 34, no. 1 (Winter 1999): 39–97.

Repak, Terry A. *Waiting on Washington: Central American Workers in the Nation's Capital*. Philadelphia: Temple University Press, 1995.

Richards, Mark. "The Debates over the Retrocession of the District of Columbia, 1801–2004." *Washington History* 16, no. 1 (Spring–Summer 2004): 55–82.

Risen, Clay. *A Nation on Fire: America in the Wake of the King Assassination*. Hoboken: John Wiley & Sons, 2009.

Robinson, Henry S. "The M Street High School, 1891–1916." *Records of the Columbia Historical Society* 51 (1984): 119–43.

Rohmann, Chris, and Jeffrey Brandon Morris. *Calmly to Poise the Scales of Justice: A History of the Courts of the District of Columbia Circuit*. Durham, N.C.: Carolina Academic Press, 2001.

Rubin, Elihu. *Insuring the City: The Prudential Center and the Postwar Urban Landscape*. New Haven, Conn.: Yale University Press, 2012.

Ruble, Blair A. *Washington's U Street: A Biography*. Washington, D.C.: Woodrow Wilson Center Press, 2010.

Sachse, Michael Judah. "D.C. Home Rule Movement, 1966–1973." Thesis, Amherst College, 1999.

Sandage, Scott. "A Marble House Divided: The Lincoln Memorial, the Civil Rights Movement, and the Politics of Memory, 1939–1963." *Journal of American History* 80, no. 1 (June 1993): 135–67.

Sandoval-Strausz, A. K. *Hotel: An American History*. New Haven, Conn.: Yale University Press, 2007.

Schaffer, Dana. "The 1968 Washington Riots in History and Memory." *Washington History* (Fall/Winter 2003): 4–33.

Schrag, Philip. "The Future of District of Columbia Home Rule." *Catholic University Law Review* 39, no. 2 (Winter 1990): 311–71.

Schrag, Zachary. *The Great Society Subway: A History of the Washington Metro*. Baltimore: Johns Hopkins University Press, 2006.

Schulman, Bruce J., and Julian E. Zeilizer, eds. *Rightward Bound: Making American Conservative in the 1970s*. Cambridge, Mass.: Harvard University Press, 2008.

Schuyler, David. *A City Transformed: Redevelopment, Race, and Suburbanization in Lancaster, Pennsylvania, 1940–1980*. University Park: Pennsylvania State University Press, 2002.

Schwartz, Joel. *The New York Approach: Robert Moses, Urban Liberals, and the Redevelopment of the Inner City*. Columbus: Ohio State University Press, 1993.

"The Second Sacking of Washington." *U.S. News and World Report*, April 22, 1968.

Self, Robert O. *American Babylon: Race and the Struggle for Postwar Oakland*. Princeton, N.J.: Princeton University Press, 2003.

Seligman, Amanda I. "'But Burn—No': The Rest of the Crowd in Three Civil Disorders in 1960s Chicago." *Journal of Urban History* 37, no. 2 (2011): 230–55.

Sellers, Cleveland, with Robert Terrell. *The River of No Return: The Autobiography of a Black Militant and the Life and Death of SNCC*. New York: William Morrow & Company, 1973.

Siegel, Fred. *The Future Once Happened Here: New York, D.C., L.A., and the Fate of America's Big Cities*. New York: Free Press, 1997.

Silver, Christopher. *Twentieth-Century Richmond: Planning, Politics, and Race*. Knoxville: University of Tennessee Press, 1984.

Simon, Jonathan. *Governing through Crime: How the War on Crime Transformed American Democracy and Created a Culture of Fear*. New York: Oxford University Press, 2007.

Singh, Nikhil Pal. *Black Is a Country: Race and the Unfinished Struggle for Democracy*. Cambridge, Mass.: Harvard University Press, 2004.

Smith, Sam. *Captive Capital: Colonial Life in Modern Washington*. Bloomington: Indiana University Press, 1974.

Soss, Joe, Richard C. Fording, and Sanford F. Schram. *Disciplining the Poor: Neoliberal Paternalism and the Persistent Power of Race*. Chicago: University of Chicago Press, 2011.

Stauch, Michael. "Wildcat of the Streets: Race, Class, and the Punitive Turn in 1970s Detroit." Ph.D. diss., Duke University, 2015.

Stevens, Sara. *Developing Expertise: Architecture and Real Estate in Metropolitan America*. New Haven, Conn.: Yale University Press, 2016.

Stewart, Alison. *First Class: The Legacy of Dunbar, America's First Black Public High School*. Chicago: Lawrence Hill Books, 2013.

Stone, Clarence N. *Regime Politics: Governing Atlanta, 1946–1988*. Lawrence: University Press of Kansas, 1989.

Sugrue, Thomas J. "Crabgrass-Roots Politics: Race, Rights, and the Reaction against Liberalism in the Urban North, 1940–1964." *Journal of American History* 82 (1995): 551–78.

———. *The Origins of the Urban Crisis: Race and Inequality in Postwar Detroit*. Princeton, N.J.: Princeton University Press, 1996.

Sullivan, Patricia. *Days of Hope: Race and Democracy in the New Deal Era*. Chapel Hill: University of North Carolina Press, 1996.

Teaford, Jon C. *The Rough Road to Renaissance: Urban Revitalization in America, 1940–1985*. Baltimore: Johns Hopkins University Press, 1990.

———. "Urban Renewal and Its Aftermath." *Housing Policy Debate* 11, no. 2 (2000): 443–65.

Thompson, Heather Ann. "Urban Uprisings: Riots or Rebellions?" In *The Columbia Guide to America in the 1960s*, edited by David Farber and Beth Bailey, 109–17. New York: Columbia University Press, 2001.

———. *Whose Detroit: Politics, Labor, and Race in a Modern American City*. Ithaca, N.Y.: Cornell University Press, 2001.

———. "Why Mass Incarceration Matters: Rethinking Crisis, Decline, and Transformation in Postwar American History." *Journal of American History* 97, no. 3 (December 2010): 703–34.

"A Threat of Anarchy in Nation's Capital." *U.S. News and World Report*, May 20, 1968.

Ture, Kwame, and Charles V. Hamilton. *Black Power: The Politics of Liberation*. New York: Vintage Books, 1992.

Tydings, Joseph D. Foreword to "District of Columbia Court Reorganization, 1970" by Wesley S. Williams Jr., *Georgetown Law Journal* 59, no. 3 (February 1971): 477–80.

Tyson, Timothy B. *Radio Free Dixie: Robert F. Williams and the Roots of Black Power*. Chapel Hill: University of North Carolina Press, 1999.

Unger, Irwin. *The Best of Intentions: The Triumphs and Failures of the Great Society under Kennedy, Johnson, and Nixon*. New York: Doubleday, 1996.

Valk, Anne M. "'Mother Power': The Movement for Welfare Rights in Washington, D.C., 1966–1972." *Journal of Women's History* 11, no. 4 (2000): 34–58.

———. *Radical Sisters: Second-Wave Feminism and Black Liberation in Washington, D.C.* Urbana: University of Illinois Press, 2008.

Van Uffelen, Chris. *Convention Centers*. Salenstein, Switzerland: Braun, 2012.

Vitale, Alex S. *City of Disorder: How the Quality of Life Campaign Transformed New York Politics*. New York: New York University Press, 2008.

Vose, Clement E. *Caucasians Only: The Supreme Court, the NAACP, and the Restrictive Covenant Cases*. Berkeley: University of California Press, 1967.

Wacquant, Loïc. *Punishing the Poor: The Neoliberal Government of Social Insecurity*. Durham, N.C.: Duke University Press, 2009.

Walker, Samuel. *Popular Justice: A History of American Criminal Justice*. 2nd ed. New York: Oxford University Press, 1998.

Walker, J. Samuel. *Most of 14th Street Is Gone: The Washington, DC Riots of 1968*. New York: Oxford University Press, 2018.

Walters, Ronald W. "Introduction: An Administered System of Government." In *Democratic Destiny and the District of Columbia*, edited by Ronald W. Walters and Toni-Michelle Travis, 1–20. Lanham, Md.: Lexington Books, 2010.

Walters, Ronald W., and Toni-Michelle Travis, eds. *Democratic Destiny and the District of Columbia*. Lanham, Md.: Lexington Books, 2010.

Ward, Jason Morgan. *Defending White Democracy: The Making of a Segregationist Movement and the Remaking of Racial Politics, 1936–1965*. Chapel Hill: University of North Carolina Press, 2011.

Weaver, Vesla. "Frontlash: Race and the Development of Punitive Crime Policy." *Studies in American Political Development* 21 (Fall 2007): 230–65.

———. "More Than Words: How 'Law and Order' Invigorated Conservatism, Did Irreparable Damage to Liberalism, and Ushered in a New Political Order." *The Forum*, July 2008.

Weaver, Vesla, and Amy Lerman. "Political Consequences of the Carceral State." *American Political Science Review* 104, no. 4 (November 2010): 1–17.

Weisbrot, Robert. *Freedom Bound: A History of America's Civil Rights Movement*. New York: W. W. Norton, 1990.

Weiss, Marc A. *The Rise of the Community Builders: The American Real Estate Industry and Urban Land Planning*. New York: Columbia University Press, 1987.

Wiebenson, John. "Symbol Power." *Journal of Architectural Education* 29, no. 2 (November 1975): 18–21.

Wilkins, Roger. *A Man's Life*. New York: Simon & Schuster, 1982.

Williams, Brian N., and J. Edward Kellough. "Leadership with an Enduring Impact: The Legacy of Chief Burtell Jefferson of the Metropolitan Police Department of Washington, D.C." *Public Administration Review* 66, no. 6 (November–December 2006): 813–22.

Williams, Rhonda Y. *Concrete Demands: The Search for Black Power in the 20th Century*. New York: Routledge, 2015.

———. *The Politics of Public Housing: Black Women's Struggles against Urban Inequality*. New York: Oxford University Press, 2004.

Williams, Yohuru. *Black Politics / White Power: Civil Rights, Black Power, and the Black Panthers in New Haven*. Oxford: Wiley Blackwell, 2000.

Wolfe, Keri. "'Maximum Feasible Participation': The Value of Community Work Opportunities for Women in the Ongoing War on Poverty." *Journal at MALS Dartmouth College* 1, no. 2 (2013): 90–104.

Woodard, Komozi. *Nation within a Nation: Amiri Baraka (LeRoi Jones) and Black Power Politics*. Chapel Hill: University of North Carolina Press, 1999.

Wright, Amy Nathan. "Civil Rights 'Unfinished Business': Poverty, Race, and the 1968 Poor People's Campaign." Ph.D. diss., University of Texas at Austin, 2007.

Wright, William M. "White City to White Elephant: Washington's Union Station since World War II." *Washington History* 10, no. 2 (Fall/Winter 1998/1999): 24–43.

Yellin, Eric Steven. *Racism in the Nation's Service: Government Workers and the Color Line in Woodrow Wilson's America*. Chapel Hill: University of North Carolina Press, 2013.

Yglesias, Jose. "It May Be a Long, Hot Spring in the Capital." *New York Times Magazine*, March 31, 1968.

Young, Andrew. *An Easy Burden: The Civil Rights Movement and the Transformation of America*. New York: HarperCollins, 1996.

Zaretsky, Natasha. *No Direction Home: The American Family and the Fear of National Decline, 1968–1980*. Chapel Hill: University of North Carolina Press, 2007.

Zasloff, Jonathan. "The Secret History of the Fair Housing Act." *Harvard Journal on Legislation* 53 (January 2016): 247–78.

Zelizer, Julian E. *The Fierce Urgency of Now: Lyndon Johnson, Congress, and the Battle for the Great Society*. New York: Penguin, 2015.

Zigas, Eli. *Left with Few Rights: Unequal Democracy and the District of Columbia*. San Francisco: Creative Commons, 2008.

Zukin, Sharon. *Landscapes of Power: From Detroit to Disney World*. Berkeley: University of California Press, 1991.

ONLINE SOURCES

Berry, Max. "Statement of Max Berry, Chairman PADC, before House Subcommittee on Government Operations and Metropolitan Affairs." 1981, Committee of 100, Box 19, folder 18. *Washington History Matters*. Accessed July 30, 2018. http://dchistorymatters.org/document.php?mod=39&doc=64.

Civil Rights Movement Veterans. "1960." Accessed June 25, 2013. http://www.crmvet.org/tim/timhis60.htm#1960sncc.

Clarke, Craig. "Washington Board of Trade: Overview." *Washington History Matters*. April 28, 2006. Accessed July 30, 2018. http://dchistorymatters.org/introduction.php?mod=29.

Council of the District of Columbia. "Office of the Advisory Neighborhood Commissions." Accessed September 5, 2013. http://www.dccouncil.washington.dc.us/offices/office-of-the-advisory-neighborhood-commissions.

Daly, Christopher B. "The Peoples Bicentennial Commission: Slouching Towards the Economic Revolution." *The Crimson*, April 28, 1975. https://www.thecrimson.com/article/1975/4/28/the-peoples-bicentennial-commission-pif-you/.

The Disaster Center. "United States Crime Rates 1960–2012." Accessed June 17, 2014. http://www.disastercenter.com/crime/uscrime.htm.

Federal Bureau of Investigation. "Uniform Crime Reporting Statistics." Accessed

June 17, 2014. http://www.ucrdatatool.gov/Search/Crime/State/RunCrimeOne YearofData.cfm.

Francisco Quakers. "Memorial Statement." Accessed June 22, 2014. http://www.sfquakers.org/arch/mem/bill_moyer_memorial.pdf.

Gordon, Karen. "Statement of Karen Gordon on Behalf of Don't Tear It Down, April 23, 1982." Committee of 100, Box 20, Folder 3. *Washington History Matters.* Accessed July 30, 2018. http://dchistorymatters.org/document.php?mod=39&doc=59.

Greater Washington Board of Trade (BOT). "Open Letter to President and Congress Urging Passage of Eisenhower Civic Center Bill," August 15, 1972, BOT records, box 238, folder 18. *Washington History Matters.* Accessed July 30, 2018. http://dchistorymatters.org/document.php?mod=29&doc=125.

"Halting Freeways and Blazing Trails: Bike-Ped Guru Tedson Meyers." *Project for Public Spaces,* September 9, 2012. Accessed July 30, 2018. https://www.pps.org/article/halting-freeways-blazing-trails-an-interview-with-bikeped-guru-tedson-meyers.

Hampton, Henry. *Eyes on the Prize II Interview with Marian Wright Edelman.* December 21, 1988. Transcript, Washington University Digital Gateway Texts. Accessed July 30, 2018. http://digital.wustl.edu/e/eii/eiiweb/ede5427.0676.044 marianwrightedelman.html.

Howe, Charles A. "David Eaton." *Dictionary of Unitarian and Universalist Biography,* November 19, 2002. Accessed July 30, 2018. http://uudb.org/articles/david heaton.html.

Huxtable, Ada Louise. "Out of a Fair, a City." *Horizon* 2, no. 5 (May 1960): 80–87, Board of Trade records, box 233, folder 7. *Washington History Matters.* Accessed July 30, 2018. http://dchistorymatters.org/document.php?mod=29&doc=113.

Jackson, Phillip. "Petey Greene Talks Down the Riots, 1968." *Boundary Stones* (blog), May 15, 2004. Accessed July 30, 2018. https://blogs.weta.org/boundarystones/2014/05/15/petey-greene-talks-down-riots-1968.

Janak, Cynthia A. "The New American Discrimination—Eminent Domain." *Renew America,* January 9, 2008. Accessed July 30, 2018. http://www.renewamerica.com:80/columns/janak/080109.

Johnson, Lyndon B. "Memorandum of Disapproval of the District of Columbia Crime Bill." November 13, 1966. *American Presidency Project.* Accessed July 30, 2018. http://www.presidency.ucsb.edu/ws/index.php?pid=28029&st=district+of+columbia&st1=crime.

———. "Special Message to the Congress: The Nation's Capital." February 27, 1967. *American Presidency Project.* Accessed July 30, 2018. http://www.presidency.ucsb.edu/ws/index.php?pid=28662&st=district+of+columbia&st1=.

———. "Statement upon Signing the District of Columbia Crime Bill." December 27, 1967. *American Presidency Project.* Accessed July 30, 2018. http://www.presidency.ucsb.edu/ws/index.php?pid=28644&st=district+of+columbia&st1=crime.

King, Martin Luther, Jr. "Statement Delivered at Press Conference Announcing the Poor People's Campaign." December 4, 1967. *Martin Luther King Jr. Papers Project.* Accessed June 3, 2011. http://www.stanford.edu/group/King/publications/papers/unpub/671204003_Announcing_Poor_Peoples_campaign.htm.

Muhammad, Khalil Gibran. "'Black Silent Majority,' by Michael Javen Fortner." *New York Times*, September 21, 2015, https://www.nytimes.com/2015/09/27/books/review/black-silent-majority-by-michael-javen-fortner.html.

———. "Power and Punishment: Two New Books about Race and Crime." *New York Times Review of Books*, April 14, 2017, https://www.nytimes.com/2017/04/14/books/review/locking-up-our-own-james-forman-jr-colony-in-nation-chris-hayes.html.

Murch, Donna. "Who's to Blame for Mass Incarceration?" *Boston Review*, October 16, 2015, http://bostonreview.net/books-ideas/donna-murch-michael-javen-fortner-black-silent-majority.

National Capital Planning Commission. "The Dwight D. Eisenhower Memorial Bicentennial Civic Center (never built)." 1971, Board of Trade records, box 240, folder 12. *Washington History Matters*. Accessed July 30, 2018. http://dchistorymatters.org/document.php?mod=29&doc=127.

Nixon, Richard. "Remarks on Signing the District of Columbia Court Reform and Criminal Procedure Act of 1970." July 29, 1970. *American Presidency Project*. Accessed July 30, 2018. http://www.presidency.ucsb.edu/ws/?pid=2601.

Tang, Joanne. "The Old Lorton, Virginia Prison Is Being Turned into Homes. Here's Its Fascinating Story." *Greater Greater Washington* (blog), September 21, 2018. Accessed October 1, 2018. https://ggwash.org/view/69004/this-old-lorton-virginia-prison-has-now-become-housing.

"The Vision Shared: The Republican Platform, Uniting Our Family, Our Country, Our World." August 17, 1992. *American Presidency Project*. Accessed July 30, 2018. https://www.presidency.ucsb.edu/documents/republican-party-platform-1992.

"Voices of Feminism Oral History Project: Narrators." Smith College Libraries. Accessed July 30, 2018. https://libraries.smith.edu/special-collections/research-collections/resources-lists/oral-histories/voices-of-feminism/narrators.

Washington Area Convention and Visitors Bureau. "Brochure for the Eisenhower Memorial Bicentennial Civic Center." 1971, Board of Trade records, box 237, folder 18. *Washington History Matters*. Accessed July 30, 2018. http://dchistorymatters.org/document.php?mod=29&doc=153.

INDEX

Page numbers in italics refer to illustrations.

FSC
www.fsc.org
MIX
Paper from
responsible sources
FSC® C008955